Tales, Rumors, and Gossip

Tales, Rumors, and Gossip

Exploring Contemporary Folk Literature in Grades 7-12

Gail de Vos

1996
Libraries Unlimited, Inc.
Englewood, Colorado

Thanks to Lillian (Taback) and Cecil Shukster for telling me these legends while I was growing up. And special thanks, Mom and Dad, for your help and encouragement while I was putting this book together.

And as always, lots of love and thanks to Peter, Esther, and Taryn.

LIBRARIES UNLIMITED, INC.
P.O. Box 6633
Englewood, CO 80155-6633
1-800-237-6124

Production Editor: Kevin W. Perizzolo
Copy Editor: Tama Serfoss
Proofreader: Jason Cook
Layout and Interior Design: Kay Minnis

Library of Congress Cataloging-in-Publication Data

De Vos, Gail, 1949-
    Tales, rumors, and gossip : exploring contemporary folk literature in grades 7-12 / Gail de Vos.
    xx, 405 p. 17x25 cm.
    Includes bibliographical references and index.
    ISBN 1-56308-190-3
    1. Folklore--Study and teaching (Secondary)--United States.
    2. Folk literature--Study and teaching (Secondary)--United States.
    3. Folklore--United States--Themes, motives. 4. Urban Folklore. I. Title.
GR105.3.D4   1995
398'.071'273--dc20   95-19553
                                                      CIP

Contents

PART
I

PART
II

PART
III
—————

12—SCARY STORIES (*continued*)

INTRODUCTION

> *A man sees a newspaper ad for a used Porsche in excellent condition for only $50. He rushes to the address and a woman shows him the car. He pays the woman and asks her why the price was so low. She explains that her husband had run off with his secretary a few days earlier and had instructed her to sell her car and send him the money.* (So there's this guy, see . . . 1991, 81)

In 1991, *Maclean's* magazine devoted several pages to contemporary legends such as the one shown above. An interesting aspect of the article in this Canadian news magazine was its placement under the section "Behaviour" rather than "Entertainment," demonstrating that contemporary legends are gaining recognition and acceptance in a world beyond folklorists and sociologists. This book focuses on these legends and the role they play in the life and belief systems of their tellers: the "common folk" and, particularly, young adults.

Storytelling is an art, and, as an art, it can be taught, perfected, and practiced by everyone. The first thing that I tell my students is that stories and storytelling techniques are the same communication tools that we use in everyday life. When you talk to someone, you are telling a story: the story of what you did that day; the story of what someone else did; or the story of what you wish you could have done. Interspersed in your dialogue with family, friends, and colleagues are traditional types of folklore. We share *gossip* about people we know, impart *rumors* about situations that we wish we knew more about, and tell *tales* to exemplify a point or attitude. The tales that we tell are often believed to be true, things that have happened—if not to us, then to someone close to us, a "friend of a friend." These tales are known as *contemporary legends*. As David Buchan, an expert in modern legends, defines them, contemporary legends are:

> Stories told as true which circulate by word of mouth in contemporary society and exhibit traditional variation. They circulate in a wide variety of social groups, on every level of the socioeconomic scale and are prevalent among the educated. They contain both ancient and modern elements: they involve the phenomena of contemporary society but often demand belief in something unlikely or fantastically horrific or on occasion even supernatural. (1978, 2)

xvii

Tales, rumors, and gossip, the genres that interrelate with contemporary legends, are natural tools we use to exchange information, both informally, in conversation, and formally, in instruction. They are speculative genres, allowing the tellers and listeners to collect "information" and formulate opinions. They also add interest to the swapping of information. These legends explore and explain our fears and anxieties about modern culture, and our fascination with the genre has escalated in the last decade. Scholarship in contemporary legends has been undertaken by such diverse disciplines as anthropology, business management, communication studies, English language, English literature, folklore, history, Native American studies, popular culture, psychology, and sociology (Smith 1991, 2). The topics studied are also extremely diverse.

Young adults, particularly people in grades 7 to 12, are fascinated with the world around them and how others react to it. Studying the reactions of others helps these young people to formulate their own responses and attitudes. Consequently, they share as much information as possible with one another to help themselves in this task. Much of this material includes local gossip and rumor and "universal" contemporary legends.

Whenever I speak with young adults and the people who work or live with them, I get a common request: Tell me more about these contemporary legends. Thus, this book!

STRUCTURE OF
TALES, RUMORS, AND GOSSIP

Tales, Rumors, and Gossip is divided into three major sections. Part I provides an introduction to the large genre of contemporary legends. The basic structure, functions, and features of the legends are discussed, as are the customary methods of telling the legends and bringing them alive.

Part II focuses on the role of contemporary legends in the world around us. Chapter 2 investigates the connections among the three conversational modes of sharing pertinent information: legends, gossip, and rumor. Chapter 3 explores the role of the mass media, as both an agent in the dissemination of contemporary legends and as the subject matter of those legends.

Beyond simply telling or believing in contemporary legends, many people act on them or act them out. These people go on "legend trips," consciously poison Halloween treats and try to redeem aluminum pop-can tabs for medical treatment. These examples, and others, of "ostensive" actions are investigated in chapter 4. Chapter 5 highlights the connections between contemporary legends and other genres such as ballads, jokes, literary horror stories, and personal experience narratives.

Discussions of individual contemporary legends make up part III. Specific legends are arranged according to both broad subject areas and availability of information about the legends themselves. Legends included in the discussion of science and technology reflect society's preoccupation with and misconceptions about technological and medical advances. The legends in the chapter on contaminated food exhibit our preoccupation with cleanliness and fears of "foreign" influences. Other chapters focus on broad issues such as theft, intentional and unintentional; animals, wild and domestic; and threats to our safety, as individuals and as a community. "Individual" threats include tales of body parts being stolen for organ transplants, AIDS lore, kidnapping of children and young adults, and LSD-laced tattoo transfers. "Community" threats include legends of satanic activity and the responses to those threats.

The last three chapters concentrate on the body of contemporary legends that particularly fascinate young adults: scary tales. Chapter 12 presents a large collection of scary legends and discusses their functions, themes, and universality. Chapters 13 and 14 are dedicated to examinations of two individual supernatural legends, "The Vanishing Hitchhiker" and "La Llorona."

An appendix follows, with discussion and research topic suggestions that can be modified for any age group or curriculum area and purpose.

Indexes are supplied for easy access to individual legends, core subjects, and literary works mentioned within the text.

RESOURCES

The recent explosion of articles and monographs dedicated to various aspects of contemporary legends provided me with a myriad of sources and resources to draw upon in putting together this book. I used the articles liberally, attempting to provide as many different points of view as possible. The content of individual chapters and discussions of individual legends is based on the amount of research and discussion available; therefore, some legends have a broader treatment than others. Obviously, some contemporary legends have been more fascinating than others! I have skewed the information presented to include only those contemporary legends of special interest to young adults and people who work with young adults, which means that some recent legends are not included.

I owe a special debt to Jan Harold Brunvand and the work he has done generating interest in contemporary legends. His analyses of contemporary legends in *The Vanishing Hitchhiker* (Norton, 1981), *The Choking Doberman* (Norton, 1984), *The Mexican Pet* (Norton, 1986), *Curses! Broiled Again!* (Norton, 1988), and *The Baby Train and Other Lusty Legends* (Norton, 1993) have been enormously helpful. Because of the popularity of Brunvand's books and their availability in public and school libraries (at least in the ones I have visited), I have not drawn extensively from them; rather, I recommend them as companion reading and resource material.

A major source of articles and contemporary legends used throughout this book is *FOAFTALE NEWS*, the newsletter of the International Society for Contemporary Legend Research (ISCLR). In addition to the newsletter, the ISCLR's annual journal, *Contemporary Legend*, and the Perspectives on Contemporary Legends series (Sheffield Academic Press, 1984–1990), five volumes of ISCLR conference proceedings on the contemporary legend were used liberally in this work.

Three other basic resources have proved to be of extraordinary help in putting together this book. The first is my daily newspaper, the *Edmonton Journal*. Several contemporary legends have received front-page coverage as "respectable" news items ("The Exploding Toilet" and "Baby Parts") while others have been retold by local columnists ("The Elevator Incident" and "The Stolen Kidney"). "The Exploding Toilet" legend is a story of a highly explosive situation in which a man sits on the toilet and lights a cigarette immediately after his wife has disposed of a volatile substance in the toilet bowl. This legend is often combined with another legendary ending—having the poor man being unceremoniously dropped off a stretcher as the result of the paramedics' loss of control as they are laughing about the cause of the accident. This legend has been the focus of several articles on contemporary legends and is discussed further in chapter 3. Chapter 9 includes the legendary "Elevator Incident," also known as "The Dog in the Elevator." "Baby Parts" and "The Stolen Kidney" legends, interrelated, are explored in detail in chapter 10.

In most newspapers, advice columnists provide an additional platform for disseminating and discussing contemporary legends. Readers often ask Ann Landers and Abby Van Buren about "true" stories such as "The Cookie Recipe," discussed in chapter 3, and "The Philanderer's Porsche," which opens this introduction and is part of the dialogue on car tales in chapter 6.

Cartoons published in daily newspapers also offer a different viewpoint on the legends. Fans of Gary Larson's *Far Side* may recognize some familiar contemporary legends as the inspiration for his cartoons, particularly "The Hook" (chapter 12) and "Spiders in the Hairdo" (chapter 9). Both of these legends have a long history and therefore are considered, by Larson and others, to be common knowledge. "The Hook," told to me by my mother when I was a teenager, warns of what might happen if you "park" in lover's lane with a member of the opposite sex. Of course, a madman with a hook for a hand *does* add to the danger! I remember, too, hearing from my mother a cautionary tale about regularly washing your hair—"After all, it could happen to you!" Spiders would find no purchase on a squeaky clean scalp.

My daughters, high school students, have been my most valuable resource. I am grateful for their discussions about the legends, about what the legends meant to them when they first heard them, and about what the legends mean to them now. They kept me up-to-date with the legends and variants circulating through our community and confirmed the importance of this work.

REFERENCES

Buchan, David. 1978. The modern legend. In *Language, culture and tradition: Papers on language and folklore presented at the annual conference of the British Sociological Association*, edited by A. E. Green and J. D. A. Widdowson. The Institute of Dialect and Folklife Studies, School of English, University of Leeds. The Centre for English Cultural Tradition and Language, University of Sheffield.

Smith, Paul. 1991. Editorial. *Contemporary Legend* 1: 1–3.

So there's this guy, see . . . 1991. *Maclean's* 104, no. 48: 80–81.

PART
I

CONTEMPORARY LEGENDS

"[A] lady picked up a hitchhiker near here and while he was riding—in the backseat—he warned her to set aside enough food and supplies to last for two years, because there was to be—is to be—a time of trouble and she should be prepared. When she tried to ask him questions, he didn't answer. When she looked in the rearview mirror, she couldn't see him. When she turned around, he was gone! (Young and Young 1991, 138–39)

Contemporary legends are important to consider for educators and communicators, not only because they articulate modern concerns in contemporary societies, but because they are told, and believed, by all segments of those societies. These legends are not the exclusive domain of any single age, race, profession, or socioeconomic group. And, unlike traditional folklore, these legends are formulated and transmitted not only by the general population, but by the mass media as well.

The very fact that contemporary legends embody the fears and concerns of Western civilization makes them a powerful tool in the classroom. Young adults recognize these legends and are willing to discuss and retell them. Even more important, students are able to relate educational activities involving contemporary legends to their "real" lives.

Young adults are prolific tellers of contemporary legends as many underlying themes in the legends speak directly to them. Contemporary legends often feed young adults' taste for the macabre and a "good" fright. They also encompass anxieties about sexuality, sex roles, guilt in violating social norms, assuming responsibility, and gaining more control over their own lives (Samuelson 1981, 138).

The study of contemporary legends presents rich educational opportunities for educators at all levels. The legends offer windows into modern society by reflecting our beliefs, concerns, and fears; they offer a passport into the worldview of other cultures and allow us to compare it to our own culture's worldview as we examine variants and analogues of the tales being

3

told today; and they invite connections to other subjects in the school curricula. But most important, contemporary legends are fun to tell and discuss and are relevant to the lives of young adults, providing an effective tool for accomplishing educational goals.

Most people who listen to and tell contemporary legends have never heard the actual term and don't know that they have been the subject of discussion and research for decades. One of the major focuses of this study, in fact, has been the quest for the most appropriate definition of contemporary legends. Although scholarship of this genre dates from the 1940s, an actual consensus of what to label these legends still has not been reached. These "true" occurrences have been called, among other terms, "urban belief legends," "urban myths," and "rumor legends." Recently, they have been labeled "contemporary legends," and though many of the narratives are neither strictly contemporary nor legends, it seems to be the most satisfactory label. As Sandy Hobbs points out, the term "contemporary legend" is not new; F. Scott Fitzgerald used the phrase in *The Great Gatsby*, written in 1925.

> Gatsby's notoriety, spread about by the hundreds who had accepted his hospitality and so become authorities upon his past, had increased all summer until he fell just short of being news. Contemporary legends such as the "underground pipe-line to Canada" attached themselves to him and there was one persistent story that he didn't live in a house at all, but in a boat that looked like a house and was moved secretly up and down the Long Island shore. (Hobbs 1989, 2)

Much of the discussion on the defining of contemporary legends focuses on what they are *not*. They are not myths, as myths are sacred stories involving the creation of the world and the gods and are regarded as true by the community that tells them. People outside a community often regard its myths as "quaint," fictionalized accounts of little actual importance. Unfortunately, because of this condescending attitude and our limited understanding of other cultures, the word "myth" is often abused and misused in the media and in ordinary conversation, becoming synonymous with "untrue" or "unreal" (Oring 1986, 124).

Contemporary legends are not folktales; folktales reside within a fictional world and, being told for entertainment, are not believed by the audience (Klintberg 1976, 69). Contemporary legends are not "urban legends" because their settings and narration do not always reflect urban centers. They are not rumor or gossip because they have narrative structure and tell a story.

Contemporary legends are normally considered a subset of the legend genre because legends are narratives that focus on a single episode presented as embarrassing, macabre, miraculous, uncanny, or bizarre. Legends reflect the real world and are told as if they are, or once were, true. The primary function of legends is to inform and reinforce a culture's beliefs and norms, requiring the audience to examine its own worldview. This subset is "contemporary" because its stories reflect the values, concerns, and worldview of today's society expressed in contemporary terms.

FEATURES OF CONTEMPORARY LEGENDS

Contemporary legends share many features with other traditional folk narratives: they are usually anonymous; they are primarily communicated face-to-face; they exist in multiple versions, adapted and recreated with each retelling and circulating among members of certain economic, family, or cultural groups. Contemporary legends, like other genres of traditional folklore, reflect both the past and the present. The narrators draw upon the language, symbols, events, and forms of the past to place present events and concerns in an understandable format or structure. Clichés, stock patterns, and traditional stereotypes and situations are incorporated into the legends. For example, in Hawaiian variants of "The Vanishing Hitchhiker," the Hitchhiker is identified as the goddess Pele. In the variant of "The Vanishing Hitchhiker" at the beginning of this chapter, the Hitchhiker is one of the Three Nephites who have appeared singularly or as a trio since the inception of the Church of Jesus Christ of Latter-Day Saints (Young and Young 1991, 183).

Contemporary legends reflect both the individual and the community at large. The teller must conform to the accepted standards of the community for the audience to listen to, and to believe, the teller of the tales, not just once, but in the future as well (Oring 1986, 122).

Although they can be told in "shorthand," where the teller can make a reference to another story and the audience knows exactly what is being referred to (e.g., " . . . *it's like the "Hook!"*), contemporary legends are usually told as narratives with a story structure (beginning, middle, and end) rather than as fragments or belief statements.

Contemporary legend narrative structure embraces several basic features: authentication, contemporary elements, and style and tone of the actual telling.

Authentication

Contemporary legends are represented by the teller as true and are, in fact, often believed to be so by the teller. They are authenticated by the use of several devices common to other traditional genres. The most frequent form of authenticating a tale is the use of the "friend-of-a-friend" (FOAF) motif (e.g., "My neighbor's mother's cousin") for the source of the tale. Because these sources are "known" to the teller, they are therefore perceived to be reliable.

A second and equally important method of authentication is the use of actual names, places, dates, and events to ground the tale in reality. This often works so well that contemporary legends are printed in the newspapers as actual news items. These details "load a narrative with spice and zest" and evoke connotations to involve the listeners in the world of the legend (Fine 1992, 27). Details change over time, usually by tellers who refresh the relevance of the legend for each particular audience and situation. The legends are stored, in our memories, in outline form (the "kernel" of the legend) and as this outline is retrieved and retold, new details are added to flesh out the narrative so that it makes sense to both the teller and the listener within the context of the conversation.

A third method of authentication attributes the source to the mass media (e.g., "I heard it on Oprah," "I read it in the newspaper"). Denial in the media or any other form of formal refutation does very little to lessen the popularity of these legends or the belief in their messages.

Because contemporary legends are so widely believed to be actual occurrences, it is also believed that they can be easily verified, if one wanted to the take the time to do so. However, when that time is actually taken, the trail mysteriously disappears, leaving the searcher stranded among a myriad of "dead-ends." Sometimes an actual event is pinpointed as the historical genesis of the legend, but, so far, when any given version is investigated, no substantiating evidence has been found (Hobbs 1978, 79).

Contemporary Elements

The incorporation of details from the everyday life of the teller and listener is one of the reasons that the legends are labeled contemporary. The legends abound with references to recent technology, modern transportation, and urban centers and institutions such as shopping malls and parking lots (Hobbs 1978, 74). The legends also reflect contemporary fears and concerns, articulating and verifying the contemporary worldview of the group circulating the legend.

Conversational Style

Contemporary legends are usually transmitted in informal, face-to-face conversations, are usually brief, and are often constructed and told communally rather than by a single teller. The invited (and expected) questions, dialogue, and comments during and at the end of the telling help to move the story along and develop its shape. Because the legends serve diverse functions, their format is flexible and is influenced by the teller's purpose in relating the legend, the situation in which it is being told, and the people who are interacting in the telling.

Film Noir Tone

Film noir, a film genre of the 1940s to the 1960s, provided audiences with steamy, dark urban landscapes and ordinary characters facing unexpected twists and turns throughout the plot. In a sense, contemporary legends emulate this film genre. The content is often macabre and features black comedy derived from the ill-fortune and the hurt and pain of its characters (Buchan 1978, 12). Contemporary legends often depend on their twisted endings and ambiguous characters and situations for effect.

Racial and Gender Stereotypes

Generalizations and stereotypes abound in contemporary legends, reflecting the attitudes of a society and of individuals within that culture. Female characters in the legends are frequently portrayed as weak and in need of protection, either by strong, forceful males or by fierce watchdogs, and as gullible and easy to mislead. Male characters can be foolish, but they are usually the heroes as well. Overall, human characters are fallible and quick to jump to conclusions, but family pets are reliable and loyal to the end (Nicolini 1989, 81). Contemporary legends often mirror racial attitudes and fears. Scapegoats, universal figures of blame, are frequently implicated as the "root of all our problems." The identity of these scapegoats changes over time and space, depending on the worldview of the legend-telling participants.

STRUCTURE OF CONTEMPORARY LEGENDS

Although contemporary legends follow a traditional narrative pattern, their structure is adapted to conform to their most common form of dissemination: conversation. These legends, told within the confines of conversation, use the story's beginning and ending as devices to take the audience out of the world of the conversation and into the world of story, and then back again into conversation. The legends have plots that have been fixed, through tradition, into a recognizable and stable pattern. Often, traditional motifs and structures from other genres are employed in the telling of contemporary legends. The use of repetition and the three-event format of folktales, hints of the supernatural and inexplicable events and mystery, and twisted, unexpected endings are all part of the legend-telling performance (Williams 1984, 217).

The structure of the legend depends on the purpose of the teller; the clarity of the teller's memory, through which details are forgotten or added because they seem to belong; and the audience to whom it is being told. Because the legends are usually stored in the memory as outlines only, generalization or specialization may take place, cultural or temporal replacement occurs, and anachronisms are discarded when the story is taken out of storage and given shape by the teller.

Introduction

In addition to serving as a transition device, taking the teller and listener out of the general conversation and into the story, the introduction performs several other duties. It provides the source of the story, the general attitude of the teller towards the content, the reason for the telling, and identification of the characters. This identification includes placing the characters into context by neighborhood, by relationship to the teller, and by the character's social standing.

"That exact thing happened to a friend of my cousin Geordie. You know Geordie, he's the one that married that dancer and moved to the city. Anyways, this friend, his name was Joseph, was . . . "

The introduction also establishes the setting of the contemporary legend. It provides the realistic and necessary details, or grounding, through which the legend may be believed. The listener is also informed by the introduction of the main problem inherent in the legend.

"Joseph was living on the top floor of a highrise apartment building, downtown, in Edmonton. His friends had just invited him to spend the weekend at their newly renovated home in the country. He had never been there before but thought he could easily find it . . . even in the dark."

Normal Event Sequence

Depending on the complexity of the legend, it can consist of only one event or a series of events that follow a logical or natural pattern. The event is usually an *unusual action* or a *mysterious event*.

"After spending hours on the dark country roads, Joseph finally found his friends' house. . . . Later that night, when he couldn't sleep, he got out of bed and, hearing a noise outside the window, he looked out to see . . . a coach with four black horses on the gravel drive below his window. He also saw the ugliest coachman anyone could ever imagine. . . ."

Climax and Consequence

The high point of the legend, the climax, is usually followed by a summing up, by the teller, of the reason for telling the legend.

> *"If he hadn't recognized that ugly face from the night before,*
> *he might have been dead, too!"*

Ending

The final comment takes the teller and the listener out of the world of the legend and back into the normal conversation.

> *"So next time someone warns you about something, remember my*
> *cousin's friend Joseph. Did you ever see his apartment . . . ?"*
> (These are excerpts from a variant of
> "Room for One More," discussed in chapter 12.)

Tellers can approach the legends in a variety of ways. They can be told as a personal experience of the teller (*"Last night when I went for a walk . . ."*); as the experience of a relative or a friend-of-a-friend (*"My best friend's mother went to get some milk and when she . . ."*); or as a tale not attached to the teller at all. In this case, the source is not identified or acknowledged at all (*"Once this guy . . ."*) (Smith 1981, 169). Contemporary legends that are not believed by the narrator can be told as a joke for entertainment or to diffuse a tense situation (Boyes 1984, 64).

CLASSIFICATION SYSTEMS FOR CONTEMPORARY LEGENDS

To better understand the genre as well as contemporary society, considerable thought has been given to the classification of contemporary legends. Two types of classification have been devised: by type and by theme.

By Type

The classification system established by David Buchan (1978, 11) organizes the body of contemporary legends into six basic types.

1. "Happy occurrence" legends are "wish fulfillment stories showing how fate can be kind" (e.g., "Philanderer's Porsche").

2. "Merry event" legends are satirical and express, through laughter, our feelings of powerlessness and unease created by impersonal establishments and institutions (e.g., "Department Store Snakes": a customer is bitten by a snake hidden in a garment or rug that has been imported from a third world country, discussed in chapter 9).

3. "Horrific" tales are concerned with contemporary fears about underlying violence in modern society. They justify our fears and help us articulate them (e.g., "The Runaway Grandmother": this legend, explored in chapter 8, is the story of a grandmother who dies while on a family holiday and the subsequent, but unwitting, theft of her body).

4. "Unlucky event" legends underline the irony of fate (e.g., "The Exploding Toilet").

5. "Unusual event" tales have a supernatural element in a contemporary setting and validate belief in the supernatural (e.g., "The Vanishing Hitchhiker").

6. "Group lore" tales are told by a particular cultural group: students, military personnel, contact-lens users, and so on (e.g., "The Baby-Sitter": told by two main groups of tellers—baby-sitters and parents—demonstrating the possible dangers of accepting or designating responsibility to another person). Buchan refers to high schools, universities, and colleges as fruitful environments for contemporary legends because this mobile population of students generates their own legends and acts as collecting points for other legends.

By Theme

Others have classified contemporary legends according to widespread themes. These include contaminated food; fearful figures such as kidnappers in shopping malls, killers in backseats and at lovers' lanes, and alligators in sewers; crime; aliens in the body and other medical horrors; unfortunate pets; and famous people (Bell 1991, 119).

Jan Harold Brunvand devised a Type-Index for contemporary legends and includes it in his fifth collection of legends, *The Baby Train*. His index gives 10 basic categories of contemporary legend: legends about automobiles; legends about animals; horror legends; accident legends; sex and scandal legends; crime legends; business and professional legends; legends about governments; celebrity rumors and legends; and academic legends (1993, 325–47).

The legends in this book are organized according to large theme groupings that are, at times, fairly arbitrary. Individual chapters concentrate on legends that reflect fear of, and the scientific knowledge responsible for, technological innovations; contaminated food; legends of theft; animal tales; threats to our children and young people; threats to our society from satanic influences; and other scary stories.

FUNCTIONS OF CONTEMPORARY LEGENDS

Contemporary legends reflect, articulate, and validate values, attitudes, fears, and anxieties of modern society that may not be easily or readily expressed otherwise. The functions of these stories are nearly as diverse as the tellers, who relate them according to their own purposes and worldview.

Where the perceived threat to the subculture was accepted by both audience and performer, the narrative would simultaneously express and validate the belief of its hearers, leading to its acceptance in an increased number of repertoires. This would in turn provide an increase in the possible number of transmissions (Boyes 1984, 66).

Frequently, the legends relate feelings of unease about strange places (e.g., cemeteries, foreign hotels), unfamiliar people (e.g., other cultures), and bewildering situations and innovations (e.g., technological and medical advances), disclosing a worldview "that often appears unscientific, distrustful of government and technology, and reliant on stereotypical views of gender and various ethnic groups" (Bird 1992, 163).

As a Tool for Socialization

Many contemporary legends address specific dangers and themes and serve a direct and narrow didactic function: offering advice to the listeners to aid in the socialization process. For example, attending to the underlying message of "La Llorona," the Weeping Woman who murders her children, dies of remorse, and then forever searches for them, and reflecting on what can happen to a child if the mother neglects it, reinforces "appropriate" behavior in the young mothers in the audience.

Having a corpus of shared stories that reflects collective anxieties brings people together and fosters the recognition of community—the commonality of fears, knowledge, and attentional focus. These stories help connect networks of people (Fine 1992, 31).

As a Means for Dealing with Our Fear of Strangers

Contemporary legends reflect the participant's anxieties about outside forces infiltrating and harming both the individuals and the family structure. These fears were once expressed in supernatural terms: a ghost, devil, or demon created havoc for people who were unworthy, who had broken social taboos, or who created disharmony within the community. For many of us, today's "demons" are human in form, depicted by the *stranger*— a sociopath, a maniac, most often found at the margins of the community: isolated lover's lanes, deserted dorms during vacations, shopping center parking lots, and rural gas stations late at night (Lindahl 1986, 12).

Unlike traditional foes, "modern" strangers, who look and act human, can easily intrude into the wider community and hide upstairs, telephone and terrorize a teenage baby-sitter, or slip into the backseat of a car driven at night by a lone female. In our crowded, impersonal world of high-rises, condominiums, and retirement communities, people are increasingly sur-rounded by strangers. These urban communities and increasing media re-ports of random violence reinforce the idea that strangers are to be feared. "For each modern legend type, the principal question is seldom, '*Can* such an event take place?' or even '*Did* such an event take place as described?' but rather '*Whom*—or *what*—can we trust?' " (Lindahl 1986, 15).

Ethnocentric legends give vent to the xenophobia of modern society. But legends that depict strangers or a stereotype of a minority group usually reflect the values, norms, and life-style of the majority group (Klintberg 1976, 73). Negative ethnic stereotypes assume a worldview opposite the valued behaviors and characteristics of the culture telling the tale. By talking about the transgressions of immigrants, the tellers express what they themselves find normal (Klintberg 1976, 75). These stereotypical legends are readily believed because they express, validate, and reinforce the beliefs that the audience already holds.

Sociocentric legends describe subcultures that conflict with the world-view and norms of the majority culture. These subgroups include people who share similar interests or life-styles (e.g., motorcycle riders), certain age groups (e.g., teenagers), and groups who share similar, non-mainstream religious beliefs (e.g., Wiccans, satanists). Whenever a minority group is seen as a "threat" by the majority, it is incorporated into contemporary legends as the "enemy," a group of strangers who would harm the larger community. This threat may be, and in most cases is, a false perception based on misun-derstanding of and miscommunication with the subgroup. Both types of strangers, individuals and groups, are equally feared and are often inter-changeable in the legends.

As a Reflection of Changes in Life-Styles

As a result of technological innovations and evolving societal expecta-tions, Western society has undergone massive changes in a relatively short time period. The changes, fast and bewildering, cause anxiety within the community, and these anxieties are often articulated through contemporary legends.

Life-style changes influence our work, our leisure, and our interaction with the community. These changes have moved us from a society grouped together by common interests, background, and history to a society that encompasses all the groupings but at the same time separates the members of the groups by space.

As society becomes more complex, and as jobs become more technical, general competence and general knowledge are sacrificed in favor of specializations in the work force. The resulting ignorance about other specialities provides a fertile breeding ground for folk beliefs. When microwave ovens were first offered on the home market, the technology was misunderstood and feared. The legends about pets exploding in microwaves demonstrate that misunderstanding.

After being caught in a downpour with her kitten, a woman decides that she doesn't want the kitten to leave wet fur all over the furniture. So she tosses it into the microwave oven to dry it off quickly, and moments later, the kitten explodes.

In fact, though the pet would quickly cook in a microwave oven, it would not explode (Fine 1980, 223).

Until recently, a community was defined by spatial proximity. Today, a community reflects shared interests, and "community" is no longer synonymous with "neighborhood." Innovations in transportation and communication, additional leisure time and economic prosperity, and increased availability and knowledge of recreational activities have fostered specialized communities, regardless of an individual's address. These shared-interest communities have their own subsets of contemporary legends that are circulated only within that community (e.g., computer users, truck drivers, or high school students). These legends reflect the specialized concerns and experiences of the one group and, even if told to other groups, may not be decipherable by them.

Because individuals are no longer self-sufficient and no longer reside in self-sufficient communities, people are connected to larger networks that reflect increasing governmental intervention and the widening influence of national mass media. The traditional functions of the community are being transferred to national institutions perceived as uncaring of and unresponsive to the needs of the people under their jurisdiction. Families no longer grow and prepare their own food. Instead, they shop at large, "one-stop" shopping centers and purchase mass-produced items that need only to be heated or combined with other prepared ingredients for consumption. These goods produce ambiguity in the minds of consumers, for while the use of supermarket products makes life easier, the products threaten family autonomy by making the family less self-sufficient and increasingly reliant on sources beyond its control (Lindahl 1986, 9). In response to this ambiguity, the general population, feeling threatened by and alienated from these huge impersonal institutions, tell stories of snakes hidden in the products of large, multinational department stores and contaminants in the food of large, fast-food, chain restaurants (Fine 1980, 224).

Normal communication with clients, customers, employees, employers, and decision makers has become impersonal and frustrating. Instead of communicating with others face-to-face, people are expected to be happy communicating with or via faceless machines. This fixed and uncompromising machinery is frequently perceived as inefficient and irrational and provides legitimization for contemporary legends: *"In such a big company, what can you expect?"*

Corporations and government agencies have assumed social functions formerly the province of family, neighbors, and the local community. As large national agencies gain power and influence, local agencies decrease and fall by the wayside. Frustration with this vast, impersonal "interference" in the social sphere by government and corporations also provides fodder for contemporary legends. To balance this distrust, some legends show how large corporations really help by redeeming product codes for community aid. But other than these few "redemption" rumors addressed in chapter 4, most contemporary legends about these large institutions reflect negative concepts and values attributed to them (Fine 1980, 225).

The recent urbanization of the population has also caused large changes in the social life of people. Urban living leads to the following conditions: anonymity, as people are largely unknown to one another; division of labor; heterogeneity of residents who have very different characteristics; impersonal and formally prescribed relationships; and symbols of status independent of personal acquaintanceships (Fine 1980, 226).

Residents react to these conditions by expressing their concern and anxiety about anonymous, impersonal settings through contemporary legends, in which anything can, and does, happen. Only in the city, for example, can young girls be abducted and sold in "white slave markets." In small communities, the assumption is that strangers would be immediately noticed and watched carefully!

Along with rapidly changing life-styles, modern society has experienced shifting values regarding the labor force and in its attitudes towards consumption, gender roles, and sexuality. Ambivalence occurs because of this shift and the legends express, indirectly, anxieties about them that cannot be expressed directly. One such fear is that if women are no longer home to prepare meals, family life will disintegrate. Therefore, legends are told in which women who eat at fast-food establishments suffer terrible consequences. The moral of these stories reflects part of society's subconscious desire: *"Nothing bad would have happened if she had just stayed home!"* It is worth noting that the victims of "Kentucky Fried Rat" are always female! The increasing number of legends about satanic cults are another form of a "credible" explanation for the fears of a population faced with moral dilemmas and change.

As a Means of Dealing with Fear
of Technological Changes

The world of science and technology has quickly pushed society in new directions. These advances, expanding at much the same rate that religious faith has been declining, have brought society labor-saving devices "that come to us without a moral code" (Lindahl 1986, 15). "Can we trust technology?" is one of the most common questions raised by legend-tellers today.

THE ART OF TELLING
CONTEMPORARY LEGENDS

Even the grimmest tale of warning or the most sincere testimony of belief has to be told effectively if it is to impress its hearers. The conscious purpose may simply be to tell them something the narrator considers true and important, but the more he or she employs artistic skills—concision, suspense, drama, and so forth—the more impact the tale will have (Simpson 1988, 5).

The effective use of facial gestures and body language brings the legend alive in imaginations of listeners. Even if the legend is very brief, the audience will lose patience with a teller who is not proficient at bringing a story alive. Sound effects and the skillful use of silence (pauses) add to the impressive telling of the legend. Setting, both within the legend and of the legend performance itself, plays an important role in the communication process. The setting in the legend must be drawn carefully. The lover's lane of "The Hook" may be generic, but the teller must still take the listener there to visualize the action. The setting of the legend-telling is also of extreme importance in achieving the objectives of the legend-teller. If the legends are being told at camps or "slumber parties," rather than in the course of regular conversation, they are being told for effect and therefore will reflect that purpose: they will be much lengthier and usually will be polished for maximum effect.

REFERENCES

Bell, Michael E. 1991. I know it's true because it happened to my best friend's cousin: The modern legend in America. In *Courtly love in the shopping mall: Humanities programming for young adults*, edited by Evelyn Shaevel. Chicago: American Library Association, 1991, 109–28.

Bird, S. Elizabeth. 1992. *For enquiring minds: A cultural study of supermarket tabloids.* Knoxville: University of Tennessee Press.

Boyes, Georgina. 1984. Belief and disbelief: An examination of reactions to the presentation of rumour legends. In *Perspectives on contemporary legends* [CECTAL conference papers #4], edited by Paul Smith. Sheffield, England: University of Sheffield, 64–78.

Brunvand, Jan Harold. 1993. *The baby train & other lusty urban legends.* New York: W. W. Norton.

Buchan, David. 1978. The modern legend. In *Language, culture and tradition: Papers on language and folklore presented at the annual conference of the British Sociological Association,* edited by A. E. Green and J. D. A. Widdowson. The Institute of Dialect and Folklife Studies. School of English, University of Leeds. The Centre for English Cultural Tradition and Language, University of Sheffield.

Fine, Gary Alan. 1980. The Kentucky Fried Rat: Legends and modern society. *Journal of Folklore Institute* 17: 222–43. Reprinted in Fine, Gary Alan. 1992. *Manufacturing tales: Sex and money in contemporary legends.* Knoxville: University of Tennessee Press.

Hobbs, Sandy. 1978. The folktale as news. *Oral History* 6, no. 11: 74–86.

——. 1989. Contemporary legends, 1924. *FOAFTALE NEWS* 15 (September): 2.

Klintberg, Bengt af. 1976. Folksagner i dag. *Fataburen:* 69–89.

Lindahl, Carl. 1986. Psychic ambiguity at the legend core. *Journal of Folklore Research* 23, no. 1: 1–21.

Nicolini, Mary B. 1989. Is there a FOAF in your future? Urban folk legends in room 112. *English Journal* 78, no. 8: 81–84.

Oring, Elliott, ed. 1986. Folk narratives. In *Folk groups and folklore genres: An introduction.* Logan: Utah State University Press, 121–45.

Samuelson, Sue. 1981. European and American adolescent legends. *ARV* 37: 134–39.

Simpson, Jaqueline. 1988. *Scandinavian folktales.* London: Penguin.

Smith, Georgina. 1981. Urban legend, personal experience narrative and oral history: Literal and social truth in performance. *ARV* 37: 167–73.

Williams, Noel. 1984. Problems in defining contemporary legends. In *Perspectives on contemporary legends* [CECTAL conference papers #4], edited by Paul Smith. Sheffield, England: University of Sheffield, 216–28.

Young, Richard, and Judy Dockrey Young. 1991. *Ghost stories from the American Southwest: A collection of over 100 spine-tingling tales.* Little Rock, AR: August House.

PART II

2

GOSSIP, RUMORS, AND CONTEMPORARY LEGENDS

A cookie lover asked to purchase the cookie recipe from the waitress. When told that it would cost two-fifty, he said fine and told the waitress to put it on his account. When he received his statement and saw the charge for $250.00, he demanded that the charge be eliminated as he had assumed that the waitress meant $2.50. When told that the charge would stand, the cookie lover took his revenge by providing the recipe free to cookie lovers all over the world through photocopies and electronic mail.

In the body of literature arising from recent scholarship on tales such as this, there is no single precise definition for these modern stories. As shown in the previous chapter, scholars cannot even agree that these stories should be classified as legends, let alone whether they should be designated as contemporary, modern, or urban! The definitions overlap, several terms are used interchangeably, and semantics are the focal point of many debates. I have found, in both the literature and in discussions with students, that one of the most perplexing questions revolves around the lack of distinction between contemporary legends, gossip, and rumor.

Definitions of terms become even more complex when we realize that a single item can be considered, at the same time, to be a legend by folklorists, unfounded malicious gossip by the group or company that may be alluded to or even named in the stories, and a "true" happening by those telling the story. The same unsubstantiated tale is often reported as rumor or hearsay by the mass media (Smith 1984, 212). A recent example of this is the "$250 Neiman-Marcus Cookie Recipe" legend (shown above) that had a wide circulation across North America in the last few years.

Folklorists recognize this story as a legend that has been circulating, in one variation or another, since at least 1949. The legend previously claimed that the recipe was from the Mrs. Field's cookie chain instead of the Neiman-Marcus chain (Brunvand 1989, 221). Advice columnist Ann Landers denounces the story as "a widely circulating fraud which falls under the category of 'urban myth.' " She states: "It never ceases to amaze me how otherwise decent people are willing to pass on these malicious stories that have absolutely no validity" (Landers 1992). Morgan and Tucker, in their book *More Rumors!* refer to the recipe legend as "commercial vengeance rumors" (1987, 123). Mrs. Field's cookie outlets posted notices denying the rumor, calling it both a rumor and a story (Brunvand 1989, 219). Those passing the tale, however, believed it, and they used a photocopy or computer printout of the recipe as evidence of the validity of the tale.

DEFINITION OF TERMS

The flying rumours gathr'd as they roll'd,
Scarce any tale was sooner heard than told;
And all who told it added something new,
And all who heard it made enlargements too.

— Alexander Pope, "The Temple of Fame"

Before exploring contemporary legends we must briefly discuss gossip and rumor and their relationship to each other and to the legends.

Gossip

Gossip is defined as "idle talk, groundless rumors, tittle-tattle; easy unconstrained talk or writing especially about persons or social incidents" (*Concise* 1976, 462). Considered nonessential and often trivial, gossip conveys news about a person and can reflect both positive and negative intent. Though gossip is largely considered an oral genre, the vast number of tabloids for sale demonstrate that gossip is equally at home in the print media.

"Gossip" originally meant "god-related" and designated a godparent. The meaning of the word expanded to include a close friend who could be considered a godparent. By the 18th century, the word gained a second meaning, that of a "tippling companion." At about the same time, gossip became connected specifically with women: "one who runs about tattling like women at a lying-in" (Spacks 1985, 25). It was not until the early 1800s that gossip was defined as a mode of conversation rather than a type of person, and became the word we use today, meaning idle or groundless rumors and talk (Spacks 1985, 26).

The word "gossip," in all its various early meanings, can be found in Shakespeare's *The Comedy of Errors*. A "gossips' feast" is held for metaphorical godparents, the baptismal sponsors (the original meaning); the Duke declares his eagerness to "gossip" as a good companion (meaning communal

merrymaking, a later definition); and the slave refers to gossiping as generalized companionship (implying talk as its chief activity, a developing definition). "Shakespeare's usage stresses positive implications: the gossiping,
in all its meanings, declares happiness and closeness, an end to misery, and
an appropriate resolution for comedy" (Spacks 1985, 36).

Rumor

Rumor is defined as "general talk, report or hearsay, of doubtful accu-
racy" (*Concise* 1976, 987). Rumor, for the most part, is considered to be a brief,
speculative message that lacks a distinctly narrative element. Allport and
Postman, in *The Psychology of Rumor*, define rumor as "a specific (or topical)
proposition for belief, passed along from person to person, usually by word
of mouth, without secure standards of evidence being presented" (1947, ix).

But while gossip typically deals with the personal affairs of individuals,
rumors may deal with places and events of great importance and prominence
(Rosnow and Fine 1976, 11). Rumor and gossip are interwoven when news
is unsubstantiated and focuses on some interesting but objectively trivial,
personal highlight. "Like rumor, gossip is also given a prominent role in mass
communications which repeat the latest exciting small talk about political,
society, professional, and entertainment personalities" (Rosnow and Fine
1976, 98).

DIFFERENCES

Although there are no clear-cut divisions between rumors and gossip,
and the two forms often overlap, several basic differences stand out. While
gossip usually travels within a defined group through existing communication circuits, rumor creates its own communication pathways and groups.
Gossip mirrors the moral code of a small group, while rumors normally
express a public moral code and may be a bit less spontaneous than gossip
(Bird 1979, 72).

Gossip is an unverified message about some *one* while *rumor* is an
unverified message about some *thing*, either trite or of great importance.
According to the literature, the major difference among gossip, rumor, and
contemporary legend is that, although the three forms are similar in function
and content, the contemporary legend tends to be a fully developed story,
with details and dramatic action.

A statement such as, "*Boy, did my boss get burned the other night when he
tried to buy a cookie recipe from Neiman-Marcus!*" would be gossip. A rumor
could contend that "*Neiman-Marcus stores charge $250.00 for a single cookie
recipe.*" The legend filled in the details and produced the recipe. The version
I received in January 1992 ended with the declaration, "*Have fun! This is not
a joke—This is a true story!*"

Each of the previous statements would be wrong because, as Brunvand points out, Neiman-Marcus does not sell cookies, let alone the recipe (Brunvand 1989, 226). Ann Landers confirms that Neiman-Marcus does not make their own cookies and does not charge for any of their recipes (Landers 1992).

SIMILARITIES

There are definite similarities among rumors, gossip, and contemporary legends. All three forms of communication are based on the person-to-person transmission of unverified information presented as "true." All three are also told as a form of diversion, as an expression of fears and anxieties, and as justification for certain beliefs or actions. All three types of communication constitute more than the giving and receiving of information. They offer clues to the participants' point of view, their sources of information, and the commonalities among the group (Spacks 1985, 21).

All three types of communication also:

1. Use concrete details and dialogue to enhance credibility. All three strain for the appearance of authority, and all three claim to convey "inside" information that rarely consists of good news.

2. Contain content about unusual experiences or events. All are realistic genres, rooted in actual experience, that focus on events relevant to the teller and the listener.

3. Are accounts that can be updated with contemporary facts and evidence, but also draw upon traditional materials and popular folk beliefs.

4. Perform informational and pedantic functions. All three forms "appraise events of the real world and seek to understand, verify, and possibly explain its workings" (Bird 1979, 94–96).

The interplay of these three genres is not new. Bird uses "facts" about the Roman emperor Nero to demonstrate an example of fluidity of rumor content. Ill feeling toward Emperor Nero, coupled with the confusion about the source of the great fire that burned Rome, led to rumors that Nero was responsible; subsequent accounts suggested that the tyrant had sung, fiddled, and composed an ode while Rome burned. This rumor generated an historical legend, proverbs, and folk wisdom used even today in a variety of social situations (Bird 1979, 83).

In spite of the similarities between legends and rumors, and although contemporary legends may explain or incorporate current rumors, legends tend to attach themselves to different local settings, have a longer life-span, and have a wider acceptance than rumors and gossip (Brunvand 1980, 51). "Rumors act as reinforcements for already existing legends; a legend which does not have oral circulation but exists in the memory of the people of a community may spring back to life when a suggestive rumor becomes current" (Mullen 1972, 98).

A legend may be clusters of rumors drawn to one focal point. In discussing the legend of "The Hatchetman," Patrick B. Mullen affirms that the legend "contains several rumors: the rumor of a murder, the prediction of a mass murder, the rumor of an escaped mental patient, and many localized details" (1972, 96).

"The Hatchetman," familiar on campuses during the late 1960s, tells the tale of a mass murderer on campus (unnamed but near a body of water) who will strike on Halloween (or another designated date). The rumors about the Hatchetman centered on where the information came from (predictions) and the actual location. The identity of the Hatchetman did not seem to be of primary concern!

The relevance of contemporary legends often depends on current rumors and gossip. Thus we will look a little more closely at the types and functions of gossip and rumor before turning our attention to the legends themselves.

GOSSIP: TYPES AND FUNCTIONS

Rosnow and Fine identified three primary types of gossip according to its function: informative, moralizing, and entertaining. Informative gossip is used for news trading and for providing participants with a cognitive map of the social environment. Moralizing gossip is a manipulative device through which one person attempts to gain social control over another. The third type is primarily for the mutual entertainment of the participants (Rosnow and Fine 1976, 130).

Patricia Spacks suggests that there are typically two modes of gossip: distilled malice and serious gossip. "Distilled malice" plays with the reputations, motivations, and proposed feelings of others, often serving a serious purpose for the gossiper. Malicious gossip, even if subconscious, can further the gossiper's own political or social ambitions, gratify envy and rage, or generate a sense of power. More commonly, however, gossip doesn't result from purposeful malice but, rather, from lack of thought (Spacks 1985, 4–5).

The second mode of gossip, at the opposite end of the spectrum, is "serious gossip," which exists only as a function of intimacy. Serious gossip is usually shared among two or three people "to express wonder and uncertainty and locate certainties, and to enlarge their knowledge of one another" (Spacks 1985, 5). Though it may use the stuff of scandal, serious gossip never goes beyond the circle of the gossipers.

Gossip serves three main functions: social control, preservation of status, and diversion and entertainment. Gossip is frequently used as "a means of reinforcing group norms, in that people are motivated to conform in order to avoid being a target of gossip" (Koenig 1985, 2). People use gossip to establish their own respectability by implicitly comparing their own behavior favorably with the subject of the gossip and behaving accordingly.

In its first function, social control, gossip acts as a catalyst of social process. It provides groups with means of self-control and emotional stability. It circulates both information and evaluation, supplies a mode of socialization and social control, facilitates self-knowledge by offering bases for comparison, creates catharsis for guilt, constitutes a form of wish fulfillment, helps to control competition, facilitates the selection of leaders, and generates power (Spacks 1985, 34).

Rosnow and Fine describe three groups that employ gossip for its second function, to preserve status: professional groups who mesh gossip and jargon to make their conversation practically indecipherable to an outsider; social groups that seek to preserve their exclusiveness by closing doors to anyone who cannot gossip about the present or past membership; and social groups that have exclusiveness thrust on them, such as ethnic or minority groups (Rosnow and Fine 1976, 90).

The third function of gossip is entertainment. Gossip is spread as a means of passing time, used for shock value and to prompt laughter. Effective gossip "delights in raising its subjects on a pedestal and then delights in their fall back to the ground" (Stephens 1988, 105). The negative connotation that "gossip" has today lies in the fact that it is often exchanged with a touch of "cattiness," a certain delight in the misfortune of others. Communication among friends and acquaintances usually revolves around people and situations that all members of the group are familiar with so that all members can participate in the conversation. Gossip as entertainment helps to maintain the fluidity of communication patterns (Rosnow and Fine 1976, 92). The tidbits of gossip provide links between both the topics of conversation and the speakers.

RUMOR: TYPES AND FUNCTIONS

There are three broad categories of rumors defined according to the effect the rumor has on the listener: "pipe dream rumors," those that express one's hopes and fantasies but are otherwise harmless; "bogies," those rumors that mirror fears and anxieties; and "wedge-driving (aggressive) rumors," those that divide groups (Rosnow and Fine 1976, 23).

In a pipe dream rumor, one may get something for nothing. For example, countless people have believed the rumor that pull-tabs from aluminum pop cans can be redeemed for free time on a kidney dialysis machine (these rumors are also known as "redemption rumors"). Bogie rumors take many forms in describing our fear and anxieties. They often cite specific products, manufacturers, or public buildings and amusement parks and are likely to cause consumers to shy away from either purchasing certain products or visiting certain sites, causing marketing headaches for those companies. The rumor of the child being kidnapped from a department store or amusement park and being found later in the washroom with her blond hair cut short and dyed black reflects parents' anxieties about large impersonal places where there are so many threats to their children, and may prompt fearful parents to avoid such places. Bogie rumors that focus on kidnapping are also called "abduction legends"; they are one focus of chapter 10. An example of the third category of rumor, the wedge-driving rumor, is the one about rat meat being served as chicken in various ethnic restaurants in Europe, or in popular fast-food chains in North America. The belief in the "Kentucky Fried Rat" often causes aggressive behavior against the food outlets and their proprietors (see chapter 7, "Contaminated Food Rumors"). Until recently, European fast-food restaurants were owned and operated by "foreign" families. The rumors of rat meat and other non-food items being served to their patrons caused many confrontations in small communities.

Jean-Noel Kapferer devised a typology of rumors that includes six basic types:

The Six Types of Rumors

	ORIGIN OF RUMOR		
	Event	Detail	Exclusively Fantasy
BIRTH PROCESS Spontaneous	1	2	3
Provoked	4	5	6

(1990, 37)

Kapferer states that these types depend first of all on the factual grounds of the rumors (1990, 37). Type 1 rumors are the spontaneous result of an event whose meaning is uncertain or ambiguous. For example, a police search for a witness to a possible slaying develops spontaneously into a rumor that the man the police are searching for is the murderer and extremely dangerous, although the police and media stress this is not necessarily the case. Type 1 rumors offer "explanations" for bewildering occurrences. After the assassination of John F. Kennedy, numerous rumors circulated as people struggled to come to terms with the actual event. Type 2 rumors are based on details or signs that suddenly come to the attention of people. Attention is drawn to these details because of the rumors, although the details have been there all along. An example of this type of rumor is the "mysterious food additives" rumor that had consumers carefully reading packaging for the first time. People's selective attention unveils previously hidden "realities" (1990, 37). Type 3 rumors are stories that crop up without any precipitating fact: contemporary legends! These rumors, according to Kapferer's typology, develop from scratch without, in most instances, even the slightest event that could be misinterpreted and therefore the genesis of the rumor (1990, 37–38). An example of this type of rumor is "Department Store Snakes." No evidence of the event taking place or of a person being bitten is necessary for the rumor to take off and take on a life of its own. As details are added, the rumor develops into a story that is told as true. "The fact that these floating stories typically become 'true,' somewhere or other, shows that some people make no distinction between fantasy and reality" (1990, 38). Kapferer claims that contemporary legends dwell almost exclusively on "the collective data bank of symbols and unconscious mythical motives and very little on factual events or details" (1990, 38). These are added later by the individual tellers of the legends.

Provoked rumors are usually more malevolent. Type 4 rumors vary from deliberate misinformation to a search for sensationalism. Events are purposely misinterpreted and spread for political or social gain. Type 5 rumors, like those about satanic activity, are spread widely once a specific group becomes "aware" of the details. "No one took any notice of the packaging [of Proctor & Gamble products] before a fundamentalist religious community not only drew attention to it but also engendered its satanic explanation" (Kapferer 1990, 37). Until the symbol was analyzed and pro-claimed, in rumors, as evidence of satanic involvement, the majority of the population paid the logo very little attention at all. Once "negative" attention was drawn to the logo, however, the logo became a detriment to the corpo-ration and was eventually discarded. Leaks and confidential information also fall into the type 5 category. Type 6 rumors, concocted by the teller to provoke a certain reaction in the audience, are told for entertainment.

Scholars suggest that several conditions are necessary before a rumor can develop. Ambiguity and anxiety about a subject must exist for rumors to flourish. There must be a demand for news on a topic and a lack of reliable information or hard evidence. Rumors grow and thrive in unusual or unfamiliar situations. These situations include major disruptions such as natural disas-ters and wars as well as local intrusions such as a stranger in the neighbor-hood or a missing child. The rumor must come from a source that is trusted by the target group and the content must be plausible and consistent with the prevailing mood (Shibutani 1966, 199). A rumor cannot survive if people do not believe or trust the person spreading the message or if it is widely inconsistent with their value and belief systems.

Rumors are usually short-lived. Many rumors die a natural death, either because people have become bored with the issue or because it is established that the rumor was unfounded. Rumors about disasters are often stopped by prompt denial from a credible source (Rosnow and Fine 1976, 48). Rumors that are not disproven are often attached to traditional folklore and grow into contemporary legends and circulate on a much wider scale.

The legend of "The Stolen Kidney," which reflects the fears and anxieties of urban living, is based on rumors that evolved around actual cases of people being mugged. The rumor embellishes the mugging to the removal of the unconscious person's kidney for organ transplants. This rumor has escalated into a contemporary legend that has a wide circulation today and is explored in chapter 10. Recently I have heard this legend referring to an Edmonton man at EuroDisney in France, to a Toronto man crossing the Canadian-American border to do some shopping, and to a woman jogging in Central Park in New York City. These legends often go into hibernation until a new rumor awakens the legend and starts it circulating again.

Two functions of rumor are similar to those of gossip. Like gossip, rumors are told as diversion and entertainment. They also function, like gossip, as a means of preserving status and enhancing images. Many people try to enhance their prestige by pretending to have access to "inside information" or by presenting themselves as focal points in communication networks, and try to maintain this reputation by giving their views (Shibutani 1966, 14).

Tamotsu Shibutani, in his sociological study of rumor, considers a third function of rumors, seeing them as a format for collective problem-solving. He states that rumors are "a recurrent form of communication through which men caught together in an ambiguous situation attempt to construct a meaningful interpretation of it by pooling their intellectual resources" (1966, 17). During disasters, any available news, verified or not, is exchanged in the spirit of mutual assistance. And, although the media are important sources of information, public opinion is shaped in local discussions, and rumors often play an important part in public opinion (131).

The fourth function rumors serve is as verification and justification for anxieties, fears, and prejudices. Allport and Postman write that "by permitting one to slap at the thing one hates, it relieves a primary emotional urge; it serves to justify one in feeling as he does about the situation, and to explain to himself and to others why he feels that way" (1947, 37). Rumors concerning a threatening and unpredictable world make a person's disturbed and anxious state seem appropriate and reasonable. Fredrick Koenig, in his exploration on commercial rumors, states that "fears are apprehensions regarding specific, recognized threats; anxiety is an apprehension that is not related to anything known to the person." He goes on to state that many people have both fears and anxieties that makes them doubly receptive to the appropriate rumors (1985, 33).

Jean-Noel Kapferer (1990, 43–47) presents six reasons to explain why people spread rumors:

1. Rumors are news. News is not narrative or anecdote but is information that has *pragmatic interest* to the audience. A reader's or listener's first reaction to news is to repeat it to and discuss it with someone else, to try and make sense of it. Attention shifts very quickly from repeating the news to interpreting the news and drawing conclusions.

2. People need to speak about issues to understand them. Because newspaper readers have confidence in the media, they believe that the facts are authentic and verified. Oral news, however, is not as

readily believed, and the listener needs to discuss the details to know what to think. According to Kapferer, "The fact of speaking about information reveals what kind of consensus there is about it in the group to which we belong" (44). We shape a consensus in our everyday conversations by contributing details, additional elements, and our own hypotheses.

3. Rumors need to be transmitted to convince people of certain things on the teller's agenda. The speaker is totally committed to the content and wants others to be aware of the facts. This happens when rumors play on personal anxieties or resolve conflicts. "Rumors become an attempt to convert people to one's own views: the more the circle of believers expands, the more one feels one is right" (45).

4. Rumors are spread to release tension. "Speaking about the [rumors] is the first step towards reducing anxiety, for our interlocutors may prove to us that the rumors are groundless or meaningless" (46).

5. Rumors are transmitted because they are surprising, funny, or shocking, and the teller wishes to entertain the listeners. Similar to the telling of a joke, the passing of a rumor provides entertainment and prestige. "That is why urban legends last so long: they are savoured at the end of a meal, or in a bar while sipping on an after-dinner drink; they provide a certain momentary pleasure in consuming" (47).

6. Talk for talk's sake. Rumors are employed as conversation ice-breakers or fillers in conversation. Rumors are transmitted because people need something to talk about!

Communal washing places and contemporary markets, hairdressers, hallways, and cafeterias are the hubs of rumors because people in these places create or transmit a host of information, whether false or true, born of the need to arouse interest, converse, or say something entertaining (Kapferer 1990, 49).

We must not underestimate the power of rumors. Strong rumors "shape or limit the effectiveness of political, economic, and cultural institutions. They are markers of public attitudes and concerns" (Fine 1991, 80). Times of stress and anxiety such as war or disaster nurture rumors and lend themselves particularly to the exercise of racial prejudice (sometimes otherwise dormant), the revival of folk belief, the creation of new myths, or the flight of rumors. A notable characteristic of all these conditions is complete disregard of consistency (Burstein 1959, 367).

RUMOR AND
CONTEMPORARY LEGENDS

Gossip and rumor are interrelated, overlap, and are terms that are consistently interchanged. Contemporary legends have a similar relationship with gossip and rumor. The basic difference among the three is that contemporary legends are narratives. The legends are closer to the definition of rumor than gossip in that they usually discuss "larger" events with a wider audience than most gossip reaches. Two essential elements in both rumor and contemporary legends are credibility of the content and the teller and a homogenic culture within which to transmit the item.

Credibility

Because credibility is generally lacking in rumors, *private* confirmation of the "truth" is often necessary before the listener will accept the information. This confirmation is usually claimed to be secondhand information from a friend known to have "actually" witnessed the event—the friend-of-a-friend of the contemporary legend. "Rumors always reach us through a friend, colleague, or relative who was not himself the firsthand witness of the event in question, but a friend of that witness" (Kapferer 1990, 6).

The opening "hook" of both rumors and legends must use attention-getting devices to capture the listener's interest. Therefore, the opening frame frequently testifies to the credibility of the source and information (Bird 1979, 42). The confirmation of the credibility of the legend or the rumor is important, as this confirmation may spark group discussions and challenges as the group members decide whether or not the information is reliable (Bird 1979, 57).

Homogenic Culture

"To be sustained, rumor normally must conform to the group's current attitudes, anxieties, expectations, and underlying culture" (Bird 1979, 58). This common cultural background, be it ethnic or social, is necessary for the circulation of contemporary legends as well. Though logic may discourage literal belief in either type of communication, rumors and legends convey a moral or symbolic truth to both the audience and the teller. If the audience does not subscribe to the teller's cultural beliefs, the rumor or legend will not be believed or circulated further (Bird 1979, 59).

The power of rumors and contemporary legends comes from their ability to influence our perceptions and give meaning to facts that we may not have noticed or whose meanings may not have been obvious to us. This process is illustrated by a Chinese parable from the third century B.C.:

> *A man couldn't find his axe anywhere. He suspected his neighbor's son of having taken it and began to watch him carefully. He looked like a typical axe thief; what he said could only be construed as the words of an axe thief; all his attitudes and behavior were charac-teristic of a man who has stolen an axe. But quite unexpectedly, in spading the ground in his garden one day, the man suddenly found his axe. The next day, when he saw his neighbor's son again, he saw nothing—neither in his looks nor his behavior— suggesting an axe thief.* (Kapferer 1990, 77)

IMPORTANCE OF GOSSIP, RUMOR, AND CONTEMPORARY LEGEND IN MODERN SOCIETY

Patricia A. Turner, in her explorations of rumor and contemporary legends in African American communities, contends that "few genres of oral discourse more tellingly reveal racial anxieties than do rumor and legend" (1987, 294). Donald Bird states that "the study of rumor is important because rumor not only influences history and reflects collective problem-solving, but expresses underlying folk ideas and tells us much about mainstream values" (Bird 1979, 1). Daniel Decotterd, in his article "Gossip, Rumour and Legend: A Plea for a Psychological and Cross-Cultural Approach," argues that

> The deep roots of rumour and gossip could no doubt be found in the fear inspired by other people and in existential jealousy. Our perception of the world is slanted by our personal wishes and desires. Seen in this light, gossip, rumour and legend, transmitted in a community or by the media, reveal a lot about the mentality of the country in which they appear. (1988, 239)

Therefore, we, as educators, parents, and concerned citizens, should be aware of gossip, rumor, and contemporary legends and the role they play in our daily lives. As Allport and Postman pointed out:

> Here too lies an argument for including a basic study of rumor in programs of social studies in the schools and colleges. Young people who know the law of rumor may be able to safeguard themselves in many types of situations where evidence is insecure. (1947, 36)

REFERENCES

Allport, Gordon W., and Leo Postman. 1947. *The psychology of rumor*. New York: Henry Holt.

Bird, Donald Allport. 1979. *Rumor as folklore: An interpretation and inventory*. Ph.D. diss., Indiana University.

Brunvand, Jan Harold. 1980. Heard about the solid cement cadillac or the nude in the camper or the alligator in the sewer or the snake in the K-Mart? *Psychology Today* (June): 50–62.

———. 1989. *Curses! Broiled again!* New York: W. W. Norton.

Burstein, Sona Rosa. 1959. Folklore, rumour, and prejudice. *Folklore* 70 (June): 361–81.

Concise Oxford dictionary of current English. 1976. 6th ed. Oxford: Clarendon Press.

Decotterd, Daniel. 1988. Gossip, rumour and legend: A plea for a psychological and cross-cultural approach. In *Monsters with iron teeth: Perspectives on contemporary legends, vol. III*, edited by Gillian Bennett and Paul Smith. Sheffield, England: Sheffield Academic Press, 239–40.

Fine, Gary Alan. 1991. The republic of rumors: Corporate targets. *Indicator South Africa* 8, no. 4 (Spring): 80–84.

Kapferer, Jean-Noel. 1990. *Rumors: Uses, interpretations and images*. New Brunswick, NJ: Transaction.

Koenig, Fredrick. 1985. *Rumor in the marketplace: The social psychology of commercial hearsay*. Dover, MA: Auburn House.

Landers, Ann. 1992. Only a crumb would repeat $250 cookie-recipe myth. Syndicated newspaper column. (June 29).

Morgan, Hal, and Kerry Tucker. 1987. *More rumors!* New York: Penguin.

Mullen, Patrick B. 1972. Modern legend and rumor theory. *Journal of the Folklore Institute* 9 (August–December): 95–109.

Rosnow, Ralph L., and Gary Alan Fine. 1976. *Rumor and gossip: The social psychology of hearsay*. New York: Elsvier.

Shibutani, Tamotsu. 1966. *Improvised news: A sociological study of rumor*. Indianapolis: Bobbs-Merrill.

Smith, Paul. 1984. On the receiving end: When legend becomes rumour. In *Perspectives on contemporary legends* [CECTAL conference papers series # 4], edited by Paul Smith. Sheffield: University of Sheffield, 197–215.

Spacks, Patricia Meyer. 1985. *Gossip*. New York: Alfred A. Knopf.

Stephens, Mitchell. 1988. *A history of news: From the drum to the satellite*. New York: Viking.

Turner, Patricia A. 1987. Church's fried chicken and the Klan: A rhetorical analysis of rumor in the black community. *Western Folklore* 46 (October): 294–306.

3 MASS MEDIA AND CONTEMPORARY LEGENDS

Oi Veh, What a Day

TEL AVIV (Reuters)—An Israeli housewife's fight with the cockroach that wouldn't die landed her husband in hospital with burns on "sensitive parts," a broken pelvis and broken ribs. The Jerusalem Post *reported Thursday that the wife was frightened by the insect when she found it in their living room. She stepped on it, threw it in the toilet and then sprayed a full can of insecticide on it when it refused to die. Her husband came home from work, sat on the toilet and lit a cigarette. He threw the cigarette butt into the bowl, igniting the insecticide fumes. This "seriously burned his sensitive parts," the* Post *wrote delicately. There was worse to come. When paramedics arrived, they quickly placed the afflicted man on a stretcher. But when told the cause of the accident, they laughed uncontrollably and as a result dropped the stretcher down the stairs. This led to the broken ribs and pelvis. The man is recovering. (Edmonton Journal, August 26, 1988, A1)*

Popular culture and the mass media are active retellers of contemporary legends. At times, the legends are the starting point or catalyst for a story idea; at other times, they are the focus of a wide-ranging, "true" news feature. Because contemporary legends maintain a consistent relevance and appeal to Western society, the mass media delight in communicating the drama, the warnings, and the humor in the tales. "Their single-episode format, coupled with their plausibility and startling plots (and what press story doesn't aim to be startling), makes them highly newsworthy" (Smith 1992, 42). This chapter explores news in various formats (in particular newspapers, representing serious news, and tabloid, representing less credible news) and its relationship to contemporary legends. "The legend is a product of modern life; it reveals the interaction of oral tradition, mass media, and written literature more directly than the venerable folklore forms and also cuts across different layers of modern society" (Degh 1968, 72).

TYPES OF NEWS STORIES

The news is relayed to the public in various forms, and the type of news is directly related to the public's conception of reliability and actuality. Moreover, the different types of news are interwoven with each other and with other aspects of popular culture. However, they all have something in common: the desire to interest their audience. People are fascinated by dramatic stories; it's dramatic stories and legends that people repeat. Therefore, the network news shows run dramatic feature stories, and reporters, talk show hosts, novelists, screenwriters, and people repeating jokes and legends emphasize dramatic, compelling images (Best 1991, 112).

"Hard" News. Stories about the day's events related in the daily newspapers and daily broadcasts on radio and television are defined as "hard" news. They focus on a particular event and are factual in content.

Feature Stories. Feature stories also appear in the daily press and news programming, but, instead of focusing on a particular event, they attempt to describe general patterns and investigate on-going situations.

Talk Show News. Largely seen as pseudo-news, talk show news stories "vary in their pretensions to seriousness and respectability" (Best 1991, 110). As the popularity of talk shows grew in the late 1980s, so did a corresponding demand for interesting and provocative guests. Common talk show topics delve into claims about new social problems, including warnings about dangerous deviants. Guests often "report having firsthand experience as victims, former deviants, or experts" (Best 1991, 111). Talk show news is often cited as the authenticating source for contemporary legends (e.g., "I heard it on Oprah").

Docudrama. Televised documentaries are constructed from hard news to provide entertainment. They vary in their fidelity to the original events from "legitimate" documentaries to "docudramas," in which "the genre shades imperceptibly into fictional, made-for-television movies about social problems" (Best 1991, 111). Frequently, docudrama incorporates contemporary legend to add credibility or shock value to the message.

NEWSPAPERS

Newspapers are an important resource for anyone interested in contemporary legends. Not only do contemporary legends often appear on the newspaper pages, but there are numerous similarities between the two types of "information."

While folklorists and other scholars consistently compare contemporary legends to traditional folktales and myths, neither of these forms truly represent the boundaries of contemporary legends. There is, perhaps, a closer affinity to news on one boundary (contemporary legends) and history on the other (traditional legends) (Oring 1990, 173). Similarities between newspapers and contemporary legend exist in form, content, and function: both are cyclical in nature; both attempt to represent the content in a factual and objective manner; and both present their audience with confirmation for their fears and opinions.

Cyclical Nature

In his article on food scares in Great Britain, A. D. Beardsworth discusses the relationship between the news and its audience, whose reaction produces additional news. Because novelty and sensation are important news values, the media reports all the new and sensational items possible and then reports, again as news, the reaction of the audience (1990, 12). Such reactions are usually presented with such drama that it produces a further reaction from the public, which is once again deemed newsworthy. A cycle develops and the media maintains it for as long as the subject is of interest. "Issues may re-emerge weeks, months or even years later when their novelty value has been re-established as the result of a period out of the public eye" (12). The circular pattern of news resembles the pattern of contemporary legends as they are constantly updated and refurbished with new prominence when, once again, they are thought to be "newsworthy" (novel and relevant).

Credibility

The major stated difference among hard news, tabloid reporting, and popular fiction is credibility, which is measured by "factuality" and "objectivity." Objectivity means separating facts from emotional responses and interpretations. Objective facts can be verified, and once interpretations (values) are attributed to a source, they can also be presented as fact. If the media is expressing its own interpretation, however, the article is not news but an editorial or opinion piece. Oring (1990, 164–67) maintains that credibility of news is an illusion because

1. the selection of what is to serve as news can be neither factual nor objective;

2. the news is organized and communicated as "stories"; and

3. the news can never be independent of the process of collecting it.

The credibility of contemporary legends also depends upon the factuality and objectivity of the tale and teller. Factuality is demonstrated by grounding the tale with people and places familiar to the audience. Objectivity is verified through attribution to an authoritative source (often a newspaper or television report).

Bizarre Messages

The qualities that modern journalists are trained to look for in news stories include: impact, emotional appeal, conflict, timeliness, proximity, prominence, and the unusual (Stephens 1988, 32). It is the unusual, the nonroutine, and the unexpected that is the focus of the news (Manoff and Schudson 1987, 168). Journalism, therefore, focuses on the bizarre events that strain credibility and deviate from normal life. This is true of the "respectable" press as well as of the tabloids. These bizarre accounts function as a counterphobia for overcoming fear and anxieties, reassuring the audience that the thoughts, opinions, and often the prejudices the audience holds are respectable and representative of the general population (Manoff and Schudson 1987, 168).

In the early history of newspaper reporting, these bizarre stories were "consigned to folklore, the oral tradition, and other underground modes of storytelling." They then took up residency in the penny press as the unexplained and unexplainable desiderata of society, labeled by the French as *faits-divers* ("fillers"), which now appear in all modes of the media. The bizarre elements in the stories, of universal appeal and significance, become more pronounced as the story travels from the most to the least respectable journal, becoming the main news of the tabloids. "What is filler in the straight press is feature in the tabloids" (Manoff and Schudson 1987, 168–70).

Jan Harold Brunvand, in a recent article, discusses both the development of the bizarre legend at the beginning of this chapter and the media's varied responses to it. Variants of the story cite hair spray, perfume, alcohol, paint thinner, kerosene, or gasoline instead of insecticide as the hazardous culprit (1993, 104). In several versions, the toilet is not a factor; rather, a motorcycle spills gasoline. While Brunvand can trace a possible history of the legend to the days of using volatile liquids to clean outhouses, he concludes that its most recent history is its circulation around the world via news services, subsequent retractions, computer and military information service networks, tabloid elaborations, and the reentry of the tale into oral traditions as people ask *"Did you hear about . . . ?"* (1993, 117).

CONTEMPORARY LEGENDS
IN NEWSPAPERS

In his article "Read All About It," Paul Smith examines the relationship between contemporary legends and newspapers and concludes that there are six basic approaches employed by newspapers when dealing with contemporary legends: reporting, exposing, retracting, educating, entertaining, and advertising. Because folklorists and behavioral scientists regularly use newspapers as sources for contemporary legends, the variety of presentational forms, and the manner in which they are employed, are essential knowledge (1992, 66).

Reporting

Reporting contemporary legends as factual news occurs when the reporter communicates what he or she believes is a true story. Often these reported legends can appear on the front page, as did the story about the exploding toilet in Tel Aviv, which appeared in major newspapers across North America during August of 1988. Smith follows the evolution of that news item from *The Jerusalem Post* to Reuters News Agency and then to other news agencies such as *Oracle* (British teletext news service) and the CBC (Canadian Broadcasting Corporation) (Smith 1992, 46). Not only did the news item appear on the front page of my local newspaper, it was also part of the national news on both CBC radio and CBC television broadcasts. The version at the beginning of this chapter was published in the *Edmonton Journal* and gave me enormous pleasure, as my telephone rang all morning: *"Did you see the story in the paper?"*

Exposing

Exposing oral or reported contemporary legends as "untrue" stories is a second way of dealing with them in the newspaper. Journalists are supposed to research the stories that they receive. Frequently, when they discover that it is one of the circulating legends, they gleefully expose it as "untrue" for their readers. For example, the following article from the *Sunday Times* "exposing" the "Exploding Toilet" legend:

> Some stories never die—they just go round and round. . . . At least 20 years ago another such story surfaced in Europe about a plumber who, in a chapter of accidents, is finally dropped down some stairs by ambulance men. Lo and behold, it appeared this week as "news"

in Johannesburg newspapers. Once the setting was Budapest, where a plumber was injured when his wife gave him a playful squeeze. The latest report is datelined Tel Aviv. . . . Very funny—in whatever guise—but don't believe a word of it! (Smith 1992, 48)

In addition to reporters, alleged "victims" of the legends, eagle-eyed readers, and folklorists also expose "news" items as contemporary legends. It was a reader of the *Edmonton Journal* who debunked the legend "The Turkey in the Hat." (Additional discussion of this legend can be found in chapter 8.)

"Letter of the Day: Another Urban Myth"

Don't believe everything you read in the paper. Likewise—if you're a journalist—don't believe everything you read on the wire services. In preparing his "People" column published by *The Journal* on June 4, Tom Sawyer came across an item that was too good to be true. The story, "The cold, hard truth," told of a Swiss shoplifter who fainted after hiding a frozen chicken in her bra.

This urban legend had been making the rounds for nearly 20 years. In 1974, Swedish newspapers were fooled by reports of a male shoplifter who tried a similar trick with his hat, and ended up in hospital with "icing up of the brain." Since then, similar stories have periodically appeared in print around the world. Professor Jan Harold Brunvand, the world's leading expert on urban legends, documented the tale of "The Shoplifter and the Frozen Chicken" in his book, *The Mexican Pet.* (*Edmonton Journal*, "Letters to the Editor," June 26, 1992)

Retracting

Newspapers sometimes retract, thereby exposing, contemporary legends previously reported as factual news. "In the case of retractions, the newspaper admits that it had failed to identify a story as a contemporary legend and instead has treated it as factual news" (Smith 1992, 51). Smith contends that such retractions are rare. This is in part because it is difficult for the general public to verify the truth of a news item, as the items usually refer to individuals or institutions outside the average reader's circle of acquaintances. Readers tend to accept what is published in the papers "because we *trust* that particular source to tell us the truth" (Smith 1992, 53).

Rumor researchers and specialists tend to assume that the media plays little role in the dissemination of rumors, assuming that its primary function is to publish denials. But denials often have the opposite effect, actually contributing to the diffusion of the rumor and even reinforcing it. In fact, the media play a leading role in diffusing and sometimes even creating contemporary legends (Renard 1991, 16).

The *Edmonton Journal*'s ombudsman explained in the paper, several weeks after the article about the exploding toilet appeared on the front page, the reasons why the story had been accepted (and printed) as true—the source (Reuters News Agency) was trustworthy, and time available to follow leads is limited. If the location of the story had been Edmonton, he states, it probably would not have passed the newspaper's system of checks and balances and would not have been published. The retraction from the wire services was not published in this newspaper for almost a week after the initial article in the paper.

Educating

Educating the reader through the presentation of contemporary legends often takes the form of incorporating news items, exposés, and entertainment into one piece. Advice columns such as "Ann Landers" and "Dear Abby" are common vehicles for this education (Smith 1992, 54). After receiving numerous variants of "the cookie-recipe" legend, Ann Landers sets her readers straight:

**Only a Crumb Would
Repeat $250 Cookie-Recipe Myth**

Dear Boiling: Your letter is an example of a widely circulating fraud which falls under the category of "urban myth." This cookie story has been in circulation for at least six years. As of this time, I have received 20 versions of your letter from various parts of the country. It's too bad that some people don't have anything better to do. . . . For openers, Neiman-Marcus does not make its own cookies and has never made a chocolate chip oatmeal cookie. Moreover, Neiman-Marcus does not charge for any of its recipes. . . . It never ceases to amaze me how otherwise decent people are willing to pass on these malicious stories that have absolutely no validity. . . . Please, readers, before you become part of the wrecking crew, ask for some proof that what "they" say is true. (Landers 1992)

Entertaining

Contemporary legends are also used by newspapers to entertain the reader. They can be published as fictional literary renditions, as items taken from the tabloids, and as content matter for cartoon strips. Frequently, the literal story is followed by these retellings, but more often, the ideas, attitudes, and concept of the legends are used (Smith 1992, 62).

Advertising

Advertising commercial products using contemporary legends is done in several ways. The legend can be the focus of the advertisement, or the beliefs represented in the legend can be incorporated into the ad. Sometimes advertisements can become the fodder for contemporary legends, as in the case of Life cereal and all the rumors about poor Mikey. The tag, "Mikey likes it," apparently covered a multitude of sins, and it was even rumored that the actor had died. Advertisements are also used to stop the spread of a contemporary legend that may be damaging to individuals or corporations, as in the following example (Smith 1992, 65):

**Tiger-Cats Tuck into Mouth-Watering Buffet
as Chinese Restaurant Tries to Tackle Rumours**

A Chinese food restaurant in Burlington, Ontario, has confirmed that it serves cats—Hamilton Tiger-Cats, that is. In an effort to quell persistent rumours that it makes its food with cat meat, the Mandarin Restaurant invited more than 20 members of the Tiger-Cats football team and their families for a big meal.

"We're just trying to add some humour to a situation that's not funny," said David Williams, one of the seven owners of the 434-seat restaurant. The Tiger-Cats purred over $2,000 worth of lobster, shrimp, and other Chinese buffet delights. "I'll spread the good word about the Mandarin," said safety Todd Wiseman. The regional health department, which has received over 150 calls about the Mandarin, has inspected the restaurant and found no violations and no cats. In the past month the restaurant has spent $3,000 on newspaper ads denouncing the three-month-old rumour and hired a private investigator to find out how the rumour began. (*Edmonton Journal*, August 10, 1991, A2)

TABLOIDS

Tabloids have, in part, taken on the role of the traveling storyteller, who would set up in the marketplace and tell of other places and people far removed from the home and friends of the audience. Referring to tabloids, Harold Schechter states that "these publications are virtual anthologies of age-old folk themes reincarnated in contemporary terms" (1988, 14). Elizabeth Bird, in her examination of the role of the supermarket tabloids in modern Western society, concludes that they continue the tradition, although obviously dependent on print, of oral folk narratives (1992, 3). Supermarket tabloids are, in fact, one of our main venues for tracking the contemporary legends today.

The tabloids cannot be dismissed lightly, as they, like film, television programs, newspapers, and the oral tradition, "reflect and feed into each other" (Bird 1992, 2). To even a casual observer, the circular dynamic of tabloids becomes obvious. Tabloids and other news media report "hot" contemporary legends as pseudo-news items, which in turn become the vehicle for introducing the legends to readers who haven't heard them before (Grider 1992, 26). Contemporary legends told as fact often grace the pages of tabloids and, because of this, are quoted liberally in the discussions in part III. Tabloids are important for more than just their role in publishing contemporary legends as fact; tabloids, themselves, bear a striking resemblance to contemporary legends.

Setting

The place names in contemporary legends are constantly being adapted to the needs of the teller and audience. Legends, regardless of where they are told, usually cite local neighborhoods as the setting. This device aids in creating verisimilitude for the legend. Similarly, references to place serve to establish authority in news reports and to make the event concrete in the minds of the readers. References to setting give readers a sense of connection with the community (Manoff and Schudson 1987, 111). Tabloid journalism adopts the legends and sets them in the most "effective" settings.

To satisfy the enormous demands of their readers for new stories, tabloids often recycled old tales with new dates and locations; undoubtedly they did much of this recycling unintentionally, publishing and republishing the apocryphal tales that later became known as "urban legends" (Bird 1992, 10).

Oral Communication

Not only does the content of the tabloids resemble oral tales, but it also works like contemporary legends in validating beliefs, uncertainties, and stereotypes (Bird 1992, 165). The readers gather these stories and use them in their own conversations and gossip. "The tabloids appear to pick up on existing ideas and beliefs, restating them in narrative form, performing much the same function as the teller of an urban legend" (Bird 1992, 188). The readers of the tabloids interact with the stories they read by taking a stand on the plausibility of the tale and, as soon as they have done so, passing on both the tale and their own interpretation of it. As with listening to stories, the reading audience fully participates in "making meaning" of the tabloids; some read for information while others read for gossip and entertainment.

Traditional Motifs

Tabloid readers prize familiar themes and stories "dressed" as original material. To help satisfy this desire for the familiar, the stories in the tabloids incorporate traditional motifs from folklore (Bird 1992, 168). An article in *The Weekly World News* (March 6, 1990) read "Poodle Squashed Flatter Than a Pancake—in Trash Compactor," telling about an unfortunate incident with a family pet and a toddler in Atlanta. The mother was quoted as saying, "He was no bigger than a cigarette pack and just as flat. . . . That could have been Benjamin [her son] in there." This example, along with many of the human interest stories in the tabloids, are reminiscent of contemporary legends about other unfortunate pets and modern technology (Bird 1992, 167). There are also curious parallels to other themes in contemporary legends. A second example, from the same issue of the *News*, relates one of the legends about foreign cultures and their eating habits:

Shocking Reason Why Stew Tasted So Bad: This Isn't Rabbit—It's DOG Meat

A wife and husband were hospitalized in shock after they found out that the rabbit they bought from a butcher and stewed for dinner was actually a dog! The victims, Paul and Melissa Gilbert, originally from Chicago, were living in Mexico City at the time of this outrage. (Bird 1992, 167)

This tale of "unfood" eaten by "alien cultures" is a familiar theme of contemporary legends canon. In the majority of the tales, the "victims" either die of shock or are deathly ill and sue for damages. The horror of these tales is that they could so easily be true! When I was living in Southeast Asia in the early 1970s, our neighbors planned a celebration feast. They purchased two live dogs and, knowing how fond Westerners are of pets, they gave me one. The other dog was slaughtered and prepared for the feast. Needless to say, I lost my appetite! The second dog was considered "sacred" because it was a pet. Unlike the legends, however, no one died of shock or was ill from the experience.

FOAF

Attribution of the source to a "friend-of-a-friend" or an "authority" in the field is important in both contemporary legends and tabloid articles. The reference to a source adds to the verisimilitude of each. Since the 17th century, much of the material in the tabloids and news sheets has been "drawn from oral tradition or relied on word-of-mouth reports, often stressing that sources were eyewitnesses or, at the very least, credible—the 'insiders' of their day" (Bird 1992, 10). This is still particularly true of the gossip columnists in the tabloids today. Though some of the anecdotes printed in tabloids may actually have been witnessed by a columnist, or have some other truly reliable source, it becomes clear upon study of the tabloids that the stories are often essentially folkloric—some incident may have occurred, but in the course of the telling, details are changed or merged (Bird 1992, 171).

However, as Bird points out, the more respectable tabloids (*Enquirer* and the *Star*), which print human interest and celebrity stories that are somewhat less bizarre than stories in the *Sun* or the *News*, are also less obviously folkloric. The former tabloids do not invent sources and events, although their sources and stories still conform to traditional narratives and motifs (1992, 170).

Anonymous

Like fairy tales and legends, popular fiction is distinguished by a special kind of immortality: what remains alive is not the language of the original text or even the name of the creator but simply the story itself (Schechter 1988, 9). While reporters and writers strive to put their own unique stamp on their creations, tabloid journalists make little attempt to do so. The mark of a successful tabloid journalist is that story after story flows and fits into the appropriate mold (Bird 1992, 169). Like contemporary legends, the content of the story is what is remembered and transmitted, not the identity of the author.

Underlying Message

Tabloids preach that there is little anyone can do to change the world, except, of course, to hope for a miracle. This lesson is similar to that of folklore. "Most folk narratives help people cope with daily existence and their position in the pecking order by telling tales that dramatize values that are essentially conservative" (Bird 1992, 207). Wish fulfillment is a large part of both the tabloid worldview and that of the contemporary legend, but it is a wish fulfillment tempered by reality.

NEWS AS MYTH

News is narrative, and as narrative, it is orienting, communal, and universal (Bird and Dardenne 1988, 70). Because news is usually categorized into two distinct types—"hard" and "soft"—with two distinct functions—"important edifying information" and "interesting and entertaining human interest story," Bird and Dardenne suggest that we consider news as myth, dissolving those distinctions. They refer to news, not as individual myths, but "as a communication process [in which] news can act like myth and folklore." This is because news, especially television news, offers more than facts. It offers reassurance and familiarity in shared community experiences and provides credible answers and explanations to the baffling and the inexplicable (1988, 70).

> Myth outlines the boundaries of acceptable behaviour by telling stories. . . . So all news media report crime and deviant behaviour, and not primarily as a duty to inform; the average reader does not require the quantities of information offered on crime. . . . A central meaning of crime news is symbolic . . . such news is a main source . . . about the normative contours of a society . . . about right and wrong, about the parameters beyond which one should not venture and about the shapes that the devil can assume. A gallery of folk types—heroes and saints, as well as fools, villains and devils—is publicized not just in oral tradition and face-to-face contact, but to much larger audiences and with much greater dramatic resources. (Cohen and Young 1981, 431)

JOURNALISM AS STORYTELLING

Journalism, like any other storytelling activity, is a form of fiction operating out of its own conventions and understandings and within its own set of sociological, ideological, and literary constraints (Manoff and Schudson 1987, 6). Any discussion of the role of mass media in the world of contemporary legends must include the journalists themselves. During this age when human interest stories have taken the place of "hard news," the journalist not only relies on traditional story structure and content, but on an "oral" presentation that talks to the readers, involving them in the lives and drama of the participants. Nonfiction is presented by setting a scene, assigning point of view, and developing the "story" through the use of extended dialogue (Barkin 1984, 31). More than ever, the press, "respectable" or tabloid, tells a story. This becomes even more pronounced when the journalist is in front of the camera talking "with" the audience. The adoption of these fictional techniques not only aids in telling the story, but is a return to the storyteller's emotional function, evoking fear, pity, and wonder in the audience (Barkin 1984, 31).

In addition to using the oral techniques of storytellers, tabloid journalists manipulate the same general themes and structures that storytellers use when constructing their tales, using established formulas to produce a coherent story (Bird 1992, 191). A framework must be established that both the teller/journalist and the audience/reader can understand, with characters that the audience can identify with easily. The journalist uses traditional structure for several reasons, one of which is the lack of time necessary for creating an original piece of writing. Also, tabloid journalists, like their readers, value the features that characterize oral narratives, such as cliché, hyperbole, and standardized language, so their stories are even more markedly oral in nature (Bird 1992, 192).The tabloid reader, too, responds to the confiding and oral tone of the articles in the tabloids.

Cultural Functions of the Storytelling Journalist

To help their reading and listening audiences make sense of the news items bombarding them, journalists must organize the items into a format that can be easily understood. That format is the narrative or story. The journalist, while telling/writing a story, also assumes several important cultural functions of the storyteller.

Stress Commonalities. Like storytellers, who link people together by stressing their commonalities, journalists personalize the news, put it into an understandable format, and make it accessible to the general public (Barkin 1984, 28). The media coverage of the marriage of Prince Charles and Lady Diana strongly resembled the sharing of a fairy tale in its narrative structure, archetypal characters, and widespread appeal. The subsequent separation and media coverage has also made reference to the fact that the prince and princess did not "live happily ever after."

Organize Events. Through their stories, storytellers help to make sense of the world and, by organizing events into scenarios, imply reasons for events. Journalists organize events as well: by placement (e.g., in the "Sports," "Finance," or "Lifestyle" sections of the paper); by tone (e.g., hard news, editorial, news analysis, feature); and by narrative structure (Barkin 1984, 29).

Explore the Inexplicable. Both storytellers and journalists focus on the significance of the individual; but, at the same time, they stress the inexplicable.

> While storytellers perform an explanatory function . . . they also stress the importance of the inexplicable. There has always been a place in storytelling for the magical—the unexplained cure, the intervention of forces or spirits. The point of such stories is to illustrate that whatever our knowledge, it is ultimately not enough to explain the mysteries of the natural environment. (Barkin 1984, 29)

News stories focus on explaining the inexplicable as well: how and why something works (or why it does not), from technological marvels to the sphere of local politics. Recent news stories, for example, explore frequent lightning strikes, random "mysterious" killer diseases, and "unnatural" weather patterns.

Education of the Audience. Both traditional storytellers and contemporary journalists present their stories for pedagogical reasons: to provide guidelines for socially acceptable behavior (Barkin 1984, 30).

Seasonal Cycles. Both storytellers and journalists follow a cyclical, seasonal pattern of story themes related to the environment. Storytellers tell summer and winter tales, harvest and hunting stories that relate to the bond between humankind and the natural environment and cosmos. While journalists rarely cast their eyes to the cosmos, seasonal stories are the staples of journalism. Feature articles are tied to holiday celebrations, the school year, or the sports calendar (Barkin 1984, 30).

Storytelling Techniques

Journalists are trained to recognize and use "news values" in reporting the news. These values are the same that a storyteller uses to create a tale: relevancy, the unusual and the dramatic, simplicity, personalization, and consequences (Bird and Dardenne 1988, 73). News stories never reflect reality and tell of mundane and boring everyday events but, instead, shout the different, the peculiar, the bizarre. Storytellers rarely tell stories about the mundane and boring, either! The wonder of the world and its inhabitants are the stuff of which storytellers and journalists create their products.

Although "hard news" has been traditionally presented in an "inverted pyramid" form, with suspense being sacrificed for the lead element, research has shown that readers do not respond well to this arrangement, preferring to find their information in story form. "The common assumption that readers prefer 'human interest' stories only because the content is more interesting overlooks that these are the same stories that are usually written in traditional story form" (Bird and Dardenne 1988, 77). In response to this discovery, journalism is focusing on presenting information in a more "user-friendly" manner: narrative form. "To explain, journalists are constantly reverting to the story form—attributed quotes take on the nature of dialogue, a point of view develops, details are added that turn into an unemployed miner or a bereaved parent" (Bird and Dardenne 1988, 78).

Another important change in the world of news is the shift of the "authoritative voice" from the newspaper reporter to the television news anchor or reporter. People tend to give the most credit to items presented orally, in story form, over all other forms of information dissemination. Television news, in which audiences can see its presenters, has co-opted the storyteller/mythmaker role so effectively that it is now regarded as the most authoritative and hence truthful source of news (Bird and Dardenne 1988, 80).

MASS CULTURE

Ronald Baker identifies mass culture as "a product of a society ordered and regimented by a technology working through mass media, such as radio, television, and graphic advertising" (Baker 1976, 367). Baker maintains that all aspects of mass culture nurture legends by providing fresh subject matter and aiding in dissemination, and that mass culture also influences contemporary legends through its products, institutions, and heroes (1976, 368). The automobile is one product of modern culture that has either generated or regenerated contemporary legends. Stories dependent on the automobile include "The Death Car," and the smell that cannot be eradicated; "The Killer in the Backseat," in which a lone female driver is terrorized by a vehicle behind her only to discover that the actual threat is traveling in the car with her; "The Hook"; "The Boyfriend's Death," which takes the action one step further than the action in "The Hook," as the boyfriend leaves lover's lane but does not return alive; and "The Vanishing Hitchhiker." (These legends are discussed in chapter 6 in the section "Car Tales," and in chapter 12, "Scary Stories.")

Baker pointed out in the mid-1970s that in a society lacking widespread automobile ownership, the transference and localization of modern forms of "The Vanishing Hitchhiker" legend would be severely limited, which helps explain why this migratory legend has been more popular in the United States than in other countries (Baker 1976, 368). Since that time, however, cars have become more accessible in other parts of the world, and the "car" tales have flourished there as well.

Other manifestations of mass culture reflected in contemporary legends include institutions such as nationally owned department stores and large shopping malls. The legends "Department Store Snakes" and "The Dead Cat in the Package" are set in local shopping centers and chain department stores. The stores in these legends sell foreign-made or "alien" products that may not have been available in the community without large corporations. As we follow the trail of the "dead cat" in chapter 8, we see the package being transported first on railroad journeys, then on shopping junkets in department stores, and most recently, in the parking lots of large suburban shopping centers.

An aspect of both mass or popular culture and contemporary legend is that they are characterized by their immediacy and ephemeralness (Baker 1976, 372). "The Spider in the Hairdo" legend is a demonstration of how, once the stiff, sprayed hairstyle of the story disappears from fashion, the legend fades as well (only to be reworked and retold in a more modern guise years later).

Mass media heroes also figure largely in contemporary legends. Elvis has been sighted many times in various locations since his death; similarily, other media culture heroes have not been allowed to "rest-in-peace." Stories still circulate about the "apparent death" of John F. Kennedy.

Non-human culture heroes are also featured in contemporary legends, especially around the celebration of Halloween. Every Halloween season sees a revival of new and old horror movies in theaters. On television, news media publish and transmit ghost stories and interview clairvoyants, Wiccans (modern witches), and psychics (Degh and Vazsonyi 1983, 21). It is only during the last few years, because of the rise of satanic legends, that ghosts, witches, fantasy, and Halloween itself have become "politically incorrect" and, at times, censored. Halloween used to be a busy time for storytelling in schools and for public performances. It is not anymore! This is happening, mind you, at the same time that a rise in popular horror fiction is noted among young readers.

POPULAR FICTION

Harold Schlechter defines popular fiction as "a category which includes comic books as well as such 'post-Gutenberg' forms as television soap operas and most Hollywood movies." He goes on to describe popular fiction as a mass-produced art whose major function is to reach the widest audience possible by telling a story that triggers a basic and powerful emotional response: wonder or terror, laughter or tears, suspense or erotic arousal (1988, 7). These popular works are, in fact, "pure folklore cast in contemporary terms and communicated through sophisticated, technological means, but essentially unmodified" (Schechter 1988, 19). The difference between serious art and popular art is that the former transforms the folk material while the latter simply transmits it (19). Needless to say, the folk material most often transmitted is the contemporary legend. Specific retellings of contemporary legends in both visual and literary popular fiction are discussed in subsequent chapters.

MEDIA NARRAFORMS

The mass media, particularly television programming, and oral tradition have a symbiotic relationship. Students often use supernatural plots gleaned from television and films to spice up both their oral storytelling and creative writing. The media provides the content, often based on folklore motifs and plots, and the oral tradition provides the performance opportunities, not only for professional storytellers, but for storytelling individuals. Regularly, when I am telling a contemporary legend to a group of students, they will tell me that they have seen something similar on television and then proceed to tell me the plot of the show. This is not a new phenomenon, but it is appearing in the classroom with increasing frequency. The term "media narraform" has been coined to refer to those retellings of mass media presentations of the supernatural, which use traditional storytelling techniques and folklore motifs (Grider 1981, 125).

Sylvia Grider (1981, 127–28) identifies the characteristics of narraforms:

1. Identification of the media as the source for the information (e.g., "I saw this on TV"; "I read it in a book of scary stories"). This acknowledgment of the source is closely related to the traditional authentication of truth that precedes a contemporary legend. Grider states that this acknowledgment in the introduction demonstrates the high status given to the media.

2. A disconnected retelling of a string of episodes, because students find it difficult to translate the visual storytelling techniques into the oral.

3. Characters that are frequently stereotypes in the retellings, resembling the characters of traditional literature more than those in popular fiction. A distance is created by the translation and, as Sylvia Grider has said, "neither audience nor narrator can really identify with and vicariously participate in the action of a narraform the way that they can in the legend or folktale."

4. Stories that are longer than most traditional narratives, because the narrator is trying to recapture as much as of the detail as possible.

The media narraforms told by all age groups, including young children, tend to dwell on the violence and grotesque dramatized on television. Such television programs—and similar comic book episodes—depict darkness, mysterious sounds, and howling winds as well as a parade of deformed old men, crazy scientists, graveyards, and dilapidated Gothic mansions. All of these elements are integral components of what folklorists call the "legend climate" (Grider 1981, 126).

Media narraforms are an important communication form for children. Because so many children are familiar with the television world, they can all actively participate in the retellings. They are also important because the world of the supernatural is new to most young students, and media narraforms aid in the assimilation and understanding of data as they discuss the stories and their interpretations of them (Grider 1981, 129). The narraforms prepare younger students for participatory and communal storytelling and lay the framework for more sophisticated tellings of legends as they grow older (Grider 1981, 130).

Like the legend-telling sessions of young adults, the narraforms of younger children help to diffuse the tension created by the television viewing. Narraforms give the narrators—and, vicariously, the audience—control over otherwise terrifying concepts. Viewing television programs in the safety of one's own living room is less frightening than being alone in the dark. And so, by extension, a story *about* that same television program would therefore be the least frightening of all (Grider 1981, 130).

CRIME-VICTIM STORIES

Not only are North Americans fascinated with the supernatural, they are equally fascinated with violence and criminal behaviour. Eleanor Wachs maintains that this obsession with violence is the source of one of the oldest storytelling traditions and is still highly visible in the North American folk and popular culture today (Wachs 1985, 275). This heritage is evident in our ballads, tall tales and legends, and sagas about notorious outlaws and criminals as well as in our everyday conversations.

While young children translate the world of television and film through media narraforms, and young adults use contemporary legends to cope with the challenges of growing up and understanding society, the primary domain of adults is the "telling of a crime-victim experience which is embedded into everyday discourse" (Wachs 1985, 275). Crime-victim stories help victims and families and friends cope with the daily threat of violence. "In general, Americans are fearful of violent crime; by talking about it and telling stories to one another, victims are able to express this common fear" (Wachs 1988, xiii).

Crime-victim stories are also "horror tales," but instead of supernatural antagonists, they feature street muggings, rapes, household burglaries, and the murders of false lovers (Wachs 1985, 275). These tales are frequently supported by media broadcasts reminding the population that the world indeed is a dangerous place. Crime-victim narratives are populated with stock characters (e.g., the simpleton policeman, the trickster offender, and the clever victim) and, like contemporary legends, crime-victim stories are localized and personalized, by including local places and names, and follow traditional story sequences and structures.

"Like the urban legend, the crime-victim story is told for truth (though it differs from newspaper accounts about crime); characterization is limited; and the setting is the real world, not the world of fiction" (Wachs 1988, 40). Though statistical studies show that most murders take place between persons who know each other, crime-victim narratives reflect society's fear of the anonymous criminal, the stranger lurking in a dark alleyway ready to pounce on an innocent victim. Like the ogre and bogeyman of older folktales, this stereotypical urban character evokes an ill-defined fear of physical assault and danger (Wachs 1988, 17). Urban folklore works because it plays on people's common responses, responses that depend on a shared set of culturally determined traits, assumptions, and expectations. These traits reflect the well-known characteristics of this world: population density, heterogeneity, alienation, anonymity, bystander apathy, and invasion of privacy, among others (Wachs 1988, x).

Function of the Crime-Victim Narrative

Crime-victim narratives, which frequently incorporate contemporary legends and other folklore motifs, are often used as entertainment, for conversational icebreakers and invitations for humorous exchange, or as a didactic means of educating the audience in "street smarts" (Wachs 1988, 1). Similar to other traditional forms, the personal-experience narrative can propose solutions to problems encountered by a group; reiterate traditional wisdom, soothing the group's fears and anxieties; and, in case of the crime-victim narrative, serve as a cautionary tale, projecting situations and providing responses for the future, the unknown, the unexpected, and the dangerous (Wachs 1985, 273).

Didactic Tales. Streetsmarts taught through crime-victim stories include safety tips such as having a good mental map of the city and neighborhood, what areas of the city to avoid, learning self-defense, being as inconspicuous as possible, and cooperating with the offender. As Wachs states:

> One of the main reasons that victims share these stories about urban life is the desire to tell and warn others how *not* to become a crime victim. Many times their advice . . . is direct; that is, they use the narrative itself as a warning device. Sometimes, their clues about protection are more subtle and are embedded within the story and deduced by the listeners. But whether implicitly or explicitly, tellers impart a form of folk knowledge—street smarts. In addition, these stories teach about the dangers of the urban world. (Wachs 1988, 75)

Cautionary Tales. Crime-victim narratives function as a warning about contemporary dangers on the street. Like traditional folktales and contemporary legends, the crime-victim narratives often employ negative racial stereotypes. The tales often reinforce and foster prejudice through their use of stock characters.

Therapeutic Tales. These tales allow the victim and others concerned about crime to handle their fear and aggression in a culturally sanctioned way. Storytelling, itself, is a sign of survival. Humor is used to comment on urban aggression as well as to distance the teller from the trauma of the experience (Wachs 1988, 5). One of the reasons for telling these personal-experience stories is so that victims can appear victorious over situations they could not control. Individuals seeking to gain power over the experience through words are simply retelling a structured narrative. Relating their role in the story is a way for them to bring the danger under control and reclaim their self-esteem (Wachs 1988, 73).

Entertainment. Stories are often used as ice breakers, as both teller and listener share the same concerns, worldview, and fears. Crime-victim stories can also be told to shock the listener. "The ordinary setting and the extraordinary event that takes place within the story frame not only lend[s] believability to the story but also insure[s] its shock value" (Wachs 1988, 6).

Traditional Stories Told as Crime-Victim Narratives

Crime-victim narratives, though presented as real cases of crime and victims by their tellers, are adaptations of urban legends with their traditional tale plots: stories such as the traditional scam or confidence game and the shaggy dog story. "In some cases, they reveal how little human ingenuity, character, and responses to such dangers have changed over time" (Wachs 1988, 32).

There is a similarity between the stock characters in both types of narratives. Victims in contemporary legends are often foolish or naïve, but in the crime-victim narrative, not only are the victims naïve, they are frightened, vulnerable, and at times unusually trusting of others. They are unaware of the dangers surrounding them. The victim characters in these stories are caricatures of urban life—the common person on the street (Wachs 1988, 44). The offenders in both types of narratives are either the "innocent-looking neighbor" or the new bogeymen: the freeway shooter, the Halloween sadist, the killer drunk driver, the stranger-kidnapper of young children, the serial killer, the copycat who duplicates crimes reported in the media, and the satanists and other ritual abusers of children (Best 1991, 110).

Michael Goss, in his investigation of "urban maniac" legends, discovers that the bogeymen are prime offenders, using "transient, unpredictable and totally irrational psychopaths as their theme, and mak[ing] all the gore, carnage and cruelty credible by engaging all preconceptions about 'psychopaths' and other dangers" (Goss 1990, 95). In the same investigation, Goss confirms that the false alarms that surrounded the threat of the "Halifax Slasher" in Great Britain were perpetuated by word of mouth. "Newspapers were an even more common source. . . . But the press did not *invent* him, and would have been unable to foist him on the public without the prior willingness to believe" (101). Today we are only too willing to believe in modern bogeymen and inexplicable behavior on the part of the criminal. To some extent, these bogeymen have replaced the traditional ghosts of folklore.

Both contemporary legends and crime-victim narratives use dialogue to add verisimilitude, to add a comic touch to defuse tension, and to focus the story line. The setting of crime-victim narratives, too, resembles the setting of the contemporary legends: the elevator, the subway, the apartment lobby or vestibule, the public street, and the public park (Wachs 1988, 18).

Both types of narratives are set in the everyday world of the teller and listener and "could happen to you" because you frequent those places as well.

The Mutilated Shopper

Well, I work in Jordan's and I heard from another salesgirl about a problem that [they] had at Sears on a Friday or Saturday night. A lady was there shopping. Her husband had left her off. And she was trying on dresses or sportswear. It was at the end of the day, possibly an hour before closing time. The husband went outside to wait for her to come out. And she didn't arrive when the store closed. So, he called security. And security went into the store looking for her. And they found her in a fitting room. And evidently she had been mugged and her finger had been cut off and her diamonds cut off her finger. And she was unconscious. That is what I heard. (Wachs 1990, 143)

"The Mutilated Shopper" is closely related to other contemporary legends that highlight physical or sexual violence against women by local deviants. They share the following motifs: a female victim; the mall or department store; the husband's search and discovery of the victim; the gruesome act of mutilation; the mention of the stolen jewelry; and the ultimate fate of the victim (Wachs 1990, 145).

Wachs's examination of this legend demonstrates that, regardless of the form of the narrative (e.g., whether in the form of a legend kernel—statement of belief or fact—or as a lengthier narrative filled with detail), tellers focus on the victim's mutation and the terrifying conditions facing people in today's society rather than on the veracity of the account (Wachs 1990, 146). She points out that this legend mirrors concerns expressed in others that are circulating in the 1990s: xenophobic fears of strangers and people of other races; fear of urban crime and physical attack; and a cultural ambivalence towards conspicuous consumption (Wachs 1990, 148). The legend tells us that it is dangerous to wear expressions of consumer power: the woman is a target for violence simply because she wears either a gold band or a diamond engagement ring. As some legend texts (and crime-victim personal-experience narratives) indicate, one avoids danger by *not* being conspicuous (Wachs 1990, 153).

REFERENCES

Baker, Ronald L. 1976. The influence of mass culture on modern legends. *Southern Folklore Quarterly Press* 40: 367–76.

Barkin, Steve M. 1984. The journalist as storyteller: An interdisciplinary perspective. *American Journalism* 1, no. 2 (Winter): 27–33.

Beardsworth, A. D. 1990. Trans-science and moral panics: Understanding food scares. *British Food Journal* 92, no. 5: 11–16.

Best, Joel. 1991. Bad guys and random violence: Folklore and media constructions of contemporary deviants. *Contemporary Legend* 1: 107–21.

Bird, S. Elizabeth. 1992. *For enquiring minds: A cultural study of supermarket tabloids.* Knoxville: University of Tennessee Press.

Bird, S. Elizabeth, and Robert W. Dardenne. 1988. Myth, chronicle and story: Exploring the narrative qualities of news. In *Media, myths and narratives: Television and the press* [Sage Annual Reviews of Communication Research, vol.15], edited by James W. Carey. Newbury Park: Sage, 67–86.

Brunvand, Jan Harold. 1993. A blast heard around the world. *Contemporary Legend* 3: 103–19.

Cohen, S., and J. Young, eds. 1981. *The manufacture of news: Social problems, deviance and the mass media.* London: Constable. Quoted in Bird, S. Elizabeth, and Robert W. Dardenne. 1988. Myth, chronicle and story: Exploring the narrative qualities of news. In *Media, myths and narratives: Television and the press* [Sage Annual Reviews of Communication Research, vol.15], edited by James W. Carey (Newbury Park: Sage), 71.

Degh, Linda. 1968. The runaway grandmother. *Indiana Folklore* 1, no. 1: 68–77.

Degh, Linda, and Andrew Vazsonyi. 1983. Does the dog bite? Ostensive action: A means of legend telling. *Journal of Folklore Research* 20, no. 1 (January–May): 5–34.

Goss, Michael. 1990. The Halifax slasher and other "urban maniac" tales. In *A nest of vipers: Perspectives on contemporary legend, vol. V,* edited by Gillian Bennett and Paul Smith. Sheffield, England: Sheffield Academic Press, 89–111.

Grider, Sylvia. 1981. The media narraform: Symbiosis of mass media and oral tradition. *ARV* 37: 125–31.

———. 1992. Tie a yellow ribbon around Elvis: Contemporary legend, popular culture and the media. *Louisiana Folklore Miscellany* 7: 22–32.

Landers, Ann. 1992. Only a crumb would repeat $250 cookie-recipe myth. Syndicated newspaper column. (June 29).

Manoff, Robert Karl, and Michael Schudson, eds. 1987. *Reading the news: A Pantheon guide to popular culture.* New York: Pantheon.

Oring, Elliott. 1990. Legend, truth, and news. *Southern Folklore* 47: 163–77.

Renard, Jean-Bruno. 1991. LSD tattoo transfers: Rumor from North America to France. *Folklore Forum* 24, no. 2: 3–26.

Schechter, Harold. 1988. *The bosom serpent: Folklore and popular art.* Iowa City: University of Iowa Press.

Smith, Paul. 1992. Read all about it! Elvis eaten by drug-crazed giant alligators: Contemporary legend and the popular press. *Contemporary Legend* 2: 41–70.

Stephens, Mitchell. 1988. *A history of news: From the drum to the satellite.* New York: Viking.

Wachs, Eleanor. 1985. A definite vision of the world: Worldview and the crime-victim narrative. *The 8th Congress for the International Society for Folk Narrative Research,* edited by Reimund Kvideland and Torunn Selberg. Bergen, Norway (June 12–17, 1984): 273–81.

———. 1988. *Crime-victim stories: New York City's urban folklore.* Bloomington: Indiana University Press.

———. 1990. The mutilated shopper at the mall: A legend of urban violence. In *A nest of vipers: Perspectives on contemporary legend, vol. V,* edited by Gillian Bennett and Paul Smith. Sheffield, England: Sheffield Academic Press, 143–60.

OSTENSION

LEGEND TRIPPING, "BLOODY MARY," POISONED HALLOWEEN TREATS, AND MERCANTILE LEGENDS

4

A marble gravestone in an old deserted cemetery in West Virginia was the legend trip site for a particular group of young adults in the vicinity. The marble statue was of a seated lady, her hands outstretched to all that pass by the resting place. The legend stated that the woman in the grave had died of a broken heart when jilted by her fiancé. The legend trip was an initiation rite: new members had to spend the night sitting in the statue's lap. But the last time anyone tried this, the young woman who sat in the statue's lap met with a tragedy. The difference, you see, was that the young woman was a direct descendant of the fiancé!

The citizens of the community did not sleep well that night. Something kept their nerves on edge. They did not know what they feared.

The next morning the young girl was discovered, still sitting in the statue's lap. She was dead. On her body were found marks as though she had been held in a superhuman clinch. Perhaps the seated lady had gained revenge. (Musick, 1977, 112)

One of the most interesting facets of contemporary legends, for me, is the reaction of people to the legends. Some people scoff at the messages, but others firmly believe in their truth. This belief often leads to believers acting out the content of the legend, an ostensive action; people make these legends come alive. Besides belief in the legend, ostension is performed because of the thrill, a defiance of authority, or because it is seen as correct or appropriate behavior.

DEFINITION OF TERMS

To better understand the world of contemporary legends coming alive, however, several terms used by folklorists and other legend scholars should be clarified:

Ostension. Ostension "refers to the process by which people act out themes or events found within folk narratives" (Fine 1991,179). People act on the legends, using them as patterns or maps for future behavior. Ostension shows that "not only can facts become narratives, but narratives can turn into facts as well" (Degh and Vazsonyi 1983, 5). The legends are believed and acted upon and then the new stories are told and retold to validate the original legends.

Pseudo-Ostension. Pseudo-ostension is defined as "imitating the outlines of a known narrative to perpetuate a hoax" (Ellis 1989a, 208). Examples of pseudo-ostension include young adults terrifying their friends at a legend-tripping site by pretending to be the homicidal maniac, children tampering with their own Halloween treats for attention, and people mimicking animal sacrifice.

Legend Tripping. Legend tripping is an organized (although sometimes spontaneous) journey to an isolated area to test the bravery of the group when faced with supernatural phenomena. The trip experience involves the telling of appropriate legends. Legend-tripping sites include cemeteries, tunnels, deserted and "haunted" houses, and remote lanes and bridges. Ideal conditions for legend tripping are dark, gloomy, and foggy nights, and the nights of the full moon around midnight (Meley 1991, 15). The peak age for legend trips coincides with attaining a driver's license and access to a car. The peak time for legend trips is summer and early fall, especially around Halloween.

EXAMPLES OF OSTENSION AND
PSEUDO-OSTENSION

A brief overview of the myriad of ostensive and pseudo-ostensive behavior demonstrates how pervasive this behavior is in modern society. The following examples are not by any means the entire corpus of ostensive action. They are, however, directly related to young adult culture and interests. Several of the examples are discussed in greater detail later in this chapter, while others are explored in other sections of the book.

Animal Mutilations

The killing and mutilation of animals is commonly associated with underground cults of witches or satanists, who periodically sacrifice and mutilate animals. "Intrigued by such stories, an individual or individuals may decide to don robes, light candles, mumble chants and really kill animals—or humans in some ceremonial fashion in the hopes of raising a spirit" (Ellis 1989a, 209). Animal mutilations are explored in the discussion on satanism in chapter 11.

Attempted Abduction

Children have claimed to have been abducted to avoid punishment by worried parents and police for their absences after school and at night. Recently, a tenth-grade student in my daughters' school claimed that she had been abducted outside of the school. Subsequent police investigation showed that she was using the story as a way to get out of attending school that day. Her claim was false, but, unfortunately, some claims are true. Others use the legend of attempted abduction to hide their more sinister behavior. After the October 1983 television movie about the Adam Walsh abduction and murder, and its subsequent reruns, were broadcast, such legends became very prominent, especially among parents and educators. Parents and children were continually reminded to take caution when attending crowded fairs or shopping centers.

Adam Walsh disappeared in Florida from a toy department while shopping with his parents. This widely publicized abduction became cited as proof that children do get abducted by strangers.

Incidents of child murders initially reported as abduction attempts demonstrate attempts to use the legend as an excuse or explanation, or to mislead police.

> *Sharon Comitz told police that she had left her month-old baby alone in her car for a few minutes; when she returned, the baby was gone; the body was found the next day in a nearby stream. Police investigation showed that Sharon Comitz had a history of abusing children and that the parents had taken out a $3,000 insurance policy on the baby's life the day before it was "abducted." Eventually the mother admitted that she had killed the child herself and had fabricated the story.* (Ellis 1989a, 214)

As in the recent Susan Smith case, police investigation exposed the murderers to be not deranged strangers, but the mothers themselves. "The abduction story was initially reported in the media as genuine and so served as a smokescreen to deflect attention away from clues that would lead back to the family circle itself" (Ellis 1989a, 214). When the mother of two boys, who had supposedly been kidnapped by a stranger, went on national television to plead for the return of her sons, hearts went out to her. Those who knew the frequent examples of ostensive kidnappings paused to await further development. The entire theme and plot, unfortunately, had been played before.

Halloween Sadism

Halloween sadism stories are "a group of consistently growing rumors, later officially confirmed, that adults hide pins, razor blades, and glass splinters in apples or inject drugs or poison into candies and other handouts" (Degh and Vazsonyi 1983, 11).

Halloween is a ritual celebration that provides examples of legends at work. The celebration is based on legends, communicates legends, and creates legends (Degh and Vazsonyi 1983, 9). Sadistic behavior involving Halloween treats combines two common themes found in other contemporary legends: danger to children and contamination of food.

The media and police appeal to parents and care givers year after year to take care of their children and to watch out for dangerous substances in Halloween treats. At the same time, the warning is directed at children and young adults to beware of strangers and adult malevolence. Today, Halloween is surrounded by suspicion and fear because the warning has been so frequently and systematically repeated and believed. The warnings (which are unsubstantiated) have become part of the Halloween ritual (Degh and Vazsonyi 1983, 11).

Bloody Mary

Ritual games and other forms of divination are also examples of ostension. The ritual games "Bloody Mary" and "Mary Worth," discussed later in this chapter, involve the ritual summoning of a witch in a mirror.

"Obligatory Wait"

A more peaceful college rumor involves the specific amount of time students are obligated to wait for late professors. The time periods are dependent on the rank of the professor. Students assume that this obligatory wait is part of the "established rules" governing student behavior and do not realize that it is, in fact, folklore.

Pin-Prick Panic

A series of incidents in New York City during 1989 involved black adolescents jabbing pins into the backs of the necks of randomly chosen white females. A panic was created by media coverage that repeatedly suggested that the pins were tainted with AIDS. However, when within a week the teenagers were arrested and charged, the police discovered that there was no validity to the media reports. Rather, the teenagers "felt it was fun to run down the street and stick females and see their reaction" (Ellis 1989b, 5). Both the legend of "The Halifax Slasher" in Great Britain and the numerous legends about "white slavery" involve mysterious attacks with needles and provide possible antecedents for the activity. Ellis feels that "the pin-prick attacks were legend performances through acts of ostension, literally 'needling' the previously dominant white culture and symbolically turning the tables on them" (1989b, 5).

Postcards for "Little Buddy"

The legend about a sick child who wants to break a *Guinness Book* world record has been circulating for years, and the legend's requests for postcards have resulted in an avalanche of mail for the non-existent child. The hoax was first exposed when a stamp collector purchased a large volume of mail at the dead-letter office and realized that the mail had been sent to the same fictional address from concerned people all over the world who believed the story and were acting on the legend's request.

Four real appeals for world records have been launched since 1987. These appeals have used the same format and distribution patterns as the legend. In all four cases, the parents found that, once their appeal became known, the public became overwhelmingly responsive and renegade appeals started circulating. "One effect of these renegade appeals was the generation of a quagmire of distorted and missing information, the consequences of which have led to speculation, and the invention and generation of numerous scenarios based on both fact and fiction" (Dying Child's Wish 1995, 7).

Craig Shergold's appeal was one of the four and was the most widely followed by folklorists in both Great Britain and North America. Just recently, a M.A. thesis by Anna Guigne has been published exploring the legend and focusing on Craig Shergold's experience. Her research states that people's perceptions about this appeal varied from positive support for the campaign to cynical views about the reality of the appeal. "This in turn led to the creation of a body of 'lore' surrounding real appeals and the resulting generation of the Dying Child's wish complex" (Dying Child's Wish 1995, 7).

Computer networks in North America received a variation of the appeal on April 5, 1990 and gave a deadline of April 15 for the get-well cards. The appeal added:

> This is such a small task for us to accomplish for a precious little seven year old. Let's put a smile on Craig's little face with a get-well card and let him know we all truly care by sending him a card as soon as possible. (Craig Shergold 1990, 8)

Appeals circulated worldwide on fax machines, computer networks in newspapers, flyers, billboard advertisements, and one was even published as a form letter in a Russian newspaper "that invited readers to cut it out, sign it, paste it on a card, and send it to Craig" (Craig Shergold 1990, 9). There are many variants of the story; facts that change include the child's age, the fatal disease, and the home town and address. The Atlanta Children's Foundation gathered 3 million cards for Craig, and upon refusal by the Shergold family, forwarded the cards to American children suffering from cancer. They were then to be recycled.

A new version of the appeal appeared in Britain in January 1991. Instead of get-well cards (for which Craig already appears in the *Guinness Book of World Records*), the faxes asked for business cards. "We should be grateful, therefore, if you would send one of your business cards to the address below and send this letter to another 10 companies of your own" (Craig Shergold 1991, 11). Craig published a personal request on February 9, 1991 to disregard any requests for business cards but to send a donation, if one wished, for leukemia research.

The Royal Marsden Hospital, where Craig received chemotherapy treatments, previously announced that more than £ 20,000 ($34,200) has been raised for leukemia research by selling the foreign postage stamps on Craig's get-well cards (Craig Shergold 1991, 11).

Ann Landers addressed the issue of the request for business cards in a column published June 23, 1991. She warned her readers not to send business cards as "they can fall into the wrong hands and become part of the mother of all mailing lists. Sharp-eyed scam perpetrators, always on the alert for suckers, may figure if you'd fall for this, you'd fall for anything" (Craig Shergold 1992, 11). The "sharp-eyed scam perpetrators" Landers mentions are practicing pseudo-ostension, using the legend to play a hoax. But the legend and the appeals are not always willful hoaxes. Because of the publicity of successful campaigns, other children (and their parents?) wish to be included in the *Guinness Book of World Records*. In 1991, a Canadian variant was spotlighted in the media:

Bernie Granger, a 10-year-old cancer victim of Winnipeg, Canada, has circulated an appeal to help make a collection of caps. The appeal got its first boost when columnist Gordon Sinclair, Jr. of the Winnipeg Free Press, *mentioned the collection in a column shortly before Christmas. The story was picked up by the CBC's* The National *and then, on Christmas night, by the Atlanta-based TV network CNN.* (Craig Clones 1991, 11–12)

By sending the cards, letters, and baseball caps, people are practicing ostension and demonstrating their belief in the truth of the rumors. Pogs may be the next item requested to fulfill a "Dying Child's Wish."

Redemption Rumors

The most frequent redemption rumor concerns the pull tabs from aluminum cans, which the rumor says can be redeemed for medical aid and charity. People who believe this legend have collected thousands of pull tabs expecting to redeem them, but the rumors were false. However, some organizations have redefined the "meaning of the legend" to develop projects that recycle the pull tabs for money, which the organization then donates to their chosen cause. The standard claim of the rumor that the soft drink or beer companies will contribute donations or services for pull tabs remains false, and the money is given as a general contribution to the Ronald McDonald House, not for kidney dialysis machines for particular individuals (Fine 1991, 180). "Redemption rumors" are explored further later in this chapter.

Roaming Gnomes

The question now is: Can nomadic Gnorman be content leading a sedentary life? He's the small, silent type. And he possess a worldliness uncharacteristic in a gnome. Especially the garden variety. But Gnorman the gnome has just returned from an 18-month odyssey in Australia, Alaska, Canada and the U.S. He's got the photos to prove it, too. The 11-kilogram lawn ornament recently arrived back on the Calgary lawn of Richard and Hazel Sorenson, both 74. After Gnorman just picked up and left in the summer of 1992, the Sorensons didn't give him much thought. Until he reappeared with his mini-diary and an album full of photos recording his adventures: at Fisherman's Wharf in San Francisco, the Sydney Opera House in Australia, Disneyland, Seattle's Space Needle, Anchorage in Alaska, Vancouver, Edmonton, Saskatoon. . . . The Sorensons have no idea who Gnorman's travelling companions were, though Hazel thinks she might have seen them on the lawn one night taking a photo of Bugs Bunny. "I'd really love to meet them," says Hazel. "This is crazy, but it's so much fun." The trip did produce one disappointment, however. Despite visiting Alaska, Gnorman didn't make it to Nome. (Edmonton Journal, Feb. 17, 1994, A2)

This example of ostension deviates slightly from the established pattern of "roaming gnomes." Usually, after the garden ornaments have been stolen, their owners receive postcards from various locations. "Whirlwind vacation was a blast, but there's no place like gnome" read another recent headline in the *Edmonton Journal* (Sept. 18, 1993). This article of the abducted gnome's pictorially documented holiday from Calgary, Alberta, to Australia, and back again, made no mention that ostensive action was at work. But I can guarantee the unknown "gnome-napper" had heard the legends of other roaming gnomes before providing the Calgary gnome with the experience of a lifetime.

Gnomes and other lawn ornaments have been disappearing, going on vacations, and reappearing for the past decade. Several variants of the legend were collected on television and in the mass media in Australia. "These stories as urban legends, while not dependent upon mass media for their survival, are given a wider dissemination via their mass media telling" (Hults 1988, 92).

A common offshoot on the "roaming-gnome" theme is the more blatant kidnapping of gnomes:

> "A host of gnomes went missing at the same time from around town. Nothing was heard regarding ransoms. Six months later, the gnomes were discovered in a clearing in a bush in a big semi-circle around the biggest gnome—obviously holding a meeting." (Hults 1988, 91)

And in the Media . . .

Sometimes the popularity of the legend has tragic results if people act upon them, as in the following letter to columnist Ann Landers:

> Dear Ann Landers: Are people becoming more insensitive, more vicious, crueler and maybe crazier as time goes by? I wonder where mankind is heading when I read about the hideous things that are happening all around us.
>
> For example: A lawyer in Maryland pleaded guilty to breaking into the home of a friend's estranged wife to look for documents that had to do with the couple's divorce. He encountered the family kitten running loose in the kitchen, became annoyed by the "nuisance underfoot," picked up the kitten and tossed it into the microwave. He then "accidently" turned the oven on. . . . The man was prosecuted for this heinous act and pleaded guilty. His defense was that he had been drinking and "wasn't thinking straight." The penalty—are you ready for this?—was probation! Richmond, Va.
>
> Dear Richmond: Check the Bible and you will find that the cruel, vicious and crazy people have been among us for a long time. Because of the advances in communication, however, we not only hear about atrocities the moment they happen, but get instant replay in our living rooms on TV. . . . The *Baltimore Sun* informed me that the lawyer was sentenced to one year in prison, which was then suspended, given 18 months probation, required to receive alcoholism counseling and do 40 hours of community service and fined $1,000 plus court costs. He also faces disbarment proceedings. ("Ann Landers," May 31, 1992)

In another case reported in the media, a young boy committed an act of ostension, causing a great deal of pain:

A Humane Society worker in Canton, Ohio, came home on 30 August to find her white Maltese Jo-Jo in her microwave oven. The dog was rushed to a veterinarian, but put to sleep after the injuries were found too extensive to treat. An eleven-year-old boy from the neighborhood was arrested; the dog's owner claimed that he had done it for kicks. (Microwaved Maltese 1990, 10)

LEGEND TRIPPING

I told this story ["The Vanishing Hitchhiker"] when I was a senior in high school to a friend who was a year behind me. We were driving through the country at night along the same route that Jeff Orr [character in story] had taken this girl home (supposedly, according to the story). The setting was perfect and I was really serious and completely unfunny, telling this story in an eerie monotone.

Just as I finished we pulled up alongside this cemetery where the girl was buried. The guy in the car with me, Joe, was visibly shaken by what he had heard, but he still refused to believe me. I offered to take him into the graveyard and show him the girl's grave as proof. . . . The beam of my flashlight went over several different gravesites before it struck the tomb of Jane Murphy at the end of the lawn, and on the edge of the tomb there was hanging an old gray sweater (which had been placed there several hours previously).

This was all that was needed, for with a double-take and a gasp of horror, Joe promptly keeled over backwards, fainting from the shock. This action was met by uproarious laughter from five of my friends who were hiding is some nearby trees. . . . To this day (it's been about three years now), Joe still turns white as a ghost when he tells about what happened that night. He fully believes that story, and as a result of this, many other people now believe it.
(A Strange Sort of Power 1990, 4)

Legend trips are journeys to sites with supernatural or scary stories associated with them. These sites, unlike parking spots, are usually in remote spots that require a considerable journey by the participants (Meley 1991, 22).

As part of the legend-tripping experience, scary contemporary legends are told to get the participants in the right mood. The legend sites themselves, may vary considerably over time. The stories around and about legend sites have cyclical pattern of dormancy and resurgence, as the legends are forgotten for a time, then are remembered, possibly with contemporary, local features added to the original legend.

Structure of Legend Trips

Although the actors and tellers change, the legends evolve, and the legend sites fluctuate, legend trips have a fixed three-part structure:

Introduction. This part sets the scene for the trippers before they arrive at the legend-trip site and includes telling spooky legends about escaped maniacs, ghosts, witches, or curses associated with the site. Told with the traditional tales are personal-experience stories about previous legend trips. Regardless of the location of the legend-trip site, the emphasis of the stories is on the "scare" factor rather than historical fact (Hall 1973, 147). After all, the belief states, "*Something* must have happened there, otherwise no legend-trip would be necessary. Or in other words, *some* legend, it doesn't matter which, is necessary to justify the traditional ritual" (Ellis 1982/83, 63). Which particular legend is told is influenced by the time and place of the legend trip, the composition of the group involved, and the personalities of the individual group members. Other factors include the storytelling abilities of the group members and the natural progression from one legend to another. One legend about an escaped maniac will suggest other legends featuring the same character. Legends are composed of familiar material and are often collaboratively told. Members of the group are free to enter into each tale, add their own details, and clarify any points to add support to the "truth" of the legend, including their own personal-experience stories (Hall 1973, 168).

Most of the legends do not seem particularly plausible when they are examined outside of the experience. However, blend them with an appropriate location (e.g., dark cemetery at night), a few beers, and a conversation centering on death and evil, and they tell a different story (Bird 1994, 200). Often, the participants view horror movies before leaving for the site, to get into the right spirit.

Enactment (what actually happens at the site). The effectiveness of the legend trip is dependent upon the threatening and remote appearance of the legend site, the effect of the legends on the way to the site, and the atmosphere of tension and uncertainty generated by the trip (Hall 1973, 170). Young adults pile into a car and, after telling each other scary legends, travel to the dark, remote site to see if the legend is true. Something usually happens, either prepared in advance or as the result of heightened anticipation, and the participants flee the scene.

Legend-trip sites are easy to recognize because the area is usually deeply rutted with tire tracks and often scattered with beer cans and the remains of campfires (Ellis 1982/83, 63).

Retrospective Personal Narratives. The telling and retelling of the events experienced are an essential element of the legend trip. Patricia Meley observed that, although the legend trip may be fairly well organized, the leave-taking "is usually abrupt and is markedly uncontrolled. Something happens, someone sees or hears something, and kids jump into the car, bury their faces, scream, and speed away" (1991, 15). It is when the teens begin to calm themselves as they drive toward safety that they begin to reconstruct the trip among themselves, developing a narrative that will become part of the legend-trip tradition and will be told at the next legend-trip event.

Types of Legends for Legend Trips

The stories attached to the legend-trip sites are of three general types:

Site of a Tragic Death That Is Haunted by Ghosts. The most popular legends involve people who died either violently or accidently and, unable to rest in their graves, haunt the place of their death (Ellis 1982/83, 62). The characters in these legends include babies who were either murdered or died when flung from the window of a crashing car, and decapitated revenants searching for their missing heads.

Haunted Graveyards. Legends about haunted graveyards comprise the second most popular type. In these stories, the dead return to punish those who disturb their graves or desecrate their tombs or grave markers. In other stories, tombstones develop strange markings or move around (Ellis 1982/83, 62). Several legend sites include statues that are supposedly haunted and will harm anyone who touches or kisses them.

Uncanny Persons or Creatures. These characters may be supernatural (e.g., witches, werewolves, zombies, and ghouls), but the more popular threats are maniacs and escaped mental patients who "prowl around 'parking' roads looking for unwary carloads of teenagers to liquidate" (Ellis 1982/83, 63).

Functions of Legend Trips

There has been a myriad of explanations offered in the literature on legend trips about their functions. Kenneth Thigpen believes that legend trips provide an introduction for the "uninitiated to the realm of the supernatural" (1971, 207). William Clements agrees with Thigpen, stating that legend trips provide a supernatural thrill as an escape from boredom (1969, 96). Gary Hall considers legend trips to be primarily a recreational activity (1973, 171). Bill Ellis, however, contends that the trips represent a "ritual of rebellion" against adult authority:

> The legend-trip is more than an initiation into the supernatural; it functions in the same way as other adolescent automobile activities—that is, as a "ritual of rebellion." The trip is the significant thing to the adolescent, and the legend serves mainly as an excuse to escape adult supervision, commit anti-social acts, and experiment illicitly with drugs and sex. (1982/83, 64)

Clements and Lightfoot, in their examination of "The Legend of Stepp Cemetery (Indiana)," conclude that the legend is "a complex network of oral narratives which interact both with each other and with other sets of legends" rather than one specific legend (1972, 128). They also find that "the stories . . . function differently for different tellers and hearers, ranging from sympathetic identification to vicarious expression of morbid fantasy" (127).

> The legend provides teenagers and college students in the area [of Stepp Cemetery] with valid reasons for driving several miles in the middle of the night to an isolated and hard-to-find cemetery. Further, the legend justifies the ritual of sitting in, or going to great lengths to *avoid* sitting in, a chair-shaped stump located there. Other forms of behavior, such as dancing around, throwing beer cans at, and shining automobile lights on the stump, mutilating dogs near the site, and overturning gravestones in the cemetery are all directly attributable to the existence of the legend. And, finally, the stories justify the, perhaps, otherwise unexplainable, existence of the mysterious stump itself. (Clements and Lightfoot 1972, 130)

In addition to giving young adults entertaining, scary glimpses into the supernatural, legend trips also serve to provide a kind of initiation ritual for the participants:

> The legend trip functions as a response to the stresses generated by the transitions inherent in adolescence, transitions that must be managed without adult guidance. The age segregation of American teens, coupled with the lack of socially approved means of ritual transition, results in adolescents finding their own standards of behavior and their own rites of initiation. (Meley 1991, 18)

OSTENSION AND BLOODY MARY

Bloody Mary, Mary Worth, Mary Whales, and Svarta Madame are all different names for the same being: a spirit who appears in mirrors as part of a ritual game played by younger children, especially elementary-school students. When discussing contemporary legends with young adults, I find that many of them have played this ritual game, and they often ask, "What about Bloody Mary? Is she a legend too?"

The ritual game to summon Bloody Mary by peering into a mirror in a dark room lit by a candle is a form of the legend trip. The players, usually female, cluster together, apprehensive but bursting with belief. The ritual will not work if the participants do not believe in the spirit. These are not independent and mobile legend-trippers; they are too young to travel to remote legend-trip sites and so find an appropriate location in the home and school bathroom mirrors!

Like the legend trips of their older counterparts, this trip also begins with a tale. Most of the game players know the circumstances of Mary's death, but the story is repeated again; in many cases, the legends echo "The Vanishing Hitchhiker" and "La Llorona." In some parts of the United States, the spirit is that of a witch burned at the Salem witch trials (Langlois 1980, 200).

As the stories are varied, so are the traditions involved in the ritual itself. Diverse incantations, ritual knocking, and turnings of the players; the lighting and placing of candles; and how one peers into the mirror (over the left shoulder, for example) all vary in different places and times. The action of the spirit also varies. Sometimes she is passive, while in other rituals, she will reach through the mirror and scratch the faces of the nearest participants, whose hair turns white. Some children have gone mad when Mary touches them (Klintberg 1988, 160).

So why do children continue to summon Bloody Mary, flirting with danger and possible tragedy? The ages between 9 and 12 are labeled "the Robinson age" by psychologists. This is the period when children need to satisfy their craving for excitement by participating in ritual games and playing in the dark. They are constantly looking for a safe way to extract pleasure and release their anxieties and fears (Klintberg 1988, 165). Bengt af Klintberg (1988, 166) states that there are three functions of ritual games such as Bloody Mary and Svarta Madame:

1. to actively challenge and conquer fears;

2. to give the opportunity of increasing status in the peer group; and

3. to develop a mechanism for coping with the supernatural.

The use of the mirror is symbolic of the entrance to an unknown world. Look what happened to Alice on her travels in *Through the Looking Glass*! There are two aspects associated with the mirror. The first is literal and "reflects the identification of the participants with the revenant" (Langlois 1980, 202). Under the ritual conditions, instead of seeing their own reflections, the girls "see" Mary. "In reality one perhaps sees the outline of one's own head or spots of color, which one interprets as having seen a ghost" (Klintberg 1988, 160). The second aspect of the mirror is the connection between the ritual game and an even larger window or mirror: the television screen. Steven Spielberg's film *Poltergeist* enlarged on this idea.

In his exploration of the Swedish "Svarta Madame" ritual, Klintberg compares the contemporary rituals of Swedish children with past Swedish folk practices and finds possible roots in earlier magical divination rites. Unmarried women, by staring into mirrors, surrounded by candles, on Christmas night or New Year's night, could conjure up the image of future husbands (Klintberg 1988, 162). As for the spirit that appears in mirrors to countless believing schoolchildren around the world, he could find no precedent.

HALLOWEEN SADISM

Contemporary legends about Halloween sadism emerged during the 1970s to give expression to growing fears about the safety of children, the danger of crime, and other sources of social strain. Such urban legends, like collective behavior and social-problem construction, are responses to social strain, shaped by the perception of the threat and social organization (Best and Horiuchi 1985, 488).

Contemporary legends associated with Halloween are much more prevalent than the legendary creatures and tales of Halloween past. Modern Halloween celebrations in North America have undergone a tremendous transformation during the last three decades. The innocent tradition of trick-or-treating from door to door, guaranteeing children a bag full of apples, popcorn balls, and homemade fudge, is a very distant memory. Today, if children are even allowed to participate in the ritual, they are bombarded with warnings about tampered treats, dangerous strangers, and other violence. The warnings come from parents, teachers, classmates, local police, and the media. These warnings are based on rumors and legends that have been circulating for more than 30 years. The legends combine two basic themes found in other contemporary legends: danger to children (e.g., "The Baby-Sitter" and abduction legends) and contamination of food (e.g., "Mouse in the Coke Bottle" and "Kentucky Fried Rat") (Best and Horiuchi 1985, 492). The fact that the rumors and legends have very little basis in reality has had no effect on quelling the fears of adults and, consequently, the children of today.

Poisoned Treats and Razor Blades in Apples

> *The Fraternal Order of Police and local pharmacies united to offer parents safety tips for Halloween. Among these tips [was] warning children not to eat any of their candy or other treats until parents could check them at home. The F.O.P. cautioned parents to "disregard [discard?] unwrapped or loosely wrapped items" and "Consider passing out stickers . . . and other non-candy treats," adding, "The other parents will appreciate your concern for their children's safety." (Halloween in America 1989, 9)*

These warnings are based on ostensive action, acting out the legends as if they are based on fact. In most cases, the ostensive act is benign. The legend is believed and transmitted without any attempt at verification. The resulting panic is also ostensive action. Parents and community leaders, acting on the legends, have devised new activities that are safe for children. Now, instead of visiting the neighborhood, children canvas salesclerks at shopping malls for manufactured and sterile treats.

The rumors and legends of adults willfully and anonymously poisoning Halloween treats and hiding pins, needles, glass splinters, or razor blades in the traditional Halloween apples have interacted with media warnings to create "the most widespread Halloween legend in America" (Grider 1984, 136). The publication and distribution of the warnings have become one of the first signs of the Halloween season (Ellis 1994, 29).

Many of these warnings had nothing directly to do with Halloween customs, but incorporated common sense advice about crossing roads or walking facing traffic. But a large number of these warnings acknowledged the presence of the sadism legends and incorporated other "horror stories" in telegraphed form (Ellis 1994, 30).

Folklorists have established that the legends surfaced in the late 1950s and were at first dismissed by the population at large as mere rumors with little substance. However, with continual repeated warnings, both orally and in the media, and the rise of anxieties regarding strangers, the public started to accept the legend as established fact. Best and Horiuchi explored newspaper coverage of Halloween sadism between 1959 and 1984, examining the indexes for *The New York Times*, *The Chicago Tribune*, *The Los Angeles Times*, and *The Frisco Bee*, as well as all entries under "Halloween" in *The Readers' Guide to Periodical Literature* and the medical database MEDLINE. They found 76 alleged incidents of Halloween sadism in 15 states and two Canadian provinces. To qualify for inclusion in their study, the reports had to include the name of the community where the incident occurred and the nature of the attack. The incidents were generally not serious, although two reports did involve death. The two deaths, however, were not the random murders of the legend. In 1970, Kevin Touston died from ingesting heroin alleged to be in his Halloween treats. It was later discovered that he had found the heroin in his uncle's home, not in the candy (Best and Horiuchi 1985, 489). The second death, that of Timothy O'Bryan, is discussed below.

Thirty-one of the incidents Best and Horiuchi investigated were reported within a span of three years (1969–1971). They conclude that this wave of reports encouraged the popular recognition of Halloween sadism. A systematic review of safety tips published in the media established that, before 1972, there was no mention of the sadists, but, after 1972, a warning to parents about possible tampering of treats was always included (Best and Horiuchi 1985, 490).

Best and Horiuchi (1985, 491) drew three major conclusions from their study:

1. The threat of Halloween sadism has been greatly exaggerated and there is no justification for the claim such behaviors are a major threat. Although two deaths were attributed to Halloween sadists, they were in fact not caused by anonymous strangers. However, the two deaths continue to be held as tangible proof of the threat of Halloween sadists while the particulars of the case are long forgotten or overlooked.

2. Many, if not most, reports of Halloween sadism are of questionable authenticity and are often hoaxes. A child who "discovers" an adulterated treat stands to be rewarded with the concerned attention of parents and perhaps police officers. Such a hoax is consistent with Halloween traditions of trickery, just as the fear of sadists resembles the more traditional dread of ghosts and witches.

3. The press should not be held responsible for the widespread belief that Halloween sadism poses a serious threat. Many of the stories received minimum coverage, often embedded in larger stories about Halloween. The authors concluded that legends about Halloween sadism are most frequently transmitted orally.

Rules governing children's handling of treats reflected fears about widespread tampering. All safety lists stressed that children should not sample candy before parents had inspected it, a point underscored in 1990 by the death of Ariel Katz, a seven-year-old girl in Santa Monica, California who collapsed while trick-or-treating. Local police, believing she had eaten candy from her bag, "conducted an intense door-to-door search" in the girl's neighborhood, blocking off streets, confiscating candy, and interviewing residents. Later reports conceded that Katz had died of congenital heart failure, not poison or drugs, but the nationwide publication of the initial fears obviously confirmed this "rule" in many parents' minds (Ellis 1994, 32).

The incidence of reports of Halloween sadism declined after 1971 to a few each year, until 1982 and the Tylenol murders. "In the weeks that followed, there were hundreds of reports of 'copycats' adulterating food, over-the-counter medications, and other household products" (Best and Horiuchi 1985, 490). And as Halloween approached, the media repeatedly broadcast the warning to care givers about the danger to treats.

In her exploration of contemporary legends, Sylvia Grider concludes that legends such as Halloween sadism stories reflect the fears of modern Western society. The legends are vehicles used to verbalize "a deep-rooted fear of strangers, a distrust of old customs and traditions, an acknowledgement of child abuse and infanticide and an ambivalence toward random, wanton violence" (1984, 132). The official warnings and commercial advertisements for tamper-proof treats reinforce these fears. The unconfirmed reports of contaminated treats are meshed with reports of other contaminated food products and repeated again and again, both orally and by the media, reinforcing the public belief that the legends are true. These warnings are now part-and-parcel of the Halloween trick-or-treat ritual! Parents everywhere examine their children's collected treats and throw out anything that is not hermetically sealed. Trick-or-treating has been restricted to close neighbors and friends, shopping malls, or community organized Halloween parties. No more homemade candy and no more Halloween apples. Bill Ellis points out that the crusade to have Halloween conform to other institutionalized holidays "corresponds to a national trend toward prohibition as a ready answer for what is perceived as adults' loss of control over the next generation" (1994, 38).

The two most popular Halloween sadism legends are obvious reversals of traditional Halloween themes. In "The Razor Blades," the treat that originally forestalled the child's trick becomes itself a cruel adult trick on the child. In "The Child Sacrifice," the custom of normal children impersonating agents of death becomes the image of murderous adults putting on the mask of normal-seeming neighbors (Ellis 1994, 38).

The Death of Timothy O'Bryan

A large majority of the population believes that Halloween sadism stories are true and try to protect their children from the presumed danger. But for Timothy O'Bryan, the danger was only too real. In 1974, in a bizarre case of ostension, one man believing that the legend represented reality, decided to insert cyanide poison into the Halloween treat of one person and blame the death on anonymous strangers. The police investigation that followed concluded that the treat was given to Timothy by his own father. "O'Bryan is the only person ever convicted of acting out an urban legend and carrying it to the ultimate conclusion—murder" (Grider 1984, 128). To add to the horror, when Ronald Clark O'Bryan, who won several stays of execution, was finally executed "shortly after midnight on 31 March 1984, Texans all over the state showed up in bars wearing Halloween costumes" (Ellis 1989a, 215). The O'Bryan murder case resulted in an intensification of the fears and warnings and is cited as proof and vindication of the warnings (Grider 1984, 136).

"Copycat" Cases

Several "copycat" cases of poisoned products have had wide media coverage in recent years. These cases, although not actually tied into the Halloween celebration, have had an effect on the public's belief in the legends.

Tylenol. In September 1982, there were several deaths from Tylenol that had been injected with cyanide. This incident had repercussions on Halloween celebrations of that year and intensified the warnings and paranoia about tampering of Halloween treats for the next decade. An Associated Press report of November 1, 1982 stated that "Halloween night climaxed a bizarre week during which more than 175 incidents of sabotaged fruits and candies were reported in more than 100 cities in 24 states" (Degh and Vazsonyi 1983, 13). The majority of incidents were later exposed as hoaxes. "Some were anonymous pranks, but [others] involved publicity-seekers or schemes to collect insurance settlements from manufactures" (Best and Horiuchi 1985, 491).

Pepsi. Reported incidents of syringes found in Pepsi cans in June 1993 were quickly exposed as hoaxes by the Food and Drug Administration. The reports came from over 20 states within 48 hours. FDA Commissioner David Kessler was quoted as saying, "Reports of possible tampering breed additional reports" (*The Edmonton Journal*, June 18, 1993, E15). The "Pepsi scare" is explored in greater detail in chapter 7.

And in the Media . . .

Shades of halloween apples? Children scooping up Easter treats at a Kelowna park Sunday also found hundreds of buns with pins and nails hidden inside. Horrified parents snatched the buns out of their children's hands, but a few kids began eating the crusty rolls. More than 500 people had gathered in the park for an annual Easter egg hunt sponsored by a radio station. Station employees had earlier distributed 650 sealed plastic eggs, containing candy, gum and chocolate, inside a cordoned-off area. But someone had also scattered hundreds of buns around the park. Signs painted with the word "buns" and directional arrows had been taped to posts and nailed to trees. Many of the booby-trapped buns had a smiling face stuck on them. No injuries were reported. ("Buns Spiked," Edmonton Journal, April 5, 1994, A3)

MERCANTILE LEGENDS

---

*It is claimed that a major international conspiracy is currently
flourishing which is specifically designed to support devil worship
and the antichrist. The way you can tell the people
and the companies involved is that they bear the mark
of the devil messenger—666. (Smith 1986, 68)*

"Mercantile legends" are contemporary legends that feature businesses
and corporations as the corrupt or evil central character and in which
something usually dreadful happens to the naïve consumer. They reflect a
public perception that there is danger from corporations and danger from
products that are mass produced and mass distributed. These legends also
demonstrate an undercurrent of fear and suspicion of size and power among
the general populace (Fine 1992, 158–59).

"The Goliath Effect"

Suspicion of big business is one of the most prevalent folk ideas in
Western society this century (Fine 1992, 141). Big business is seen as a threat
because it has such an enormous impact on people and communities economically, regionally, psychologically, and in terms of prestige. Gary Fine
(1992, 141) attaches the label "the Goliath Effect" to the folklore that incorporates the following characteristics:

1. refers to the dominant corporation or product in a particular area;

2. the larger the corporation, the wider the dissemination of the legends
   associated with it; and

3. legends may change target from a smaller corporation to a larger
   one.

Psychological Dominance. Corporate dominance is achieved in several
ways. One is size. Some product markets are so dominated by large corporations that their names become almost generic. For example, we say "Xerox"
to mean any brand of photocopiers; "Kleenex" to refer to any brand of facial
tissue, and "Jell-O" for all flavored gelatins (Fine 1992, 146). In legends and
rumors about these types of products, the "generic" names are used without
necessarily meaning that a particular corporation is the only one involved.
Most people speak of going for a "Coke," even if they normally drink another
soft drink product, while the terms "Kentucky Fried Chicken" and "Colonel
Sanders" represent all other fried chicken outlets in most conversations. The

fact that these corporate names are used in place of the general product name reflects their psychological dominance.

Economic Dominance. Other corporations, such as McDonald's, have established economic dominance over their competitors, and this is reflected in the legends. Even though some rumors and legends (e.g., earthworms in hamburgers) may originally be attached to another fast-food outlet (e.g., Wendy's or Burger King), the general population transfers the legend to the more economically dominant chain. This phenomenon is examined in chapter 7.

Regional Dominance. Regional dominance of a corporation is another factor in assigning corporate names and products in the legend corpus. A story about a particular corporation will not travel outside the economic territory of a corporation—people don't know the company, so they aren't interested in the legends about it. If the story does move into a different region, it does so with the name of the corporation that dominates in that area (Fine 1992, 152). If a narrator is telling the legend to someone from elsewhere, he or she may change the target either deliberately or unconsciously so that the audience will appreciate its significance. For a story to make sense, both teller and audience must share a "universe of discourse" about its major features. The central images and symbols must be meaningful to the audience (Fine 1992, 152).

Prestige. The content of mercantile legends can also be influenced by prestige. "In those markets in which the largest corporation or best-selling product is not widely known, the most prestigious corporation may become the target" (Fine 1992, 155). The content in some of these legends is only plausible when it refers to the "best" product or corporation. Whenever car legends are told, for example, the product named reflects the type of car that is prestigious for the environment of the teller and listener (e.g., Rolls Royce, Cadillac, or Porsche).

Types of Mercantile Legends

Mercantile legends are classified on the basis of the source of contamination: evil, greed, or carelessness. The fourth type of mercantile legends is remarkable in that it reflects benevolence toward rather than trauma for the consumer.

The Evil Corporation

In the evil corporation legend, the claim is made that the corporation itself, and not the product, is contaminated by evil. Both Reebok and Snapple have been targets of this type of legend. Other examples are discussed in chapter 11, "Modern Concerns: Satanic Legends."

Reebok Sneakers. Many evil corporation rumors during the late 1980s and early 1990s focused on the highly visible Reebok sneakers:

> As the price of the athletic footwear and celebrity attention to South African politics increased, a rumor merging these seemingly disparate phenomenon began to circulate. In its most popular versions, the rumor maintains that Reebok, manufacturer of one of the best-selling lines of athletic footwear, is owned by South Africans or manufactured in that country. Subscribers to the rumor claim that the white power structure of South Africa is surreptitiously profiting off young African-Americans' lust to have the right shoe; that is, it is essentially engaged in an anti-African-American conspiracy. (Turner 1993, 128)

This rumor differs from the other conspiracy rumors circulating in African American communities in that the product is popular with all young fashion-conscious North Americans and that the "officially sanctioned oppressor" is not the Klu Klux Klan but South Africa. As discussed later, the Klu Klux Klan has been the targeted oppressor in the background of many of the mercantile legends circulating in African American communities. The function of the rumor remains the same, however, acting as a harness against a highly popular luxury item that most African American parents could not afford to purchase for their children.

Patricia Turner investigates the repercussions of the Reebok legend in *I Heard It Through the Grapevine* (1993). In 1988, three weeks after purchasing an expensive pair of Reeboks that her teenage son *had* to have, his stepmother found them in the garbage. His reason for this behavior was that his classmates had upbraided him for "wearing South Africa on his feet." The stepmother, personally committed to anti-apartheid activities, did not insist that he wear the shoes, which she nevertheless rescued. She brought the issue to Turner's attention and was told that research indicated no South African ties with the Reebok manufacturing firm. "Reebok was not owned by South Africans, nor were their products made by South Africans or even sold in South Africa." Buoyed by this answer, the woman asked her stepson to wear his shoes again. "Nevertheless, he continued to be verbally accosted by peers who were not satisfied with his explanation that his mother's college professor's research debunked the rumor. Concerned for his personal well-being, his stepmother soon bought him another brand of sneakers" (Turner 1993, 132). Consumer values are being reshaped by the community. The outcry against the cost ("expensive," "over $50.00") of the shoes is validated by its South African "connection" (133).

Snapple. As new products are offered for sale, consumers circulate new stories, coloring the products with "ulterior motives." The rumor tells us that "apparently Snapple (the popular flavored ice-tea drink) contributes to

Operation Rescue." The drink is quite popular with young adults, many of whom are likely to oppose Operation Rescue, a Pro-Life group that pickets abortion clinics (More Corp Rumors 1992, 12).

Although this particular legend has apparently not harmed the introduction of Snapple into the market, this early attempt to alienate possible consumers is important to note.

The Deceptive Corporation

Deceptive corporation legends tell about companies that regularly adulterate their products with foreign substances such as worms in hamburgers or that corporations are aware of the long-term harmful effects of commonly used products such as microwave ovens. "These stories reflect the public's implicit conclusion that the post-industrial state is dangerous, since greedy corporations do not care about the health of the general public" (Fine 1992, 142).

The Careless Corporation

These legends are about one-time product contamination resulting from the carelessness of the corporation. Examples of this type of contamination are "Department Store Snakes," "Mouse in the Coke Bottle," and "Kentucky Fried Rat." "Typically the corporation is not blamed for being intentionally evil but is seen as lacking concern, being careless, and employing apathetic and indifferent workers" (Fine 1992, 143).

The Benevolent Corporation

This type of mercantile legend has been labeled the "redemption rumor" and depicts corporations as benevolent benefactors, redeeming parts of the product package to aid needy individuals. These legends and rumors provide redemption for the corporation involved (for all of the sins associated with wealth and power) and for the consumers as well, freeing them from blame, debt, or sin (Fine 1992, 189). Redemption rumors are discussed in depth in the following section.

REDEMPTION RUMORS

A thrifty housewife saved all her empty cans and, after a quantity had accumulated, shipped them off to Detroit. After a few weeks, she was delighted to receive the following letter: "Dear Madam, In accordance with your instructions we have made up and are shipping you today, one Ford. We are also returning eight cans which were left over." (McConnell 1989, 239)

Several automobile legends are attached to the character of Henry Ford I, who encouraged legends and jokes about the Model T. The above story adds to these legends by claiming that Ford was the inventor of redemption rumors as well. This legend circulated in the early part of this century and is presented as a possible antecedent for today's redemption rumors. A more plausible antecedent is the actual redemption of the tinfoil found in cigarette packages. Prior to and during World War II, this tinfoil could be recycled for money (Fine 1992, 197).

Product packaging is a fairly recent phenomenon. But by the beginning of the 20th century, unit packaging, rather than bulk sales, had become the norm. Soon the packaging was being used to entice a prospective purchaser to buy that particular product; it became an advertisement for itself and the company and a basis on which selection of products was decided (Fine 1992, 190). All the major forms of packaging, with the exception of plastic, were in wide use by the early 20th century.

Coupons and other forms of product-redemption incentives also date back to the 19th century. Benjamin Talbot Babbitt, a soap manufacturer in the 1850s, decided to market his laundry soap in individually paper-wrapped bars. Until that time, laundry soap had been sold in a long unwrapped bar that the grocer would cut as pieces were sold. When first introduced, Babbitt's innovation floundered because consumers wished to purchase soap, not paper. Babbitt then conceived a redemption scheme: for 25 wrappers, consumers would receive an attractive colored lithograph. Manufacturers have not looked back since! By the 1890s, many product lines had premium catalogs, and trading stamp companies were established. Grape Nuts offered consumers a 1-cent coupon for their next purchase of the cereal, and, for the first time, the coupons had a monetary value (Fine 1992, 190).

In 1929, General Mills began a coupon-redemption program in which a coupon for a free teaspoon was offered in every bag of Gold Medal flour. This program expanded into the Betty Crocker Coupon Plan, which is still going strong today. These promotions were very successful in promoting brand loyalty, and other companies soon joined General Mills with various redemption and coupon programs.

These programs eventually led to such redemption rumors as the pull-tab rumor: *You can redeem the pull tabs from aluminum cans to get free time on a dialysis machine for a kidney patient.* The rumor is not completely unfounded. Historical precedents for such cooperation between the corporate world and medical technology do exist. Perk Foods, between 1948 and 1979, sponsored a program whereby Vets Dog Food labels could be redeemed for 1 or 2 cents to the Pilots Guide Dog Foundation in Chicago. This program raised over $1 million in contributions to help train seeing-eye dogs (Fine 1992, 191). Other programs are offered by H. J. Heinz Company (6 cents for each baby-food label to a specific hospital) and Campbell Soup Company (soup-can labels for sports equipment for schools). Some local Kidney Foundation chapters have sponsored the collection and redemption of aluminum cans to help purchase kidney dialysis machines (Fine 1992, 191).

The Betty Crocker Coupon Program was approached by consumers who wanted to earn items not available in the redemption catalogue. General Mills responded by assigning each coupon point the value of ½ cent. Groups were given 18 months to complete a program that had been approved by the manufacturer. The more than 3,000 groups involved earned such diverse products as televisions, school buses, swimming pools, a tiger for a local zoo, and hospital beds.

In 1969, the Kidney Foundation of Ohio asked for approval of a coupon drive for dialysis machines. General Mills was delighted to comply, but problems quickly developed. Not all of the groups registered complied with the terms set by General Mills. At first, the corporation, fearing bad publicity, honored all the collections, but they soon called a halt to the entire program. Their initial participation in the redemption scheme had a backlash as well: General Mills was accused of "trading on human misery" (Fine 1992, 192). During the brief time that the program was in effect, approximately 300 dialysis machines were purchased. But although the program was discontinued in 1971, the redemption rumors still circulate!

These rumors, by their very longevity, have proven to be very adaptable. The diseases change depending on which are the subject of public concern at the time, and as medical technology advances (from seeing eye dogs to dialysis machines), what is collected changes as a function in packaging (e.g., the emphasis on pop-can tabs). Further, redemption rumors have a great appeal for consumers (Fine 1992, 193).

According to Gary Fine (1992, 195), the products that are the targets for redemption rumors have several common features, including:

1. they all come in packages that can easily be saved—whole, or in part.

2. they are all products one consumes in large numbers.

3. some of these products are believed to have negative health effects. Many of the rumors concern the three legal "drugs" in our culture: caffeine, nicotine and alcohol.

By collecting these items, the general public believes that it has a chance to get involved and help others. By providing benevolent action, "doubtful" products and the people who consume them are "morally redeemed." "This 'redemption' is perhaps most obvious in those cases in which the product has some connection to the disease being treated: as when cigarette packages are redeemed for an iron lung (even though those machines do not treat lung cancer) or a vague 'cancer machine,' or when soft drink can tops are saved for dialysis machines" (Fine 1992, 196).

Although, in some sense, people who respond to redemption rumors feel that they are getting something for nothing, because otherwise they would merely discard the packaging, it is not truly "something for nothing." The companies benefit from these rumors because some consumers decide the beneficent corporation should receive their business, as a small economic token of thanks (Fine 1992, 201).

Variants of Redemption Rumors

The variants are as diverse as the type of packaging and service or product being received as result of redeeming actions.

Seeing Eye Redemptions. *The Seeing Eye Foundation will provide a free seeing eye dog to a needy blind person for every collection of 25 thousand empty matchbook covers brought in to them.* This variant began circulating in the United States in the 1940s, "evolving along the way to apply to empty cigarette packages, quantities of tinfoil, and even string" (Morgan and Tucker 1984, 44).

Bar Codes in France. Since 1982, rumors have circulated throughout France that by collecting 5,000 product codes beginning with the number 3 from food packages, an organization would win a free wheelchair. Variants of this rumor cite different amounts of labels needed as well as the number with which the codes must begin. The rumors were direct replicas of rumors circulating in 1963 stating that by saving empty Gitanes cigarette packages, a wheelchair could be obtained (Kapferer 1990, 118).

Pop-Can Tabs. This is the most prevalent redemption rumor/legend of all time. Schools, community leagues, and hospitals have been conscientiously hoarding tabs for redemption.

These narratives have led to so much ostensive behavior because they depict nonmagical, seemingly plausible scenarios. It is relatively simple for people to believe them and to translate that belief from story to action. Unlike supernatural legends or rumors, people *can* perform the actions depicted with little cost (Fine 1991, 180).

In researching several of the stories about groups actually redeeming their product proof-of-purchases for medical technology, it was found that while the population saved pop-can tabs and turned them in, firm in the belief that they were redeeming them for time on a dialysis machine, the organization had made arrangements with an aluminum recycling center to take the tabs and forward a check directly to the organization as a donation. Cans are also accepted as donations, but "the idea was to get people's private collections of tabs out of basements and convert them into funds that really helped kidney patients" (Redeemed After All! 1989, 10).

And in the Media . . .

Bar Codes

John Rimmer of Magnolia writes that in June he "had to convince a work colleague that our local [London] hospital probably does not actually want a million bar codes off supermarket packages and old library books in order to buy some expensive piece of equipment." (More Redemption Rumors 1989, 5)

Coca-Cola

On June 12, the Louisville (KY) Courier-Journal reported finding six projects (one at the paper itself) to collect Coca-Cola tab tops in the belief that every three tabs would pay for one minute of kidney dialysis treatment needed by a boy in a local hospital. In one case, second-graders in a Clarksville, IN, school collected thousands of tabs before a Coca-Cola spokesperson debunked the rumor, noting that it had been circulating for at least ten years.

The project began when a parent received a computer message from a co-worker in another city who was involved in a similar collection. The parent mentioned it to her son, who was looking for a Cub Scout project, and he suggested it to his teacher. In two months, the children collected enough tabs to fill several grocery bags, but when the teacher tried to elicit a thank-you note from the sick boy, the co-worker could not locate the family and assumed that they had moved away from the area. After further calls determined that the story was not true, the tabs were sold to an aluminum recycling center for $27, which the teacher donated to the National Kidney Foundation.

The Foundation commented, "Hardly a day goes by that we don't get calls about the pull tabs. . . . It's something that had just mushroomed. All these people are well-intentioned, and it's hard to tell them that there's nothing to it. I wish I could tell them it's true." (Good Intentions Pave Way for Old Can-Tab Rumor to Mushroom Anew 1989, 6)

Campbell's Soup

The Navaho Lutheran Mission recently succeeded in collecting one million Campbell's soup labels. The total collection weighed 1300 pounds (590 kg.) and would measure 56.5 miles (91 km.). Children of the mission brought in the labels, which were supplemented by donations across the U.S. Campbell's Soup agreed to accept the million labels in exchange for a new Dodge mini-van. (Labels Beget Van 1989, 42)

Free Insulin

[Subject of story] has about 50 kg of aluminum pop and beer can tabs which he believed would qualify his daughter for free insulin for a lifetime. The family had heard that if 27 kg of tabs were collected, some organization would provide free insulin to a diabetic child. The catch is no one had heard of any organization that actually supplies free insulin in exchange for pull tabs.

Because his daughter requires two kinds of insulin, he has been trying to collect double the quota. He and scores of other people across Alberta are apparent victims of an urban myth or a cruel hoax. . . . Officials of pop companies, the Canadian Diabetes Association and the Juvenile Diabetes Research Foundation say they have no such program and they don't know of anyone who does. The diabetes association's offices across Alberta were inundated with calls last week from people offering to collect tabs after an item aired on the "good question" item of CBC Radio's morning program. Exhaustive inquiries were made . . . and staff did their best to debunk the myth. . . . "We were just trying to lay the issue to rest but it just doesn't seem to want to die. . . . Calls are still coming in." (Edmonton Journal, Sept. 24, 1991)

REFERENCES

Also heard. 1990. *FOAFTALE NEWS* 19 (October): 9–10.

Best, Joel, and Gerald T. Horiuchi. 1985. The razor blade in the apple: The social construction of urban legends. *Social Problems* 32, no. 5 (June): 488–99.

Bird, S. Elizabeth. 1994. Playing with fear: Interpreting the adolescent legend trip. *Western Folklore* 53, no. 3 (July): 191–209.

Clements, William M. 1969. The chain on the tombstone. *Indiana Folklore* 2, no. 1: 90–96.

Clements, William M., and William E. Lightfoot. 1972. The legend of Stepp Cemetery. *Indiana Folklore* 5: 92–141.

Craig clones. 1991. *FOAFTALE NEWS* 22 (June): 11-12.

Craig Shergold. 1990. *FOAFTALE NEWS* 18 (June): 8.

Craig Shergold. 1991. *FOAFTALE NEWS* 21 (March): 10–11.

Craig Shergold. 1992. *FOAFTALE NEWS* 26 (June): 11.

Degh, Linda, and Andrew Vazsonyi. 1983. Does the dog bite? Ostensive action: A means of legend telling. *Journal of Folklore Research* 20, no. 1 (January-May): 5–34.

Dying Child's Wish. 1995. *FOAFTALE NEWS* 37 (June): 6–7.

Ellis, Bill. 1982/83. Legend-tripping in Ohio: A behavioral survey. *Papers in Comparative Studies* 2: 61–73.

———. 1983. Adolescent legend-tripping. *Psychology Today* (August): 68–69.

———. 1989a. Death by folklore: Ostension, contemporary legend and murder. *Western Folklore* 48 (July): 201–20.

———. 1989b. Needling whitey: The New York City pin-prick incidents as ostension. *FOAFTALE NEWS* 16 (December): 5–6.

Fine, Gary Alan. 1991. Redemption rumors and the power of ostension. *Journal of American Folklore* 104 (spring): 179–81.

———. 1992. *Manufacturing tales: Sex and money in contemporary legends.* Knoxville: University of Tennessee Press.

———. 1994. "Safe" spooks: New Halloween traditions in response to sadism legends. In *Halloween and other festivals of death and life*, edited by Jack Santino. Knoxville: University of Tennessee Press, 24–44.

Good intentions pave way for old can-tab rumor to mushroom anew. 1989. *Courier-Journal* (Louisville, KY) A1, 6. Quoted in More redemption rumors. 1989. *FOAFTALE NEWS* 15 (September): 5.

Grider, Sylvia. 1984. The razor blades in the apples syndrome. In *Perspectives on contemporary legend: Proceedings of the conference on contemporary legend* [CECTAL Conference Papers #4], edited by Paul Smith. Sheffield, England: University of Sheffield.

Guigné, Anna Elizabeth Kearney. 1993. The "Dying Child's Wish" Complex: A case study of the relationship between reality and tradition. M.A. thesis, Memorial University of Newfoundland [St. John's, Newfoundland]. Available through UMI Dissertations Service, catalogue number 0-315-91654.

Hall, Gary. 1973. The big tunnel: Legends and legend-telling. *Indiana Folklore* 6: 139–73. Reprinted in Degh, Linda. 1980. *Indiana folklore: A reader*, edited by Linda Degh. Bloomington: Indiana University Press, 225–57.

Halloween in America. 1989. *FOAFTALE NEWS* 16 (December): 9.

Hults, David S. 1988. Roaming gnomes. *Australian Folklore* 2: 87–92.

Just in. 1989. *FOAFTALE NEWS* 15 (September): 4–7.

Kapferer, Jean-Noel. 1990. *Rumors: Uses, interpretations and images.* New Brunswick, NJ: Transaction.

Klintberg, Bengt af. 1988. "Black Madame, come out!" On school children and spirits. *ARV* 44: 155–67.

Labels beget van. 1989. *The Lutheran* (September 27): 42. Quoted in Redeemed after all! 1989. *FOAFTALE NEWS* 16 (December): 10.

Langlois, Janet. 1980. Mary Whales, I believe in you. *Indiana folklore: A reader.* Edited by Linda Degh. Bloomington: Indiana University Press.

McConnell, Brian. 1989. The corporate legend: Marketing invention or consumer response. In *The questing beast: Perspectives on contemporary legend, vol. IV,* edited by Gillian Bennett and Paul Smith. Sheffield, England: Sheffield Academic Press.

Meley, Patricia M. 1991. Adolescent legend trips as teenage cultural response: A study of the lore in context. *Children's Folklore Review* 14 (fall): 5–25.

Microwaved maltese. 1990. *FOAFTALE NEWS* 19 (October): 10.

More corp rumors. 1992. *FOAFTALE NEWS* 28 (December): 12.

More redemption rumors. 1989. *FOAFTALE NEWS* 15 (September): 5.

Morgan, Hal, and Kerry Tucker. 1984. *Rumor!* New York: Penguin.

Musick, Ruth Ann. 1977. The seated lady. *Coffin Hollow and other ghost tales.* Lexington: University Press of Kentucky.

Redeemed after all! 1989. *FOAFTALE NEWS* 16 (December): 10.

Smith, Paul. 1986. *The book of nastier legends.* London: Routledge Kegan Paul.

A strange sort of power that I had in my possession: An ostensive version of "The Vanishing Hitchhiker." 1990. *FOAFTALE NEWS* 20 (December): 3–4.

Thigpen, Kenneth A., Jr. 1971. Adolescent legends in Brown county: A survey. *Indiana Folklore* 4, no. 1: 141–215.

Turner, Patricia A. 1993. *I heard it through the grapevine: Rumor in African-American culture.* Berkeley: University of California Press.

5

RELATED GENRES

The Boyfriend's Death

After parking in Lover's Lane for some time, Pam told her boyfriend Jeff that it was time to leave. He grumbled a bit but tried to
start the car. . . . It wouldn't turn over. At first Pam felt that he
was just stalling for time, but the car truly would not start. . . . It
was out of gas. Because Pam was dressed up and was wearing
heels, Jeff told her that he would walk to the first house and see if he
could get some help. "Stay in the backseat," he told Pam, "and
don't open the door unless you hear me knocking three times." Jeff
left after making sure that Pam was secure in the backseat; she had
a blanket around her to keep her warm. He did not return and Pam
actually fell asleep waiting for him. She woke with a start as she
heard a knock on the roof of the car. "Jeff," she thought. But there
was no more knocking! "The wind. It must be the wind." Too
disturbed to fall asleep again, Pam waited. She heard strange
dripping sounds and scratching but no Jeff.

Eventually, a large light shone into the car and caught her in its
glare. A man spoke gently to her, "Please get out of the car. I am a
policeman. Please, let me help you." He turned the light on his identification and Pam opened the door. He helped her out of the car and
propelled her down the road. "Don't look back," he warned. Too
late! In the glare of the lights, Pam could see the car and the swaying body of Jeff hanging above it. His fresh blood still dripping on
the windshield and his steel-toe boots still scratching the roof.

84

Throughout the literature on contemporary legends, references are made to similarities between these legends and other genres. These similarities are often noted in attempts to define what a contemporary legend is, and what it is not. The category of contemporary legend seems "to be a happy borrower of the features of other genres. It combines, in one form, characteristics of legend, fable, tall tale and personal experience story" (Bennett 1985, 66). The function of the contemporary legend is very like that of a fable; the content is closely linked to that of tall tales; and the manner of telling incorporates the same devices as those of personal-experience stories (Bennett 1985, 67). Besides rumor and gossip, already discussed, contemporary legends have been likened to pourquoi tales (how and why stories, tales that explain how something came to be or why animals have certain characteristics and not others), jokes, proverbs, ballads, and other forms of traditional folklore. Resemblances have also been noted to several literary genres as well, most notably, mystery stories and horror tales.

Nevertheless, each of these is a separate and distinct genre, defined by whether its stories are believed or not; whether they occur in the distant past, recent past, or present; whether the tales are transmitted orally or in writing; and whether they are motivated by fear, embarrassment, wonder, orality, or speculation (Nilsen 1989, 6).

BALLADS AND FOLK SONGS

There is a definite relationship between the stories told in ballads and the tales retold in contemporary format. One such tale is "The Mistletoe Bough," a Christmas ballad sung in Scotland. The ballad tells the story of the young bride who, on her wedding night, becomes lost forever during a game of hide-and-seek. Her skeleton is discovered years later; her death was caused by her accidently locking herself in a large trunk. Several collections of scary tales for young adults contain prose variants of this sad tale ("The Missing Bride"). Young adult workshop attendees have enjoyed "locking" their nemesis in lockers, car trunks, and old freezers in their "active" retellings of this ballad!

"Dunderback's Machine" is another old folk song that has had many rejuvenations over the years. Echos of various legends resonate throughout this "children's" song about Dunderback, a butcher, who gathers a wide assortment of items to make his famous sausages. Dogs, cats, and the odd child disappear before justice is served.

His wife she had the nightmare,
She walked right in her sleep,
She grabbed the crank, gave it a yank,
and Donderback was meat. (Schwartz 1984, 91)

FABLES

Although fables feature animal characters rather than humans, these short didactic tales, like the contemporary legend, are commentaries on social, political, and sexual fears and anxieties (Bennett 1985, 67). The stated moral of the fable, as we know it today, is a relatively recent innovation, tacked on when the wisdom and understanding of audiences was assumed to be insufficient to see the point unaided, and publishers of fable collections deemed it necessary to add the "morals" at the end of each tale. (To see how each collection follows its own political, social, or educational mandate, compare several different collections and the appended morals.) Contemporary legends also serve to impart wisdom to the audience, implying the morals that the storyteller wishes to communicate. Both fables and contemporary legends are told to socialize their audience through humor, wonder, and fear.

FABLIAUX

"One subtype of contemporary legend that has not been studied so intensively is what we might call . . . the fabliau legend." These brief, humorous narratives focus on some type of intrigue that allows one or more of the characters to violate some social taboo. Part of the delight in these tales is the fact that the character often exposes himself (Ellis and Hays 1994, 1).

Two contemporary legends that are favorites with young adults, "The Surprise Party" and "The Fart in the Dark," fall into this category. A potential embarrassing incident is one of the greatest concerns facing young people as they make their way in society, so they revel in embarrassing tales that "happen" to others.

"The Surprise Party"

A young, recently engaged couple are baby-sitting. After the parents leave, the amorous couple undress. The mother phones to say that she has forgotten to turn on the washing machine. Still naked, the young man piggybacks his fiancée downstairs. There, they encounter their family, friends—and the local priest—who have arranged a surprise party for them. (So there's this guy, see . . . 1991, 80)

In contrast to jokes, which they closely resemble, modern fabliaux are told as true occurrences and the proverbial friend-of-a-friend is given as authority. Due to the intended audience and purpose of the material, and because of the nature of their content, very few fabliaux appear in this book.

In fact, very few of them are actually studied. "In addition, their themes— often bawdy or scatological—mean that they do not often show up in sources consulted by folklorists" (Ellis and Hays 1994, 1).

Another version of this legend is the story of a boss who celebrates his birthday by going to lunch with his secretary. After lunch they retire to her apartment. While he's making himself comfortable in the living room, his secretary goes to the bedroom with a promise of a surprise. The man assumes he knows what the surprise it, but unknown to him, his wife, children, parents and co-workers are waiting for him in the bedroom; they enter the living room to shout "surprise" and find him with only his socks on!

Ann Landers published this version several years ago while I was on a school tour. At one of the schools, the janitorial staff were discussing the morning paper. One woman stated, "I showed this to my husband this morning and told him he better never do anything like that!" The others agreed that the story provided a good warning. When I casually mentioned that it was not true, I barely survived. The next day I returned to the school only to overhear the same woman: "Someone told me it wasn't true, but I know it was. Men just behave like that!" Regardless, then, of the truth of the tale, modern fabliaux connect with members in the audience who are easily convinced of their truth because of their preconceived notions and understanding of human nature.

"The Fart in the Dark"

> *A victim of stomach gas is alone in either a darkened room or the front seat of a car at night. The person relieves themself of the gas by breaking wind. However, much to their embarrassment, they quickly learn that they are not alone at all.* (Brunvand 1981, 148)

Variants of this legend circulate in the world of Xeroxlore, usually billed as "The Gastronomical Bean Story." One variant is related in *The Heart Is a Lonely Hunter* (1940) by Carson McCullers. The legend strikes terror into the hearts of the audience (after they laugh in embarrassment) because this embarrassment could easily happen to anyone.

It is interesting to note that at one time breaking wind was considered socially acceptable in European society. *An Essay of Farting* (1787) contains numerous ways to bring about this condition. During the following century, such "musical interludes" were incorporated into stage performances. As time passed, however, the activity became socially unacceptable and therefore many contemporary legends highlight this anti-social behavior (Smith 1986, 32).

JOKES

Contemporary legends and jokes share similar functions, structures, and themes. Both function as socially acceptable methods of releasing tensions, fears, and anxieties of the general population. However, while the joke uses humor, the contemporary legend relies on both fear and humor as a means of release (Greenburg 1972/73, 136). Beyond functioning simply as a release, however, the actual existence of legends and jokes signify those underlying tensions inherent in society (Nilsen and Nilsen 1992, 664). This is one of the reasons why sick jokes and contemporary legends immediately follow any type of disaster, natural or man-made.

Contemporary legends, sick humor, and ethnic jokes have two outstanding common themes: consumption of objectionable foods and disasters involving modern technology (Davies 1990, 49). "Grandma's Ashes" has circulated as both a contemporary legend and a joke for many years.

"Grandma's Ashes"

When the family moved to North America, they kept in constant touch with their European relatives. Letters and parcels regularly made their way from one shore to another. After a long period of silence, a small box arrived from the U.S. Inside, carefully wrapped in tissue paper, was a jar of grey powder. There was no note, but since many of the previous parcels had contained ready-to-make packaged mixes, the European family members thought that this powder, too, was a mix that would be prepared by simply adding water. The sauce was made and served, but it wasn't the best they had eaten! Several days later, a letter arrived from the U.S. explaining that the father had died, and because he had always been home-sick, he wished his ashes to be spread over his home town. Grandma hoped that the rest of the family would not be inconvenienced and that the letter would get to them before the ashes, which were being sent separately in a jar and were securely wrapped in tissue paper.

Whether we class a particular telling of a tale as a joke or a legend presumably depends on the rather arbitrary and subjective question of what is in the mind of the teller at the time and how his audience perceives and classifies his account (Davies 1990, 51). These legends and jokes play on the element of shock—incorporating cannibalism, death of pets, aggression, and the threat or reality of death and destruction. Shock is frequently caused by the casual way that the horrible surprise is parachuted into the ordinary world of the audience. In both genres, outsiders are key players. In the contemporary legends, the outsider provides a plausible explanation for a bizarre episode; in the joke, the outsider is employed as the key "whose punch-line is going to switch a plausible narrative into palpable farce" (Davies 1990, 64).

Disaster Jokes

> The prevalence and popularity of disaster jokes, particularly among young people, is neither evidence of their extreme callousness nor of the use of jokes as catharsis, as a means of coming to terms with the pain of the tragedy. . . . Such jokes are best seen as related to the reporting of these events in the mass media rather than directly to the events themselves. (Davies 1990, 55)

The mass media has invited the general population to view disaster as it occurs, or very shortly thereafter, from the safety of their homes. We are swept into the tragedy along with the eyewitnesses, victims, and family members, but are buffeted by banal commercial messages and programming all the while (Davies 1990, 55). This incongruity is the stuff of which jokes are made. Sick humor closely follows the onset of large-scale epidemics as well as largely publicized incidents such as the "Bobbitt" incident and trial and the televised chase and trial involving O. J. Simpson.

Sick jokes that grow out of the paradox of real disasters viewed from a safe and uninvolved distance are paralleled by nasty legends (imaginary, though plausible disasters that are alleged to have overtaken the "friend-of-a-friend") (Davies 1990, 56).

Ostensive Pranks

The temptation to act out contemporary legends has been discussed in the previous chapter. What was not addressed was the deliberate staging of a legend as a prank or practical joke. A variant of "The Boyfriend's Death" (told at the beginning of this chapter) was told to a group of female university employees by a group of male students in the early 1970s after they had made some preparations. The men seemed very agitated, and claimed that they had got back to the lodge just in time, because the police were setting up road blocks to try and apprehend an escaped lunatic who was in the area and was thought to be "heading this way."

The men departed, leaving the female staff disturbed by what they had been told. They decided to lock themselves in their rooms as a precautionary measure, something they normally did not do. During the night, loud, thumping footsteps were heard on the flat roof above their rooms. They rushed out of their rooms, hysterical, and gathered in the communal area. One brave soul went to summon help. No sign of anyone was found. In the morning, they discovered that an elaborate practical joke had been played on them: there were no road blocks, no escaped lunatic, and the footsteps were caused by a student walking across the roof (Bowman 1987, 172).

The practical joke was a huge success. For the men to tell the women about an escaped lunatic, to relate an incident confirming their preconceptions about the sort of dreadful thing that might happen when a madman is on the rampage, and then to add footsteps in the night was a winning combination (Bowman 1987, 172). For those on the receiving end, however, the incident was anything but funny.

LITERARY HORROR STORIES

Horror must be overwhelming at some point in the plot of a literary horror story. This horror cannot lose the element of horror and still be effective, and must carry the reader away simultaneously with the characters in the story. One of the reasons that horror stories are so popular today is that they allow the reader to create the images, actions, and terror in their imagination, making everything seem even more horrifying. Movies, though popular, do not allow for this collaboration between reader and author, as everything on the screen has already been created for the viewer and allows no chances for participation in their creation (Bodart 1994, 25).

The demand among students for scary stories, not always sanctioned by educators and care givers, is constant. My personal rule of thumb is not to tell scary tales to audiences below grade six. This is an arbitrary rule I devised observing my own children and their nightmares. Younger audiences are often quite put out with me. Their demand for scarier and scarier tales and novels have revolutionized the publishing industry. "Everything is getting pushed down: junior high kids read Stephen King, middle schoolers read YA thrillers, so the real market for these thrillers [scary story series] will probably be upper elementary kids" (Jones 1993, 30). These collections are meant to recreate the thrill and fun of telling ghost stories. "The hook in all of these is the trick ending; the meat is the gross-out" (30).

Horror stories are adaptable to all aspects of communication media. The tales are successful told in the dark around a camp fire; they sell well in the movie and video market; more and more horror literature, for all ages, is being published; and amusement park rides thrive on horrifying their patrons (Stewart 1982, 33).

Like oral tales, horror literature builds slowly on audience expectations and tensions, leading the audience through the text step by step. The ending can never be revealed before its time, as that would negate the entire experience (Stewart 1982, 34). Horror fiction follows the convention of allowing the reader to know no more than the victim of the story. This is evident in scenes where the reader and the character are presented with a letter that is read at the exact same moment. In oral tales, the direct quote and sound effects serve the same function: audience as victim (Stewart 1982, 39).

There are differences, though; the literary tale "preys on the solitude of reading" while the oral tale is most effectively told in settings of ambiguity: in the dark or around a fire (Stewart 1982, 40). Whether oral or written, the horror story often depicts scenes of those ambiguous suburbs between nature and culture, or between categories of the natural: the dungeon (part basement, part cave), the swamp (part land, part water), the woods (part garden, part wilderness), and, perhaps most significantly, the haunted house, a powerful example of the domestic being overtaken by nature (Stewart 1982, 41). One of the earliest examples of horror fiction, *Frankenstein* by Mary Shelley, is a landmark book. It gave birth to the genre of science fiction and also introduced an important theme that is used again and again: "the scientist who meddles in forbidden things and creates a monster that cannot be controlled" (Kies 1992, 46). A secondary theme, also introduced by Shelley, is the sorrow of the monster as it realizes that it can never be truly human.

The theme of good versus evil, underlying all universal mythology and legends, is also an important component of horror fiction. In mythology, the characters involved in the struggle are superhuman gods. In horror literature, evil is frequently portrayed as an occult force attempting to corrupt the good (ordinary citizens). Evil may also take the form of ancient evil beings of legends, of alien worlds, of scientific and technological terrors, or of psychological evil innate in humankind (Kies 1992, 60).

MYSTERY STORIES

The connection between contemporary legends and mystery lies in the structure of the tales. To be effective, the contemporary legend plot must *conceal* its functions, as do the literary plots of the mystery genre. "In both urban legends and detective stories, what is to be dis-covered (un-covered) is the 'real plot,' as opposed to the 'apparent plot.' Plots themselves thereby become metaphors for mystery" (Barnes 1984, 70). Contemporary legends often do not offer all the primary details needed to correctly interpret the action. Sometimes these details are purposely withheld by the teller for maximum impact on the audience.

PERSONAL-EXPERIENCE NARRATIVES

Personal-experience stories are tales that come from within the teller's realm of experience: things that have actually happened and the teller's interpretation of that event.

The narrator usually tells both contemporary legends and personal-experience narratives as if they are true and, in many cases, believes they are, in fact, so. Both genres are "person-centered narratives, telling of a single occasion in the near past, and featuring a cast of ordinary people" (Bennett 1985, 67). As in contemporary legends, both personal-experience narratives and tall tales use local details and setting to authenticate the experience. Names of people, places, dates, and relationships, as well as explanations of how the characters came to be participants in the adventure, are all incorporated into the tale to add verisimilitude (Bennett 1985, 67). The media and authority figures are also woven into all three types of tale to impress upon the audience the truthfulness of what is being presented. Contemporary legends, like personal-experience narratives and tall tales, are informal presentations told, in the most part, as part of ordinary conversations.

William Labov, in *Language in the Inner City: Studies in the Black English Vernacular*, establishes six basic structural elements of personal-experience narratives (1972, 370). Not all personal-experience tales are composed of all six elements. Labov considers narrative, essentially, as a series of answers to underlying questions (1972, 359–60).

1. *Abstract*: a brief summary of the whole story in one or two clauses at the beginning of the telling. *What is this about?*

2. *Orientation*: the introduction of the setting, characters, and problem addressed in the story. *Who, when, what, where?*

3. *Complicating Action*: the narrative proper, the main body of the story. *Then what happened?*

4. *Evaluation*: "that part of the narrative which reveals the attitude of the narrator towards the narrative by emphasizing the relative importance of some narrative units as compared to others." *So what?*

5. *Result or Resolution*: follows the evaluation to wrap up the problem or conflict. *What finally happened?*

6. *Coda*: returns the audience to the "real" world and out of the world of the story. The coda is found less frequently than other elements of the narrative.

The structure of contemporary legends resemble Labov's scheme very closely. A successful telling of a contemporary legend, however, deliberately represses an essential portion of the orientation until the telling of the complicating action. This assures maximum effect on the audience (Nicolaisen 1987, 72). Labov's structural elements are referred to throughout the discussions of individual legends in part III.

TALL TALES

Contemporary legends are the natural descendants of the tall tales of the Old West. Both genres resonate with real-life details and mix exaggeration with "touches of fear, titillation, and wish fulfillment" (Nilsen and

Nilsen 1992, 668). Contemporary legends are based on plausible occurrences that are exaggerated just beyond probability. As with the tall tales, they begin in the world of ordinary people having ordinary adventures. But, again like the tall tale, potential hazards in that very ordinary world become actualized, usually in a gross and frightening form (Bennett 1985, 67).

Many of the elements that are used to define tall tales can just as easily be used to define contemporary legends:

> The tall tale is based on the humor of lies and exaggerations; its narrative content is traditional in nature. It exists in certain contexts or traditional situations and serves certain functions within those contexts; it is characterized by certain formal patterns which reinforce the functions it serves; one may consider both context and function as part of a traditional performance. The tall tale is a genre which relies on dramatic presentation and is thus normally told in the first person. (Thomas 1977, 7)

Tall tales use the local setting to add verisimilitude, at least at the beginning. "The tall-tale teller . . . attempts to convince his audience of the truth of his narrative" (Thomas 1977, 33). The tall tales, although they function as a form of entertainment and a way of creating a group identity, primarily functioned as a method of dealing with the fears and anxieties surrounding the mysterious new environment that the settlers had to contend with in their daily lives. Contemporary legends fulfill the same function for the "pioneers" of today, who are trying to come to terms and make sense of their "new" world. Both genres share longevity, have a wide acceptance, and preserve traditional themes (Nilsen 1989, 7).

Notable differences between the two genres are generally superficial, but they do exist, as noted by Don Nilsen (1989, 7):

1. Contemporary legends take place in the very recent past, while tall tales are typically tales from the distant past.

2. Contemporary legends, essentially an oral form, are frequently circulated in print (usually by the media); tall tales, often reprinted in "lifeless" collections, are spread by word of mouth. Tall tales take their life from the art of narration; they are of little substance on the printed page.

3. Tall tales are usually associated with the Western states and provinces. Contemporary legends are not regional.

4. Contemporary legends, reflecting the urbanization of Western society, tend to take place in urban or suburban areas; tall tales take place in the wild open spaces.

5. Contemporary legends often revolve around sex and other conversational taboos; tall tales are never sexually titillating.

6. The heroes of tall tales are bigger-than-life while those of contemporary legends are ordinary, smaller-than-life, friend-of-a-friend characters. The bigger-than-life characters in the tall tales are reflected in the bigger-than-life forces that interrupt their lives. In the ordinary world of the contemporary legend, the settings are more trivial and normal.

7. Once-in-a-lifetime events are the occasions of the tall tale cycles but contemporary legends can happen to anyone at anytime.

OTHER LITERARY GENRES

Contemporary legends occasionally surface in poetry, science fiction, and fantasy. Research has also uncovered contemporary legends (reflecting another contemporary time) in works of the classics: Dickens, Boccaccio, and Chaucer. Suggestions for studies incorporating novels and legends can be found in the following chapters under the section, "Literary and Visual Adaptations."

Students can explore their favorite reading genre and compare the structure, content, and function of the genre with the world of contemporary legends. Frequently, authors allude to the idea of contemporary legends within the body of their stories, assuming that their readers will understand what they are talking about, as in this example from John Dunning's mystery, *Booked to Die*: "They had had one run-in last year: the story had gone through the trade like a shot and quickly taken on the characteristics of an urban legend" (1992, 47-48).

Other writers use a specific contemporary legend as a generic "brand," again assuming that readers are knowledgeable about the genre, as in this example from Emma Bull's fantasy, *Bone Dance*: "I've never heard if they let him out. I've never heard that the thing got video release. I've never heard it proved that it was released, period. File the whole story next to Hitchhikers, Comma, Vanishing" (1991, 5).

Still others make a commentary on the genre and folklorists who study the legends. The following example is from *Dreams Underfoot*, a fantasy collection by Charles de Lint (1993, 107; 400). The character speaking is also a fantasy writer.

> We'd be just another urban legend. . . . I was thinking more of that Brunvand guy with his choking Doberman and Mexican Pets. . . . I called them urban legends—independently of Jan Harold Brunvand, who also makes a living collecting them. But he approaches them as a folklorist, cataloguing and comparing them, while I retell them in stories that I sell to magazines and then recycle into book collections. . . . And Brunvand does such a wonderful job. The first time I read his *The Vanishing Hitchhiker*, I was completely smitten

with his work and, like the hundreds of other correspondents Brunvand has, made a point of sending him items I thought he could use for his future books.

UFO-LORE

The U.S. Air Force has discovered the true nature of UFOs (Unidentified Flying Objects) but is keeping it a secret in the interest of national security. (Dickson and Goulden 1993, 107) *After the U.S. Air Force investigation of UFOs,* Project Blue Book, *came to an end in 1969, the government's interest in the phenomena did not wane as reported. While the government officially abandoned all interest in UFOs, a secret military underground was hot on the trail of suspicious radar blips, saucers and even the aliens themselves.* (Rayl 1994, 49)

What folklore and UFO-lore have very much in common is the same kind of evidence. In both cases, such evidence is overwhelmingly anecdotal, the verbal testimony of narrators describing extraordinary occurrences (Bullard 1988, 9). The focus has shifted recently from a debate between "believers" and "debunkers" over the physical reality of UFOs and alien abductions to a discussion of the psychology, myth, and culture of the sightings (Menefee 1993, 37). In her article "UFOs: True, False, or Does It Matter?" Christine Menefee suggests the need for teachers and librarians who work with young adults to be aware of the growing realm of UFO literature. The wonders of technology and the prominence of popular culture icons like *Star Trek, Star Wars,* and the *X-Files* have created an intense interest in the world beyond our frontiers. "Popular culture abounds in good, bad, and mixed-up aliens, and it's not difficult to see why young people find them so interesting. I know teachers, a priest, and a social worker who have found story lines from *Starman* (movie and TV series) useful in communicating with troubled children" (Menefee 1993, 38).

Like contemporary legends, UFO stories told around the world share common elements, regardless of place or time of origin. However, unlike contemporary legends, the alien characters do not always behave in a consistent manner. Those who experience the encounters have their own interpretation of the experience: some perceive it as a threat, while others feel that it will ultimately benefit humanity.

There are two basic types of UFO stories: reports of sightings and abductions and reports of conspiracies. Contemporary legends, and folklore in general, share many conspiracy elements with UFO-lore. The conspiracy stories contain two basic plots: governmental "cover-up" and "secret treaties" between the government and the alien culture.

Omni magazine ran a six-part series on the UFO conspiracy in 1994. (Editorial 1994, 10) Their mandate for the series states:

> We are not speaking of tabloid sensationalism or special-effects wish fulfillment. No E.T. No supermarket flying saucers. It's a simple question. Is there evidence of alien presence on Earth and have governments suppressed that evidence? . . . The essence of science is skepticism; the watchword of the scientific method is proof. Hearsay and rumor—which run rife in the UFO community— don't count.

The articles delve into six decades of supposed government UFO cover-ups, citing authoritative personal-experience narratives as well as classified documents and the attempt to obtain them.

An alternative explanation for the suppression of the "truth" is that of the "secret" conspiracies and treaties established between our governments and the alien cultures. According to this theory, the treaty allows trades of advanced technology for "the right to abduct and conduct biological experiments on a number of humans. The EBEs [extra-terrestrial biological entities] feed on human blood, and the experiments involve implanting mind-control devices in ordinary citizens' brains" (Ellis 1990, 6).

Many of the elements within this body of UFO-lore are similar to the conspiracy stories derived from anti-Semitic rumors of plots by Jewish-dominated groups for taking over the world. The parallels between the UFO conspiracy rumors and the legend known as "Stolen Baby Parts" also demonstrate that these reports are part of a larger corpus of conspiracy beliefs that are reflected in the contemporary legends (Ellis 1990, 6).

REFERENCES

Barnes, Daniel R. 1984. Interpreting urban legends. *ARV* 40: 67–78.

Bennett, Gillian. 1985. What's modern about the modern urban legend? In *The 8th Congress for the International Society for Folk Narrative Research*, edited by Reimund Kvideland and Torunn Selberg, June 12–17, Bergen, Norway, 65–70.

Bodart, Joni Richards. 1994. Booktalks: In defense of horror fiction. *The Book Report* 12, no. 5 (March/April): 25–26.

Bowman, Marion. 1987. Contemporary legend and practical joke. In *Perspectives on contemporary legend, vol. II,* edited by Gillian Bennett, Paul Smith, and J. D. A. Widdowson. Sheffield, England: Sheffield Academic Press.

Brunvand, Jan Harold. 1981. *The vanishing hitchhiker: American urban legends & their meanings.* New York: W. W. Norton.

Bull, Emma. 1991. *Bone dance.* New York: Ace.

Bullard, Thomas E. 1988. Folklore scholarship and UFO reality. *International UFO Reporter* 13, no. 4 (July/August): 9–13.

Davies, Christie. 1990. "Nasty" legends, "sick" humour and ethnic jokes about stupidity. In *A nest of vipers: Perspectives on contemporary legend, vol. V*, edited by Gillian Bennett and Paul Smith. Sheffield, England: Sheffield Academic Press.

de Lint, Charles. 1993. *Dreams underfoot*. New York: Tor.

Dickson, Paul, and Joseph C. Goulden. 1993. *Myth-informed: Legends, credos, and wrongheaded "facts" we all believe*. New York: Perigee.

Dunning, John. 1992. *Booked to die*. New York: Charles Scribner's Sons.

Editorial. 1994. *Omni* 16, no. 7 (April): 10.

Ellis, Bill. 1990. The UD-EBE "secret treaty": Folklorists should be appalled. *FOAFTALE NEWS* 17 (March): 6–8.

Ellis, Bill, and Alan E. Hays. 1994. Art Linkletter and the contemporary legend: A bibliographical essay. *FOAFTALE NEWS* 33/34 (June): 1–8.

Greenburg, Andrea. 1972/73. Drugged and seduced: A contemporary legend. *New York Folklore Quarterly* 28/29: 131–58.

Jones, Patrick. 1993. Have no fear: Scary stories for the middle grades. *Emergency Librarian* 21, no. 1 (September/October): 30–32.

Kies, Cosette. 1992. *Presenting young adult horror fiction*. New York: Twayne.

Labov, William. 1972. *Language in the inner city: Studies in the black English vernacular*. Philidelphia: University of Pennsylvania Press.

Menefee, Christine C. 1993. UFOs: True, false, or does it matter? *School Library Journal* (June): 37–38.

Nicolaisen, W. F. H. 1987. The linguistic structure of legends. In *Perspectives on contemporary legend, vol. II*, edited by Gillian Bennett, Paul Smith, and J. D. A. Widdowson. Sheffield, England: Sheffield Academic Press.

Nilsen, Don L. F. 1989. Contemporary legend: The definition of a genre. *Kansas English* 75: 5–9.

Nilsen, Alleen Pace, and Don L. F. Nilsen. 1992. Barbs of the west: Humor of the western United States. *The World and I* 17 (April): 663–70.

Rayl, A. J. S. 1994. Inside the military UFO underground. *Omni* 16, no. 7 (April): 48–59.

Schwartz, Alvin. 1984. *More scary stories to tell in the dark*. New York: Harper & Row.

Smith, Paul. 1986. *The book of nastier legends*. London: Routledge Kegan Paul.

So there's this guy, see . . . 1991. *Maclean's* 104, no. 48 (December 2): 80–81.

Stewart, Susan. 1982. The epistemology of the horror story. *Journal of American Folklore* 95, no. 375: 33–50.

Thomas, Gerald. 1977. *The tall tale and Philippe D'Alcripe*. St. John's: Memorial University of Newfoundland.

PART
III

6

SCIENCE, TECHNOLOGY, AND THE CONTEMPORARY LEGEND

It was during a cold spell in the middle of last winter when a van driver passed a motorcyclist who had broken down. It was snowing and, although the bike rider was well wrapped up in leathers and a helmet, the van driver decided he had better stop and offer his assistance. There was very little wrong with the motorbike—it had just run out of petrol [gas]. Although the driver had a spare can of fuel, unfortunately the petrol cap had frozen shut. Being a resourceful chap (and brave), the van driver unbuttoned his fly and peed over the cap to thaw it out. He refilled the tank and the bike rider, still wrapped up against the cold, mumbled a thank you and they both went their separate ways.

Some days later the van driver was called into the office at work and the boss showed him a letter he had received from a local vicar. It praised his helpfulness and expressed gratitude for the assistance he had given the vicar's daughter *when she had broken down.*

(Smith 1986, 35)

The legend of "The Empty Gas Tank" circulated throughout Alberta and England during the mid-1980s. It was told to me, of course, by someone who knew the brother of the sister's boyfriend who drove the van. The story is an example of a contemporary legend based on our society's response to modern technology.

One of the primary functions of contemporary legends is to explain or "handle" the anxieties caused by society's misapprehension and misunderstanding of science and technology. Creating and telling stories as a way of coping with these anxieties is nothing new—the earliest tales explained natural and scientific phenomena and helped a fearful audience cope with the terrors of everyday life. These early stories circulated as myths and *pourquoi tales*, stories that explained how and why certain things were the way they were. Jan Harold Brunvand demonstrates this similarity, saying that:

> In modern folklore our present-day technology may substitute for the supernaturalism in myths from earlier epochs, as a result, we hear urban horror stories concerning microwave ovens, fast foods, and elevators rather than monsters, omens, or evil spells. (1989, 189)

Today's version of myths, contemporary legends, still serve this explanatory function. They answer our questions about how and why certain things work and, even more importantly, what would happen if they did not work correctly.

Certain "modern inventions" (e.g., the automobile, the shopping center, suntan salons) affect the content of the legend, while others (e.g., the telephone, the photocopier, the computer, and the information superhighway) affect the transmission and dissemination of legends. Mass culture, which David Buchan calls "a product of a society ordered and regimented by a technology working through mass media, such as radio, television and graphic advertising," plays a fundamental role in nourishing legends, both in providing the fodder and in speeding its digestion (1978, 367).

In this chapter we will explore diverse contemporary legends, focusing on how advances in technology transform the legend corpus, on how fear of technology produces legends, and on how technology aids in the creation and dissemination of the contemporary legend. Technological advances and the public's misapprehension of this new technology are demonstrated in the case study at the end of the chapter (see p. 123).

LEGENDS ABOUT TROUBLE WITH MODERN GADGETS

Contemporary legends often reflect the general public's misunderstanding and mistrust of new and rapidly changing developments in today's technology. Once people understand the invention or principle behind the device, legends about the device usually lose their appeal and are discarded. Sometimes a legend hibernates until a similar anxiety arises, needing to be vented and discussed; then the legend circulates again with new adaptations and vitality.

Microwave Ovens

It was originally believed that the story about pets being dried off in microwave ovens with explosive results had emerged with the invention of the household microwave oven, reflecting people's fear of the new technology. But, as several scholars inform us, the legend, though popular at the time microwave ovens were first being offered on the market as home appliances, is merely a modern adaptation of older stories about pets being placed in regular ovens, dryers, and washing machines. Sometimes the animal, looking for warmth, would crawl into these "caves" on its own. The microwave oven, therefore, would be a natural addition to the list of household appliances that could be dangerous for the family pet. My editor's South African sister-in-law swore that this story happened in the 1970s near or in Johannesburg.

The tale of "A Roast Cat for Breakfast" (1942) by Cornelia Berry in the Virginia Writers' Project (VWP) has been cited as a clear predecessor to "The Cat in the Microwave." The VWP was a subsidiary of Virginia's Work Projects Administration and, during its existence (1937–1942), VWP workers collected more than 3,850 examples of oral and material folklore from 62 countries. When VWP was closed down, the files were deposited at the University of Virginia's Alderman library in Charlottesville. Thomas Barden, in his work with the collection, documented several predecessors of contemporary legends, of which Berry's tale is one:

> *The next morning she made her fire and made her bread dough and in a hurry jerked open the oven and shoved in the dough in the pan. The fire got hotter and she called her grandson to his breakfast. As he walked into the kitchen putting on his shirt, she reached down and opened the door to take out the hot biscuits as usual. When the door was opened an awful smelling cloud of smoke floated up into her eyes and she almost fainted on the spot. Her grandson saw that something was amiss and went to the door of the oven, and inside he found the biscuits brown in front and just below them back in the far corner, a fine roasted tom cat. She has the stove to this day, cooking on it as usual and says it cooks as good as ever.*
> (1992, 157)

Because of this early connection, it's possible that the common interpretation of the story as reflecting fear of technology should be reassessed. However, Berry's version is highly unlikely, and in fact, the microwave oven is much more feasible, as it cooks so quickly (Barden 1992, 157).

An early Russian tale tells of a mother who is bathing her child in a tub of warm water setting on an apparently unlit stove. She goes into the yard to gossip, leaving the front door open. To her horror, she returns to discover that the breeze that came through the door rekindled the fire, and the baby was cooked to death (Smith 1983, 65).

Another early variant was being told in Australia around 1949. It was a story about

---

a machine that used "a new form of energy" to melt metal. Strangely, it appeared to give off no heat, and since it had no door on the front, a hand could be put into it while it was operating without any feeling of warmth. One day a student placed a plate with metal on it while it was running, and "suddenly the heavy gold signet ring that he was wearing melted around his finger! As a result of the horrible burns . . . he lost the finger."
(The Microwaved Signet Ring 1989, 4)

One variant has a curious similarity to a legend that circulated when suntan salons became the rage.

In the kitchens of a large hotel a microwave oven had been installed. However, rather than being set at eye level, like the majority of such ovens, this one was fitted down low—almost at waist height in fact. One day a young pastry chef, who worked at a table across the aisle from this cooker, was suddenly taken ill and in seconds collapsed and died.

On investigation it was discovered that every time he stepped back to admire his handiwork he stood with his back against the microwave oven door. Unfortunately, the oven door did not seal properly and over a period of time it had slowly cooked his kidneys and it was this that had eventually killed him. (Smith 1983, 64)

Regardless, however, of its historical antecedents, the legend about the microwaved pet was extremely popular at the height of the public's discovery of microwave ovens. The legend peaked in 1976, when microwave ovens were no longer "new" (Belanus 1981, 67). Just how common an appliance microwaves are today was recently demonstrated when our family received an 18-year-old, hand-me-down microwave oven. Although the younger members of the family had requested a microwave quite vocally over the years, my husband and I managed to ignore the request. When the microwave arrived, my daughter announced to her classmates that we finally had one. The response was quite surprising—"How have you ever warmed anything up without a microwave?" Her classmates did not remember a time that the microwave had not been a regular appliance in their kitchens!

This legend is not the property of any particular age group and is told with relish for a varied number of reasons. The comedian Robin Williams firmly understood the universality of the legend when, on a take-off on the television program *Mr. Roger's Neighborhood*, he announced: "Welcome to my neighborhood. Let's put Mr. Hamster in the microwave oven. OK? Pop goes the weasel!" (Belanus 1981, 68). Younger children, when told the legend by an authority figure, believe it as scientific fact, an illustration of "what would happen if. . . ." Young adults are a skeptical audience and tend to view the legend as a gross joke told for entertainment. A group of university graduates believed that the legend was plausible (Belanus 1981, 71). This last group were skeptical, not of the legend, but of the safety standards of both the manufacturer and the United States government (73).

Suntan Salons

> *There are stories of countless young people with beautiful suntans dropping dead just like that. When autopsies are performed, it is found that they all acquired their tans artificially while in a tanning salon. While they were doing so, their insides had been cooked alive.*

This cautionary legend came to light during the summer of 1987. It warns people of the dangers of the technology behind the artificial suntanning craze. There is a connection to earlier tales about suntan lamps with malfunctioning timers and to the tales of microwaved pets "which are a part of the lore warning against modern technology and product misuse" (Brunvand 1989, 33). Perhaps these warning were in response to misunderstanding of ultraviolet rays used in suntan salons and the microwaves needed for cooking.

As demonstrated previously, letters to advice columnists Ann Landers and Abby Van Buren often contain variants of contemporary legends. At times, the stories are accepted as fact but at others, the two sisters are quite adapt at the art of debunking:

Dear Abby: I just received a letter from my daughter. . . . She related the following story that I found so horrifying, I want to share it with you so that you can warn others: "A 17-year-old girl won a trip to Hawaii. She wanted a really nice tan for the trip . . . she went to a tanning parlor . . . [she asked] the maximum time she could stay in, and they said half an hour. Well, she wanted a really dark tan, fast, so she went to seven places and spent a half-hour in each—three and a half hours total! Well, this poor girl is now in [the hospital]. They estimate she has about 26 days to live. She's totally blind, and they say it's as if she had 'microwaved' herself—it's basically the same principle. Anyhow, she just cooked herself from the inside out. And the worst part is, there's not a thing they can do for her. Not a thing. Her poor family!"—Anita.

Dear Anita: Thanks for writing. I wondered how "they" could estimate the number of days "this poor girl" had to live, so I called the [hospital] and its spokesperson . . . stated that there was no such patient in the facility, but that the story had been circulating at the Brigham Young University . . . but [they] were unable to confirm it.

Well, friends, so much for the "tanning" story.
    Incidently, after that item appeared, I heard from folklorist Jan Harold Brunvand. . . . He wrote (in part): "I was pleased to see that you debunked the tanning story. I have heard many different versions of that legend—it's been around for a long time." (Advice to the Legendary 1989, 2)

Other times, you are just not sure . . .

On May 24, 1989, Patsy Campbell of Portage, IN, died at the University of Chicago Medical Center of burns suffered in a 25-minute tanning booth session 11 days earlier.
    Campbell had been taking Psoralen, a drug used to increase the skin's sensitivity to light as part of a program to treat psoriasis. Soon after visiting the parlor, she began to itch all over, and blisters soon developed. A burn expert from the University of Alabama thought it was the first verifiable case of fatal burns suffered in a tanning booth. (Tanning Booth Death 1989, 5)

Contact Lenses

Beware of radiation from electric arcs or sparks which can cause contact lenses to fuse to the eye.

This rumor circulated via phony health bulletins in 1983. Similar to the more recent bulletins about LSD-laced tattoo transfers, at least one insurance company issued a loss prevention memo to counter the rumor (Brunvand 1986, 165).

Lie Detectors

The suspect is put in a metal-framed chair with the colander inverted in his head and wires running from it to the photocopy machine. The [police] officers have prepared a sheet of paper with the word "lie" (or in some versions, "false") neatly inscribed on it. The suspect is told that he's hooked up to a lie detector, and officers start to ask him questions like "Where is the gun?" or "Did you do this alone?"

When he answers with what the officers can tell is a lie, one officer pushes the print button on the machine and out comes a sheet saying "lie."

Believing that he can't fool the machine, the suspect starts confessing his crimes, at which point an officer surreptitiously switches the "lie" paper with one saying "true." (Brunvand 1993, 139)

While watching an episode of the television program *Homicide*, I started laughing so hard that my family became quite concerned. There, in front of my eyes, was the above contemporary legend being played out in all its glory. The legend involves two things found in every police station in North America: a photocopy machine and a suspect who may not be as bright as he thinks he is. The colander, however, is not a usual police station item. However, the idea of a metal "helmet" to help extract the truth from someone's brain comes straight out of old science fiction movies! Put this fear of technology into play by adapting household items, add an anxiety-filled situation, and "presto": a new legend! Brunvand tried to trace this legend to a source but has had no success as yet (1993, 139–45). The legend has been circulating for several years and is included in an article in the newsletter of the International Society for General Semantics. The 1986 article quotes an unidentified published report and worries about the violation of the suspect's rights.

In a lighter vein, an article in the *National Law Journal* (April 27, 1992) reports that the "photocopy caper" was included in a comedy show held at a meeting of the Association of the Bar of New York ("The Photocopy Polygraph" 1992, 9).

Friday the 13th Computer Virus

> *On 13 October [1989], users of IBM-compatible personal computers braced for widespread attacks from the Datacrime or Columbus Day virus. This was supposed to activate itself when the computer's internal clock hit 12:01 A.M. on Friday the Thirteenth; it would disable computers by wiping out the hard disk's directory so that the computer could no longer access programs.* (Friday the Thirteenth Computer Virus 1989, 6)

This virus was supposedly attached to "certain types of system files circulating through computer bulletin boards or informally transmitted by amateurs trading software" (6). Although more than 50 reports of damage were received on October 13 , most of them "proved to be false alarms caused by operator error" (7). Many experts claim that, though this particular warning proved to be false, it is entirely possible that such attacks can happen in the future. "The viruses are out there" (7).

Many computer security experts advise personal computer owners to back-up all important programs and to use a "vaccine" program to locate viruses already in place. Based on advance notice of where viruses are attached and how many bytes are added to the program, vaccines warn the user and destroy the virus.

Telephones

Telephones not only help to disseminate legends but also provide storylines for tales as well. Accompanied by early stories of people shouting into the telephone because they were calling long distance, and stories of telephones being buried in mausoleums (in case of an emergency?), the telephone has become a fixture in our modern society. Without the telephone, for instance, how would the baby-sitter become so terrified? Or the young woman escape at the gas station? ("The Baby-Sitter" and "The Killer in the Backseat" are both discussed in chapter 12.) Or, how could the veterinarian warn his patient's owner of the lurking danger in the house? (See "The Choking Doberman" in chapter 9.)

CAR TALES

*I heard several years ago about this real rich guy who was driving
down a real deserted road in his Corvette and had a heart attack
and died. They say he laid there for months before anyone found
him. His body had decomposed, and the smell was terrific, I guess.
A car dealer fixed up the car and put in new upholstery and everything, but the smell of death just would not go away no matter
what they tried. I think it was for sale on some car lot in Chicago or
Indianapolis. But no one would buy it because of the awful odor, so
the car dealer put it up for sale for $25, and still it didn't sell.*

(Baker 1982, 196)

    The automobile, in North America, is a symbol of the modern age in
which the average home contains two cars and people commute long dis-
tances to work via highways and roadways that have been constructed to
accommodate our dependency. Contemporary folklore also reflects our interest, our fascination, with the car. The car has two roles in contemporary
folklore: as an item of material culture upon which older traditions and
legends have been transferred and as a technology upon which a new body
of legends has arisen (Sanderson 1969, 241).

    Cars are extremely important to young adults, and many of the car tales
that they tell are macabre and "revolve around themes of violence, mutilation
or death" (Sanderson 1969, 249). However, the car is also important to other
age groups, and these legends cross all age barriers. Car tales traverse time,
as some of them are older than the technology that they reflect. Several
legends have been circulating since at least the 1940s ("The Death Car," "The
Philanderer's Porsche") and some have been adapted from a much older
tradition. "The Vanishing Hitchhiker" legend is older than the car, but the
dissemination and realism of modern variants of the legend would be
severely limited without cars and the highways on which they travel (Baker
1982, 31). Other legends inspired by, or built around, the car (e.g., "The Killer
in the Backseat," "The Hatchet in the Handbag," "The Dead Cat in the
Package," and "The Runaway Grandmother," discussed in subsequent chapters) have also been influenced by enhanced mobility created by cars. The
custom of necking in cars is credited with influencing such legends as "The
Hook" and "The Boyfriend's Death" and legend trips (Baker 1982, 31).

"Ankle Slashers at the Mall"

In some mall parking lots, muggers hide under cars, particularly high-riding cars or minivans. They've been known to grab a woman by the ankles to pull her down and attack as she approaches her car, or they might slash a woman's Achilles tendon so she can't run away. (Ankle Slashers at the Mall 1993, 10)

Hiding under vehicles is now more plausible when you regard all the minivans parked at a shopping center. Rather than a fear of technology, however, this legend reflects a fear of large impersonal areas and the threat of "petty" theft and personal attack. The question of why muggers would stoop to such a precarious position is answered with a recent addition to the legend: gang initiation rites. Now the legends has it that gang members slash ankles in parking lots so that when the victims bend down to grab at their ankles, the gang member can cut off their fingers. "Allegedly, this was going on all the time, and newly fingerless people were flooding the area hospitals" (Ankle Slashers at the Mall 1993, 11). A television reporter checked hospitals, police, and shopping malls to find that there was no such epidemic occurring. This initiation-rite legend variant was making the rounds in Chicago in 1991. On September 23, 1991, when the legend was reported on the air, the police had to establish a hot line to counter the rumor as they received more than 600 calls from concerned citizens in one week. Most people believed that the rumor was true and that the news of the attacks was being suppressed to avoid panics and scaring customers away from the shopping malls (Mall Slashers in Chicago 1991, 11).

"The Death Car"

"The Death Car" was first linked to a 1929 Model-A Ford in which the driver committed suicide after being rejected by his lover. Richard Dorson was told, in 1953, that the suicide occurred in 1938, and that the car was painted with distinctive hunting and fishing designs. Clifford Cross bought the car but could not eradicate the lingering smell of death. "One time a little white dog got inside when Cross wasn't looking and barked from the backseat, scaring Cross into thinking there was a ghost in the car" (Brunvand 1990, 18). Dorson made no attempt to trace the legend as it circulated and adapted itself to local areas. He offers no explanation, either, for the loss of the unique detail, such as the paintings and the white dog (19). Brunvand states that this legend is primarily a story about buying a seemingly wonderful car for a bargain price, as the legend, in all its variants, centers on an expensive car rather than an old clunker (19). The Model-A Ford has been transformed, in subsequent reincarnations of the legend, into Buicks, Cadillacs, Corvettes, and Jaguars since Dorson was told of the "real" incident that took place in Michigan (Baker 1982, 32).

While the make of the car changes over time as perceptions of prestige change, the overall theme or message does not. The offensive smell is perhaps not only the smell of death but that of filthy lucre. The prestigious sports car symbolizes wealth; the legend suggests that the only way working-class people can obtain such a product is if it is defective—in other words, if it *stinks* (Fine 1992, 157).

Structure of "The Death Car"

Richard Poulson (1985, 158–59) notes that variants of this legend all follow the same narrative plot:

1. A new car is purchased.

2. The owner suffers a fatal accident, suicide, or death by natural causes in which the driver is killed but the car is unharmed.

3. A long time passes before car and body are discovered.

4. Because of warm weather, the body quickly decomposes and the car is filled with a most horrible odor.

5. The car is cleaned and sold but returned because of the smell.

6. The car is repeatedly resold and returned until the last image of the story, which pictures the car, beautiful, new, and undamaged, standing abandoned on the used car lot, unsold and unsalable.

Variants of "The Death Car"

Other researchers maintain that the story is not new, but instead is an updated version of a classic legend about age-old evil, represented in "The Death Car" by the smell. The vehicle undergoes constant revisions, much like the vehicle in "The Vanishing Hitchhiker," "not because of historical events, but because of the modes of conveyance a culture assumes, while the image of evil is constant" (Poulson 1985, 159). Thus, the vehicle may be a cart, a wagon, a ship, or a car. A legend circulating among airline pilots about former pilots who return to haunt restored planes is a technological update of the same legend (160).

Cars have played an active role in the contemporary folklore of Poland and Russia since cars have become everyday commodities. Variants collected in Poland, between 1989 and 1990, all involve the death of the driver (usually from a heart attack) in an isolated area. The body is not found for quite some time, and the smell insinuates itself into the car, proving to be impossible to remove and, thus, the car is impossible to sell. The legend is also told in at least four former Soviet republics: Russia, Byelorussia, Ukraine, and Lithuania (Czubala 1992, 2). The question always hovers at the edge of our minds, however, as we wonder: Did this actually happen?

On Saturday, February 3, Tracy Ziegenfuss of Bethesda, Maryland, was driving her 1985 Subara when it broke down. The local dealership towed it to their lot but left the door unlocked. That night, a homeless drifter named Gilbert Davis crawled inside the car for shelter. The next morning he was found dead on the front seat. The dealership cleaned the seat, but the Ziegenfusses refused to take the car back, claiming that it "still smells of death." Bob Ziegenfuss said that he contacted the dead man's family, saying that he "was sorry about his death and hoped that our automobile provided him a comfortable place to make his transition." ("Stop Me If You've Heard This," Legends in the Tabloids 1990, 10)

Contemporary issues are also incorporated into the legends, as in this variant told by a Mexican American teacher who heard the story in 1979 from her aunt. In 1985, the story was still being told about smuggling.

It is said that one time there was a drug gang who always bought cars. The reason for this was so the police would never find out which car they drove. One day they found one of their cars in an alley, and in the car was a dead body. The gang still owed on the car, so the dealership took the car back. They tried to sell the car, but the smell of the dead body would not come off. They painted it, put [in] a whole new inside, but to no avail. The smell was so bad no one wanted it for free. To this day, it is said that the same car is going from one dealership to another. (Glazer 1985, 296)

"The Driver's Revenge"

> *A trucker went into a 24-hour cafe and ordered a meal. He had just started eating when three young men, wearing leather jackets, came into the cafe and began to make fun of him. One picked up his coffee and drank it. Another ate one of his sandwiches while the third grabbed a handful of fries. The trucker said nothing, just calmly got up, paid his bill and left the cafe.*
>
> *One of the trio turned to the cafe owner and said, "He isn't much of a man, is he?" "No," was the response, "and he's not much of a driver either. He just backed his truck over three motorcycles in the parking lot. They looked pretty messed up!"* (Smith 1986, 39)

Movie fans may recognize this scenario; it has been dramatized in several popular films. The legend first began circulating in North America in the 1960s before crossing over to Europe, where it was told as a "true" story and reported in the media (Smith 1986, 39).

"Enhanced Mileage"

> *A carburetor has been invented that results in a passenger car's getting 50 to 75 miles to the gallon. However the rights to the unit were purchased by General Motors and/or Ford and/or the Japanese and/or the Germans who is/are keeping the invention secret.*
> (Dickson and Goulden 1993, 135)

Winnipeg inventor Charles Nelson Pogue announced in 1937 that he had designed an economical carburetor that got 200 miles to the gallon of gasoline. Ford of Canada reportedly found the device effective and a patent was issued on the design in the U.S. patent office, but after the initial publicity, nothing was heard of it again. Rumors ran rampant: the device cremated the engines; the whole thing was a hoax; or the oil companies were suppressing the device. The "true" story has never emerged because Pogue adamantly refused to speak to reporters (Ellis and Mays 1994, 2).

My father told me this tale just recently. The reason that the carburetor was never offered to consumers, he said, was because the oil companies did not want to lose their profits. When I told him it was a legend, he was disappointed. He was quite sure it was true, and maybe it is . . . my dad is from Winnipeg!

"Gravity Hill"

Russel Moody, a resident of San Antonio, Texas, had gone often to the Shane Road railroad crossing to test a local legend. In the 1930s, a tradition goes, a school bus stalled on these tracks and ten children were killed when a train hit it. Nowadays, if a car stalls on these tracks, the ghosts of these children push it off to save the driver. Moody tested this legend one morning and was surprised to find "tiny handprints and hoof marks in the heavy dew on my rear bumper." The next day, he dusted the bumper with baby powder and tried again; once more the handprints and hoof marks appeared. The legend explained the handprints, but the hoof prints remained a mystery until a psychic was invited to contact the spirits. She learned that the children's ghosts were having difficulty getting some heavy cars to roll, so they had captured a demon, whose strong hoofed feet could start the vehicles moving.
("Stop Me If You've Heard This," Legends in the Tabloids 1990, 11)

The above narrative has four basic elements:

1. The accident between a train and a school bus.

2. The legend that the ghosts of the young accident victims will push a stalled vehicle off the tracks at the site of the accident.

3. The decision to test the belief.

4. The test itself, which always proves the "truth" of the legend.

The legend and the legend-trip story "show[s] a clear association between legend, belief and . . . behaviour" (Glazer 1989, 165). Some variants in Texas include a religious element: the children are from an orphanage and are accompanied by nuns and priests. This element accentuates the helpful character of the ghosts (166). One of the most common elements in the legend is the handprints that are left on the back of the car. Less common is the element of the driver using baby powder to "collect" the prints.

Mark Glazer (1989, 167) documents three subtypes of this legend:

A. Narratives that tell of the accidental death of the children.

B. Legends that relate the story of the accident and speak of the belief that stalled cars will be pushed over the tracks.

C. Stories that include the accident, the belief, and the pushing of the car over the tracks.

Very few variants examined in Glazer's study are type A, stopping at the accident itself. Approximately two-thirds are type B. Along with an account of the accident, they include "the belief, conditionally stated, that *if* a car stops or stalls on the tracks, *then* it will be pushed to safety" (1989, 168). Almost a third of the tales are type C, containing all four parts of the legend.

Variants in other parts of the country lack the sequence that explains *why* the car would be mysteriously pushed out of danger. The difference in the structure is directly related to the Mexican American traditions about helpful ghosts. These beliefs about helpful ghosts change the meaning, or essence, of the legend without affecting its configuration as a migratory legend. Though the legend in South Texas is in some aspects equivalent to versions from other parts of the country, Texas narrators add a preamble (or postscript) to explain *why* the car moves (Glazer 1989, 170).

The majority of tellers of this legend are females between the ages of 19 and 30. While cars and car tales are traditionally the domain of males, the involvement of children and other "feminine" aspects of the tale attract female tellers (Glazer 1989, 172). "Gravity Hill" appeals to both young adult and adult audiences because of its rather sentimental air, and also because it can be used as the excuse for a dare or a legend trip (173).

"Gravity Hills" in other localities are not tied to any particular legend. They are scientific "oddities" that demonstrate that the force of gravity will pull a car up a hill:

> There is this hill that is in South Bend. You drive to the bottom of the hill; it's not real steep, but it is a hill. You can see it. You park your car at the bottom, and you put the car in neutral. The car coasts up the hill for about 100 yards. They say that it has been checked by scientists from Notre Dame and that they cannot figure it out. There is only one other place in the world like it. It's some-place in Florida. It sure is weird. (Baker 1982, 200)

My husband and I, on a holiday in Nova Scotia, sat in our car while it was "pulled" up the hill. The sensation provided by this optical illusion is truly "weird." In this instance, however, there was no mention of legends or railway tracks and certainly no mention of young helpful ghosts.

"Note at Accident Site"

> A man returned to his car and found a dent in one of his fenders along with the following note under his windshield wiper: "The people who are watching think I'm writing my name and address on this note, but I'm not." (Attbury 1970, 452)

This legend has been circulating probably as long as automobiles have been on the road and is often told as a joke.

"The Nude in the RV"

According to a story told to the press by Officer Robert Glass, police in three states had to collaborate to reunite a husband and wife accidently separated at a gas station on May 10. The couple was driving their van from Delaware back home to Colorado, when in the middle of the night the husband stopped in Rostraver Township (western Pennsylvania) for gas and a sandwich. While he was inside, the woman, who was asleep in the back of the van, awoke and went into the gas station's restroom. She came out just in time to see him drive off. Four hours later he stopped, went into the van to awaken his wife and realized that he must have left her behind. Driving back to Pennsylvania, he hit a deer just west of Wheeling, West Virginia, and disabled the van. He walked a mile to the nearest truck stop and told police his problem. A deal was arranged in which state troopers in Pennsylvania, West Virginia and Ohio drove his wife in shifts to the truck stop, where the two were united. Glass said, "She told us she wasn't going to say much to her husband about the situation, since he had told us the truckers at the truck stop were teasing him about stranding his wife on Mother's Day. . . . She felt he had suffered enough." No report was filled; Glass also told the press he could not recall the couple's names. (Stranded Wife 1992, 11)

People continually tell me that this story "really" happened and, in fact, one student wrote that it actually happened to her and her son on Mother's Day. When the student was asked about the truthfulness of her tale, she staunchly repeated that it really happened to her! Although there is no nudity in this version, the usual scenario is of a nude or partially clothed person stepping out of the RV unbeknownst to the driver, leaving the person stranded on the highway.

"The Philanderer's Porsche"

The headline of Ann Landers's column read "Strange but true; Porsche sold for $50," and the letter retold an embellished version of the "Philanderer's Porsche" (see p. xvii). Ann Landers commented that, although the newspaper that claimed to have printed the original story could not find it, "the incident did happen as reported" (Landers 1990, D2). This legend has been circulating in Great Britain since 1948 and still has the power to intrigue people, who are convinced that it is true. When conducting a contemporary legend workshop at a high school in Alberta, I watched with amazement as a teacher's face blanched as I discussed this tale. When I spoke to him later, I asked him what had happened. His answer: "Well, you know that car you were talking about? I heard about it here in town and I spent all last week trying to find it."

An antecedent for this legend may be found in this anecdote of a pious miser:

> [A pious miser] leaves his widow with the task of selling a rooster and a cow. The money from the cow is to be donated to the church, and the money from the rooster she is allowed to keep. What does the woman do? She offers the cow for five florins and the rooster for fifty, on the condition that both are bought together! (Petzoldt 1990, 55)

"The Philanderer's Porsche," with a gender twist, has also found its way into popular culture, as in the novel *The Lies That Bind* by Judith Van Gieson:

> "What was Michael doing with a Porsche?" I asked him. "You won't believe this Nellie. . . . It was the weirdest thing. Miguel found this ad in the newspaper for a Porsche for $500. I said it was a mistake, there had to be some zeros missing, but he said, what the heck, he'd give the guy a call. There was a divorce going on that the husband didn't want. He'd agreed to sell all the couple's possessions and give his wife half as a settlement, so he sold them all dirt cheap. It was his way of getting even." (1993, 101)

"The Severed Fingers"

> A woman was driving on Horsholm Road on her way home from Copenhagen. When she got to an area where there are not many houses, a gang of motorcyclists drove up behind her. Her car was small and not very fast. The motorcyclists passed her and tried to push her to the side of the road. They were trying to get her to stop. Just to scare her, one of them drove right up to her slowing car and struck the windshield with a chain, knocking a hole in it. Of course she was terrified, but she pushed the gas pedal to the floor and drove away from the motorcyclists. To her surprise they did not follow her. She drove to the nearest police station to report what had happened. There she realized that the chain was tangled in the windshield, and two of the motorcyclist's fingers were stuck to one end of it. (Kvideland and Sehmsdorf 1988, 381–82)

This legend appeared in Scandinavia in the early 1970s when "long-haired" hitchhikers and motorcycle gangs first appeared. This legend is closely related to others that articulate the society's fear of foreigners and strangers.

"The Solid Cement Cadillac"

A cement-mixer operator has a job in his own neighbourhood and decides to pay a surprise visit to his wife. To his surprise, he sees an unfamiliar convertible in his driveway. He peeks through the window and sees his wife talking to a strange man. Assuming that she is having an affair, the husband fills up the convertible with cement. It turns out that the man was a car dealer and the convertible was a birthday present for the husband. (So there's this guy, see . . . 1991, 81)

This legend depends on a "soap-opera plot" in which the characters are threatened with the discovery of a supposed infidelity. It also functions as an example of a just punishment for jumping to the wrong conclusion (Brunvand 1980, 55). The plot is realistic and the characters so ordinary, that it is highly possible that not only could the story happen but that it could happen to anyone. Its continual appeal clearly derives from the belief that philandering spouses should "get what they deserve," a viewpoint tempered by the warning that a person ought to be absolutely sure of the evidence before doing something drastic (Brunvand 1980, 59).

This legend, too, became firmly fixed in popular culture when a cement-encased 1946 de Soto was used to advertise the Centennial Concrete Company of Denver, Colorado in 1960. Sanderson cites this as an instance of "applied folklore," in which a pre-existing oral tale is "exploited in advertising, and the oral circulation of the oral tale was itself, in turn, reinforced through dissemination of reports of the de Soto by the news media" (Sanderson 1980, 379).

The make of the car is an essential element in the tale. In North American versions of the legend, the car is usually a Cadillac, while in Britain, it is a Jaguar. Both types of cars are expensive symbols of affluence and worldly success and add to the plausibility of the tale. Knowledge of the details of the incident, including the make of the car, means that the teller can tell the tale with confidence, and that this confidence is communicated to the audience (Sanderson 1980, 381). "A concrete image!"

ROLE OF TECHNOLOGY IN THE DISSEMINATION OF CONTEMPORARY LEGENDS

Technology has not only influenced the content of the legends, it has affected their transmission and consequently, the narrative style of the legends. Face-to-face conversation is still the most common manner of dissemination of the legends; it is the optimum situation because both the teller and the listener can rely on facial gestures and body language to help decode the message being transmitted. While telephones allow for aural transmission, neither the teller nor the listener can tell if the other believes the tale, as they are deprived of nonverbal communication signs. Both "Xeroxlore" and legends told over computer networks depend on a written (or drawn) text for transmission. "Xeroxlore" transmissions are usually directed, as are oral versions, to people within a legend conduit—people the teller (or sender) actually knows, but the computer networks are open to a wide group of strangers (Fine 1992, 13). The mass media can be considered the "nodes," or central transmitters, in an enormous undiscriminating network (14).

"Xeroxlore"

Lost: dog goes by the name "Lucky," has three legs, is missing one eye and has been recently castrated. If you see this dog please call . . .

A circular with the above information has been circulating around Alberta for the past few years. It had been photocopied and sent (and most recently, faxed) to several of my colleagues, who laughed and filed it away. But the tale of "Lucky" took a twist a few years ago, when a colleague of my brother-in-law placed it as an advertisement in the lost-and-found section of a local newspaper. The published name and phone number belonged to another colleague of theirs. Immediately after publication, the unfortunate victim of the prank, "Fred," was flooded with telephone calls. Some of these callers reported sightings of the imaginary dog, while others threatened to report his cruelty to animals! This practical joke took a long time to lose its impact, much to the chagrin of the victim.

"Xeroxlore," so called after the most well-known manufacturer of photocopier machines, is "a category of folklore that circulates in the form of copy-machine duplicates of typed or handwritten accounts" (Brunvand 1981, 142). Xeroxlore legends, not a new phenomenon, were initially called "typescript broadsides" and include, as noted by Paul Smith (1987, 178), items that encompass the following criteria:

1. They exist in multiple and variant forms.
2. They are photocopied texts, graphics, or a combination of the two.

3. They are essentially anonymous, although they may be attributed to "credible" authors or may have discoverable sources.

4. They are produced, regardless of the nature of the "parent" document, for free circulation.

The content of such a transmission is usually a humorous treatment of social or cultural values incorporating anti-establishment views of business and governmental practices and commentary on taboo topics (such as excretory or sexual behavior) (178).

In the past 20 years, the increased availability and decreased cost of photocopy machines and facsimile (fax) machines have diminished the time, effort, and cost necessary to duplicate a "parent" document to such an extent that an explosion of Xeroxlore has been the result (Smith 1987, 179).

Smith notes (1987, 191) several points of comparison between Xeroxlore and contemporary legends:

1. They are part of a system of unofficial information dissemination.

2. They exist in multiple and/or variant forms.

3. They deal with anonymous materials, although spurious authors or sources may be attributed to them.

4. Regardless of their source, they are usually presented at no cost to the recipient.

5. They draw on oral and literary traditions for source material and have a constant interrelationship with popular culture and all forms of "official" media dissemination.

6. They are communicated to impart information, although they may also have an entertainment value.

Both Xeroxlore and faxlore have an increasing emphasis of visual material:

> [It may be] a characteristic of both the increasingly visual sophistication of youth in our society and the capacities of the fax machine which sends images rather than alphanumeric messages; in contrast, one finds an inverse proportion of verbal to visual xeroxlore transmitted over computer networks. (Preston 1994, 156)

Xeroxlore has been particularly influential in the dissemination of rumors and legends warning people about complex dangers, such as LSD-laced tattoo transfers. Flyers and leaflets are necessary whenever a large amount of information must be transmitted. The written word is much more persuasive and authoritative. "As they circulate they often acquire *Good Housekeeping* 'seals of approval' from influential people who believe them and decide to collaborate" (Kapferer 1990, 59).

"Computer as Disseminator"

Using computer bulletin board on FreeNet (USENET) such as "alt.folk-lore.urban"(AFU) and "alt.folklore.computers" to debunk contemporary legends has become very popular. Approximately 70,000 people around the world delve into AFU to read about and discuss "the Misappliance of Science, Stupid Academia Tricks, Stupid People Tricks, Kill Your Television, and unprintable legends about sex and relevant body parts" (Dube 1993, E4). Dube reports that Terry Chan, a California economist who has been monitoring AFU for the last several years, has noticed two new trends in the subjects of legends: AIDS-lore and gang initiations (E4). Debunking legends on the network is often as simple as making a few telephone calls to "resident" experts in science and technology. Often a debunker need only consult one of Brunvand's books. " 'Debunking urban legends won't kill them off,' says Hiscock [a folklorist from Newfoundland], 'because even for the debunkers, the fun is in the telling, and new ones are constantly springing up' " (Dube 1993, E4).

"The Cookie Recipe," introduced in chapter 2, was transmitted over communication networks several years ago. The legend spread with amazing rapidity. When my husband brought a printout of the message home, he was quite excited, and so was I, but for different reasons. His office had informed the food editor of the local paper hoping that she could publish the story. My husband and his co-workers believed the story, and thought that printing the recipe in the paper would serve as justice. I, however, was ecstatic to hold concrete evidence of a contemporary legend in my hand. After discussion, however, the office staff telephoned the newspaper to withdraw their request—but they were not happy with my debunking the tale. It was just too "delicious" for words.

Mass Media

Newspapers and magazines are choice mediums for the dissemination of contemporary legends, but radio and television also communicate these legends as both news items and items for entertainment. The appearance of legends in the media has had a double role in that it both demonstrates the gullibility of the press (for publishing the legends as actual news items) and provides tellers with verification of the content ("It's true, I read it in the newspaper") (Smith 1987, 196). Often the mass media will supply new details and twists to the plots, or as with phone-in shows, allow callers to transmit legends to a much wider audience. Several legends have been the subjects of television investigations attempting to trace the source of the tales, while others "make guest appearances" on talk shows. "The Kentucky Fried Rat" was the subject of discussion on *The Tonight Show* on May 23, 1979, when host Johnny Carson claimed that it was not "the place run by the guy with the white hair and the beard—the trademark of *this* outfit is the Pied Piper. . . . They'll ask you, 'Do you want a breast or a tail?' " (Brunvand 1980, 81).

Techniques in structuring news reports have developed over time, shaped by changes in both technology and audience expectations. The "inverted pyramid" reporting style of the newspaper evolved in response to a developing, and often unreliable, technology. This inverted pyramid, in direct opposition to the structure of most oral and written stories, organizes stories around facts rather than ideas or chronologies. The reports lead with the most newsworthy facts and are followed, in descending order, by supporting data (Stephens 1988, 254). This technique was developed during the American Civil War when reporters, relying on unreliable telegraph lines, transmitted the most important facts first in short, paragraph-long dispatches (253).

Oral transmission of stories soon gave way to the written reporting style of the newspapers:

> The telegraph, therefore, led to the disappearance of forms of speech and styles of journalism and storytelling—the tall story, the hoax, much humor, irony, and satire—that depended on a more traditional use of language. The origins of objectivity, then, lie in the necessity of stretching language in space over the long lines of Western Union. (Manoff and Schudson 1987, 164)

Radio gave news reporters their voices back, and television, their faces. "The television newscast seems to resemble that most ancient of methods for communicating news: a person telling other people what has happened" (Stephens 1988, 280). Technology changed the face of news reporting once again. Because of the time limitations of television, news broadcasts became more superficial, producing less in-depth coverage of events, and were presented in a conversational style.

Newspapers reacted to the loss of their role as the breakers of news by moving away from pure news reporting toward in-depth analysis of events and coverage of opinion and popular culture. The traditional inverted pyramid started to topple as anecdotes and "turned phrases" began to be used as leads to the front-page stories. To maintain the interest of their readers, newspapers published bizarre stories as front-page leads and fillers that are picked up and reported on the air. Many of these bizarre stories are contemporary legends.

CASE STUDY:
CONTEMPORARY LEGENDS,
TECHNOLOGY, AND THE MASS MEDIA

The following case study is based on research by Barbara Allen on technology, tradition, and the emergence of folklore.

"The Face in the Window"

A friend of mine told me about an abandoned house on the next block. A girl who was a senior in her high school lived there. This girl had all the luck: not only was she beautiful, but she was popular with the male population and, because she was also clever, with the teachers as well. The only downfall was that she expected everything to fall in with her wishes—she was so spoiled. On the night of the big dance a couple of years ago, there was this tremendous storm—rain, wind, and lightning. The sky was black, and of course, there was no power. In fact the weather was so bad that, although she was almost ready to go out, her parents wouldn't let her go. They finally put their foot down. The girl couldn't believe it—she couldn't even phone her date as the telephone lines were down too. Her disappointment quickly turned to anger and she swore at her parents and dashed upstairs to her room. Frustrated and angry, she ran to the window and cursed God for sending such a storm. A bolt of lightning struck her dead. She fell against the window pane.

Her parents and friends were devastated. But soon they were also horrified as they looked up at the window in her room. There on the glass window pane, they could see the girl's image as clear as day. Her face was twisted in rage, or maybe, horror. Her parents tried everything they could to get rid of that image, even changing the glass . . . but it didn't help. Her image kept reappearing. Finally they boarded up the window and moved away. No one bought the house and it stands there today with that one bedroom window boarded up.

The legend of "The Face in the Window" has had a long history. News-paper reports of the phenonema flourished in the latter part of the 1880s in the United States. The earliest variants of the legend involved the image of a wrongly convicted man etched in the window glass or mirror of his cell, just after he was hung. Four common threads appear in the variants examined by Barbara Allen (1982, 95). They are

1. The image is of a human face or body.
2. The glass surface that the image appears upon is usually a window pane or occasionally a mirror.
3. Lightning is the agent which causes the image to appear.
4. There is a frequent comparison of the image on the glass to a photograph, particularly in the newspaper accounts.

The first three elements involve traditional folklore motifs. It is the fourth element that is the focus of this case study. Allen concentrates on the history of the technological advances in photography and the reaction to these advances in both the general population and in the dissemination of the legend.

The newspaper accounts of this legend always compared the image to a photograph, but this comparison became less pronounced with time and has almost completely disappeared in the modern oral variants. This also raises the question of why newspaper accounts of the phenomena flourished between 1871 and 1892 and have virtually disappeared today, while oral accounts continue to be told. "Photography as an essential element in the 'image on glass' texts can be directly correlated to the time period in which the stories first began to appear—the heyday of studio photography" (Allen 1982, 95).

Glass plates were introduced in 1851, revolutionizing the world of photography. Because reproductions of prints could now be made easily and inexpensively from a single negative, family portraits became the rage. However, even though the photographs became popular and easily available, the general population had no understanding of the mysterious process that produced the photograph. Allen feels that part of this ignorance was encouraged by the photographers themselves; the process was kept a darkroom mystery. Because the general public did not understand the photographic process, they imbued it with powers far beyond its actual capacity. Speculation of the potential of photography was the focus of many a newspaper article:

> Given the mental associations between photography, images, glass, and light (particularly a dramatic flash of light) coupled with a general lack of understanding of the photographic process, it seems logical for people to have believed that lightning could produce a photographic image on a pane of window glass. (Allen 1982, 99)

The face of photography changed again when, in the late 1880s, George Eastman perfected a flexible film as an alternative to the awkward and expensive glass plates. Coupled with this innovation was the appearance of the Kodak camera. Photography was now in the hands of the amateurs, and the mystery surrounding photography was diminished. Allen formulates that this technological advance is the key to understanding why newspaper accounts of the legend ceased to appear after the mid-1890s (Allen 1982, 99).

It is, according to Allen, the supernatural elements of divine retribution and the ineradicability of the haunting image that carry the legend into the present. These aspects of the legend are not mentioned in the newspaper reports but are found in the oral tradition:

> This difference is one of emphasis: the newspaper accounts, in their enthusiastic amazement over the strange images, focus on the phenomenon itself, while the oral versions emphasize the chain of events which led up to the creation of the image. (Allen 1982, 101)

The traditional themes of love, justice, revenge, and retribution are the focus of the oral tales and are melded with the imperfectly understood process of photography (Allen 1982, 101). Long after the newspaper accounts ceased to be published, the legend flourished as the technology of photography was subtly but surely transformed to fit traditional molds: ordinary portraits become ghostly images, prepared glass plates become windows and mirrors, the slow steady exposure to light becomes the dramatic flash of lightning (101).

The photographic image is no longer a random occurrence but serves as a warning, a cautionary tale. According to Allen (1982, 102) these narratives

1. fuse some new element of the sociocultural environment (such as an innovation in technology, business practices, or living conditions), with

2. traditional ideas and themes (such as retribution or the suffering of innocents) or motifs (such as loathsome creatures)

3. by means of an emotion (such as fear, anger, or curiosity) aroused by the unfamiliar phenomenon that is the subject of the narrative, and

4. in so doing, they describe in realistic terms the imagined potentialities afforded by that unknown quantity.

The popularity of video cameras and players heralds another variation of the legend. In the video version (but not the large-screen version) of the film *Three Men and a Baby*, a ghostly image can be seen behind the curtain. Speculation ran rampant and escalated as people attempted to explain this image. The most common explanation is a suicide or murder victim who died in the apartment long before the film was shot. When the boy's parents saw the video, the rumor explains, "they noticed the image, played it back in slow motion, and identified the figure as the ghost of their son, wearing the clothes he died in" (Three Men and a Baby Ghost 1990, 8). However, the stories do not take into account that the actual filming was done in a studio and not on location at all. The rumor was a hot topic of conversation in many university campus dormitories. The variant at Marshall University stated:

It seems that the apartment in which the movie was filmed was owned by a family with a young son [about 8—sometimes 4, 6 or 10 years old]. Because of the publicity and crowds of on-lookers during the filming, the family bought a shotgun to protect themselves from crazy fans trying to break in when the filming was over. The child accidentally shot himself with the shotgun. (Three Men and a Baby Ghost 1990, 8)

As with the earlier legends and rumors of images on the glass and spirits in photographs, the unknown grabbed the attention of the general population and speculation became quite a sophisticated procedure:

These legends begin with a genuinely novel situation, the unexplained figure of the boy in the film—but most of the narratives go far beyond description of the curious phenomenon. With fantastic details about the circumstances surrounding the supposed death, the legends create an elaborate *explanation* for the appearance of the specter. (Kelley 1991, 6)

In Chula Vista, California, a largely Hispanic Catholic community near San Diego, the image legend has recently transferred to another form of media:

The image of a murdered girl has appeared on a blank billboard since July. Crowds estimated that up to 25,000 have visited the billboard . . . looking for the face of nine-year-old Laura Arroyo, who was abducted on 19 June from her home in San Diego. Her body was discovered the next day at an industrial park, and her murderer has not been apprehended. Shadows cast on the vacant billboard by spotlights resemble Laura Arroyo's features, according to some, but others have spotted crosses, a dove and other faces. . . . Some believe that the face of the murderer will appear on the sign. . . . "Off to the right you can see his face, too. Eventually, her face will fade away, and all we'll see is his face. That's when he'll be caught."

To discourage crowds at the site and avoid liability for any accidents that might occur, the owners of the billboard plan to put up a picture of Laura Arroyo and the number of a telephone hotline that police have established. (Miraculous Billboards 1991, 12)

Traditional Beliefs

In her exploration of the "Face in the Window" legend, Barbara Allen established that the first three elements of that legend (images, glass, and lightning) are fairly common traditional beliefs in many cultures. Christian legendry includes many references to mysterious images of a human face or body, the most notable being the Shroud of Turin, but there are also secular manifestations with images on gravestones and walls. Glass, in the form of mirrors, plays a large role in superstitions and folk beliefs, as does lightning. Broken mirrors bring seven years bad luck and at the death of a family member; after a death, mirrors must be turned to the wall to avoid having a permanent reflected likeness of the deceased etched on the surface. Lightning is usually interpreted in oral tradition as a warning and also as an agent of retribution or punishment (Allen 1982, 94). Exploring these and other traditional motifs referred to in the case study above demonstrates the universality of the images.

Traditional Motifs

Motifs are considered to be any one of the elements that make up an item of folklore. They can be very simple concepts that are regularly found in tales, such as cruel stepmothers, success of the youngest, and magic mirrors. Motifs are assigned identification labels in a classification system developed in 1932 by Indiana folklorist Stith Thompson. This internationally accepted classification system was published by Indiana University Press as the *Motif-Index of Folk-Literature*. The listing of motifs is as inclusive as possible to facilitate comparisons and identification of folktales from around the world, regardless of language or title of the tales. Twenty-three general categories comprise the index; these are further subdivided by numbers into more specific classifications. For example, category A contains Mythological Motifs; B, all motifs to do with animals that are not part of the creation myths; and C contains the motifs concerned with Tabus. Magic is classified as D and subdivided as follows: D0–D699 Transportation, D700–D799 Disenchantment, D800–D1699 Magic Objects, and D1700–D2199 Magic powers and manifestations. The motif index was revised, 1955–1958, and published in six volumes. For an abridged version of the Motif-Index I suggest that you use Margaret Road MacDonald's *Storyteller's Sourcebook*, a reference tool found in almost every library.

Motifs are used as the components to create "new" literary folktales. "The Face in the Window" includes the following elements and motifs:

1. beautiful girl dresses to go to a party
2. violent electrical storm—cloudburst
3. realization that she cannot go to party

4. approaching window and cursing God [M414.1—God cursed; M represents those motifs that *ordain the future*, and numbers between M400-M499 are for *curses.*]

5. bolt of lightning strikes her dead [D2060—*magic; manifestations of magic power;* C984.5—*taboo; disastrous lightning for breaking taboo.*]

6. fall against window pane

7. image remains on the pane of glass [E532(a)—*the dead;* all those included in E500 refer to *phantom hosts;* E532(a) specifically refers to *ghost-like portrait etched in glass*] and remains whether glass is changed or window is boarded up (Wilgus 1970, 251). [Motif E532(a) identifies the process referred to as "photographic lightning." It is closely related to D1323.1.1—*magical mirror which shows the face of whoever dies* and E532(d)—*imprinting of a ghostly face on a tombstone*] (Taylor and Weldy 1976, 93).

LITERARY AND VISUAL ADAPTATIONS

"Ankle Slashers at the Mall"

Pet Sematary (1990). Based on Stephen King's novel of the same name, this film includes a cinematic allusion to the legend. However, the culprit hides beneath a bed instead of a car.

"The Death Car"

Christine (1983). Based on Stephen King's novel of the same name, this film depicts a supernatural variant of the "Death Car" in which the ghosts of several people who died in a car manifest themselves as a foul smell and bring death to those who pester the teenager who buys it at a cheap price.

Mr. Wrong (1984). The purchase of a secondhand car that turns into a nightmare when the new owner realizes that a murder had taken place. Based on the short story of the same name in the collection by Elizabeth Jane Howard titled *Mr. Wrong: A Collection of Short Stories* (Penguin, 1979).

"The Driver's Revenge"

Every Which Way But Loose (1978). This film starring Clint Eastwood contains two sequences involving motorcycles and the disposition of them.

Fried Green Tomatoes (1991). Middle-aged Evelyn rams her car into that of two teenaged girls who mock her about her age.

Smokey and the Bandit (1977). Cletus, a friend of the Bandit, drives over a gang's parked motorcycles after they throw him out of a bar.

"Microwave Ovens"

Gremlins (1984). This movie contains a brief segment when one of the gremlins is destroyed by it being thrown into the microwave oven and exploding.

Medium Rare (1987). A low budget film about a hoodlum who gets his kicks from microwaving poodles.

The Wild Life (1984). This movie has one of the characters tell the legend and then later prevent two of the "party animals" from acting it out.

"The Nude in the RV"

With Six You Get Eggroll (1968). A film in which this legend is the climatic sequence.

"The Severed Fingers"

Mad Max (1979). A futuristic film, set in Australia, incorporates this legend in its storyline about a time when the countryside is plagued by motorcycle gangs.

REFERENCES

Advice to the legendary. 1989. *FOAFTALE NEWS* 13 (March): 2.

Allen, Barbara. 1982. The "image on glass": Technology, tradition, and the emergence of folklore. *Western Folklore* 41: 85–103.

Ankle slashers at the mall. 1993. *FOAFTALE NEWS* (March): 10–11.

Attbury, Louis W. 1970. It was a de Soto. *Journal of American Folklore* 83, no. 330: 452–57.

Baker, Ronald L. 1982. *Hoosier folk legends*. Bloomington: Indiana Press.

Barden, Thomas E. 1992. Early Virginia analogues of some modern legends. *Contemporary Legend* 2: 155–64.

Belanus, Betty J. 1981. The poodle in the microwave oven: Free association and a modern legend. *Kentucky Folklore Record* 26: 66–75.

Brunvand, Jan Harold. 1980. Heard about the solid cement Cadillac or the nude in the camper or the alligator in the sewer or the snake in the K-Mart? *Psychology Today* (June): 50–62.

——— 1981. *The vanishing hitchhhiker: American urban legends & their meanings*. New York: W. W. Norton.

———. 1986. *The Mexican pet: More "new" urban legends and some old favorites*. New York: W. W. Norton.

———. 1989. *Curses! Broiled again!: The hottest urban legends going.* New York: W. W. Norton.

———. 1990. Dorson and the urban legend. *Folklore Historian* 7: 16–22.

———. 1993. *The baby train & other lusty urban legends.* New York: W. W. Norton.

Buchan, David. 1978. The modern legend. In *Language, culture, and tradition: Papers on language and folklore presented at the annual conference of the British Sociological Association,* edited by A. E. Green and J. D. A. Widdowson. The Centre for English Cultural Tradition and Language. Sheffield, England: University of Sheffield.

Czubula, Dionizjusz. 1992. The death car: Polish and Russian examples. *FOAFTALE NEWS* 25 (March): 2–5.

Dickson, Paul, and Joseph C. Goulden. 1993. *Myth-informed: Legends, credos, and wrongheaded "facts" we all believe.* New York: Perigee.

Dube, Francine. 1993. Debunking myths. *Edmonton Journal* (October 31): E4.

Ellis, Bill, and Alan E. Mays. 1994. Art Linkletter and the contemporary legend. *FOAFTALE NEWS* 33/34 (June): 1–8.

Fine, Gary Alan. 1992. *Manufacturing tales: Sex and money in contemporary legends.* Knoxville: University of Tennessee Press.

Friday the thirteenth computer virus. 1989. *FOAFTALE NEWS* 16 (December): 6–7. [This is a compilation of several Wall Street Journal articles plus others quoted from Computer virus countdown ends. 1989. *Wall Street Journal* (October 13): B1, B2; Michael Selz. 1989. Claims of cures for data killers aren't proven. *Wall Street Journal* (October 13): B1, B2; Virus busters profit from PC panic. 1989. *Denver Post* (October 13): C1; Abram Katz. 1989. Computers survive virus scare unscathed. *New Haven Register* (October 14): 1–2.]

Glazer, Mark. 1985. The traditionalization of the contemporary legend: The Mexican-American example. *Fabula* 26: 288–97.

———. 1989. Gravity hill: Belief and belief legend. In *The questing beast: Perspectives on contemporary legend, vol. IV,* edited by Gillian Bennett and Paul Smith. Sheffield, England: Sheffield Academic Press, 165–77.

Kapferer, Jean-Noel. 1990. *Rumors: Uses, interpretations, and images.* New Brunswick, NJ: Transaction.

Kelley, Charles Greg. 1991. Three men, a baby, and a boy behind the curtain: A tradition in the making. *Midwestern Folklore* 17 (spring): 5–13.

Kvideland, Reimund, and Henning K. Sehmsdorf, eds. 1988. *Scandinavian folk belief and legend.* Minneapolis: University of Minnesota Press.

Landers, Ann. 1990. Strange but true; Porsche sold for $50. *Edmonton Journal* (August 24): D2.

MacDonald, Margaret Read. 1982. *The storyteller's sourcebook: A subject title, and motif index to folklore collections for children.* Detroit: Gale Research.

Mall slashers in Chicago. 1991. *FOAFTALE NEWS* 24 (December): 11.

Manoff, Robert Karl, and Michael Schudson, eds. 1987. *Reading the news: A Pantheon guide to popular culture*. New York: Pantheon Books.

The microwaved signet ring. 1989. *FOAFTALE NEWS* 12 (February): 4.

Miraculous billboards. 1991. *FOAFTALE NEWS* 23 (September): 11–12.

Petzoldt, Leander. 1990. Phantom lore. In *Storytelling in contemporary societies*, edited by Lutz Rohrich and Sabine Wienker-Piepho. Script Oralias series, volume 22. Tubingen, Germany: Gunter Narr Verlagg. [Based on a paper presented at the International Congress of Folk Narrative Research, 1989, Budapest, Hungary.]

The photocopy polygraph. 1992. *FOAFTALE NEWS* 26 (June): 9–10.

Poulson, Richard C. 1985. Legend: An image in time. In *The 8th Congress for the International Society for Folk Narrative Research: Papers IV*, edited by Reimand Kvideland and Torunn Selberg, June 12–17, Bergen, Norway.

Preston, Michael J. 1994. Traditional humor from the fax machine: All of a kind. *Western Folklore* 53, no. 2 (April): 147–69.

Sanderson, Stewart. 1969. The folklore of the motor-car. *Folklore* 80 (winter): 241–52.

———. 1980. Why was it a de Soto? In *Folklore studies in the 20th century: Proceedings of the centenary conference of the folklore society*, edited by Venetia J. Newall. Lanham, MD: D. S. Brown, Roman and Littlefield.

Smith, Paul. 1983. *The book of nasty legends*. London: Routledge Kegan Paul.

———. 1986. *The book of nastier legends*. London: Routledge Kegan Paul.

———. 1987. Contemporary legend and the photocopy revolution: An exploration. In *Perspectives on contemporary legend, vol. II*, edited by Gillian Bennett, Paul Smith, and J. D. A. Widdowson. Sheffield, England: Sheffield Academic Press, 177–202.

So there's this guy, see . . . 1991. *Maclean's* 104, no. 48 (December 2): 80–81.

Stephens, Mitchell. 1988. *A history of news: From the drum to the satellite*. New York: Viking.

"Stop me if you've heard this," legends in the tabloids. 1990. *FOLKTALE NEWS* 18 (June): 10-11.

Stranded wife. 1992. *FOAFTALE NEWS* 26 (June): 11.

Tanning booth death. 1989. *FOAFTALE NEWS* 15 (September): 5.

Taylor, David L., and Mary Helen Weldy. 1976. The woman in the window: A local legend. *Kentucky Folklore Record* 22: 91-94.

Thompson, Stith. 1955–1958. *Motif-Index of Folk-Literature*. rev. ed. 6 vols. Bloomington: Indiana University Press.

Three men and a baby ghost. 1990. *FOAFTALE NEWS* 20 (December): 8–9.

Van Gieson, Judith. 1993. *The lies that bind*. New York: HarperCollins.

Wilgus, D. K. 1970. The girl in the window. *Western Folklore* 29: 251–56.

7

CONTAMINATED FOOD

Before going to the movies, a young man and his date stopped at a fast-food chain fried chicken stand, purchasing a bucket of fried chicken to eat at the show. The girl complained that one of her pieces of chicken was rather tough and "rubbery." Toward the end of the film she became violently ill. The boyfriend was so concerned at her sudden and intense condition that he drove her to the nearest emergency hospital. The examining physician said that she appeared to have been poisoned, and he asked the young man if he knew of any probable cause. The boy raced out to the car and began burrowing through the half-consumed bucket of chicken and discovered an odd-shaped piece, half eaten. He broke off the batter and realized that it was the remains of a rat, poisoned and fried along with the chicken. The girl, receiving a fatal amount of strychnine from the rat's body, died. (Fine 1980, 230)

LEGENDS ABOUT CONTAMINATED FOOD

One of the greatest fears of modern Western society is of contaminated food products. Reports in Great Britain from the Environmental Health Department state that "covering the past five years, on average, fifty percent of the complaints they received related to contamination of foodstuffs, frequently with so called 'mouse droppings'" (Smith 1984, 207). In the majority of cases the "mouse droppings" are actually small particles of burnt food. Contaminated food legends reflect our fears, not only of contamination, but of our distrust of mass-produced food products and fast-food restaurants. Recent reports of tampering with medications and packaged foods reflect and intensify these concerns.

However, neither the anxiety nor the naming of scapegoats responsible for the behavior portrayed in these tales is new. In the 14th century, blame

132

for the Black Death in Europe was laid at the door of Jews, who were rumored to have poisoned local wells. This purposeful "mass poisoning" has since become associated with wartime sabotage. The Chinese warned that the Japanese, during the Sino-Japanese hostilities in the 1930s, put ground glass into food tins. Closer in time and space, American soldiers in Saigon claimed that Vietcong sympathizers put ground glass into Coca-Cola bottles (Fine 1980, 228). The growth of the food industry at the beginning of this century created anxiety among the public, who suddenly had less control over the production and handling of their food. Upton Sinclair's *The Jungle* (1906) documented the extreme levels of contamination found in Chicago's slaughterhouses, reinforcing the public's fears. His story describes the crying of rats as they are pulled into the big meat mills (Klintberg 1981, 156). After public outcry over the conditions in *The Jungle*, the government examined the slaughterhouses and found Sinclair's novel to be based on fact. This examination led to the regulations and inspections that are part of the production of food in the industry today. The book also gave credibility and reinforcement to the public's fears about contaminated food that echos in our contemporary legends today. Most people are not familiar with the numerous checks and balances that are in place to make sure that these conditions could never again exist.

Legends about contaminated food reflect some legitimate health concerns. Pre-packaged foods with extended shelf life contain substances that, although not dangerous to humans, are not actual sources of nourishment either. Here again, it is people's lack of understanding about the technology of modern food manufacturing that lies behind the anxiety demonstrated in these legends. There is also an underlying concern that our emphasis on pre-packaged, fast-food nourishment may be wrong, either morally or nutritionally. "Food may be contaminated with substances which poison not our physical being, but which corrupt our social, cultural, and moral identities" (Clements 1991, 42). Contamination legends reflect modern society's fears of flouting traditional mores about food and about ignoring more recent nutritional guidelines, such as the low-fat diet.

Structure of the Core Legend

Regardless of the type of contamination or foodstuff, Susan Domowitz (1979, 86) notes that the core legend is remarkably static:

1. Packaged or canned food is purchased, or someone orders food from a fast-food or ethnic restaurant.

2. Something horrifying and disgusting is found in the food, usually after some of it has been consumed.

3. The contaminant is usually a part of a human being or animal.

4. Evidence is produced either for or against the truth of the reported incident.

Other recurring elements in contaminated food legends are the fact that the legend is usually associated with the largest corporation or manufacturer of the product in the community's marketplace, the hospitalization or death of the victim, and the resultant legal action (Fine 1980, 242).

In many variants, the disgusting substance is found in the most ordinary of foods; foods that can be considered staples of the North American diet. In contrast, other variants target foreign or ethnic foods that are either contaminated or contain foods that are taboo in Westerner culture. Thus there seems to be a double message operating. On the one hand, the stories warn: "beware the exotic," unfamiliar foods prepared by foreign strangers. On the other hand, the legends warn against "the familiar" and remind us that one cannot be too careful in today's world (Domowitz 1979, 94). "The motif of unwitting cannibalism serves to remind the listener that he can never be absolutely *sure* about anything" (94).

Variants of the Core Legend

In 1979, Susan Domowitz presented a brief historical overview of the variants of contaminated food legends in an article titled "Foreign Matter in Food: A Legend Type." In the article, Domowitz (1979, 86–89) demonstrates that, although the variants all combine elements of the core structure, they are considerably different from each other. The variants include:

1. Legends that include the motif "human flesh eaten unwillingly." Stories about consuming human flesh are the most horrifying of all contamination legends. Accidental ingestion of mice (and their droppings), spider eggs, and other foreign matter is not as repulsive as cannibalism.

   a. 1951: a finger found in spaghetti in a unnamed Italian restaurant
   b. 1954: a human thumb found in can of tomatoes (brand name not included)
   c. 1955: a human finger found in chop suey in a named Chinese restaurant

2. Legends about entire bodies and/or human body parts in vats:

   a. 1955: a body in a vat at the Aunt Jane's Pickle company. The adaptation of the legend to a household name (especially in Michigan) adds immediacy, as most listeners to the legend would, at the very least, have heard of the company but would, more likely, have consumed their fair share of the product
   b. 1955: rats in vats of (unnamed) pickles

3. Legends that offer variants on both the contents and the containers of the above examples:

   a. 1955: cremated remains eaten unwittingly. This version of the legend "Grandma's Ashes" describes a situation in which the ashes were sent with food packages to war-torn Germany. Before the delayed accompanying letter is found, the relatives bake a cake with the "flour" that they had received from North America.

   b. 1948: mouse found in Coke bottle

   c. 1955: body found in barrels of alcohol. The barrels were discovered and their content drank before the drinkers discover that the alcohol was being used to preserve a body.

   d. 1955: dead cats found in barrel of cider (unnamed).

"KENTUCKY FRIED RAT"

The legend of the rat in the chicken has close parallels to the legends labeled "Chinese Restaurant" stories in Europe in the 1970s. The core legend, according to Graham Shorrocks (1975, 30), is as follows:

1. The victim, with a bone stuck in the throat, is taken to the hospital after eating at a local restaurant.

2. The bone is identified as a bone from a rat.

3. The restaurant is inspected by the Health Inspector or the police and is found to be stocked with the meat of other animals, particularly German shepherds.

There are obvious differences between the European and the North American variants. In Europe, ethnic restaurants are typically implicated and the "foreign" substance is used deliberately, but in North American variants, the rat (in the majority of tales) accidently falls into the batter of a nationally known fast-food chicken outlet (Fine 1980, 231). In France and Great Britain, the usual settings are Oriental restaurants, while in Scandinavia and Germany, Mediterranean restaurants are the culprits (Campion-Vincent 1989, 103). The introduction of the fast-food outlets is a recent phenomenon; early North American variants cited Italian and Chinese restaurants as the locality (Fine 1980, 230).

Most North American variants do not include an explanation for the rat's presence but, when offered, this explanation falls into two broad categories: deliberate sabotage by disgruntled employees and unsanitary conditions (Fine 1980, 231).

Symbolism of Key Elements

Researchers suggest an explanation for the widespread popularity of "Kentucky Fried Rat" tales and "Chinese Restaurant" stories. Anxieties about lack of control in food preparation, "unorthodox" foodstuffs, the impersonalization of fast-food outlets, and changing lifestyles and values have all had a part in the transmission of the legend. Our "new" values, which include increased leisure time and women in the work force, both coexist with and contradict traditional values (Fine 1980, 237). "No matter how soothing and inviting the advertisements for fast-food restaurants (and advertisements attempt to address these fears by portraying the establishments as homey), the public subconsciously depicts them as sources of danger" (Fine 1987, 4). This legend is frequently told while the participants are eating or thinking about food. Several versions are explicit in their warning about the consequences of fast food while others implicitly warn about corporate greed and employee sabotage (Fine 1980, 235–36).

Foreign Food Culture

The European variants of contamination legends are mostly xenophobic, reflecting the universal belief that people of foreign cultures eat certain animals that are taboo to our own culture (Klintberg 1981, 155). Therefore, the belief goes, it is quite understandable that rats, dogs, and cats would be served as food in such establishments. The proprietors, knowing that these animals are not considered fit for consumption, try to keep the general public from discovering their meat source. Until, of course, someone gets a bone stuck in her throat. Early rumors about "alien" restaurants were quite specific about what took place behind the scenes as well. In 1936, "the police had found three skinned cats, labeled as rabbits, in the restaurant's refrigerator" (Bird 1979, 180).

Female Victims

In most variants of the legend on both continents, females are the usual victims. This is partially due to the fact that women are perceived as more vulnerable to attack than their male counterparts; they are the traditional victims in other legends as well (e.g., "The Roommate's Death," "Department Store Snakes," and "The Killer in the Back Seat" [chapter 12]). Female victims eating at fast-food restaurants also symbolize the loss of traditional values that tell women to stay at home and prepare the meals for the family. She, by neglecting her traditional (and proper) role, helps to destroy the family by transferring control from the home to "amoral profit-making corporations." According to the legends, therefore, she deserves to be appropriately punished! (Fine 1980, 233).

The rumor persists because it has become a moral tale. In effect, it is telling that such rumors involve a woman, i.e., a housewife whose responsibility it is to feed her family. The rumor reminds her that in neglecting her traditional role, she makes her family run risks: the rat is a form of symbolic punishment. The rumor more generally aims at woman's liberation: thanks to new forms of nourishment, woman are no longer obliged to spend hours and hours preparing meals. (Kapferer 1990, 153)

Impersonal Corporations

North American variants reflect the anxieties that Americans have about large corporations usurping the role of small, local businesses with large chains, replacing family-owned restaurants (Simons 1990, 193). The large chains are symptomatic of the erosion of traditional institutions and values.

Rats

There are three credible interpretations for the role of the rat in the legend. First, rats and small rodents have been reported in milk cartons, soft drink bottles, and in areas of food preparation. Second, the structure of the legend calls for a plausible substitute for a piece of chicken that might be found in a fast-food outlet. Finally, rats symbolize "urban decay." "The rat, an animal attracted by filth, represents the decline of community and morality in the neighbourhood or small town" (Fine 1980, 231).

Sabotage by Employees

Workers in large food-processing plants and fast-food outlets are alienated from their employers, who often have their offices elsewhere and have virtually no contact with their underpaid and overworked staff. Therefore, the legends suggest, in today's immoral climate, where anything goes, employees retaliate against the innocent—the consumer. The only resource for the consumer is the court system as "the moral code of small town life is transformed into the formal bureacracy of the courts" (Fine 1987, 4).

"Setting"

The setting in contamination legends is often the dim interior of a car, or a dark restaurant. Not only does darkness provide a plausible explanation for why the consumer fails to recognize the rat, but it is also symbolically significant. Quickly grabbing something to eat in the car, a symbol of mobility and freedom, acknowledges the changes in eating habits caused by conflicting time schedules. The family dinner, credited with uniting families, has been transformed into a secondary, hurried, and isolated activity (Fine 1980, 234).

"Catflesh in Tacos"

The legend of "Catflesh in Tacos" is a curious blending of the European and North American variants of "Kentucky Fried Rat." Xenophobia seems to be the motivating factor behind this variant, reflecting fear and distrust of the Hispanic community in the United States. The legend addresses cultural issues and the cultural order that defines not only what we eat but our perception of ourselves in the social order (Clements 1991, 49):

> The catflesh at a Mexican restaurant rumor says, in paraphrase, that lazy, lower-class ethnic "others" are offering a substance . . . as if it were food to their social and cultural superiors. They thus violate the rules of food exchange while treacherously suborning their trusting victims to undercut the culture order. As the Mexican restaurateurs trick their hapless customers into violating one very fundamental categorical distinction, they themselves violate another: that between social classes. (Clements 1991, 46)

The substitution of cats for rats is also symbolic. Eating catflesh has as many negative connotations as eating rats. Consuming cats, which are carnivores, is taboo in Judeo-Christian cultures. Their typical food supply, rats and mice, are also repugnant, causing cats to be considered nonfood. But even more important than the fact that cats would not produce much meat (particularly in proportion to the effort required to process) if they were deemed edible, cats are treasured pets and, as such, are viewed anthropomorphically. Just look to the comic pages of the daily newspapers, populated with such cats as Garfield, Bill the Cat (*Outland*, formerly *Bloom Country*), Jesper (*Sam and Silo*), and Hobbes (*Calvin and Hobbes*) (Clements 1991, 44–45). Cats, beyond their function as pets, provide numerous valuable services as live entities rather than dead food: "rodent control, status indication, entertainment, education, sport, protection, and companionship" (46).

While Clements feels that the catflesh variant is indicative of anti-Hispanic attitudes, it must be noted that this version of the legend has been popular in other parts of the world, reflecting racist attitudes against minorities everywhere.

Variants

"A New Taste Sensation"

According to the British Daily Mirror, *one Eric Schneider "from Long Island" went to a McDonalds restaurant and ordered its new McRib sandwich (a barbecued simulated pork rib with no bones). Finding that it had an unusual taste, he opened the sandwich and found the two back legs of a half-eaten mouse. Schneider allegedly vomited and then had to wrench the rest of the meal away from restaurant workers, who were trying to confiscate the evidence. He is said to be suing McDonalds because of mental problems caused by the experience.*
(More Corp Rumors 1992, 12)

"Paris in the Springtime"

The sister-in-law went to eat at a Chinese restaurant [in Paris] and got something stuck in her teeth and could not get it out. She had to see a dentist who managed to get it loose, and found that it was a splinter from a rat's tooth. Later the police raided the restaurant, and there they discovered fifty rats in the deepfreeze. After hearing this I would not eat at Chinese restaurants in Paris anymore. I was afraid those strips of meat in Chinese dishes might be rat meat.
(Kvideland and Sehmsdorf 1988, 380)

"KKK CONTAMINATED FOOD LEGENDS"

Political groups such as the Ku Klux Klan (KKK) are also the focus of legends. The major thrust behind identifying the KKK with food contamination legends is the idea that they are attempting to control the African American population through their eating habits.

At least four contemporary legend cycles, according to Patricia Turner (1993, 82), have identified the Ku Klux Klan as the villain in pursuing the bodies of African Americans:

1. Church's Fried Chicken, allegedly owned by the KKK, reportedly includes a secret ingredient in their recipe that sterilizes the black male consumers of their product.

2. Troop clothing company, popular among young African American male consumers, is also rumored to be owned by the KKK. So black

men who purchase clothes from the company are unwittingly supporting an organization dedicated to white supremacy.

3. Marlboro cigarettes, a popular brand in the African American community, is allegedly owned by the KKK, which uses the profits to support its policies, and is responsible for causing cancer in the black consumers.

4. Tropical Fantasy, a soft drink manufactured by the Brooklyn Bottling Company, is also rumored to contain a secret sterilizing ingredient that only affects black men.

Church's Fried Chicken

Church's Fried Chicken has been identified with the Ku Klux Klan and its secret plan to render black men sterile. The overall plot, say the legends, is to "depopulate" black neighborhoods with the secret ingredient in the chicken (Morgan and Tucker 1984, 137).

Although the public company has no connection with the KKK and tests conducted by the Food and Drug Administrations have found no evidence of harmful chemicals (especially any that would make men sterile), the rumor was prolific in the early 1980s. The primary reason for the wide acceptance of the story is the location of the chicken outlets. Because of Church's low-budget attitude towards advertising, their profile on the American market is understandably low. Many white consumers not only were unfamiliar with the rumor and legend cycle but were completely unaware of the company.

> In an age when most fast food companies bombard us nightly with their televised pitches, however, a company with little or no advertising becomes conspicuous, to those who know it, precisely because of its anonymity. Perhaps, the folk assumption is that a company that doesn't boast about its product has something to hide. (Turner 1993, 87)

The cheap, poor, and largely black inner-city locations of Church's restaurants are the result of a company policy designed to gain a high return on investment. The lack of a well-developed public image, due, in part, to a low advertising budget, helps to feed the legend (Morgan and Tucker 1984, 138). Also, fast-food products produce a certain amount of ambivalence among their consumers. Fast-food represents convenience at the same time as it represents a misuse of budgeting because the same items could be made at home for a fraction of the cost (Turner 1993, 3). "Anxiety and guilt arise from the change from eating personally prepared food to eating what profit-making enterprises serve; these emotions have been projected onto the commercial establishment, and transformed into fear" (Fine 1980, 232).

Tropical Fantasy

Tropical Fantasy, a line of low-priced soft drinks intended for the poor, inner-city market was introduced in September 1990 by a small family-owned soft drink manufacturer, Brooklyn Bottling. The suggested retail price was 49 cents for a 20-ounce container. Initially, sales were successful. However, late in 1990, rumors began circulating in black neighborhoods that the soft drink had, as a secret ingredient, a sterilizing drug. The rumor also maintained that the Ku Klux Klan was responsible for the manufacture of Tropical Fantasy (Tropical Fantasy and the KKK 1991, 11).

The resemblance between Brooklyn Bottling and the other companies linked with the KKK is twofold. First, the advertising strategy was perceived as "for blacks only" as the location of outlets was in predominantly inner-city neighborhoods and the company did not have an active advertising campaign. Second, the name of the product was ambiguous, as a large proportion of the target market was from the "tropics," the Caribbean islands, and therefore, the white company was treading on "symbolically significant terrain" (Turner 1993, 104). A flyer posted in stores and passed around in the streets proclaimed the charge:

> *Attention! Attention! Attention!*
> *Please be advised, Top Pop, and Tropical Fantasy, also 50 sodas are being manufactured by the Klu Klux Klan. Sodas contain stimulants to sterilize the black man, and who knows what else!!!*
> *You have been warned. Please save the children.* (Dickson and Goulden 1993, 39)

Brooklyn Bottling's attempts to debunk the rumor were no more successful than those of Church's Fried Chicken earlier. Customers did not buy either the disclaimers or the product. Instead, they threatened distributors and delivery drivers. Then rumors circulated that Pepsi and Coke officials were deliberately spreading the rumor to regain their market share. This was also denied by representatives of both companies. Finally, New York Mayor David Dinkins, an African American, agreed to drink Tropical Fantasy on television and, within the month, business was back to normal (Dickson and Goulden 1993, 39).

> While the most potent folklore genres of the postindustrial age—rumor, graffiti, Xeroxlore—were being put to work to spread the notion that Tropical Fantasy was a KKK-inspired anaphrodisiac, the company fought back with all the standard damage-control tools. (Turner 1993, 169)

Among their campaigns were hiring a black public relations firm, hiring someone to drive a truck, with a large billboard denying the allegations, around black neighborhoods; testing their products with the FDA and making the results public; and gathering testimonies from individuals respected in the African American communities. Eventually the rumors died away and business resumed.

COKELORE

His eyes fixed on the clean concrete walk, Gant strode on, muttering dramatically, composing a narrative of the picture. . . . The window on the corner was filled with rubber syringes and thermos bottles. Drink Coca Cola. They say he stole the formula from an old mountain woman. $50,000,000 now. Rats in the vats. Dope at Wood's better. Too weak here. He had recently acquired a taste for the beverage and drank four or five glasses a day. (Wolfe 1929, 225)

Legends and rumors are so plentiful about Coca-Cola that the term "Cokelore" has been coined to refer to the phenomenon. These legends range from fanciful stories concerning the secret formula to rumors of foreign objects found in Coke bottles.

Coke was first sold only at soda fountains. A man approached the executive of the company and told them that for $500 he would reveal the secret of untold corporate riches. His secret, after he pocketed the money, was "Bottle it!" (Dickson and Goulden 1993, 60)

The folklore about Coca-Cola containing cocaine is based on historical fact. The name was registered as a trademark in 1893 and reflects the names of two of the ingredients of the soft drink, revealed in this story about the accidental invention of the soft drink:

Once upon a time, in the days when a snake-oil salesman could still make a respectable living and when every druggist concocted his own syrups for the soda fountain in his store, there lived in Atlanta a druggist named Pemberton. Pemberton sold such patent medicines as Triplex Liver Pills, Globe of Flower Cough Syrup, and "French Wine Coca-Ideal Nerve Tonic Stimulant." In 1886, he went into his kitchen and devised a "new" proprietary elixir, a syrup containing extracts from the Andean coca leaf and the African kola nut. By chance, the elixir got mixed with soda water and was discovered to be not just a medicine but a beverage as well. (Smith 1991, 128)

After the Food and Drug Act of June 30, 1906, cocaine was eliminated from the manufacturing of the drink. Dickson and Goulden quote the U.S. Supreme Court in their decision between Coca-Cola Company and the Koke Company of America:

> Coca leaves still are used, to be sure, but after they have been subjected to a drastic process that removes from them every characteristic substance except a little tannin and still less chlorophyll. The cola nut, at best, on its side furnishes but a very small portion of caffeine, which is now the only element that has appreciable effect. (1993, 60)

With the elimination of cocaine from the recipe, the company began stressing the abbreviation "Coke" in their advertising, and the word "Coke" is now the property of the Coca-Cola Company (Dickson and Goulden 1993, 61).

As with other large corporations and other rumors and legends about manufacturing, Coca-Cola, the leading seller of soft drinks, is the company identified with the tales, regardless of what company may have been cited originally.

"The Mouse in the Coke Bottle"

> *On opening a bottle or can of coke (any pop or beer), a whole or part of a mouse is found inside. The purchaser takes the manufacturer to court and is awarded huge amounts of money in compensation for the resulting shock (hospitalization).*

An examination of court records of the decisions of state appellate courts was undertaken to find evidence of whether the legend of "The Mouse in the Coke Bottle" had any basis in reality. And it does! The first recorded case found was in 1914 in Mississippi. Harry Chapman's win against the Jackson Coca-Cola Bottling Company was appealed and the appeal denied. Since that time, from 1914 to 1976, 45 cases involving mice found in soft drink bottles reached the courts. This number does not include the cases that were settled out of court or not appealed (Fine 1979, 479). The cases, in fact, appeared quite regularly: four cases between 1914 and 1920, three in the following decade, nine between 1931 and 1940, eight in the 1940s, 15 in the 1950s, and two between 1971 and 1976 (Fine 1979, 479). The rise in cases between 1931 and 1959 could have resulted from a variety of things: increasingly unsanitary bottling conditions, the growth of the soft drink industry, the "sue syndrome," or a greater legal pugnacity on the part of the soft drink manufacturers (Fine 1979, 479).

Mice were not the only "foreign" objects found in the bottles. Other named objects include: roaches, maggots, worms, putrid peanuts, cigarette butts, kerosene, concrete, glass slivers, hairpins, safety pins, paint, and a condom. Containers other than soft drink bottles were also cited: milk cartons, beer bottles, pies, and meals served at Chinese restaurants (Fine 1979, 480). Though the majority of cases cite Coca-Cola, this large number is attributed to the fact that Coca-Cola is the largest manufacturer of soft drinks and that "Coke" has become a folk-generic term for "soft drink," along with "pop" and "soda" (Bell 1976, 63).

There are close similarities between the accounts of legal action and the contemporary legends. When the discovery of the object occurs in the dark, the parallels to "Kentucky Fried Rat" are striking. "Because of the dramatic, horrifying qualities of the event, along with its functional value for express-ing real fears about the industrialization of America, each of these versions is likely to be widely diffused" (Fine 1979, 481). Eventually, as the stories were related by "uninvolved" tellers, they were altered and embellished to pro-vide a "better story" (481). Each new occurrence brought forth the legend cycle, with new additions and new authorities to quote. New cases also brought about fraudulent claims as well. These cases may have been sug-gested by the circulating legends and by the perception that the "likely" occurrences can easily be faked (481).

Not all urban belief tales are the products of actual events, or of dupli-cations of these actual events. However, the data from the "Mouse in the Coke Bottle" story suggests that such an origin must not be discounted (Fine 1979, 481).

While the legend may be based on real facts,

> The anecdote is now a part of the American oral tradition, belong-ing to a series of stories now told about Coca-Cola; it is a sort of warning concerning the power of the mysterious drink whose recipe is kept such a secret. (Kapferer 1990, 30)

Other Aspects of Cokelore

An analysis of Cokelore and interaction of elite, popular, and folk culture shows "that in one way or another, the contemporary legends and beliefs recorded to date make comment on *every* aspect of Coca-Cola from its *creation* to its *use*" (Smith 1991, 148). Other elements in the body of Cokelore include:

1. The corrosive properties of Coca-Cola: *"If you put a tooth in a glass of Coca-Cola overnight, it will have dissolved by morning. That is also true of a nail or a penny"* (Dickson and Goulden 1993, 59). Many experi-ments have proven this rumor wrong but the belief persists. Last year, at my daughter's school science fair, the experiment was attempted once again—with galvanized nails!

2. The use of Coca-Cola as a solvent: *"Tar can be removed with Coke . . . the only thing that can remove tar"* (Bell 1976, 59). The largest variation in versions of both these legends is the amount of time required for the Coke to do its "thing."

3. *"That the mixture of aspirin and Coca-Cola is (a) a powerful intoxicant or (b) a powerful aphrodisiac, but, either way, (c) can kill you."* (Dickson and Goulden 1993, 59)

The following results were compiled from a Cokelore survey of 100 folklore students conducted at the University of Colorado in 1975. Coke was believed by those surveyed to have the following properties:

Corrosive Properties		*Non-Corrosive Properties*	
Dissolves teeth	8	Coke + aspirin = intoxicant	7
Dissolves meat	2	Contraceptive douche	4
Dissolves nails	12		
Cleans rust from metal	12		
Dissolves stomach lining	10		
Dissolves car paint	9		
Dissolves pennies	4		

(Bell 1976, 65)

Case Study: "The Mouse in the Coors Beer Can"

"The Mouse in the Bottle" legend does not cite only Coca-Cola as the culprit. Numerous stories (and tellers?) have graduated from Coke to beer. The following discussion centers on a recent alleged case of "The Mouse in the Coors Beer Can."

This episode first made headlines in the business section of *The Denver Post* (Aug. 4, 1988). The story, with the headline "Rat Allegedly Found in Can of Coors," reported that a man claimed to have found a rodent in a 16-ounce can of Coors beer. Upon examination by health officials, the animal appeared to be either a baby roof rat or a mouse. James Harvey claimed that, upon drinking from the can, "[I] felt something against my mouth. I looked in the can in the sunlight and saw feet and a tail" (Preston 1989, 1). The following day, an article in *The Denver Post*, "Coors Wants Rodent in Can Tested," was accompanied by a photograph of the mouse, the can, and a glass of beer. Preston confirms that this was the second time in six years that Coors had been involved with a claim of a rodent in their beer. The previous case was settled in 1982 out of court for an undisclosed amount of money.

Two articles appeared in the August 6 issue of *The Denver Post*: "Coors Fans Smell a Rat in Scandal" and "Story Chokes Coors Sales in Florida." Editorials and letters to the editor began appearing, all supporting the manufacturer. Anecdotal reports of fraudulent claims began to circulate both orally and in the media. *The Denver Post* reported on September 3, 1988 that Coors was filing suit against James Harvey for fraud. "A court ordered autopsy by University of Florida veterinary pathologists later indicated the mouse had died no more than a week before the Aug. 5 examination. Coding on the can indicated the beer was packaged May 13 in Golden" (Preston 1989, 2).

October 26, 1988 saw the last newspaper article in Colorado about this case: "Mouse in Beer Lands Stuffer in Prison." Harvey was sentenced to 18 months in jail. Coors officials were pleased with the verdict, saying that they were out "not for revenge, but to restore consumer confidence on our products" (Preston 1989, 2).

Preston discusses the case as "life imitating legend," another example of ostension. He refers to other legends mentioned in connection with this case, particularly those about Corona beer, and also cites several examples of jokes and Xeroxlore that reflect the incident. For example, on a Halloween broadcast, there was a shot of a costume that was "a body-length Coors Beer can; the trick-or-treater's face was made up to look like a mouse and upon his head was perched a pair of Mouseketeer ears" (Preston 1989, 2). The later news articles read more like news-releases from Coors, "carefully shifting the episode in the media paradigm from 'legend' to 'product tampering,' thus associating the episode with the Tylenol scare, not the 'Kentucky Fried Rat'" (3).

MISCELLANEOUS CONTAMINATED FOOD LEGENDS

The following legends are arranged alphabetically and do not represent the entirety of the body of contaminated food legends. This is a rapidly growing body of legends, and students are encouraged to add to the list with examples of their own.

"The Cat and the Salmon"

A woman cooks an elaborate salmon dish for a dinner party but just before the guests arrive she finds the cat nibbling at the fish. She tosses the cat outside and quickly makes cosmetic repairs to the salmon. When the party is over, the woman takes the garbage outside and finds the body of her cat. Fearing her guests ate tainted fish, the woman calls them and they all rush to the hospital to have their stomachs pumped out. The next morning, the woman's neighbor telephones to apologize, "Last night I ran over your cat as I drove out of my driveway. I didn't want to ruin your party so I put its body next to your house and waited until morning to telephone you." (Dickson and Goulden 1993, 159)

Contaminated Water

Precious supplies of fresh, potable water have been the focus of contamination anxieties throughout history. But what may not be as commonly known today are legends about the danger of drinking contaminated water and "vomiting frogs." Frogs are not the only water creatures that can be accidently swallowed when offering explicit and implicit warnings about drinking contaminated water, but they are the most prolific. Paul Smith, in his article "Vomiting Frogs," provides an early analogue to this legend in a letter describing an incident that occurred in 1780 when Archdale Wilson Taylor vomited a toad after eating watercress in Matlock, Derbyshire.

> *He in general ate Water Cresses twice a day; and for some days before he left that place he had pains in his Stomach, which pains continued with frequent inclinations to vomit until the fifteenth of October last, when . . . [advised to] take an Emetic . . . he found something stuck in his Throat . . . [it] proved to be a living Toad of about two inches and an half long and an inch and an half broad, which was afterwards laid upon the floor and crawled towards the fire in the presence of the Doctor and several other persons.*
> (Smith 1987, 2)

And then there are those who supposedly contaminate their water on purpose:

> *Marianne Kosse, 29, from near Arles, France, began suffering from an odd illness: "No matter how much I ate," she said, "I kept getting weaker and weaker, as if I was being deprived of food." When her physician, Dr. Giles Lebideux, found a circular mass in her stomach, he feared a cancer and immediately decided to operate. Once into the stomach, however, he watched in horror as a four-pound frog jumped out onto the operating room floor. Afterwards, Kosse recalled that a few months before she had swallowed a tadpole from a nearby pond on a dare during a birthday party.* (Legends in the Tabloids 1990, 10)

Diet Pills

A few years ago there was a company who put out surefire diet pills, guaranteed to lose weight in no time. People began to take these pills, and in no time the people were losing weight. After a few weeks these people began to lose too much weight. So the government investigated. They opened the pills and found the head of a tapeworm. They had the person starve himself for days. Then they set a bowl of hot milk in front of the person. He had to keep his mouth open. After a while the tapeworm began to come up his throat because he smelled the milk. They kept moving the bowl further away until the tapeworm was completely out. (Baker 1982, 226)

The legend that diet pills or other "appetite suppressant candies contain worm eggs, which hatch in the stomach and eat the food there, thus causing weight loss" has been circulating for several decades (Morgan and Tucker 1984, 65). However, the active ingredient in appetite suppressants is not tapeworms (the most commonly identified species), but benzocaine, "a local anesthetic that numbs the stomach and quells hunger pains" (65). The above legend was collected in 1969. When I presented it recently to a group of junior high students, I expected to hear jeers and laughter. Much to my surprise, however, I heard one student say, "But it wasn't hot milk, it was chocolate. I know 'cause that's what happened to my aunt."

"Doggie Dinner"

An English couple went out one evening for a Chinese meal. As they did not want to leave their dog in the car, they took it into the restaurant with them. The waiter, who didn't appear to know much English, showed them to a table and they indicated that they would like him to take the dog to be fed. He smiled, bowed and went away with the dog. Another waiter came, they ordered their meal and sat back relaxing while they waited for the food to arrive. Eventually, the first waiter came back bearing a large platter which he placed in the center of the table. When he lifted the lid the couple were mortified to find their dog—cooked and served with full trimmings. (Smith 1986, 95)

The "Doggie Dinner" legend circulates in Europe rather than in North America, where dogs are not allowed into establishments that prepare and sell food. It also reflects Europeans' fears and misunderstandings of non-European immigrant culture. While these fears could not be expressed directly against the non-Europeans, the legends refer to one of the major ways that people are differentiated: their culinary "foodways" or traditions (Fine 1987, 6). When pets disappeared, their bones were allegedly found in the garbage cans of newly arrived residents. Because local residents were not really sure of the habits and traditions of their new neighbors, anything was possible! (Fine 1987, 61). This story is related to the Gomez family tale about their dog. According to the *Inquirer*, the Mexico City family bought meat from the butcher next door, only to discover that they were dining on their missing pet (Bird 1992, 25).

> A prejudice has arisen against eating rats, because the doctors say that their flesh is full of trichinae. I own for my part I have a guilty feeling when I eat dog, the friend of man. I had a slice of spaniel the other day, it was by no means bad, something like lamb, but I felt like a cannibal. Epicures in dog flesh tell me that poodle is by far the best and recommended me to avoid bull dog, which is coarse and tasteless. (Smith 1986, 95)

"Grandma's Ashes"

Unlike the "body in the vat" and other human contamination legends about food, the consumption of "Grandma" is an unwitting act committed while the body is in an unidentifiable state. The horror attached is not as vivid as that experienced when faced with other cannibalistic tales (Domowitz 1979, 89). Early variants included information about post office regulations that state that letters could not accompany parcels and had to be sent separately. This information, along with family names and addresses, added to the plausibility of the legend actually taking place. "The sending of food and clothing packages to war victims provides a plausible framework for the horrible mistake: eating the ashes of one's own kin" (Domowitz 1979, 89). Another "interesting" variant is as follows:

> *Then there is the woman who is accidently locked in a house for a month. She survives by eating corn chips or potato chips. When the owner returns he learns what she has been eating and gasps, "Those boxes weren't filled with corn chips! Those were pieces of my dead skin when I had leprosy!" (Knapp 1976, 246–47)*

Jack-in-the-Box Burgers

The 1992 incident in which this regional fast-food chain served improperly prepared and cooked hamburgers, resulting in a child's death, brought to the surface other legends and rumors that had been attached to other restaurant chains. Computer networks resurrected an earlier story in which Gary Underhill, a police officer in Phoenix, Arizona, ordered hamburgers from Jack-in-the-Box in 1990. The cook on duty allegedly blew his nose into one of the burgers, commenting to a co-worker, "That's what the cop gets." Underhill took three bites of his burger, noticed the mucus on his hands and face and arrested the cook. The cook tested negative for AIDS and was fined. He also lost his job. Jack-in-the-Box announced three days later that they were suspending all radio and television advertising, citing "jokes being made on various radio stations" (Tainted Jack-in-the-Box Burgers 1993, 10).

In March 1993, newspapers re-publicized another case from 1990. Tacos were the culprit this time. The couple bit into a taco from Jack-in-the-Box only to discover that there was blood all over the wrapper and food. They returned to the fast-food outlet to find an employee with one hand covered in a blood-soaked towel. They alleged that the employee was diagnosed positive for hepatitis (communicated through contact with blood) and are suing for damages for emotional stress and medical expenses.

Pop Rock Candy

The lady at the store says that a kid a couple of blocks away saved up his allowance to buy Pop Rocks. He was so greedy that he ate all of them at one time—just swallowed and swallowed. . . . They all popped in his stomach and he died. Now they aren't supposed to be sold—they are really dangerous! (Fine 1992, 95)

Although "Pop Rocks" have lost favor with today's consumers, legend tells of how they exploded in the stomach, often causing death. The candies, small sugar pellets that had been treated with carbon dioxide to make them "explode" or "tingle" in the mouth, were natural targets for the concern of a public ambiguous about mass-produced foodstuffs. They were manufactured by one of the big companies, General Foods, and were the dubious invention of modern technology.

Spider Eggs in Bubble Gum

Apparently some little kids in either New York or Chicago started telling people that the reason Bubble Yum was so soft was because the gum had spider legs in it. It spread all over the country apparently because as I was chewing a piece of Bubble Yum talking to the clerk, someone came in and asked for some Spider Leg Gum. (Fine 1992, 153)

Bubble Yum was the first soft bubble gum to be marketed and was popular with its intended market: young children. Shortly after its successful launching, Squibb, which owns Bubble Yum, became the leading manufacturer of bubble gum and the legends began circulating in an attempt to "explain why this new gum, so different from traditional gums, felt and tasted as it did" (Fine 1992, 154). The legends used spider eggs and spider legs interchangeably as the "magic" ingredient to explain this phenomenon. This was probably due to the similarity in sound between the words *eggs* and *legs*. Squibb spent more than $100,000 trying to debunk the spider-leg/egg tale (Dickson and Goulden 1993, 36).

Sushi Grubs

The envious West, jealous of the continuing economic successes of Japan, would naturally be a breeding-ground for anti-Japanese urban legends. So we have had reports that the raw fish used in sushi and sashimi contains minute grubs that can enter the blood stream and contaminate the brain. Certain chopsticks exported from Japan are said to have poisoned tips. (Kirkup 1989, 3)

Urine in Corona Beer

"Americans see Mexico as both an underdeveloped nation—an exotic location filled with danger and poverty—and recently as an economic rival" (Fine 1989, 158). American reactions to their southern neighbor have resulted in numerous rumors and legends, including rumors that began circulating in 1986 that the distinctive bright yellow color and copious foam in Corona beer are the result of Mexican workers urinating into bottles designated for export to the United States (Fine 1989, 159). Although at the time that his article was written there were no narrative variants of this rumor, Fine stated that he has no doubt that it would evolve into a legend (159).

The rumor's plausibility is essential for believability and the fact that the bright yellow beer is sold in clear bottles enhances the chance that the rumor will be believed (or at least commented upon). Fine comments that "underlying these facts is the reality that United States citizens find it credible that Mexican workers might be capable of such contamination and motivated to do it" (Fine 1989, 160). He further states that American fears about disease from "bodily fluids" and lack of proper hygiene is reflected in this rumor, as he asks, "What could be a more archetypal body fluid than urine?" (160).

During the time that this rumor surfaced, Corona Beer was the fastest growing imported beer and was considered a high-prestige beer (Fine 1989, 160). "The one thing you're dealing with in a beer is image, and if that image is sullied, that can have a severe effect," said Michael Mazzoni, executive vice president of Barton Beers in Chicago. Barton Beers is the major U.S. importer of Corona Extra Beer. Corona traced the source of the rumors to a competitor, won a lawsuit, and instituted a publicity campaign to reeducate the consumers (Preston 1989, 1).

Worms in McDonald's Hamburgers

The rumors about ground worms in hamburger meat was originally attributed to Wendy's, who advertised the *"juiciness"* of their hamburgers, but was quickly transferred to McDonald's, a much larger fast-food franchise. This story circulated primarily between 1978 and 1982 and warns, metaphorically, of the risks of eating "junk food" and reflects other anxieties relating to changing eating habits of North Americans (Kapferer 1990, 85).

The concept of ground earthworms is a concrete symbol of our phobia of rotting insides caused by a constant diet of soft drinks and hamburgers. Worms are the symbols of both garbage and inner destruction that follows its absorption (Kapferer 1990, 85). The legend warns the general population that hamburgers are potentially dangerous and that large food franchises recognize this fact and do nothing about it other than, of course, promote the products further.

And in the Media . . .

The following articles appeared in my local newspaper during the past few years. In some cases, the articles were used as fillers and were never followed up by the newspaper. In others, the articles were a series of reports of possible contaminated food that occurred "elsewhere."

"Are Canadians Ready Yet for Hormones in the Milk?"

In this front-page article, Philip Day discusses recent biotechnological developments such as tomatoes that stay ripe for a month because the "softening" gene is blocked, genetically altered canola that produces biodegradable oils and detergents, and cows that produce more milk. The first test of government and consumer approval is laboratory-produced bovine somatotropin, known as BST. Years of testing in the United States showed no harmful effects from BST, but angry protests have followed the decision. Murray McLaughlin, president of a Saskatchewan company that works in biotech development, "compares the current debate to the firestorm that greeted the sale of microwave ovens" (Day 1994, A1).

"Convict Suffered Too Little"

An inmate's lawsuit over an allegedly defective Pop Tart turned out to be fruitless. Christopher Lyons, 28, a drug dealer serving nine to 18 years, said he bit into a Pop Tart in July 1993 and a sliver of glass lodged in his gum for 18 hours. Lyons sought almost $350,000 Canadian for pain, suffering and mental anguish including "emotional trauma for loss of sleep for 72 hours due to nightmares" in which he was "dead in a coffin in prison from eating Pop Tarts." U.S. District Judge Benjamin Gibson dismissed the suit in Grand Rapids, Mich., against Kellogg Co. and J. M. Smucker Co. He ruled Lyons failed to prove that his suffering was worth at least $50,000, the minimum claim for a federal lawsuit. (Edmonton Journal, July 10, 1994, A2)

No concrete evidence about the glass was mentioned in the news item.

Gerber Baby Food

A mother who says her baby choked on plastic in Gerber's baby food expected an explanation and an apology from the company but received, instead, coupons to buy more of its products. "Does Gerber think my baby's life is worth three $1 coupons?" asked an angry Susan Sewell of Delta, B.C., whose six-month-old daughter choked, gasped and turned red during a feeding March 11. "She couldn't breathe," Sewell said Monday. "I was going to phone 911 but first I put my finger in her mouth and was able to dislodge a round piece of hard plastic from the back of her mouth. I was scared for her life." Sewell said she called Gerber's toll-free line that day and was urged to send the plastic to Gerber's lab for analysis. She did so immediately.

Gerber spokesman Nancy Lindner at head office in Fremont, Mich. said the company intends to send Sewell another letter after the tests are completed. But she insists it would be impossible for a piece of plastic to find its way into Gerber's baby food. ("Mother Ticked Off," Edmonton Journal, March 22, 1994, A3)

Syringe in Pepsi Bottle

---

*Health and Welfare Canada has launched an investigation to
determine how a syringe got into a bottle of Pepsi at a Steinberg
grocery store. The ministry began the investigation Friday after
learning the unsealed bottle was returned to EastCan Beverages
Ltd., an Ottawa company that bottles and distributes Pepsi,
Seven-Up and Pure Spring products. "A syringe represents a
potentially serious health concern," said Dave Hanna of the
ministry's health protection branch. He said several factors,
including tampering, will be investigated. "Anything's possible."*

*The syringe was found two weeks ago by a grocery clerk while he
was stacking shelves at the eastern Ontario store. "At first I
thought it was a straw that someone left in a bottle," said Jason
Nixon, 17. He said the syringe has a needle attached to it which
was bent. The syringe may have been put in the bottle by a
disgruntled employee, said Mario Galang, vice president of
EastCan. "With the control systems Pepsi has, I'm confident it's an
isolated incident," he said. "Nobody likes to find a syringe because
who knows what it was used for." ("Syringe in Pop Bottle
Prompts Probe," Edmonton Journal, September 2, 1990, A12)*

Three years later, the syringe appeared in the news again—this time in
a Pepsi can. "Syringes reported found in Pepsi cans. . . . People reported
finding syringes in Pepsi cans in five more states in the United States,
bringing the number of cases of possible tampering to 10" (*Edmonton Journal,*
June 16, 1993, A12). The next day, the topic received more prominence as it
appeared closer to the front page. "Soda-can needles reported in 20 states:
Two suspected hoaxers could face up to five years in federal jail" (*Edmonton
Journal,* June 17, 1993, A5). The first reported syringe incident was in Tacoma,
Washington on June 9, but officials had not yet confirmed any tampering.
"Still, the U.S. Food and Drug Administration has advised consumers to pour
soda into a glass before drinking it or to buy bottles and look inside before
drinking" (A5). The specific cans involved were manufactured in several
different plants over several months and yet the telephone calls were received within a period of just 48 hours "immediately following the news in
Seattle" (A5). There were no reports in Canada (this time).

A headline on June 18, 1993 stated that "U.S. Food Regulator Dismisses
Allegations of Pepsi Tampering: Four Arrests Follow Wave of Copycat Claims
Against Pop Maker." The article went on to explain that "Kessler [FDA
Commissioner] said there have been four arrests so far of people who alleged
they found syringes, nails or other objects in Pepsi cans, and other people
who made such claims are recanting" (*Edmonton Journal,* June 18, 1993, E15).

Local news media accounts indicate more than 50 reports of tampering in at least 23 states during this time. An interesting adjunct to this discussion is the positioning of the news report within the newspaper. The first two articles appeared in the front section of the paper but the final outcome was not considered of equal importance—hence its appearance in the E section! Most newspaper reports of "true" contemporary legends are rarely recanted within the newspaper at all, leaving the impression that it truly was a news event.

LITERARY AND VISUAL ADAPTATIONS

"The Cat and the Salmon"

Her Alibi (1988). Starring Tom Selleck, this film contains an adaptation of the legend.

"Coke and Aspirin"

Grease (1978). This film included the legend that aspirin in Coke acts as an aphrodisiac.

"Kentucky Fried Rat" and Other Contaminated Food Legends

The Pickwick Papers by Charles Dickens.
Full of improvisions, inset tales, and anecdotes, many of which Dickens represents as having been told to Mr. Pickwick by other characters in the book . . . early examples of modern legends. . . . Particularly "The Kentucky Fried Rat." (Simpson 1983, 462)

Poison Flowers by Natasha Cooper (New York: Crown, 1991), 30.
"No one could imagine how the aconite had got into Titchmell's breakfast cereal unless either some lunatic had put it in during packaging or storage of the cereal, *as various people had put ground glass and pieces of metal in babyfood a year or two earlier,* or the victims had done it themselves."

"The Mouse in the Beer Bottle"

Strange Brew (1983). The McKenzie brothers manage to get a job in a beer factory as a result of finding a (previously placed) mouse in a beer bottle.

"The Pet That Was Eaten by Mistake"

Rich and Strange (1932). Film released in the USA as *East of Shanghai*. Hitchcock describes the scene:
They huddle up in the front of the junk, and after a while the Chinese bring them some food and chopsticks. It's delicious, the best meal they've ever tasted. When it's over, they walk to the rear of the junk where they see the cat's skin being pinned out to dry. Stunned as well as nauseated, they rush over to the side. (Truffaut 1978, 87)

REFERENCES

Baker, Ronald L., ed. 1982. *Hoosier folk legends*. Bloomington: Indiana Press.

Bell, Michael. 1976. Cokelore. *Western Folklore* 35: 59–65.

Bird, Donald Allport. 1979. *Rumor as folklore: An interpretation and inventory*. Ph.D. diss. Indiana University.

Bird, S. Elizabeth. 1992. *For enquiring minds: A cultural study of supermarket tabloids*. Knoxville: University of Tennessee Press.

Campion-Vincent, Veronique. 1989. Complots et avertissements: Legendes urbaines dans la ville. *Revue Fracaise de Sociologie* 30: 91–105.

Clements, William M. 1991. Catflesh in Mexican food: Meaning in a contamination rumor. *Studies in Popular Culture* 14, no. 1: 39–51.

Day, Philip. 1994. Are Canadians ready yet for hormones in the milk? *The Edmonton Journal* (March 10): A1.

Dickson, Paul, and Joseph C. Goulden. 1993. *Myth-informed: Legends, credos, and wrongheaded "facts" we all believe*. New York: Perigee.

Domowitz, Susan. 1979. Foreign matter in food: A legend type. *Indiana Folklore* 12: 86–95.

Fine, Gary Alan. 1979. Cokelore and Coke law: Urban belief tales and the problem of multiple origins. *Journal of American Folklore* 92: 477–82.

———. 1980. The Kentucky fried rat: Legends and modern society. *Journal of the Folklore Institute* 17: 222–43.

———. 1987. The city as a folklore generator. *Urban Resources* 4, no. 3 (spring): 3–6, 61.

———. 1989. Mercantile legends and the world economy: Dangerous imports from the third world. *Western Folklore* 48 (April): 153–62.

———. 1992. *Manufacturing tales: Sex and money in contemporary legends*. Knoxville: University of Tennessee Press.

Kapferer, Jean-Noel. 1990. *Rumors: Uses, interpretations and images*. New Brunswick, NJ: Transaction.

Kirkup, James. 1989. Truth stranger than legend: Contemporary legends in Europe and the Orient. *FOAFTALE NEWS* 15 (September): 2–4.

Klintberg, Bengt af. 1981. Modern migratory legends in oral tradition and daily papers. *ARV* 37: 153-60.

Knapp, Mary, and Herbert Knapp. 1976. *One potato, two potato . . . The secret education of American children.* New York: W. W. Norton.

Kvideland, Reimund, and Henning K. Sehmsdorf, eds. 1988. *Scandinavian folk belief and legend.* Minneapolis: University of Minnesota Press.

Legends in the tabloids. 1990. *FOAFTALE NEWS* 18 (June): 10.

More corp rumors. 1992. *FOAFTALE NEWS* 28 (December): 12.

Morgan, Hal, and Kerry Tucker. 1984. *Rumor!* New York: Penguin.

———. 1987. *More rumor!* New York: Penguin.

Preston, Michael J. 1989. The mouse in the Coors beer can: Goliath strikes back. *FOAFTALE NEWS* 14 (June): 1–3.

Shorrocks, Graham. 1975. Chinese restaurant stories: International folklore. *Lore and Language* 1, no. 6: 30.

Simons, Elizabeth Radin. 1990. *Student worlds! Student words! Teaching writing through folklore.* Portsmouth, NH: Heinemann.

Simpson, Jacqueline. 1983. Urban legends in *The Pickwick Papers*. *Journal of American Folklore* 96, no. 382: 462–70.

Smith, Paul, ed. 1984. On the receiving end: When legend becomes rumour. In *Perspectives on contemporary legend, vol. 1* (CETAL Conference Papers #4). Sheffield, England: Sheffield Academic Press, 197–215.

Smith, Paul. 1986. *The book of nastier legends.* London: Routledge Kegan Paul.

———. 1987. Vomiting frogs. *FOAFTALE NEWS* 6 (July): 1–2.

———. 1991. Contemporary legends and popular culture: "It's the real thing." *Contemporary Legend* 1: 123–52.

Tainted Jack-in-the-Box burgers. 1993. *FOAFTALE NEWS* 29 (March): 10.

Tropical Fantasy and the KKK. 1991. *FOAFTALE NEWS* 22 (June): 10–11.

Truffaut, François. 1978. *Hitchcock.* London: Granada.

Turner, Patricia. 1993. *I heard it through the grapevine: Rumor in African-American culture.* Berkeley: University of California Press.

Wolfe, Thomas. 1929. *Look homeward, angel.* New York: Scribner's.

8

THIEVES

A woman living in a bed-sit was concerned as to how she should dispose of her recently deceased cat. So when a friend suggested that they bury it in his garden she took up the offer straight away. She carefully laid the little corpse in a shoe box, placed it in a carrier bag, and set off for the bus station. When she discovered that she had just missed her bus, she popped into the large store on the High Street to find a little something for her friend. She found it, took it to the desk, paid, and was about to leave when she missed her bag. The assistant immediately noticed that something was amiss, and within moments had alerted the store detective while a growing throng of staff and onlookers began to search the floor. When the store detective arrived she seized her chance: "Quick! Up to the Ladies," she said, "we'll catch her this time." And so they did. The cleaning lady unlocked the cubicle door, and there was the would-be thief, unconscious, with a dead cat in her lap.
(Dale 1984, 68–69)

Is this a chapter glorifying thieves? Not really. Contemporary legends, however, recognize the fact that theft and other "domestic" crimes are in the forefront of people's consciousness today. These legends, for the most part, reaffirm the belief that "crime does not pay" while they emphasize the comic, ironic, and satirical aspects of any given situation. "At the same time they convey a sense of uneasiness about the disintegration of traditional norms and values in modern society" (Kvideland and Sehmsdorf 1988, 389).

Several of the legends ("The Runaway Grandmother," "The Dead Cat in the Package," and "The Disappearing Room") convey our physical fear of the dead, while others ("The Unwitting Thief," "The Double Theft," "Free Tickets," "Kit Kat," and "Stuck with the Bill") demonstrate our joyous response to the ancient trickster character who has reappeared in our modern tales. It is this trickster who reminds us that humans are not perfect, that we still tend to jump to conclusions, and that we still expect something for nothing. Our sense of justice is fed by several other legends: "Missing Lottery Ticket," "Stolen Police Car," and "The Turkey in the Hat." By telling and listening to these tales, we give voice to our fears and concerns but, at the same time, experience healing laughter.

"THE RUNAWAY GRANDMOTHER"

A young couple from Holte [Denmark] was vacationing in Spain, and they had taken the husband's mother along. During a car trip high up in the Pyrenees, the mother-in-law got sick from the cold and the thin air, and within a short time, she died. Because the temperature was so low, the body became rigid rather quickly, and not being able to get her back into the small car, they wrapped her up in a tent they had brought, and put her on top of the luggage rack. They now drove as quickly as possible to the nearest town to report the death to the authorities and to take care of all the necessary formalities. Because of the language difficulties, it took some time before they managed to tell their story to the police. But the worse was yet to come! When they went back outside, they found the car had been stolen, and it has not been found yet! Imagine the thief's fright when he found the dead mother-in-law inside the tent. What did he do with the body? The one who is most interested in this question is, of course, her son. He cannot prove to the Danish authorities that his mother is dead, and, consequently, he cannot claim his inheritance, which supposedly amounts to around 300,000 Kroner. Who can help this unhappy man? (Kvideland and Sehmsdorf 1988, 390–91)

Is there really an unhappy man to help? This legend has achieved wide popularity in the past few decades in North America and Europe. Although folkloric antecedents exist, because of the apprehensions of Europeans crossing "unfriendly" borders, the legend reached its present form during or shortly after the Second World War (Kvideland and Sehmsdorf 1988, 391). It is still too early to tell how European storytellers will adapt the legend to incorporate the formation of the European Common Market. Not only abundant in oral communication, "The Runaway Grandmother" has made cameo appearances in numerous novels, short stories, and television and movies scripts.

While the above example faithfully follows the basic structure of the legend, it is an amalgamation of the distinct North American and European versions. For the most part, European variants concentrate on the difficulties and tensions involved in crossing international borders, while the North American variants rarely discuss border crossings at all. The major focus in the American tales is the inconvenience of death and the resulting dead body, as well as greed for an inheritance that may not be forthcoming.

Structure of "The Runaway Grandmother"

In both North America and Europe, storytellers begin this tale with enough concrete details that the listeners can appreciate the transformation of a family vacation into a nightmare. The primary difference between the two cultural variants is in the emphasis of the storyteller and the evaluation or coda that is attached to the legend. The basic form of the legend, according to Linda Degh (1968, 75), is as follows, arranged according to Labov's structural elements but without the various evaluations.

Orientation: (*who, what, when, where?*) Family takes vacation and old (sick) grandmother or other family member is taken along.

Complicating Action: (*why did this happen?*) She dies suddenly (heart attack because of the heat, strain, or other). Obstacles hinder the disposal of the body, which causes frustration (remoteness of the area, the unavailability of mortuary facilities, crossing a national border). Body is wrapped in rug (tent) and strapped on top of the car for return trip home.

Result: (*what finally happened?*) The family has almost made it and relaxes at a restaurant (after driving day and night without food) or enters the police station or other place where help is secured. The car is parked outside and its contents (or car itself) are stolen.

Functions of "The Runaway Grandmother"

Folklorists Linda Degh and Alan Dundes explore the functions of "The Runaway Grandmother." A brief summary of their conclusions illuminate the cultural and geographic differences in interpretation and focus of the basic legend.

Fear of the Dead

Degh interprets the legend as communicating fear of the dead. The fear evident in the story is different than most tales serving the same function. The body must have a decent burial and must (for a variety of reasons) be taken home (Degh 1968, 75). When the body disappears, the family becomes terrified that the grandmother will come back to haunt them because she has not had an honorable burial (Kapferer 1990, 154).

This interpretation does not seem valid in North America. Although the legend demonstrates fear of the dead, the North American family is concerned with the tasteful disposal of the corpse, and is not really worried about the potential of an unhappy ghost haunting them. Rather, their concern is with the immediate transportation problems that they must face while dealing with a dead body. In our sanitized society, most individuals do not have (or desire to have) any experience with the laying out of a body.

Disgust with the Elderly

Dundes claims that the legend is one of wish fulfillment, one of the principal characteristics of folklore. This function is particularly evident in the North American variants, which focus on capitalistic gain rather than the dangers of border crossings. There are two aspects to the wish fulfillment: to be rid of the older generation and not to have to contend with their funerals when they die. Dundes states that not only are North Americans

> chiefly interested in monetary gain, but [they] have little desire to be hampered with an older (and possibly, ailing) generation. There is no place for the older generation in a society that worships the future and rejects the past! "The Runaway Grandmother" legend gets rid of the grandmother and her body with a minimum of effort by those who would benefit most from her death. (Dundes 1971, 34)

One of the reasons that this legend is so popular is the fact that there is a twisted ending or trickster aspect to the North American variants. After the "easy" disposal of the corpse, the greedy family members cannot benefit from their fulfilled wish: without the corpse as evidence, they cannot prove the grandmother dead and therefore cannot collect their inheritance. Dundes remarks that the fear is not that grandmother will return, but the fear that she will *not*! (Kapferer 1990, 154).

Distrust of Authorities

Fear of custom and border officials is evident in the European versions of this legend. The legends often involve a crossing of an "Iron Curtain" border and the tension involved in transporting grandmother (both alive and dead). These variants focus on the successful smuggling of the body across the border and often end abruptly after the corpse is stolen. The climax is in shocking contrast to the preceding description of the happy family vacation (Degh 1968, 75).

Variants

Variants of the legend have been gathered from all corners of the world and demonstrate both the popularity of the legend and the cultural differences in the core legend.

The first version I myself [Sanderson] *heard was set in France in 1940 and involved a Belgian family (friends of the narrator's), who were escaping by car from Brussels into France ahead of the invading German armies. Their luggage was restricted to easily portable valuables— jewelery, silver, and two or three oriental rugs that were rolled up on the roof rack of their car. The grandmother died of a heart attack, brought on by stress and exhaustion, on the third day of their journey. They wrapped the body in the rugs and placed it on top of the car until they could find a priest and arrange for the burial. When eventually they stopped in a small town to have a hurried meal and a couple of hours of sleep and to look for a priest, the rugs were stolen from the roof rack.*
(Sanderson 1981, 5)

Another variant also displays problems and fears about crossing international borders:

It concerned a young and impecunious [penniless] couple on their honeymoon, travelling in Spain with the girl's aunt, a great favorite of them both, in the aunt's car. The aunt unfortunately died of a heart attack; it was impossible to arrange for cremation—her well-known wish—in Spain; the body, with a travelling rug pulled well up to the chin and a hat pulled well down over the brow, was driven with some trepidation from Spain to France during the siesta hour; and while the young couple were steadying their frayed nerves with a glass of cognac in a bistro before looking for the British Vice-Counsel, the car was stolen. (Sanderson 1981, 5)

Sanderson found an earlier version in a evening's conversation described by neurologist Sir Walter Russell Brain in *Tea with Walter de la Mare*:

> *Leonard told him (W. J. de la Mare) a story which was current at the time about a couple who were touring with their car in Spain when an old lady they had with them died unexpectedly. To avoid all the local complications they wrapped the body up and tied it on top of the car. They left the car unattended while they went to consult the British Consul, and when they came back it had been stolen. W. J. enjoyed the gruesome details. "What a horrible story!," he said.* (Sanderson 1981, 5)

Some North American variants also reflect trepidation over border crossings:

> *A family plans to spend its vacation in Canada on a canoe trip and decides to take Grandma, who is a spry eighty. After arriving at a remote river, the grandmother keels over dead. The local constable is notified, and he tells the family that the paperwork associated with recording the death and shipping the body out of the country is so great that they would be better if they just packed her up and made a beeline for the border. Taking this advice, the woman is wrapped in canvas and strapped into the canoe, which is tied to the roof of the family car. The family drives all day and at dark pulls into a motel near the U.S. border. They rise early to get a fresh start and find the car and the canoe have been stolen.*
> (Dickson and Goulden 1993, 158–59)

In the following case, the legend became blended with a series of practical jokes played out on the roadways of Great Britain in which a group of young people would pretend to be driving around with a corpse. Another example of ostension?

Within the years I recall, 1957–66, though, I believe it was reproduced as a parallel to an actual series of occurrences. Young people, not always students, developed the habit of riding around in motor cars with one of their colleagues lying in the boot [trunk], with the boot lid slightly raised, and a limp hand hanging over the number plate. Other motorists would pursue the car and/or report it to the police who investigated the matter and dismissed it as a prank. There was no stolen corpse but the actual sight or reporting of a human hand poking out of the boot gave rise to the legend that the everlasting grandmother who had died on holiday and been stolen with the vehicle had been traced and her body recovered with the motor car. Thus we have an incident repeated often enough, no doubt reported in the occurrence book at the local police station, tied in legend to give it further verisimilitude. (McConnell 1982/83, 226)

Sanderson (1981, 5) briefly identifies additional variants that were also circulating around in England in the 1960s:

The theft of the body from a trailer that slipped its tow on a hill near Brighton one Bank Holiday.

The theft of the body from the luggage compartment on a holiday tour bus in Cumbria.

The loss of the body from the roof of a bus traveling from Lagos to Calabar in Nigeria.

Several versions set in motor-cars transversing the Australian desert or the Sahara.

A tale about a Brazilian collecting a new car from a dealer in Argentina— the mother-in-law goes along for the trip; she dies and both the car and the mother-in-law are stolen.

"THE DEAD CAT IN THE PACKAGE"

I heard a version of this legend from an American relative who thought she was telling us a true story. It happened during a family reunion, and I had been listening patiently, knowing that someone in my storytelling family would provide me with a contemporary legend. I admit I crowed a little when it happened within a few hours of everyone getting together! That "The Dead Cat in the Package" was the tale told did not surprise me either; the tale has a long history. Rumors have circulated about other packages that have mistakenly been delivered to the wrong address, often shocking the recipients with gruesome contents. The infamous Burke and Hare of Edinburgh, Scotland were subjects of legends after their arrest in 1829. In their zeal to make a living supplying corpses for dissection to local medical schools, they often produced their own corpses by murdering street vagrants. Rumors also circulated about doctors involved in bodysnatching rings bent on the same financial rewards. Ruth Richardson, in *Death, Dissection and the Destitute*, tells of a legend of "a mis-delivery of a fine ham and other edibles which arrived as many other hampers had done, without an address. The body in a hamper in the same consignment never appeared" (Richardson 1987, 136). Three fresh corpses had been expected to arrive at the medical school in unmarked hampers. Speculation circulated about the whereabouts of the third corpse as only two hampers contained their promised goods. The third hamper contained the foods but no one ever claimed to have received the third corpse.

A modern variant cites National Institutes of Health as the sender, and the expected contents of the containers three fetal pigs for an advanced biology class. When the container was opened, a severed human head was discovered. Two versions have been posted on the Forteana News List (forteana@primeNet.com) on the Internet (Legends and Life 1995, 9). Apparently, the human heads were destined for a medical school dissection lab and the shipments got mixed up.

The more benign legend of "The Dead Cat in the Package" involves the theft of a package that contains a dead pet, a urine sample, or human or animal solid waste. One of the early versions circulating in 1906 and discussed in Jan Harold Brunvand's *The Vanishing Hitchhiker* (1981) tells of a package being exchanged through an honest mistake. Apparently, the man was supposed to throw his package overboard from the ferry he road each morning. The ground was frozen and the pet could not be properly buried. The man's wife wrapped the cat in a very neat package. However, the man forgot to dispose of the package and took it with him to the office, intending to do so on the ferry trip home. Once again, he became distracted and almost left the package on board. He "rushed to exit, remembered his package, ran back and grabbed the package over the seat they [he and his friends] were occupying, and got off." Unfortunately, or fortunately for the man perhaps, he forgot that when he first got on board and put the parcel on the rack, he had been sitting elsewhere in the crowded commuter ferry. The parcel he took home contained a 14-pound ham (1981, 110–11). Subsequent versions involve pickpockets, thieves, and shoplifters willfully taking these packages only to find that "crime does not pay." Morgan and Tucker comment that this 1906 version is "the only version in which the victim is innocent of any wrong doing" (1987, 121). They felt that the trickster-ending on the more recent legends developed as the legend matured (120).

Another recent innovation of "The Dead Cat in the Package" legend is its setting in a shopping mall. The majority of the versions told today involve the theft of the package from a car in the parking lot of a large shopping center. Previous renditions had the shoplifter operating in downtown department stores or on public transportation.

Structure of "The Dead Cat in the Package"

The basic structure of all the variants includes the following elements:

1. Unwanted item that must be disposed of (dead pets, garbage, etc.).

2. Problem with disposal (apartment dweller who cannot bury dead animal in garden, sanitation workers' strike, etc.), so item is packaged in some manner for transportation.

3. Theft of item from a store or vehicle.

4. In later versions, the shoplifter is punished; otherwise, punishment is implied as the listeners imagine the thief's reaction.

The following variant, noted by Paul Smith (1986, 88), demonstrates how this legend follows Labov's pattern of narrative:

Orientation: An elderly woman had been ill for some time and eventually the doctor sent her to see a specialist at the hospital and gave her strict instructions to take a [urine] specimen with her.

Complicating Action: This she did but all she could find to put it in was an empty whiskey bottle. Not wanting to spill or break the bottle, she placed it upright in the top of her shopping basket and set off to the hospital. On the way she stopped to so some shopping.

Result: However, imagine her surprise when she arrives at the clinic to find that the bottle has been stolen from her basket.

Evaluation: I'll leave the outcome to your imagination.

Functions of "The Dead Cat in the Package"

The story is usually related with relish as the teller anticipates the reaction of the audience. On a more serious level, the legend reflects our anxieties regarding the disposal of unwanted (and "unclean") items. The most common variant of the dead cat reflects a frustration with an antiseptic world that does not allow its population to properly look after the final remains of treasured pets. The recent marketing of pet cemeteries shows that this frustration is being heeded somewhat. The legend also functions as a warning to potential thieves that "all is not what it seems!"

Variants of "The Dead Cat in the Package"

Historical antecedents of the legend are discussed by Brunvand in *The Vanishing Hitchhiker* and include variants published on the front pages of newspapers along with variants told about train travel and shoplifters. Other variants exclaim the "vanishing" of items other than a dead cat:

This happened to the aunt of a friend of mine. I heard it directly from my friend whose aunt it was. She was a rather elderly woman and had a pet poodle— a toy poodle, you know, one of those little ones— and it died. She lived in New York City, and you know, there was no ready means of disposing of it, and she decided to take it to the park and bury it herself. So she put it in a shoe box and wrapped it carefully so that it would be inconspicuous and she could take it on the subway. When she got off the subway, there was a long flight of stairs up. The package was fairly heavy, and a man came along and said, "May I carry your package for you?" She was grateful and thanked him and gave him the package. With that he bounded up the steps two at a time and disappeared out of the subway. . . . I may have forgotten a few details, but I'm sure something essentially like this really happened. (Bynum 1990, 198)

Sometimes the thief is encouraged to steal the package:

> *During a garbage collector's strike in New York City, one enterpris-*
> *ing citizen got rid of his trash by putting it in a bag from a fancy*
> *store every night and leaving it on the backseat of his unlocked car.*
> *Each night the trash was stolen.* (Morgan and Tucker 1984, 118)

> *The little old lady decides to wrap the dead cat in brown paper and*
> *take it downtown, where she can leave it so that someone else can*
> *worry about burial. She first tries to leave it on the bus, but this*
> *doesn't work, for another passenger notices and runs after her to*
> *give her the package. This is repeated all day, as the woman leaves*
> *the package on the corner, in coffee shops, on another bus. Defeated,*
> *she returns home and decides to open the package and take a last*
> *look at her beloved tabby. She unties the package and finds a leg of*
> *lamb.* (Dickson and Goulden 1993, 177–78)

Other stories revolve around hospital specimens:

> *This is a true story. J— (another physician) told me about it. This*
> *lady was supposed to bring a stool specimen to the hospital. She*
> *had to ride on the bus, and she was embarrassed to take on the*
> *carton on the bus, so she wrapped it as a Christmas present. When*
> *she got on the bus, she put it on the seat beside her, and on the way*
> *to the hospital, someone stole it.* (Bynum 1990, 199)

> *A lady was going to the doctor for an examination. The doctor had*
> *asked that she bring a sample of urine. She looked around the house*
> *for a bottle to put it in. Finally she found an empty whiskey bottle,*
> *so she put the urine into it. When she got into the car she laid the*
> *bottle in the front seat. On the way to the doctor's, seeing that she*
> *had time, she stopped at the K-Mart to get some things. It was*
> *summertime; the car windows were down. After she got back to the*
> *car from her shopping, she became almost hysterical from laughter,*
> *for her bottle of so-called whiskey was gone.* (Baker 1980, 212)

A variation concerns the man who lives in the suburbs and works in the city, and who wishes to fertilize a struggling sidewalk tree near his office. On the weekend he goes to a stable and collects five or so pounds of horse manure, which he bundles into a sack so he can take it into town on Monday. Again, a snatch-and-run thief on the subway —hopefully the same sneak who is still trying to figure out what to do with that dead cat. (Dickson and Goulden 1993, 178)

And in the Media . . .

The legend of the "Dead Cat in the Package" and its variations appear often in the media. The following tales are from various tabloid newspapers. As you certainly realize by now, they are all true . . .

In Sydney, Australia, a thief surprised a 25-year-old mother changing her baby's diaper in the backseat of a car at a shopping mall. The man beat the woman and made off with the bag she had in the car with her. He ran away before he could discover that his booty was a bag full of dirty diapers. ("Left Holding the Bag— At Arm's Length," *Philadelphia Inquirer,* June 13, 1992, A3)

In Mexico, a woman was walking her dog when a boy jumped from a truck and grabbed a shopping bag the woman was carrying. Unaware that he was swiping a bag of freshly scooped dog droppings, the youth raced back to the truck, but not before the dog bit him in the leg. ("Messy Theft," *National Examiner,* March 24, 1992, 22)

In Seattle, Washington, a brazen thief reached into the window of a car at a light and stole a box from the seat as the driver watched. According to a police dispatcher, "The package contained dog doo that this good citizen had picked up." ("Doo-Gooder's Revenge," *Philadelphia Inquirer,* August 10, 1990, 3-A)

> *In the streets of the Bronx, New York City, an armed gunman accosted an elderly lady holding a brown paper bag. The woman had just finished cleaning up after her dog when the man pulled up in a car and ordered, "Give me the bag or I'll blow your head off!" She complied and the man drove off. After the woman contacted the police to report the incident, policeman Charles McGowan said, "I can see the punk now, reaching his hand into the paper bag and then jerking it out, yelling: 'It's s——!' And he would have been right!"*
> ("A Stinker of a Stickup," *National Examiner,*
> August 7, 1990, 17)

> *It's really true . . . that I was watching MTV, the music video channel, and they had a 15-second cartoon of "the dead cat in the shopping bag." This version had an elderly woman who was carting her deceased dog in a suitcase to the pet cemetery via the subway when a man pretending to help her steals the suitcase and runs off. The cartoon started with the words, "It's really true . . . "* (*The Story Bag Newsletter,* vol. 11, no 7/8 [June/July 1991]: 6)

"THE UNWITTING THIEF"

> *An elderly lady went shopping with a twenty pound note. She took a train to town and during the journey nodded off to sleep. When she woke, she found another lady in the compartment, also asleep. She took out her purse to check her shopping list, and her twenty pound note was gone. On an impulse she looked into her companion's bag and there on top— no attempt to hide it— was the note. She removed it quietly, for she had no intention of getting the old lady into trouble, and left the compartment. After her day's shopping, she was met by her husband at the station. "How did you ever manage to buy all this stuff?" he asks. "You left your twenty pound note on the mantelpiece."* (Dale 1984, 14–15)

This legend is so established that it has been assigned a motif number. Baughman states, in the *Type and Motif-Index of the Folktales of England and North America,* that the legend can be found in a March 3, 1946 newspaper story in the *Indianapolis Sunday Star* (Baughman 1966, 372). The motif number is N360(a). Items classified under N (*chance and fate*) 300–399 relate to "unlucky accidents." Motifs classified as N360 involve a man who unwittingly commits a crime. The entry for N360(a) reads:

> Woman has lunch in a restaurant with a new acquaintance met on train. She goes to rest room, returns; the new acquaintance goes to rest room. The first woman looks in her purse for a $50.00 bill, finds that it is gone. She looks in the purse of the stranger, finds the bill, takes it, leaves the restaurant. That night she finds her missing bill on the dresser where she had forgotten it that morning. (Baughman 1966, 372)

Structure of "The Unwitting Thief"

The core legend has remained the same during the various adaptations and renditions it has undergone. The most recent variant, noted by Eleanor Wachs (1988, 35), is sometimes called "The Central Park Jogger":

Orientation: A jogger is taking his usual run through the park.

Complicating Action: A fellow jogger brushes by him. Paranoid and incensed, the jogger thinks that the man has stolen his wallet. He picks up his pace, determined to catch him. He runs up to him, looks him in the eye, and yells: "Give me the wallet!" Frightened, the second jogger quickly hands over a wallet that the first man puts in his pocket. The first jogger continues his run and heads home.

Result: When he arrives there, he finds his own wallet, which he had absentmindedly left on his bureau.

Evaluation: Thinking that he was the victim of a crime, the jogger finds that he himself has committed one.

Functions of "The Unwitting Thief"

"The Unwitting Thief" involves humor and the irony of mistaken conclusions, but it is actually human frailty and suspicion that give the legend its power (Wachs 1988, 36). Buchan states that this legend "plays on the anxieties of the moral person that one might unwittingly steal" (1978, 10). The ironic nature of the tale contrasts the apparent logic of the unwitting thief with the reality of the situation.

In her *Crime-Victim Stories: New York City's Urban Folklore*, Eleanor Wachs states that "though cast as crime-victim stories by their tellers, they are adaptations of urban legends, traditional tale plots, stories about the traditional scam—the confidence game—and the shaggy dog story" (1988, 32). According to her findings, both crime-victim stories and the adapted legends serve the same function: "both address human predicaments by showing how people act in times of crisis and danger. In some cases, they reveal how little human ingenuity, character and responses to such dangers have changed over time" (1988, 32). Wachs identifies the "ideal" setting of New York City, as this city symbolizes violence and victimization. The most contemporary version, that of the jogger, was circulating at a time when running fever was particularly high, not only in New York City, but across the continent.

Wachs states that a clear difference can be seen between the early versions of this legend and the more contemporary ones. "While both falsely accuse a stranger of theft, in the Briggs version (told at the beginning of this section), the woman clearly expresses concern and remorse for her action." However, the modern jogger and the storyteller demonstrate no remorse, but certain righteous pride, about the mugging (Wachs 1988, 35).

Variants of "The Unwitting Thief"

Unlike many other contemporary legends, there is no trend to a gender-specific victim or protagonist in variants of "The Unwitting Thief."

An elderly brother and sister lived together, and one day the sister wanted to go to town to do some shopping. So her brother gave her a five-pound note, and she set out. She travelled third class, and the only other passenger was a shabby old woman who sat opposite her and nodded. Miss M— was sleepy too, after her early, hurried start, so she dozed a little too. Then she woke up and thought it wasn't very safe to go to sleep in a railway carriage, alone with a stranger. She opened her bag to make some notes of what she had to buy, and the five-pound note wasn't there. She looked at her neighbour, who was sleeping heavily with a big old shabby bag beside her. Miss M— bent forward and, very cautiously, she opened the bag. There was a new five-pound note on top of everything.

"Old scoundrel!" thought Miss M—. Then she thought, "She's poor and old, and I oughtn't to have put temptation in her way." She wondered what she ought to do. It would cause a great deal of delay and bother to call the police, and it seemed cruel to get an old woman into trouble, but she must have her money. So, in the end, she quietly took the five pounds out of the bag, and shut it up again.

At the next stop, the old woman got out, and Miss M— got to town and did her day's shopping, and came home loaded with parcels. Her brother met her at the station. "How did you manage?" he said, "I expected to find you up a gum tree. You left your five-pound note on the dressing table." (Briggs and Tongue 1965, 101–2)

Katherine Briggs heard the above anecdote from a friend in London in 1912. An even older version has been documented below.

On Wednesday afternoon a married woman, living in Masbrough, was standing in a crowd at a sale by auction in Psalterlane, Rotherham, when, putting her hand to her pocket, she missed her pocket book, containing three sovereigns and three crown pieces. A policeman was called in, and she told him that her pocket had been picked, and pointed out three young men who stood near her as being likely to be the guilty parties. The young men protested their innocence; but, with two others, they accompanied the policeman to an adjoining beer house. The landlord locked the door, and a general turning out of pockets took place. The missing purse, however, could not be found; the door was unlocked; the suspected pick pockets were set at liberty, and the lady returned to Masbrough disconsolate. When she got home she found her pocket-book on the chest of drawers. (Early version of "The Five-Pound Note" 1989, 3)

And of course the purloined gold may be in another form.

Peter was down in London on a business trip and, after being out for dinner one evening, he decided to travel back to his hotel on the last tube. He was just settling into his seat when he realized that his gold watch was missing. On the platform stood a young man who was grinning at him and, jumping to the conclusion that this was the thief, Peter leapt up and tried to get off the tube before the doors closed. Unfortunately, he did not quite make it. Nevertheless, he managed to grab hold of the man's lapels only to rip them clean off his suit as the tube moved away. When he got back to his hotel the first thing he did was phone the police and report the theft. Then he phoned his wife to tell her of the loss. Before he could say anything she said, "Oh! I'm so glad you rang, I've been trying to get hold of you. Did you know that you left your watch behind on the dresser this morning?" (Smith 1986, 24)

An infrequent ending to the following version is supplied by folklorist Linda Degh, who was told the "true" tale by her Uncle Peter in Hungary in the early 1950s. After discovering his mistake, the man went to the police to report his error, and arrived just as the real owner of the watch, who had recognized the thief, was filing suit against him:

> *Once, when he [Uncle Peter] came off the ferry boat and made his way through the crowd he felt someone's hand in his pocket, taking his gold watch. Grabbing the hand of a man he yelled, "Give me the watch!" The man immediately obeyed. After awhile, feeling his pocket, Uncle Peter found two gold watches therein.*
> (Brunvand 1984, 189–90)

New York City is always a great setting for theft!

> *This is supposed to be a true story. A man, we'll call him Mr. Jones, is riding to work on the subway in New York City and there's a guy who keeps bumping into him. After a while Jones gets apprehensive and thinks, "This can't be what I think it is!" He checks his wallet—and it is gone. "That's it! Nine o'clock in the morning and I get mugged in the subway. Things are getting really bad." He grabs the guy, shakes him hard, and says, "All right, cough up, give me that wallet." The guy is petrified and he hands over a wallet. So Jones goes off to work and when he gets to the office his wife calls and says, "Honey, you left your wallet on the bureau this morning." (Brunvand 1989, 189)*

Canadians have similar adventures.

> *A Canadian visitor to New York City was warned about people "accidently" bumping into him—they might well be pickpockets. So when somebody did bump into him on the sidewalk he immediately felt his pocket where he usually carried his wallet. It wasn't there. "Stop, thief!" he shouted, giving chase. "Give me back my wallet." He caught up with the bumper who threw him the wallet and made off. Feeling both clever and relieved at having retrieved his stolen goods, he returned to the hotel and ordered himself a drink. It was then that he discovered that he had two wallets.*
> (Dale 1984, 15)

And woe to the unsuspecting hitchhiker.

> *Then there is the hitchhiker who asks the driver the time; subsequently the driver, realizing that his watch is gone, pulls a revolver and says: "Give me that watch and chain!" The hitchhiker submits, is put out, and flees. When the driver gets home he finds his own watch; he has robbed a stranger. (Clough 1947, 692)*

"RELATED" THEFTS

The remaining contemporary legends involving theft are also prevalent in both the oral tradition and in the media.

"The Disappearing Room"

A girl staying in a hotel with her mother finds that not only she but also her room has disappeared. The hotel staff claim no knowledge of her; later it becomes clear that they are concealing the fact that she has been struck down with a serious illness, because of the harm it might do to trade. (Hobbs 1978, 82)

This legend has been extremely popular in the literary and dramatic arts; Smith and Hobbs collected several visual retellings and cameo appearances. They refer to the legend as "The Vanishing Lady" and select this tale to demonstrate "that film reviewers and critics frequently identify links between films, and also to associated literature" (1992, 3). In an earlier article, Hobbs identifies the function of this tale as "dealing with feelings of uneasiness in strange places such as a foreign hotel" (1978, 83).

"The Double Theft"

A middle aged lady from the suburbs goes into the city one Saturday in December to do her Christmas shopping. She visits a department store and, while there, she finds that she needs to visit the toilets. Instead of hanging it on the hook, she puts her handbag down on the floor. Without any warning, a hand shoots under the door and steals the handbag. Of course, by the time she had adjusted her clothing there is no sign of anyone, the thief having disappeared into the crowd.

She reports the theft and is interviewed by the store detective and the police. Her concern is not particularly with the small amount of money the bag contained but rather the fact that her driving licence, address book and keys were also in there. The police were very sympathetic and informed her they would look into the matter, and she eventually makes her way home.

> *When she arrives the phone is ringing; it is someone from the store to say that they have found her handbag with the contents intact and could she come and collect it. She immediately returns to the shop, but finds that the store detective knows nothing of the telephone call and certainly does not have the bag.*
>
> *Rather confused she returns home yet again only to find that in her absence the person who had stolen her handbag had visited her home and stripped it of all valuables.* (Smith 1986, 56–57)

Paul Smith states that "The Double Theft" legend has been circulating throughout the English-speaking world for more than 30 years and is usually associated with the largest store in town (1986, 57). In England, the store is usually Harrods, but a quick glance at the bathroom facilities would show that it could not take place on those respectable premises. "Mrs. Newall informs me that nothing of the sort can really have happened at Harrods, where the lavatory walls are solid; she suggests that [the legend] may have originated in America, where gaps at the base of such walls are common" (Simpson 1972, 339). David Buchan believes that the setting "emphasizes the thief's cleverness by reducing the possible sympathy for the victim, since, it would be felt, Harrod customers are well able to stand such losses" (1978, 6).

Two noteworthy elements within this tale have contributed to its long success as a legend. The listener and teller have an appreciation of the thief's trickery, cunning, and cleverness; they also have a vicarious enjoyment that comes from identifying with the "underdog" and enjoying the harm suffered by this upper-class store's reputation and patrons (Buchan 1978, 6).

An interesting variant of this legend follows:

> *I have heard this story from my father, who picked it up at the police station in Deurne-Zuid. It was about an older woman who went shopping in Antwerp and made use of the public toilets. She had put her handbag on the floor, and it was grabbed from under the door. Ultimately she went back home, where she received a telephone call from a man who pretended that his wife was a kleptomaniac. He said that he would return the handbag to her. An appointment was made in a pub for the stolen property to be restored to the owner. However, the man failed to show up, and when she returned back home, she found her home robbed empty.*
> (Top 1990, 275)

And in the Media . . .

A double dose of bad news awaited a city woman Thursday when she was robbed of her purse, then went home to discover her apartment had also been looted. Police believe the same man committed both crimes, police spokesman Kelly Gordon said. The 43-year-old victim was coming out of the Grandin LRT station at 8:05 a.m. when a man carrying a knife asked her for the time, Gordon said. The man didn't directly threaten the victim with the knife but demanded her purse, which she turned over. He fled and police were unable to pick up his trail. In the purse was the woman's identification and the key to her apartment, Gordon said. Police told her to call the building caretaker to advise him of the robbery, but she chose not to, Gordon said. When she got home her apartment had been entered and a small amount of cash and some cigarettes taken. ("Woman Is Robbed Twice in a Day," *The Edmonton Journal*, December 7, 1991, B2)

"Free Tickets"

A Surrey couple had their car stolen from their front drive. Four days later it reappeared—with two theatre tickets on the front seat and a note which read: "Sorry. We had to take your car in an emergency. Please accept the tickets with our apologies." A few days later they used the tickets and returned to find their home stripped, even to the curtains. (Dale 1984, 14)

A close relative of "The Double Theft," this legend offers only prestigious tickets. The type of tickets (ballet, symphony, sold-out rock concerts, and sports events) vary from telling to telling, depending upon the recreational and cultural interests of the teller and audience. A variant from Norway has been embellished with great detail.

A married couple were returning home from Spain or some other country in the south. I guess they had been away for quite a while. They were glad to be back in Norway. They drove their heavily loaded car through Oslo to their villa, somewhere in Holmenkollen or in some other fashionable place a little way beyond the city. They unloaded their bags and blankets and soon had taken possession of the old homestead once again. They tried the red wine they had smuggled across the boarder, and I imagine that the wife fried some eggs Norwegian-style and unwrapped the goat cheese she had bought on the way home. The husband happened to be looking out the window, when suddenly he gasped. Their car was gone!

He rushed into the street and asked children and neighbours whether anyone had seen the thieves. No one could help him, and he raced back into the house, cursing this miserable country of thieves and crooks. He called the police, and they said they were sorry, very sorry. If they got the chance, they would happily arrest the crooks.

But the next morning, the man gasped once more. While he was sitting at the breakfast table, he looked out the window and saw that the car had been returned! The couple rushed outside and unlocked their beloved car. The thieves had left a note on the steering wheel. And there they read these lines:

"We are terribly sorry that we stole your car. Can you forgive us! We filled up the gas tank. And we enclose two tickets to the Chat Noir [The Chat Noir is a popular music hall and vaudeville theater in Oslo] *for tonight. Please use them! Then we'll know that you are not angry any more."*

The couple was very moved. There were still sweet and honest people in this country after all! And those theatre tickets, what a great idea! They decided to celebrate by dressing up in tux and evening dress. A half hour before showtime, they drove off and three hours later, they returned and found their house stripped. Everything had been taken from the villa. The neighbours had seen the moving van to be sure, but they had assumed that the "foreigners" had decided to leave the place for good! (Kvideland and Sehmsdorf 1988, 391–92)

"Kit Kat"

A traveler buys a cup of tea and a packet of biscuits at a station buffet in Liverpool Street station. The traveler sits down at the same table as a West Indian man. The traveler drinks the tea and begins to eat the biscuits. The man opposite helps himself to one. Somewhat shaken at this effrontery, the traveler takes another biscuit. The uninvited companion does the same and these actions continue until only the last biscuit is left, which the man opposite breaks in two so it may be shared. The angry traveler screams abuse at the man in unforgivable terms. The other man remains stoically silent. Suddenly, each realizes that the traveler's own packet of biscuits lies, still unopened, on his suitcase by his side. (Smith 1975, 139)

The Kit Kat chocolate bar has undergone metamorphoses from a cookie (biscuit) to an easily divisible chocolate bar and back into a cookie in a *Washington Times* column of January 26, 1990. In this variant, Air Force second lieutenant Mitchell W. Clapp inadvertently shared a package of Oreo cookies with a Marine Corps brigadier general, only to discover later that the general was the generous soul (Dickson and Goulden 1993, 188).

Two films, Adam Davidson's Oscar-winning *The Lunch Date* and an independent Dutch film *Boeuf Bourgignon*, were involved in a plagiarism claim. Both present an identical plot:

> A well-dressed white woman buys a tray of food in a cafeteria, leaves it on a table, then leaves to get silverware. When she returns, a shabby black man is eating her lunch. The two stare at each other, both picking at the same meal, until the man gets up and returns with two cups of coffee. After he leaves, the woman finds that she has stolen the black man's meal; her own meal lies on a nearby table.

When notified of the plagiarism charge, Davidson said that he did not know of the earlier Dutch film and had based his film on an "urban folk tale" he had heard as an undergraduate in 1985. Several members of the Academy committee also recalled hearing similar legends and decided to take no action on the plagiarism claim. "When [the] film was screened on Japanese TV, it was shown alongside a Japanese film with a similar plot" (The Lunch Date: CL or Plagiarism? 1992, 11).

Another variant of this tale was told in a sermon on the perils of greed:

A woman went to a mall and bought a box of cookies. She sat down at a table in an eating area, opened her box of cookies, and began reading the paper. She looked up suddenly to find a scruffy-looking man, whom she assumed was a bum, was taking cookies from her box. Although the woman was furious, she said nothing, and the exchange continued until there was only one cookie left. She made a grab for it, but the man got to it first, calmly broke it in two, gave half to the lady, and left. Feeling this was too much to endure, the woman got up to follow, picked up her paper—and found under it her own box of cookies.

The pastor concluded, "She knew the price of cookies, but the man knew its value." (The Lunch Date 1992, 11)

In a recent excursion into the books of Art Linkletter, Bill Ellis discovers three cousins of "The Kit Kat" legend:

> *A lady in a restaurant sees that the man at the next table has left a chop on his plate and takes it for her dogs; the waitress tells her he had just stepped away for a phone call.* (Ellis and Mays 1994, 7)

> *A lady follows her husband into a movie theater and begins eating from his bag of popcorn; when she hears a meek voice ask, "Save some for me, will you lady?" she realizes she is in the wrong seat.* (Ellis and Mays 1994, 7)

> *As part of a prank, a* People Are Funny *staffer goes to a restaurant and, on a pretext, samples food off diners' plates; despite obvious uneasiness, nobody protests.* (Ellis and Mays 1994, 7)

"Missing Lottery Ticket"

> *A Russian trade union paper reported that an Alexandra Sergeyevana had her dead husband's coffin exhumed; in the pocket of his best suit was a winning lottery ticket good for a new car. When the grave was opened, the coffin was gone, stolen by unscrupulous undertakers who stripped and reused the casket. The prize car was claimed by a man who said that he had found the winning ticket in a suit he had purchased in a thrift shop. Alexandra eventually was given the car, but sold it to give the proceeds to Chernobyl disaster victims.* (Criminal Wrong Doo-ings 1992, 11)

"The Stolen Police Car"

> *A friend of a friend of mine who drives a large white car arrived home after a night on the town, locked the car in the garage and just as he was about to go to bed there was a knock at the door. To his surprise there were two policeman standing there. "Excuse me, sir, do you drive a white car?" "Yes." "Can we see it?" When the garage was opened, there was a white police car. Automobiles were duly swapped and the police drove happily into the night. Now this friend of mine in Aberdeen is positive that it happened there but the Aberdeen City police deny all knowledge and the county spokesman claimed it was a jolly good story but wasn't true.* (Hobbs 1978, 76)

"Stuck with the Bill"

*A business man picked up a hitchhiker and after stopping at a
rather expensive roadside restaurant offered to buy him dinner.
After they finished, the driver said, "You go ahead and enjoy
another cup of coffee, I'm going to have the tank filled with gas so
we won't have to stop again. You wave back when I get to the
cashier's so that he'll know that you're with me." The hitchhiker
waved as directed, finished his coffee, fretted when the driver didn't
return in fifteen minutes or so, and finally decided he'd go on outside. The cashier stopped him at the door. "Hey," he said, "you
haven't paid the bill." The hitchhiker told him that the other man
was going to pay. "That's not what he told me," the cashier said.
"He said you would take care of the check, and that you would wave
to me to confirm it." Sure enough, the driver and his car were gone
when the cashier and the hitchhiker went outside. The restaurant
owner eventually accepted the hitchhiker's story but only after a
long wrangle.* (Dickson and Goulden 1993, 175)

The location of the scam has shifted in some versions to the grocery
store, where an elderly woman strikes up a conversation with the young man
in the checkout line. She tells him that he is the image of her dead son and it
would make her feel better if he would call her "Mom." Feeling rather
foolish, the young man calls out, "Bye, Mom" as the woman leaves the store.
He feels even more foolish when the cashier explains that "Mom" has left her
"son" to pay for her groceries. Dickson and Goulden suggest, along with
Brunvand, that the shift in setting is due to the vanishing of hitchhiking as a
regular mode of transportation (Dickson and Goulden 1993, 175).

"The Turkey in the Hat"

*One day a woman went to Ahlen's grocery store to shop. After
walking around the store for awhile, she stopped by one of the deep
freezers and took out a frozen turkey and stuffed it in her hat
without anyone noticing. It was a big, broad-brimmed hat. Then
she put it back on and continued to shop as if nothing had
happened. But there was a line for the cashier, and she had to wait.
While she was standing there, she suddenly passed out. Her hat fell
off, and the turkey rolled out onto the floor. The cold turkey had
been too much for her, and therefore she lost consciousness.*
(Kvideland and Sehmsdorf 1988, 391)

A variant of this legend also appears in Art Linkletter's *Oops! or Life's Awful Moments* (1967):

> *A woman tries to smuggle a watch through customs in her brassiere; agents announce that one of them is carrying drugs, so all passengers will be searched; the dope dealer is found directly in front of the woman in line, but she has perspired so much that the watch is ruined.* (Ellis and Mays 1994, 7)

LITERARY AND VISUAL ADAPTATIONS

"The Dead Cat in the Package"

"The Cat in the Bloomies Bag" by Daniel Cohen. From *Southern Fried Rat & Other Gruesome Tales*. New York: M. Evans, 1983.

"The Cat in the Shopping Bag" by Alvin Schwartz. From *More Scary Stories to Tell in the Dark*. New York: Harper & Row, 1984.

"Who Let the Cat Out of the Bag in Austin, Texas" by Diane Rutt. From *The Folktale Cat* retold by Frank de Caro. Little Rock: August House, 1993.

"The Disappearing Room"

Bunny Lake Is Missing (1957) by Evelyn Piper. London: Secker and Warburg. This is not a retelling of the legend but makes explicit reference to it in the text. Wilson, a writer, points out the analogy between the legend and the circumstances facing Bunny's mother. The motivation for the disappearance is different from that of the other films and the contemporary legend. (Smith and Hobbs 1992, 5)

So Long at the Fair (1950). Based on the novel of the same name by Anthony Thorne (1947), this movie has the identical setting as the German film *Verwehte Spuren*. Smith and Hobbs state that is difficult to know whether Thorne was directly influenced by the film or whether this is another interpretation of the legend (1992, 4). They surmise that Thorne may also have been influenced by earlier writers who have used this legend.

The Torrent of Spring by Ernest Hemingway. New York: Charles Scribner's Sons, 1926. Reprinted in 1972. Hemingway provides the answer to the character's mysterious vanishing room introduced in chapter 5 in his "Final Note to the Reader."

"The Vanishing of Mrs. Fraser" by Sir Basil Thompson. From *Mr. Pepper Investigator*. London: J. Castle, 1925. Reprinted in Dorothy L. Sayers, ed. *The Second Omnibus of Crime*. New York: Coward-McCann, 1932.

Verwehte Spuren [Like Sand in the Wind] (1938). This German film, set at the
Paris Exposition of 1868, closely follows the legend plot.

While Rome Burns by Alexander Woollcott. New York: Viking, 1934.

"The Runaway Grandmother"

Another Roadside Attraction by Tom Robbins. New York: Doubleday and
Company, 1971; Ballantine Books, paperback edition, 1972. Amanda is
reminded of a story after hearing the problems of Captain Kendrick's
Memorial Hot Dog Wildlife Preserve. In Part IV of the novel, the story
she tells, of course, is "The Runaway Grandmother."

National Lampoon's Vacation (1983). In this film, Aunt Edna, as a corpse, arrives
at the destination of her "loving" family, but is left in the rain on the
patio when Cousin Normie is not there to greet them.

The Pianoplayers by Anthony Burgess. New York: Arbor House, 1986. Near
the end of the novel, Hellen, the narrator, tells the adventure of her son
and daughter-in-law's fateful trip through Italy. Her son's mother-in-
law, who is traveling with them, dies in the car, is wrapped in a raincoat
and the corpse is hit by crossfire from a police car. "Though not stolen,"
as in the standard legend, this mother-in-law seems otherwise to qualify
as a literary version of "The Runaway Grandmother." (Barnes 1991, 181)

REFERENCES

Baker, Ronald L. 1980. *Hoosier folk legends.* Bloomington: Indiana University Press.

Barnes, Daniel R. 1991. The contemporary legend in literature: Towards an annotated
checklist. *Contemporary Legend* 1: 173–84.

Baughman, Ernest W. 1966. *Type and motif-index of the folktales of England and North
America* (Indiana University Folklore series, no. 20). The Hague: Mouton.

Briggs, Katherine M., and Ruth L. Tongue. 1965. *Folktales of England.* Chicago: University of Chicago Press.

Brunvand, Jan Harold. 1981. *The vanishing hitchhiker: American urban legends & their
meanings.* New York: W. W. Norton.

———.1984. *The choking doberman and other "new" urban legends.* New York: W. W.
Norton.

———.1989. *Curses! Broiled again! The hottest urban legends going.* New York: W. W.
Norton.

Buchan, David. 1978. The modern legend. In *Language, culture and tradition: Papers on
language and folklore presented at the annual conference of the British Sociological
Association,* edited by A. E. Green and J. D. A. Widdowson. The Centre for
English Tradition and Language, University of Sheffield, 1–15.

Bynum, Joyce. 1990. Modern urban legends of stolen debris. *Etc.* 47 (summer): 198–200.

Clough, Ben C. 1947. *The American imagination at work: Tall tales and folk tales.* New York: Alfred A. Knopf.

Criminal wrong doo-ings. 1992. *FOAFTALE NEWS* 27 (September): 10–11.

Dale, Rodney. 1984. *It's true, it happened to a friend: A collection of urban legends.* London: Duckworth.

Degh, Linda. 1968. The runaway grandmother. *Indiana Folklore* 1, no. 1: 68–77.

Dickson, Paul, and Joseph C. Goulden. 1993. *Myth-informed: Legends, credos, and wrongheaded "facts" we all believe.* New York: Perigee.

Dundes, Alan. 1971. On the psychology of the legend. In *American folk legend: A symposium,* edited by Wayland D. Hand. Berkeley: University of California Press, 21–36.

Early version of "the five-pound note." 1989. *FOAFTALE NEWS* 12 (February): 3.

Ellis, Bill, and Alan E. Mays. 1994. Art Linkletter and the contemporary legend. *FOAFTALE NEWS* 33/34 (June): 1–8.

Hobbs, Sandy. 1978. The folk tale as news. *Oral History* 6, no. 11: 74–86.

Kapferer, Jean-Noel. 1990. *Rumors: Uses, interpretations, and images.* New Brunswick, NJ: Transaction.

Kvideland, Reimund, and Henning K. Sehmsdorf, eds. 1988. *Scandinavian folk belief and legend.* Minneapolis: University of Minnesota Press.

Legends and life. 1995. *FOAFTALE NEWS* 37 (June): 9.

The lunch date. 1992. *FOAFTALE NEWS* 27 (September): 11.

The lunch date: CL or plagiarism? 1992. *FOAFTALE NEWS* 25 (March): 11.

McConnell, Brian. 1982/83. Urban legends in Fleet Street. *Folklore* 93–94: 226–28.

Morgan, Hal, and Kerry Tucker. 1984. *Rumors!* New York: Penguin.

———. 1987. *More Rumors!* New York: Penguin.

Richardson, Ruth. 1987. Death, dissection and the destitute. London: Routledge Kegan Paul. Quoted in Criminal wrong doo-ings. 1992. *FOAFTALE NEWS* 27 (September): 11.

Sanderson, Stewart F. 1981. *The modern urban legend.* (The Katharine Briggs Lecture No. 1) London: Folklore Society.

Simpson, Jacqueline. 1972. Another modern legend. *Folklore* 83: 339.

Smith, A. W. 1975. Yet another modern legend. *Folklore* 86: 139.

Smith, Paul. 1986. *The book of nastier legends.* London: Routledge Kegan Paul.

Smith, Paul, and Sandy Hobbs. 1990. Films using contemporary legend themes/motifs. In *Contemporary legend: The first five years: Abstracts and bibliographies from the Sheffield conferences on contemporary legend, 1982–1986,* compiled by Gillian Bennett and Paul Smith. Sheffield, England: Sheffield Academic Press, 138–48.

———. 1992. Contemporary legend on film: The vanishing lady. *FOAFTALE NEWS* 26 (June): 3–6.

Top, Stefaan. 1990. Modern legends in the Belgian oral tradition. *Fabula* 31: 272–78.

Wachs, Eleanor. 1988. *Crime-victim stories: New York City's urban folklore.* Bloomington: Indiana University Press.

9 SPIDERS, SNAKES, AND ANIMAL TALES

A girl managed to wrap her hair into a perfect beehive. Proud of her accomplishment, she kept spraying it and spraying it, never bothering to wash it again. Bugs began to live in her hair. After about six months, they ate through her brain and killed her.

Although the majority of people in Western society live in urban centers, the natural world still plays a prominent role in our lives and, therefore, in our contemporary legends. Tales about snakes, spiders and other insects, and alligators, as well as stories about familiar household pets and wild animals reveal our unease with the natural world as we perceive it. These contemporary legends illustrate more than unease with the natural world however. An examination of traditional victims in these stories, for example, demonstrates that much of Western society still retains sexist attitudes towards females. If this was not the case, the victims would have changed over time to include men as well as women and children. Other attitudes also surface and are transmitted through the retellings. The perpetrator, animal or human, is often cited to be from a third-world country or a minority group reflecting homophobic and racist fears. By considering the traditional symbolic meaning of insects, reptiles, and animals and the roles these creatures play in our legends today, we can chart Western society's attitudes and values towards people as well as nature.

SPIDERS

After conducting a workshop on spiders in contemporary legends with seventh-graders, I received a telephone call from the principal of the school. A parent had complained. Her child was terrified of spiders and was now having nightmares. Arachnophobia is not uncommon, which is why we often hear (and tell) stories about spiders invading the human body through the hair, cheeks, and ears; arriving stealthily in household plants and cacti; and being ingested with our food and bubble gum! Although these legends reflect modern life and anxieties, they are not new—spiders have been the focus of fears and stories throughout the centuries.

The symbolic interpretation of spiders has varied in different times and in different cultures:

> The frightful, cunning and dangerous spiders in these well-known children's verses ["Little Miss Muffet" and "The Spider and the Fly"] stand in marked contrast to the helpful holy figures who in Zuni and Navajo mythology are said to have taught both children and adults how to manipulate diverting and instructive string figure "webs." (Weigle 1982, 3)

According to the *Oxford English Dictionary*, "the cunning, skill, and industry of the spider, as well as its power of secreting or emitting poison, are frequently alluded to in literature [and classical mythology]" (Weigle 1982, 7). Classical myths that directly involve the spider and weaving or spinning include: the Moirai or Fates, the three goddesses who spin the thread of life, weave it in with the lives of others, and cut the thread when the person's life is to end; Ariadne, who gave Theseus a ball of thread to find his way out of the Minotaur's maze; and Arachne, who challenged the goddess Athena to a weaving contest. Athena wove into her tapestry the stories of those who had aroused the anger of the gods, while Arachne chose to represent stories of the errors of the gods. Enraged at the excellence of her work, Athena tore Arachne's web to tatters. Arachne hung herself in grief and was transformed by Athena into a spider. The scientific name for spiders, arachnids, comes from this myth. The myth is told in detail in Ovid's *Metamorphoses* and by the English poet Edmund Spenser in *Muiopotmos*.

Spiders play a large role in the mythology of other cultures as well. In Egyptian mythology, the spider is an attribute of the goddess Neith, the weaver of the world. Norse god Odin's horse Sleipnir (Slippery) was grey and had eight legs, like a spider; it also represented Odin's "Fate" and was associated with the gallows on which he was hanged.

In Christianity, spiders have been considered "evil," representing the "sinful urges that suck the blood from humanity" (Beidermann 1992, 316). But in some alpine regions of central Europe, the garden spider, because of the markings of a cross on its back, is considered a good-luck symbol and a sacred creature that must not be killed (316). In ancient China, a spider was also an omen of impending good fortune, but in Western culture, killing a spider, especially a "daddy-long-legs," will bring rain.

The culture hero of Spider, Spider Man, and Spider Woman represent a powerful, nearly always beneficent character in the myths of many Plains,

Southwestern, and Western American Indian tribes. Unktomi (the Sioux name for the Spider Man; other variants are Iktomi, Ikto, Ictinike, and Ictcinike) is identifiable as a spider and, although there is some belief that he is a culture hero and creator, the tales told about him are typical trickster tales, ridiculous and often obscene (Leach 1972, 1151).

Probably the most widely recognized spider hero is Anansi, the Spider, who is the culture hero and trickster of West African tales. Anansi is known by various names: Kwaku Ananse, Nansi, Miss Nancy, Aunt Nancy, and 'Ti Malice. In all Anansi tales, his dominant role is that of the crafty and cunning trickster who prospers by his wits. Several Anansi stories are more commonly known to North Americans as Brer Rabbit tales, which were originally retold in the southern United States after the advent of slavery.

Psychoanalysts interpret "the spider as a basically malevolent symbol when it appears in myths, tales, dreams, beliefs, and behaviours" (Weigle 1982, 22). When the poem by Mary Howeill (1829) invites: " 'Come into my parlour,' said the spider to the fly," the listener knows that the spider is a treacherous creature that can never be trusted. However, early settlers discovered many beneficial attributes of this common "pest": spider webs are efficacious for stopping bleeding, a crucial ability that everyone, not just healing specialists, needed to know during the early periods of settlement in North America. Native populations were aware of the beneficial properties of the webs, and historian Virgil J. Vogel reports that spider webs were used to stop bleeding by "such widely scattered groups as the Mohegans, Kwakiutls, Mescalero Apaches and white settlers from Tennessee to Oregon" (Weigle 1982, 17).

In French Canada, as elsewhere in the Catholic New World, priests serving parishes without doctors also acted as physicians, often to good effect, as in the case of "Father Pierre-Joseph Compain (1740–1806) [who] wrote down for the nuns of the Hotel-Dieu of Quebec in 1799 his cure for cancer and a remedy for cankers in which spider webs played an important role" (Weigle 1982, 17).

Spiders were considered helpful in the Old World as well. For common contagion, people in England were advised to carry a spider in a silk bag around the neck or in a nut shell in a pocket, and for ague, the folk beliefs said, a spider should be tied up and bound on the left arm. (Ague is a malarial fever, with cold, hot, and sweating stages; a shivering fit.) Other folk cures included rolling live spiders in butter and then swallowing them. One popular folk cure for asthma was to swallow a handful of spider webs rolled into a ball. "This is not as far-fetched as it may sound; in 1882 a substance called *arachnidin* was isolated from spider webs which proved to be a remarkable febrifuge (medicine to reduce fever, cooling drink)" (Leach 1972, 698).

Contemporary legends involving spiders essentially ignore the helpful aspects of spiders and concentrate exclusively on our phobias. The legends also point to a difference between the Western "civilized" world and the third-world countries where poisonous spiders and snakes can be easily found, reflecting our fears of mysterious, alien countries. "[Spiders] are smuggled into our everyday world hidden in bananas and potted plants, undermining our security" (Klintberg 1985, 286).

The primary victims (and players) in spider legends are female. These tales express a "typical" feminine aversion to spiders and other creeping and crawling insects. Klintberg states that in Western civilization, our society allows [and perhaps, promotes] such "female" behavior while contacts with such creatures elsewhere are everyday occurrences and gain no reaction (Klintberg 1985, 287). Because contact with poisonous spiders and snakes is so rare in our urban communities, "they have come to assume mythical proportions in our narrative tradition" (287).

Young adults concentrate on legends that involve revulsion and have a good scare factor. Although they usually laugh at the idea of anyone wearing their hair in such a fashion ("Madge Simpson, heh"), the legend of "Spiders in the Hairdo" starts them talking not only about the dictates of fashion, but also about fears of spiders and other "creepy crawlies." However, everyone knows someone who went on a holiday and woke up with a bite. . . . She might even be related to the woman they all know who purchased a new cactus!

"Spiders in the Hairdo"

Esquire Magazine published the legend of the "Spiders in the Hairdo," told at the beginning of this chapter, in 1976 as an example of folklore from the 1950s for the benefit of today's generation of teenagers. The story of the "Fatal Hairdo," as it is often labeled, is tied to the fashion industry. When the beehive hairdo became passé, the story dropped out of sight for decades, only to be revived again in the 1990s. I recently heard, from a colleague in Edmonton, about an elderly woman who had been living on her own quite satisfactorily.

However, the last time they went to check on her, they realized that she no longer could live on her own . . . it seems that she stopped taking care of the house, and herself. When she was found she had not washed her hair for a very long time and a spider had built a nest in her hair. Thank goodness that the eggs had not time to hatch.

Structure of "Spiders in the Hairdo"

Orientation: The main character (in the original group of legends) is inevitably a high school student whose hair is arranged in a beehive style and sprayed to stay.

Complicating Action: She becomes mysteriously ill in school one day. "Usually the illness involves fainting, sometimes the teacher or another student sees blood running down the girl's neck" (Marchalenis 1976/77, 173).

Result: She is rushed to the hospital where she dies. Her death is discovered to be from spiders (or other insects) that have built a nest in her hair. She either has been poisoned by their bites or they eat through her skull and into her brain.

Antecedents to "Spiders in the Hairdo"

An early analogue to this tale was discovered in the late-13th-century collection of English exempla, *Speculum Laicorum*:

> There is a sermon story of a certain lady of Eynesham, in Oxford-shire, who "took so long over the adornment of her hair that she used to arrive at church barely before the end of Mass." One day "the devil descended upon her head in the form of a spider, gripping with its legs," until she well-nigh died of fright. Nothing would remove the offending insect, neither prayer, nor exorcism, nor holy water, until the local abbot displayed the holy sacrament before it.
> (Marchalenis 1976/77, 174)

A second early example was found in Robert of Brunne's *Handlyng Synne* (1308):

> A lady who was proud of her appearance and especially of her elaborate hair arrangements and headdresses died, and after her death she appeared to her husband's faithful squire.
> (Marchalenis 1976/77, 174)

The exempla warns against pride and vanity. The cause of the woman's death and spiders are not specifically named; however, like the later tales, her death centers around her fashionable hairdo! Marchalenis attributes the justice of the punishment for her pride in her hairdressing to the medieval audience's understanding of the sin of pride: the First of the Deadly Sins (1976/77, 174). The modern versions still serve the same didactic function, although the focus has changed from godliness to cleanliness. The women in both centuries offend contemporary standards and are punished for their offense. The story, therefore, serves as both a warning and an example (Marchalenis 1976/77, 174). The most recent rendition of the legend is not so condemning. The elderly woman is not entirely to blame for her predicament and therefore does not have a fatal experience, merely an uncomfortable one which could have been avoided if her care givers had been a little more efficient. For this legend to be plausible, of course, the victim must have enough hair for the insect to be "comfortable." Traditionally, perhaps, this is why victims were always female. But even in the time when a large male population sported long hair, spiders never seemed attracted to them, at least not in any of the variants that I have heard. Perhaps it is the hairspray.

Variants

Kenneth Clarke (1964, 250) documents variants of the legend circulating in the 1950s and 1960s, which include the following elements:

Type of Insect: ants, spiders, cockroaches.

Identity of Victim: high school girl, college girl, secretary.

Mode of Introduction of Insect: introduced by beauty shop comb infested with eggs, attracted by dirt.

Type of Injury: poison from spider bite, blood poisoning from ant bites, infection and sores caused by cockroach bites, cockroaches chewing through skull.

Final Outcome: died at once, died in hospital, infestation treated and girl returned home, hair shaved off for treatment.

"Spider Bites"

Toward the end of a holiday in Spain, a girl received a rather nasty bite on her neck. She had planned to ask her doctor if it was serious, but when she returned home it began to heal quite nicely. A week or so later, she was drowsily sunbathing in her garden when the scab began to itch. Absentmindedly, she scratched it, the scab fell off, and a newly hatched family of baby spiders ran down her neck.
(Dale 1984, 68)

"Spider Bites" has been classified as a woman's story, told by women to women, because it reflects their prevalent disgust and revulsion towards insects. This particular revulsion is due in part to the fact that women, rather than men, are indoctrinated to worry about their looks. The legend about the spider bite "not only expresses a general anxiety about dangerous tropical parasites but a specific feminine fear of little crawling creeping things as well as of losing one's beauty" (Klintberg 1985, 281). Skin infestations from insects and larvae are not an unknown phenomena, and fantastic versions of these "experiences" are widely circulated in oral tradition and in the mass media. The location of the bite on the cheek is also of traditional significance, as the cheek represents, in classical literature, youthful, feminine beauty. Perhaps the story would not be as plausible if the bite appeared on a man's cheek—how could he shave every day.

Structure of "Spider Bites"

This legend is guaranteed to get a reaction and is always told for effect. Details are sometimes given about the actual location of the holiday spot, but often all that is said is that the victim is on holiday in a warm "foreign" country with wonderful beaches.

Orientation: A woman goes to an exotic place for a holiday. She is so relaxed that she can spend hours on the beach sleeping.

Complicating Action: While she is sleeping, an insect bites her on her cheek. It is a small bite and hardly noticeable. She ignores it. Upon her return to the "real" world, the bite becomes more noticeable and the woman goes to a doctor to see what can be done. He tells her that he does not know exactly what it is and that they should keep it under observation for awhile. The bite becomes more and more painful and aggravating.

Result: The woman rips open the scab on the bite (either while she is in the shower or washing her face) and countless newly hatched spiders swarm out.

In the variants I have heard, the storyteller doesn't go any further. It isn't necessary; the audience automatically screams and squirms in revulsion.

Antecedents to "Spider Bites"

The legend has many parallels in traditional folklore. Pre-industrial society had a variety of legends about animals penetrating into the human body—from serpents biting the bosom to earwigs entering the brain (Klintberg 1985, 286).

A possible antecedent is the gothic short story by Jeremias Gotthelf, *Die Schwarze Spinne*, published in 1842. In the medieval community of the story, the villagers make a pact with the Devil, sealed by his kiss on a woman's cheek. When the Devil is cheated by the villagers, a black boil begins to grow on the woman's cheek. The boil continues to grow until it eventually bursts and poisonous spiders crawl out of it. Although the story is not the same, the black boil and spider sound very familiar. However, the short story probably owes more to a legend from Switzerland than anything else:

The little man came behind him and, smiling as if there was nothing to worry about, said the mother was going to get a kiss anyway, so he kissed her on the cheek. Soon the woman in childbed had a badly swollen cheek with a black blister on it. She suffered very much and finally she died. But a frightening black spider came out of the blister and crawled onto someone else. This person got the same blister and died soon afterward. And it went on like this, without missing a house. (Lindahl 1986, 2)

Spiders are not the only threat; earwigs, too, have also caused fatalities in these stories. Samuel Simpson Adams told this version on September 9, 1940:

You know these little old earwigs that you see crawling around, mostly find them under bark of dead trees and on old rotten logs. Lork sorty like a thousand leg; them old hardshelled kind. Well, sir, them things will sure get in a body's ears. Or that's what I've always been told. I've heard pap and mother tell a tale about one time there was a man in the neighborhood that got to complaining with the headache. He done everything he could for it, but it just got worse and worse. They even got a doctor, but he couldn't do nothing for him. He just kept gettin' worse and worse; got so he just went into fits nearly. Said it just felt plimeblank like there was something crawling in his head all the time. He couldn't sleep, and it got so he was in such misery that he couldn't eat. And he finally died. The doctor wanted to know what was the matter with him. So he begged his folks to let him cut his head open to see what was the matter with him. They didn't want to, but he kept on until at last they said, "All right." Well sir, when he cut that man's head open they was a measured pint of earwigs in his head. They allus'low'd that one had craw'd in his ear when he was asleep and had young'ns in there and they just kept breedin' an' increasin' till they was that many. My Lord, that man must a-suffered a sight in this world! (Barden 1991, 308)

Variants

An Australian variant relates the tale of a tourist staying in a beach hut in Bali who gets a strange lump on her neck:

By the time she returned to Australia, she was quite distressed, so she went to a casualty ward. The doctor decided to cauterise the swelling. When he made the cut, dozens of tiny black spiders tumbled out of the lump and ran down the woman's neck. (Bishop 1988, 86)

"The revulsion this story causes has had no apparent effect on Bali's tourist industry, despite the story's popularity in recent years" (Bishop 1988, 86).

Another variant tells of a woman who falls asleep while sunbathing. While she's sleeping, an ant climbs into her nasal passages. When the eggs hatched, the itching was so bad that the woman scratched the flesh off her cheeks (Morgan and Tucker 1984, 51). Also, there's the story of a young boy who has a constant itch under a plaster cast. When the cast is finally removed, the cause of the itch is apparent; ants (or termites) had gotten into the cast and were eating away at the leg!

And in the Media . . .

In March 1980, the Oslo newspaper *Dagbladet*, along with several other Norwegian papers, published a note from the news agency *Norsk Telegrambyra*:

> *A lady of Bergen who shortly before Christmas went to a southern country on a holiday, had a shock some weeks after she had come back, Bergens Arbeiderblad reports. On her right cheek a boil developed, judged by a physician as "not malign." A salve was prescribed, but it did not help. The boil on the lady's cheek grew bigger, and one morning when she was standing in front of a mirror in order to camouflage the boil with the help of a make-up stick, the boil burst and out came a big spider.* (Klintberg 1985, 280)

"Spiders in the Cactus"

> *Have you heard the story about the woman who bought a yucca plant? When she was watering it, it began to make funny noises—a hissing or clicking. She was confused and telephoned a local plant authority who told her to bring in the plant. He examined it and found, inside, a nest of tarantula spiders.*

While various types of cacti have been identified with this legend in North America, European variants cite a yucca plant, which is not a cactus but a kind of lily from Central America and the southwestern United States. This "new and exotic" plant arrived in Europe during the late 1970s and became a sensation. When the plant was identified as a cactus, the legend did not capture the Scandinavian imagination, but as soon as the yucca plant was incorporated into the tale, the "Spider in the Cactus" legend flourished. The yucca plant has a "conspicuously thick stem, about whose consistency little was known. Was it solid, or perhaps, hollow?" (Klintberg 1985, 285). This plant indeed could host all sorts of creepy crawly things.

Structure of "Spiders in the Cactus"

As with most legends that refer to the business world, this legend has been attached to large, well-known corporations such as Marks and Spencer in Great Britain and, in the United States and Canada, IKEA, the Swedish home furnishing chain.

Orientation: A woman buys a new cactus (yucca plant) from a major store and brings it home.

Complicating Action: After some time she (or her child) notices that the plant is moving (pulsating). She phones the store (or plant expert) who tells her to leave the house immediately and that exterminators are on their way.

Result: The cactus is filled with tarantulas that have just hatched. The eggs were laid in the cactus and lie dormant until the woman brings it into the warmth of her house. Sometimes the plant actually explodes.

Variants

Alternative infestations have also been incorporated into the legend. Roy Vickery, editor of *Plant-Lore Notes & News*, reports receiving the following story in April from the managing director of a company based in Poole, Dorset:

> This was told to us in good faith by one of our employees. A friend of a cousin had bought a yucca from Marks and Spencer. The plant, despite care, died. [The customer] returned it to Marks and Spencer in exchange for tokens. Marks and Spencer analyzed the plant and found a dead male tarantula in the pot. Two experts arrived at [the customer's] house stating that where there is a dead male, there will be a female with offspring. The search duly revealed the female and eight babies inside the duvet. Marks and Spencer replaced free of charge all the bed linen and also the bed, but insisted on a secrecy agreement, agreeing to no disclosure to the press. (Spiders in Plants 1992, 10)

In early 1992, a less traditional variant circulated on a computer network:

> *A lady buys STACKER software for her home computer,*
> *a programme that compresses data on her hard disk at a ratio of*
> *1:1.8, giving her more useable storage space. One day she finds her*
> *computer buzzing and vibrating, even though it was turned off.*
> *A computer service man warns her to leave the house at once, but*
> *before she can do so, the monitor glows green and explodes,*
> *scattering tarantulas all over the house.*

> *What had happened is this (the version continues): The STACKER*
> *program was shipped from Carlsbad, California, where these deadly*
> *arachnids are an indigenous creature. A breeding pair had inadver-*
> *tently been shipped in the box with the software. When [the lady]*
> *installed STACKER on her hard disk she also unknowingly in-*
> *stalled this pair of deadly tarantulas. Being on the same disk as*
> *STACKER these deadly creatures were also compressed 1.8:1. That*
> *meant that by the time the full-sized AT cabinet was full, there*
> *were literally millions of them. When the case ruptured, the spiders*
> *were immediately decompressed and back to normal size.*

> *By the way, my lady friend only needed four pallbearers.*
> *It seems that the spider bites had compressed her 1.8 to 1.*
> (Spiders in Plants 1992, 10)

And in the Media . . .

> *A woman buys a potted cactus at the store and later her child says,*
> *"Mommy, the plant waved at me." The store (or a local conservatory)*
> *advises the woman to leave the house or else burn the plant immediately.*
> ("Tarantula Rumor Gives Cactus Customers the Creeps,"
> *Pittsburg Press*, May 23, 1990, B1. *See also* "Tarantula Horror as
> Cactus Explodes!" *National Examiner*, April 14, 1992, 5)

SNAKES

Snakes also figure substantially in mythology and in the contemporary legends and, like spiders, can play various roles. For many ancient cultures, the snake represents the underworld, the realm of the dead, because of the snake's ability to shed its skin and grow a new one and shed the old, and because it lives under the earth (Biedermann 1992, 310). The snake plays a large role in Egyptian, Hindu, Greek, Christian, and Sumerian mythology and is quite possibly the most feared creature in the Western world. Much of this fear is based on misunderstanding of snakes and erroneous beliefs such as the belief "that snakes use their tongues to bite, that they can charm animals (including humans) into paralysis, that they can jump at their victims or spring from the ground, that they can milk cows by sucking their udders, and that they swallow their young to protect them from danger and expel them, alive, when danger is past" (Ammer 1989, 189). Christine Ammer discusses the above tales (and yes, they are all tales!) and explains such phrases as "snake in the grass," "snake oil," and "snake eyes," among others, in common usage that demonstrates our feelings towards these reptiles.

Christianity identifies the snake as the embodiment of Satan in the Garden of Eden; the Greeks and Romans saw the snake as a symbol of rejuvenation and healing, represented by the caduceus of Mercury and the staff of Asclepius, which is the present-day symbol of pharmacy and the medical profession. Traditionally in Western culture, snakes are thought of as fear-inducing. Mythic dragons and basilisks are actually magnified snakes, and psychoanalysts equate snake phobias with fear of phallic symbols (Biedermann 1992, 312).

Although spiders are more common in urban environments than snakes, snakes are featured in the tales in almost the same frequency. Like the spider, the snake in contemporary legends represents fear of different cultures and fear of the unknown. The snakes, in the legends, are always poisonous, regardless of where they are found, and snakes, like many of the spiders, hitch rides into North America on "luxury" imports.

"Department Store Snakes"

I heard this one from Mom, and the lady that told her swore to God it was true. It's the same old story about the snakes in the discount store. She went—where was it?—to K-Mart and tried on a blouse or a dress or a coat or something, and when she got home there was a welt on her arm, and she didn't know what it was. And it got to hurting her, and she went to the doctor, and he said, "There's nothing that can be but a snakebite." No, he didn't tell her what it was, but kept asking her where she had gone and where she had been.

Well, she went back to the store and looked for the dress, and it was still there. She got the dress and took it to the manager's office and told him that she thought that they should tear open the dress because there was something suspicious about it. So they tore it open, and found these little baby snakes in it. The fabric had come from Singapore or somewhere. The eggs had been in it, and the heat in the store hatched them out. The store gave her so much money to shut up about it. It was about $200 they gave her, I think.
(Baker 1982, 213)

Often the legend involves a woman who is shopping for a rug that has been imported from the Far East; she is bitten by a snake and either sues the store or dies from the venom. The legend circulated extensively during the 1970s and may have been associated with the Vietnam War. "It would be the symbolic expression of the fear of revenge by Far Eastern peoples, taken through imported goods" (Kapferer 1990, 153).

Structure of "Department Store Snakes"

Early versions always involved a female shopper:

Orientation: Woman goes to a well-known department store to purchase a specific item (rug or clothing).

Complicating Action: As she passes her hand through the material to check the quality, the woman feels a jab in her arm but disregards it, thinking it is only a needle or staple. Upon arrival at home, she becomes dizzy and disoriented. She is rushed to the hospital.

Result: She has been bitten by a poisonous snake that has been hibernating in the imported material.

Evaluation: As punishment for her "unpatriotic" shopping habits, the woman is either severely ill or dies from the venom.

Although the legend had been circulating during the 1970s, it did not arrive in France until the early 1980s—with a definite change: the victim, instead of a female shopper, was inevitably a young child who died in the supermarket or on a merry-go-round in the shopping mall (Campion-Vincent 1990, 246). Again, the specter of anti-consumerism rears its head to strike a blow against large department stores and shopping malls. The audience for this tale is suburban and contains all those concerned about the safety of innocent children. An interesting switch in victims is one avenue to explore when discussing this legend. Are women shoppers no longer "innocent"?

A parallel between this tale and that of the poisonous snake (spider) in the produce, discussed later, is easy to draw. The snake "has been brought into our safe Western everyday environment hidden in a product which was imported from a distant exotic country" and reflects an obvious Western ethnocentric character (Klintberg 1985, 278).

Variants

The "Department Store Snakes" moved to the merry-go-round in Knoebels Grove:

> Joe Muscato, Public Relation director at Knoebels Grove amusement park near Bloomsburg, PA, asked local newspapers to dispel rumors about children killed by snakes in the park. Muscato said that the rumor crops up about every twenty years at Knoebels Grove and takes three forms: "A copperhead snake crawls out of the merry-go-round horse's mouth and bites a little girl. A snake slithers out of the horse's tail and bites the girl. The snake bites a boy." Although two small blacksnakes were spotted in the park this year, the rumor has no basis in fact. Brunvand reports that in the United States this widespread legend often involves merry-go-round horses supposedly imported from overseas or stored during the winter in the warmer American south, where the snakes take refuge in the horses. (Snakebite Rumor at Knoebels Grove 1991, 12)

Another variant of the legend says that you should be careful of fur collars:

Rumours circulated in March 1991 in Nebraska about a woman who became suddenly ill after trying on coats at a Burlington Coat Factory outlet (a clearing house for inexpensive imported clothing). Young poisonous snakes, found in the fur collars of the coats, were unknowingly imported (as eggs) along with the coats. Numerous calls were made to the local health authorities who could not substantiate the claim and a check of hospitals provided no evidence of someone being treated for snake bites.
(Department Store Snakes 1991, 12)

And, in a blend of both the spider and snake tales:

A lady friend went to the doctor with an abdominal rash. "Aha!" said the wise medic. "Have you bought a new skirt lately?" The patient said that she had. "Then I should go home and examine it very carefully," said the good doctor, who must have felt like Conan Doyle on a good day. So the patient returned home, and examined the garment carefully. She noticed some irregularities in the waist-band. Curious, she started to unpick it, and found that it was "full of lice." The skirt, of course, had been made somewhere in the Far East. (Dale 1984, 68)

And in the Media . . .

"Snakes in Mattresses"

According to a lawsuit filed in Bucks County, Pennsylvania, Gladys Diehl and her husband John Brehm bought a mattress from Hess' department store in May 1988 and soon after noticed unusual movements in their bed, which they "suspected could be a living creature." They exchanged the mattress for another, but found odd movements in that one as well. After four months, they took the second mattress to a laboratory, where workers found the remains of a dead 26-inch ribbon snake. Diehl and Brehm asked more than $20,000 in damages from the store and the mattress manufacturer. (John P. Martin, "A Mattress with the Wrong Coils," *Philadelphia Inquirer*, April 4, 1991, 3B; "Yikes! That Lump in Their Mattress Was . . . a Snake," *National Inquirer*, July 30, 1991, 32)

"Snakes in the Produce"

A woman from Pecs [Hungary] ate a snake-bitten banana. She became so ill that she needed a lengthy hospitalization. The lady called the Pecs radio station after her recovery in order to share her accident with the audience on a live broadcast. The woman said that later she found traces of the snake's fang on the banana. Then she mentioned that she had heard about a little girl who recently died of a snake-bitten banana. The interview ended with her saying that since her accident someone had seen little green snakes among bananas in an ABC [food] store. (Snakes and Bananas 1992, 10)

The reporter explains that he followed up the story: not only had the store *not* stocked bananas for the last three months, but the woman herself had not called the radio station, the station had called her. But "how could the radio have heard of her illness when she had told it only to her best friend?" She also had not been hospitalized and had definitely not seen any evidence of snakes in the bananas—not even a fang!

Structure of "Snakes in the Produce"

The legend is often told of a mother and her young child. The child becomes the victim and the mother, the innocent agent of death!

Orientation: A mother hands her child a banana while she is driving the car (or cooking supper or to keep the child occupied and on the back step).

Complicating Action: The child complains that the banana "bit me." The mother tells the child not to be silly, but when she checks on the child a little later, finds the child collapsed (dead).

Result: The child is rushed to the hospital but does not survive.

Evaluation: The mother realizes that if she had only paid attention to what the child said, the tragedy could have been avoided.

Variants

Once again an old tale resurfaces and circulates with additions and adaptations that reflect the culture of the teller and the audience. The version that has small black snakes breeding in the bananas, being shipped while the bananas are green, and becoming active enough as the fruit warmed up to bite the hand that moved them, was popular in Great Britain in the 1930s. It died a natural death in the 1950s (Snakes and Bananas 1992, 10). The legend was resurrected and then made the rounds in Sweden in 1973. A newspaper article, at that time, includes an interview with a curator at the Museum of Natural History at Gothenburg:

> He admits it happened in earlier times, before banana stems were dipped into preservatives in the exporting countries, that snakes and—above all—poisonous spiders were detected in cargo spaces and storage rooms. Nowadays such discoveries are rare. And snakes hiding inside the peels of bananas simply do not exist. (Klintberg 1985, 276)

With the passage of time and through the ingenuity of countless retellers, the snake inside the banana was transformed into a poisonous spider and then a worm. "The snake was too fanciful, the spider was more credible but the story about the worm was the easiest to believe especially since the ends of a peeled banana bear some resemblance to worms" (Klintberg 1985, 278).

If worms in bananas, then why not "Black Widow Spiders in Grapes"?:

> *On June 24, Carol Woodman of Sebago, Maine, bought a bunch of green grapes at a local Shop 'n Save grocery store. On unpacking them at home, she noticed a small, shiny black spider, and when it jumped onto her kitchen table, she placed a mason jar over it. When Woodman complained, store officials told her to bring the spider back to the store; meanwhile it "spun a web [in the jar] and laid several eggs." She was disappointed by the store's apparent lack of concern: when she handed the spider over to a clerk at the courtesy desk, "She doubled my money back for the grapes and handed me a coupon for ice cream. I was insulted." Officials positively identified the spider as a deadly black widow and called in "a local pesticide company." After two more black widows were found at the company's distribution center, all grapes were removed from store shelves in five New England states. Officials from Shaw's Super-markets, Inc., had also found a black widow in a recent grape ship-ment and likewise halted sales of all varieties. A week later another spider was found in grapes sent to Massachusetts; eight in all turned up. The grapes, officials said, originated in California's Coachella Valley, "which is north of the Mexican border." They blamed the finds on consumer pressure to cut down pesticide use on fresh fruits, which in turn attracts insects that black widows eat.*
> (Black Widow Spiders in Grapes 1991, 14)

This time the blame is placed not on foreign imports but on consumers who are attempting to be politically correct and environmentally friendly.

ALLIGATORS IN THE SEWER

> *Did he remember the baby alligators? Last year, or maybe the year before, kids all over New York bought these little alligators for pets. Macy's was selling them for fifty cents; every child, it seemed, had to have one. But soon the children grew bored with them. Some set them loose in the streets, but most flushed them down the toilets. And these had grown and reproduced, had fed off rats and sewage, so that now they moved, big, blind, albino, all over the sewer system. Down there, God knew how many there were. Some had turned cannibal because in their neighborhood the rats had all been eaten, or had fled in terror.* (Pynchon 1963, 42–43)

From "natural" threats like spiders and snakes in consumer goods and vacation spots, we travel to underground sewers in urban centers to encounter—alligators. Kapferer, in his discussion of these rumors, states:

> The fact that this trivial item was handed down for more than fifty years—and is now part and parcel of current folklore, i.e. of the contemporary urban legends—shows to what extent it struck imaginations, fascinated by the shrouded mysteries of the underworld. (1990, 31)

Historical Connections

The legend of alligators in the sewer may be based on a real incident. *The New York Times* printed several reports of alligators caught around the city between 1932 and 1938. On August 16, 1938, five alligators were caught in Huguenot Lake in New Rochelle. One successful fisherman theorized that the creatures "had been put there by some resident who had bought them in Florida as pets and then tired of them" (Morgan and Tucker 1984, 149). An article, "Alligator Found in Uptown Sewer," that appeared in *The New York Times* on February 10, 1935 is important to the genesis of the legend that we know today. The report spawned similar reports and is, in fact, the first documented source of this motif (Coleman 1979, 338). Although toilets are not mentioned in these early variants, they seem a feasible addition to people who live in urban centers and have few options for getting rid of unwanted materials. (Consider the many panic flushings of marijuana—and the resulting legends of potent weed flourishing in the sewer system!)

A British television program that ran in March 1987 refers to an alligator caught in the "sewers" of Orlando, Florida. The item was possibly based on a news item from *The Daily Telegraph* ["Alligator Snared by Florida 'Dundee,' " March 3, 1987] and confused "storm drains" with "sewers":

It has long been a part of the folklore of American cities that there was once a fad for keeping baby alligators and crocodiles. When the owners got tired of them they flushed them down the lavatory into the sewers where the reptiles grew into 15-foot monsters, preying on city workers. In Florida, the alligators stray from their natural habitant and as Orlando's terrified sanitation workers can testify, they can be a bit of a nuisance. (Smith and Roemer 1988, 1)

Storm drains are not sewers but large (108-inch-diameter) pipes that drain run-off rainwater into a small lake nearby. It is quite common for alligators to live in the mouth of these storm drains and venture out into the lake for food (Smith and Roemer 1988, 2).

Symbolic Implications of Alligators and Sewers

There have been several discussions about the similarities between this contemporary legend and those of another age: dragons in caves! The alligator is the figure in nature that most resembles dragons, and sewers are very like the caves and labyrinths of the dragonslaying quests of folk tradition (Thigpen 1979, 100). While "most modern audiences (having learned much of their dragon lore from the Disney studios) probably think of dragons as pudgy dinosaurs, traditional British dragons were seen more as worms than anything else," and many of the place names associated with dragons contain the word "worm": Wormstall, Wormelowe Barrow, Wormingford, Wormhill, and so on (Carroll 1984, 70).

Kapferer refers to possible symbolic implications of the "Alligator in the Sewer" legend for society today and offers the following question for contemplation: "Is it a metaphor that means under a thin gloss of civilization (the city), a world of violence, instinct and aggression lives on (the jungle is just under the black top)?" (Kapferer 1990, 159).

And in the Media . . .

Regardless of the various explanations, the sewer system is still thought of as a hospitable haven for unwanted pets:

> *Winnipeg [Manitoba] hopes to shed a growing problem with surplus serpents with its new $1,200, climate-controlled home for snakes banned or seized under city bylaws. "If we don't take them, people dump them," says animal control officer Lawrence Anonychuk, adding discarded snakes could conceivably survive in the warmth and humidity of the city's sewers. "What would happen if a snake came up through the drain in your home? There'd be a panic across the city." Last Tuesday, police called to an apartment by a tenant who heard noises beneath the floorboards spotted part of a snake, which was never found. In June, a man working on a house grabbed what he thought was a section of hose, only to be bitten by a snake which disappeared into a drain. The house was torn apart and the sewer system searched, but the rogue reptile was never found. (The Edmonton Journal, September 14, 1993, A2)*

Earlier, in another Canadian city:

A horrified woman fled the washroom of her west-end apartment Saturday night after coming face to face with a cold-blooded intruder. The metre-long snake was lurking behind the toilet of the bathroom where she planned to take a shower. Running to the kitchen, she perched on a chair while she called police. Patrol officers who arrived at the walkup in the area of 181 Street and 96 Avenue [Edmonton], found the snake holed up in a closet. City bylaw enforcement officials took the animal away. The building has a no-pets policy. Police believe the animal was a wayward resident which crawled up through the walkup's plumbing system. (Edmonton Journal, April 16, 1990, B2)

BEASTS IN THE WILD

A woman out riding with her daughter claimed yesterday they came face to face with a puma . . . in Wales. Ann Phillips and 20-year-old Lorna watched the brown animal—the size of a great dane—in the bright sunlight for several minutes. The Beast of Margam had been reported for several years in the Margam Forest, West Glamorgan. Mrs. Phillips, of nearby Cwmavon, added, "I think it was a puma." Police said, "Mrs. Phillips and her daughter are not prone to exaggeration." (Goss 1992, 184)

This news item from *The Daily Mirror* (January 24, 1990) is only one instance of reporting of wild beasts where none are thought to exist. This legend is distinctly European, as sightings of wild beasts are not so rare in North America. Research in both England and France attempts to understand this "new" manifestation of anxieties.

"Big Cats in Great Britain"

Michael Goss (1992, 188–89) documents twelve common elements in the media reports of "big cat sightings" in British newspapers:

1. An identified witness sights a large species of non-native cat.
2. The sighting usually occurs by an area of open land (also urban settings such as golf courses and parks).
3. The sighting may occur at any time of the day or night and is very brief.

4. The description in the reports are consistent in only the size of the animal and the fact that it is cat-like.

5. The media plays a large role in connecting the various reports, which may be separated by long periods of time (days, months, or years).

6. A local identity, name, or popular label may be given to the animal.

7. There is an assumption, stated or tacit, that the animal is, or could be, dangerous to children.

8. Physical evidence may be included in the report but seldom does this evidence include photographs.

9. Credibility is established by quoting authority figures.

10. The big cats are said to have escaped from zoos or wildlife collections or are released as "unwanted" pets.

11. Unsuccessful hunts, official or unofficial, are undertaken to locate the animal.

12. The cat drops simultaneously out of sight and out of the media.

Unlike North America and most parts of Europe, Britain has virtually no large wild animals of any sort. "Perhaps this total absence of large and potentially dangerous predators makes reports of 'phantom felines' more attractive—and exciting for us" (Goss 1992, 190). Scholars have suggested that the "big cat" legends may reflect a wish to return to a wilder, less urbanized environment. Others reflect that the reports of "Big Cats" have traditional antecedents. The twelve elements correlate with traditional stories of dragon sightings.

It is probable that the accounts described by Michael Goss are part of a long tradition of encounters with non-native or unfamiliar animals that were perceived, and described, as fantastic beasts. We no longer believe in dragons, but a non-native big cat is all too believable (Monger 1992, 205).

"Cats and Vipers in France"

Pro-ecology groups were said to be dropping venomous snakes by plane into certain countries in order to preserve these virtually extinct species as well as (depending on which version one heard) to feed hawks and other birds of prey or destroy rats and field mice.
(Kapferer 1990, 70)

The appearances of beasts and mystery cats in France may be linked to "social resistance towards the new French policies of nature conservation insofar as these policies lead to measures affecting sensitive wildlife animal species" (Campion-Vincent 1992, 160). Protected birds (seagulls, buzzards, or herons) are said to be proliferating at a harmful rate, but at the same time, there is equally passionate opposition to deliberate releases of predators (vipers, foxes, or big cats) that lead to the demise of the fowl (Campion-Vincent 1992, 160). The mysterious beasts and large cats have been featured in rumors for the past 10 years and are a direct reaction to the new policies of protecting the fauna and reintroducing wild predators. The reported sightings are ambiguous and beget arguments about their real or fantastic nature.

The viper release stories can be summarized in one sentence: "*Ecologists rent helicopters to release vipers in French countryside*" (Campion-Vincent 1990, 242). The tales have the major characteristics of contemporary legends:

1. They are incorporated into personal-experience narratives, and the point of view of the teller is dependent on the locality (village or micro-region) and profession of the participants (sheep farmers, whose possessions are damaged, or pro-ecology supporters).

2. While the stories are technically implausible, the majority of the urban population accept them as entirely plausible fact. The motives seem praiseworthy and it would not be the first case of reintroducing animal populations into the backwoods of France. There was wide media coverage of the reintroduction of lynxes in the Vosges Mountains in eastern France. Also, most people have only an abstract knowledge of snake physiology, so do not realize that, like any animal dropped from a great height, snakes die on impact. "They probably think they bounce" (Kapferer 1990, 71). The general population also find it easy to accept that the vipers are dropped to "reinforce the species to have more raw material allowing the making of anti-venom serum (a double-barreled operation for the laboratories since people, being bitten, would consume more serum)" (Campion-Vincent 1990, 243).

   For concerned individuals in the rural communities, the rumor substantiates several widely held beliefs and is therefore easily accepted by that population.

   a. Ecologists, as well-meaning though they may be, are dangerous because their plans always backfire. They are people with no real contact with either the land or reality (which is why they can drop snakes from airplanes with no remorse.)

   b. But most of the danger lies in the fact that ecologists are totally incompetent: "they should know that in order to feed birds of prey, longer snakes are better, i.e., garter snakes—not to mention the fact that they are less dangerous" (Kapferer 1990, 83).

   c. The frustration, in rural communities, over major decisions
      made by "absentee landlords," administrators living in Paris
      who have no concept of expense (hence the use of airplanes)
      and no concern for their rural constituents (hence the poisonous
      vipers rather than harmless snakes) (Kapferer 1990, 83). Deci-
      sions made in the capital, it is thought, seriously harm those
      who truly know nature and who live in it: farmers and hunters.
      Releasing wild animals means killing off domestic ones, making
      unworkable the land it took so many centuries to control (148).

3. The stories are a collective performance, with the entire group
   creating the tale along with the principal teller.

4. There is an integrative influence on the group that disseminates the
   tale. Group dynamics are established and confirmed (Campion-
   Vincent 1990, 245).

Function of "Beasts in the Wild" Legends

Frustration with an uncaring government, harmful ecologists, and the
perishing countryside has resulted in story cycles of "werewolves, the beast
of Gevaudan, hordes of venomous snakes and even crocodiles in the river"
(Kapferer 1990, 148). Although the sightings have been witnessed and hunts
have been organized, no evidence has been collected to prove the allegations.
Thus, these tales represent allegories and reflect the fear that the countryside
of European civilizations is becoming deserted and thusly, nature is becoming hostile and dangerous (148). "Peasants feel that they are an endangered
species, in deserted villages surrounded by untilled land" (Campion-Vincent
1990, 246).

It is only through a thorough study of the stories themselves that
we can understand their meaning and account for their success.
These stories are exemplary stories, tales of protest, parables that
denounce the mighty. Through the detour of narration, they are the
voice of the forgotten, of the humble ones who do not influence
public policy. (Campion-Vincent 1990, 248)

And in the Media . . .

"On the Twisting Trail of a Fox Folk Tale"

*A plague of foxes in the Berwyn mountains has a sinister explana-
tion the Welsh Farmers' Union believe. It is convinced of the truth
in stories that the most ignorant sentimental type of urban animal-
lover is rounding up foxes in towns and driving them out to mid-
Wales in vans to free them in the wild—where they fall ferociously
on every lamb and pheasant chick in sight. But a hunt along the
spoor of anecdote suggested by last night that the story could be no
more than a folk tale. . . . "I have not seen anyone myself. But I've
heard a lot of rumours about it. I think there must be some truth in
it. There certainly are a lot more foxes around." [Estate game-
keeper] . . . Neither Bala nor Lanfyllin police, nor the RSPCA, had
heard reports of van sightings or fox smuggling. "But there are a
lot of foxes around," Bala police added.* ("On the Twisting Trail of
a Fox Folk Tale, " *The Guardian*, Feb. 1, 1986, 2)

PET TALES

It is not a long journey from the wilds of the countryside to the cozy
hearth of home and loyal pets. Legends featuring the fate of dogs, cats,
rabbits, and other familiar household animals appear frequently in the
conversations of Western civilization. The pets may be dead ("Microwave
Ovens," "The Hare Drier," and "The Dead Cat in the Package"); may be
heroes ("The Choking Doberman"); or may be companions in adventures
("The Dog in the Elevator"). Regardless of their role in the legends, the
abundance of pet legends demonstrates that pets are taken seriously in our
culture.

Several "pet tales" were discussed in earlier chapters in reference to
technology ("Microwave Ovens"), contaminated foods ("Doggie Dinner"),
and thieves ("The Dead Cat in the Package").

"The Choking Doberman"

*A woman returned from work to find her dog lying on the floor
gasping for breath. She rushed him to the vet, who immediately
said, "Tracheotomy," and told her to leave the pet overnight. She
had no sooner returned home when the vet phoned and said, "Get
out of the house immediately. Go next door to the neighbor's and
call the police." The vet sounded so alarmed that the woman did as*

> *she was directed without asking any questions. The vet, when he*
> *began operating, found two human fingers lodged in the dog's*
> *throat. The police upon searching the house, found an intruder*
> *hidden in the closet, two fingers missing from his hand,*
> *bleeding to death.* (Dickson and Goulden 1993, 173–74)

This version of "The Choking Doberman" was reported in the Phoenix paper *New Times* in early March 1983. When the reporter attempted to verify the story, he found, instead, that it had a long history as a migratory legend as well as historical antecedents. Several elements in this legend are reminiscent of other legends. Many tell of "suffering pets" and many include the urgent warning relayed by telephone (Brunvand 1984, 80). It also conveys a familiar warning: Make sure your house is locked and secure. The "consistent themes in variants point clearly to fearful concerns about threats of burglary and violent crimes, especially when these take place in private homes and are directed against women by men" (Brunvand 1984, 85).

Dogs are symbols of both demonic and beneficent forces in mythology and folklore. The dog is referred to some 40 times in the Bible, and in many ancient and modern tales, dogs help to solve crimes. Because of these tales and the frequency of mention in the Bible, Christianity saw the dog as a symbol of conscience. The dog has long been associated with loyalty and vigilance and figured often as a guardian at the portals of the underworld: Cerebus, the guardian of the underworld in Greek mythology, is a three-headed dog. Dogs also have a reputation of being able to "sense ghosts" and to warn people of invisible danger.

While conducting a contemporary legend workshop in a local junior high school, I discovered for myself how well the underlying message of this legend works. After relating the story of "The Killer in the Backseat" and the story of "The Choking Doberman," one of the teachers excused herself and left the library. Upon her return 20 minutes later, she apologized and explained what had happened. After listening to the story of "The Choking Doberman" she started to wonder, Did I lock my house today? Because she could not remember doing so, she became frightened and left the school. In the parking lot, she walked completely around her car—checking the backseat, front seat, and underneath (for possible slashers) and then drove home. There she checked every door and window to make sure all was well before returning to the school, embarrassed, but with peace of mind.

Structure of "The Choking Doberman"

Fashions and fads affect legends. During the 1980s, the dog in the story was usually a Doberman, "the watchdog choice of the decade." However, 1990s versions featured the pit bull instead (Dickson and Goulden 1993, 174). In the versions told by North American young adults, the human protagonist is a young woman who lives alone with her loyal (and fierce) dog to protect her. In Europe, the tale is not directed at the same segment of the population and often involves a large (but not necessarily fierce) pet. Paul Smith (1983, 98) documents the structure:

Orientation: A young couple lived in the suburbs of a large city. They were fond of the city night life and used to go up to town as many evenings as possible. Every night they would leave the lights on and let their large Labrador dog have free run of the house—an adequate insurance against intruders.

Complicating Action: One evening they returned from the theatre quite late and were shocked to find the dog choking on the floor of the entrance hall. They bundled the dog straight into the car and took it round to the vet. Whilst not too pleased at being disturbed so late at night, the vet told them not to worry, he would see to the dog and they were to return home. On their return, as they opened the front door, the phone was ringing. It was the vet, and, without any explanation, he told them to get out of the house immediately. They protested but he insisted, adding that he had called the police and would be round himself straight away to explain. Very shortly the vet arrived, closely followed by the police.

Result: By way of explanation the vet announced that when he had examined the dog he had found that it was, in fact, choking on two human fingers. The police decided to search the house and in a cupboard in the hall they found a burglar—unconscious, with two fingers missing from his right hand.

Historical Antecedents

"This tale is contemporary in its expression of the types of fears felt by us today, such as fear of theft and violence" (Smith 1983, 98). But these fears are not new and the legend, itself, has a connection to similar but ancient tales.

Early one morning Gelert, the favorite hound of Prince Llewellyn of Wales, refused to leave the crib of the master's young child. Llewellyn was upset as he was on his way to a hunt, but he could not get the dog to follow him. When Llewellyn returned from the hunt, he immediately went to see his child, only to find the crib overturned, blood splattered on the walls, and an exhausted Gelert, muzzle covered in blood, lying on the floor. In anger and anguish, Llewellyn drew his sword and killed the dog. It was only then that the uninjured child cried from the corner of the room Gelert had been protecting. As the grief-stricken father picked up his child, he saw the bloody body of a large wolf in the opposite corner.

William Robert Spencer, before writing *The Ballad of Beth Gelert*, tried following an 18th-century trail to find concrete evidence for the legend, but to no avail. This ballad is traditionally set in a village at the foot of Snowdon where Llewellyn the Great had a house. The greyhound named Gelert was given to him by his father-in-law, King John, in the year 1205, and the place to this day is called Beth-Gelert, or the grave of Gelert (Crossley-Holland 1985, 282).

The theme of the owner rashly slaying the dog who had just saved his child is firmly established in older tales. Parallels have been found in Asia and Europe, including tales in *The Fables of Bidpai* and *The Book of Sinbad*. This legend, therefore, was well-known in Wales long before the time of Llewellyn the Great or Beth Gelert (Crossley-Holland 1985, 282).

"The Choking Doberman" has close connections to two other traditional motifs as well. The first, "The Robber Who Was Hurt," reflects the fact that it is the robber who loses, while the dog becomes a hero. The modern burglar represents the

> old, rural, supernatural motif [transformed] into [a] modern, urban, rationalized form. . . . For the modern town-dweller, especially women living alone, the burglar is a dreaded figure who may be lurking at any time and in any guise, just as the witch once was in rural communities. (Brunvand 1984, 93)

A second connection is with older supernatural accounts of shape-changers, like witches, who lose their fingers and hands while they are in animal form (Brunvand 1984, 93). Natural events, including the behavior of animals, were often considered omens in classical times. "Ancient accounts of omens and rumors associated with them offer a provocative avenue for comparative and historical research in contemporary folklore" (Mayor 1992, 253).

The story of "The Omen of Wolves" tells of an event that took place in A.D. 402. While the teenaged emperor Honorius was preparing for battle, his guard was attacked by a pair of wolves, which were immediately killed. When the beasts were opened, each was found to have a human hand in its belly (Mayor 1992, 254). Witnesses took the aggressive behavior and last meal of the wolves as a sinister omen and could not stop discussing it. The resulting rumors spread panic throughout Rome. The poem "The Gothic War" by Claudian was written in an attempt to negate these rumors and lessen the panic.

The wolf was associated with the war-god Mars and served as a protective civic symbol for the city of Rome. The myth of the she-wolf who rescued and nurtured the city's founders, Romulus and Remus, was being tarnished by the likening of the barbarians by the late empire, to ravishing wolves. The wolves that attacked their weak emperor in A.D. 402 had terrified Romans on four levels: a) fear of the actual wild predator; b) fear of the wolf-like Visigoths; c) distrust of the "human wolf," the barbarian general; and d) the dissonance elicited by the disfavor with which the traditional wolf-guardian now seemed to regard Rome (Mayor 1992, 260).

"The Omen of Wolves" exhibits parallels to "The Choking Doberman" and the two separate themes of the legend: the ambiguous guardian and the severed hands:

> When ferocious guardians are distrusted but nevertheless relied upon for protection against intruders, it seems psychologically fitting to imagine a scenario in which the guardian is unable to completely prevent a break-in but manages to destroy only part of the intruder, namely the part that carries out the intrusion. (Mayor 1992, 255)

A comparison of the elements of the two legends illustrates the parallels between the two. The motifs, characters, themes, plots, and outcomes of both legends coincide quite closely, despite the symbolic interpretations dictated by time and culture (Mayor 1992, 259). "The Choking Doberman," a tale reflecting our modern age, stresses individual fears, while the ancient legend is not concerned with individuals but with the public realm.

"The Choking Doberman" (1980s)	"The Omen of Wolves" (A.D. 402)
woman	Roman populace, emperor
house	city, empire
shopping	wealth
guard dog	wolves, she-wolf, Stilicho
dog's odd behavior/choking	attacking emperor
consult vet	divination process
fingers in dog's throat	hands in wolves' bellies
phone call	omen interpreted as warning
woman goes to neighbor	battle at Pollentia
police	Roman army
criminal	Visigoths, Alaric
successful break-in	Gothic invasion of empire's borders
fear of rape, burglary	Gothic lust for Roman women, greed for Roman riches
racial details	Goths as "uncivilized outsiders"
failure to prevent crime	failure to prevent invasion
criminal detained	Goths forced to retreat
woman saved	Rome saved
retold as an urban legend	omen disseminated by rumor
media, authorities	Claudian, Roman authorities
exposed as "folklore"	Claudian's counterinterpretation

(Mayor 1992, 259)

An interesting similarity between the legends is the opening up of the animal to discover the human fingers or hands. "In the crisis atmosphere before a battle, the traditional method of auguring the future from animals' entrails would have been employed to determine the appropriate action" (Mayor 1992, 261). The "augury" in "The Choking Doberman" follows the same sequence. The vet is consulted about a puzzling event, he observes the behavior of the dog (choking), he opens the animal to find the explanation, and interprets his findings accordingly. He immediately issues a warning about impending danger (261).

Folklore and rumor in different societies can create similar tales to express similar fears, but with a culturally specific emphasis on precisely what is at risk. Through her comparison of "The Choking Doberman" and "The Omen of the Wolves," Mayor (1992, 263) found three interrelated issues that clarify the values perceived as endangered in each culture:

1. Personal and public fears for safety rise as confidence in traditional protectors and authorities wanes. Traditional protectors in ancient Rome included city walls, soldiers, commanders, the emperor, and the nurturing she-wolf of mythology.

2. During such crises, unusual events may be intuitively and/or traditionally read as signs explaining the present or predicting the future.

3. Rumors and contemporary legends arising from such readings provoke controversy, especially when authorities attempt to establish their "real" meanings. "The popular validation of ancient omens and modern legends depends on their *metaphorical* aptness to anxiety-laden situations."

"The Dog in the Elevator"

Four matrons from York, Pennsylvania, although apprehensive about crime, go to New York for a shopping trip. Their husbands warn, "If someone wants your pocketbook or jewelery, don't put up a fight. Do what they ask." The women stay at the Plaza. As they ride the elevator to breakfast, a well-dressed black man with a Doberman pinscher gets on the elevator. "Sit," he commands. The women immediately sit on the floor.

In the lobby, the black man asks their room number. "Ten-sixteen," one of the women blurts. He nods and walks away. The other women berate her. "Now we'll have to change rooms," they say. At the desk the clerk says, "Oh, you're the ladies from 1016. Mr. Reggie Jackson thought his dog might have frightened you; he would like to pick up your checks for breakfast." (Dickson and Goulden 1993, 153)

Although the Doberman is mentioned in this example, the breed of dog is not a major factor. The dog, however, must be sufficiently large for the legend to be effective. But then, in some variants, the dog is not there at all! There is a close connection to the legend of "The Killer in the Back Seat" because of the final realization that the suspected assailant is actually the benefactor. However, regardless of whether the dog is identified as a Doberman or not, there is also a close connection to "The Choking Doberman." All three of these legends exhibit the same contemporary concerns: racial stereotypes, fear of crime, and people's thwarted efforts to prevent angering an assailant (Brunvand 1984, 87). The celebrity named in "The Dog in the Elevator" follows the dictates of fashion. Legends about Reggie Jackson gave way to identical tales of Lionel Ritchie, Michael Jackson, Arsenio Hall, and Eddie Murphy in correspondence to their popularity.

One of the functions of the legend, for North American audiences, is the reminder not to jump to conclusions based on racial stereotypes. It reflects other fears for people from other places.

This story is told of a South African woman on holiday to New York City. She was terrified of all black people as she felt they would realize that she was South African and would penalize her for this. Well, she was staying at the Sheraton in New York City, when she had to get into the lift with a black man and his dog. As soon as the lift closed, the black man said "Down, Lady!" The poor woman, nearly wetting herself with anxiety, sank down on the floor. The man started to laugh and said, "I was talking to my dog. Her name is Lady." The woman burst into tears and got out at her stop. The black man happened to be Lionel Ritchie, and the next day the woman went to pay her bill prior to leaving for South Africa when she found the bill paid by Ritchie. (South Africans in Elevators 1990, 10)

Cynthia Hind states "there are various versions to this story, but it is typically South African—who else would be so terrified" (10).

Others have adapted the legend to reflect their own major concerns.

*A housewife ran away to the excitement of Atlantic City to escape
the dismal monotony of her daily routine. Within the sea of slot
machines, she gazed in amazement as the 3 spinning wheels of her
machine halted to reveal 3 gold bars; coins spurted wildly from the
machine. In all of the excitement, she gathered the coins and ran to
the elevator, which led to the cashier's table. [Note: at Atlantic City,
players have to buy tokens good only in the slot machines, then
redeem their winnings for cash.] As the elevator doors closed
behind her, she looked up from her treasure to see that the other
passengers were two Afro-American men (both of whom were very
muscular). The thought of having her newly won riches stolen from
her forced prayers to St. Jude [the patron saint of hopeless causes]
to echo in her head. Those prayers were shortly interrupted by a
deep voice murmuring, "Hit the floor." With that, she threw the
coins in the air and buried her face in the plush carpeting on the
floor. When the coins stopped ricochetting off the walls of the elevator car, she peered up to see Eddie Murphy fall to the ground beside
her, in a fit of frenzied laughter. Once he was able to control
himself, he explained he was only telling his bodyguard to press the
button to indicate the floor they wanted. He was so amused by her
reaction, he sent her roses with a card, which thanked her for
making him laugh.* (Elevator Incident 1992, 11)

The housewife was obviously so worried about being robbed that she
forgot to mention the dog they had with them! Or at least the one they had
with them when I heard this variant. A variant from England's Houses of
Parliament also is missing the dog:

*The British are wizards of pomp and ceremony. Even innocent
bystanders and spectators sometimes feel themselves involuntarily
caught up in and reacting to the drama of the moment, though they
may know little or nothing of the ritual itself. . . . Parliament's
equivalent of the U.S. Speaker of the House is called the "Keeper of
the Woolsack," who wears resplendent gold-and-scarlet robes
topped with a ceremonial wig. At the time of the story . . . the office
was held by Sir Quentin Hoff, Lord Halisham. After Parliament
adjourned, Lord Halisham strode into the corridor, passed an
American tour group, and saw an old friend, the Honorable Neil
Matten, an MP with whom he wished to speak. "Neil," Lord
Halisham called, "Neil." There followed an embarrassed silence,
as all the tourists obediently fell to their knees.* (Dickson and
Goulden 1993, 154)

"The Hare Drier"

One day a woman is horrified to see her dog holding a dead rabbit in its mouth. Her neighbors have always kept a pet rabbit in a cage behind the house, and she recognizes the dead animal as their pet. The woman takes the rabbit from her dog, cleans it up as best she can, blow-dries its fur, and—her neighbours being gone—sneaks into their yard and replaces the restored rabbit in its cage in a life-like position. The next day, she sees a police car parked in front of her neighbor's house. Curious, she goes outside and asks what's going on. "A nuisance call," the officer says. "Their pet rabbit died yesterday, and some weirdo dug it up and put it back in its cage." (Brunvand 1989, 151)

The versions of this legend circulating since 1988 ("The Year of the Rabbit" as Brunvand calls it) do not vary greatly. The breed of the dog may fluctuate as does the neighborhood. (In Edmonton, Alberta, this "true" tale took place in at least seven neighborhoods and several surrounding communities!)

A close relative to this legend, "Airfreighted Pet," has been circulating for even longer. When the airline employees discover that the poodle (rabbit, cat) in the carrying case has died, they replace it with a living replica. Unknown to them, however, the animal had died before the flight and the body is being taken home for burial.

"The Elephant That Sat on the VW"

Some contemporary legends about not-so-domestic animals also enjoy a wide circulation:

A woman "somewhere in the South" attended a circus and returned to the parking lot to find the front of her Volkswagen smashed. An apologetic circus official told her that a trainer had been exercising an elephant in the parking lot as the music began. The elephant "began its act" and, lacking the normal props, perched on the front of the car. The woman was able to drive away because the VW has its engine in the back. But her trouble didn't end at the circus; friends and relatives guffawed in disbelief when she explained what had happened, accusing her of making up a wild story as an excuse for sloppy driving. (Dickson and Goulden 1993, 172)

A variant of this tale involves the thrashing of the car—from the inside:

> *A man takes his family to a wildlife park. The young son opens the electrically operated rear window of the station wagon and the friendly elephant sticks its trunk through it, delighting the children until it sneezes, producing a large volume of fetid gases and semi-liquids. The terrified son closes the window on the elephant's trunk. The enraged animal trashed the vehicle until the son releases the trunk and the family narrowly escapes.* (So there's this guy, see . . . 1991, 81)

"The Bump in the Rug"

> *A couple who were moving house lost their canary in transit. When checking how well the carpets had been laid in the new house, the husband notices a lump near one edge. He simply levels it by beating it with a hammer. . . . The lost bird is finally laid to rest.*
> (Smith 1983, 66)

"The Dog on the Balcony"

> *Ace Bragan was reportedly killed outside a Dallas, Texas, high-rise apartment when a Great Dane puppy fell on his head. Police believed that Jim Sweeny, 9, was playing ball with the puppy in his 13th-floor apartment, when the ball bounced out an open sliding door and onto a balcony. The dog apparently chased the ball and tried to catch it as it went over the 30-inch balcony wall. The mother commented, "I know this is a selfish thing to say, but thank God it wasn't Jimmy who fell off." Bragan's widow is suing the Sweenys for negligence; the fate of the dog was not reported.*
> (Puppy Jumps off High-Rise Balcony 1992, 11–12)

"The Mexican Pet"

> *A couple on holidays down in Mexico fall in love with a cute Mexican hairless dog. When their holiday is over, they can't bear to leave it behind, so they smuggle it over the borders. After a few days the dog becomes ill so they take it to a vet. The vet takes one look at it and says, "That's not a dog, that's a RAT."*

I always dedicate this legend to people in Alberta. Living in a rat-free province, we may be the only people who do not know what a rat looks like!

However, in France, they have problems too:

A very small, sweet dog was brought back from holidays in western Africa by a couple who were charmed by the animal. It had followed them in an affectionate manner during their entire stay. After smuggling it home, they find that the new arrival has cut the throat of the house cat. The animal was not a dog, but a large, sick rat.
(Campion-Vincent 1989, 103)

LITERARY AND VISUAL ADAPTATIONS

"Alligators in the Sewer"

Alligator (1980). This movie is based on the legend of alligator-in-the-sewer. "A *Jaws*-style horror movie which concerns a 25-foot renegade reptile on the loose beneath the streets of a small midwestern town" (Schechter 1988, 16).

Hip-Deep in Alligators by Robert Campbell (New York: New American Library, 1987). A mystery novel in which series character Jimmy Flannery inspects an old abandoned sewer and muses on all the dangers presented by such underground tunnels (Barnes and Smith 1992, 169).

Night Moves (1975). This movie mentions the legend when discussing other "throw away" pets such as dolphins.

V by Thomas Pynchon (Philadelphia: J. B. Lippincott, 1963). Several motifs included in Pynchon's story have become firmly attached to the contemporary legend: the alligators have become blind and albino from lack of light, and they grow to enormous sizes on their diet of rats (Morgan and Tucker 1984, 153). A companion tale is that of enormous and potent albino marijuana plants (that sprouted from seeds flushed down the toilet) growing in the sewers (Morgan and Tucker 1984, 153). Pynchon "wove the fabric of the alligator-in-the-sewers motif throughout the pages of his book, and thus brought this tale into modern popular culture as no one before him had" (Coleman 1979, 336). Pynchon adapted a story he had first heard in the winter of 1958–59. In the version he was told, from an acquaintance from New York City, the alligators were flushed down the toilet (Carroll 1984, 59).

The World Beneath the City by Robert R. Daley (Philadelphia: Lippincott, 1959). A nonfiction exploration of New York City that includes a chapter on alligators in the sewer system during the 1930s. Daley writes that they appeared in the sewers as the result of people disposing of unwanted alligator pets in storm drains and manholes rather than toilets of the more recent stories. This chapter is based on interviews with the Commissioner of Sewers, Teddy May (Fergus 1980, 182). Morgan and Tucker feel that it was the book reviews, rather than the book itself, that alerted the population to this phenomena. In Daley's newspaper articles, he never stated that the alligator "problem" was eliminated (1984, 152).

"The Choking Doberman"

"Juno" by Judith Gorog. In *On Meeting Witches at Wells* (New York: Philomel, 1991), 30–33. In the author's note (p. 119), Gorog states that this short story is "based on something my children heard on the radio and believed at the time was a true news story. I wrote 'Juno,' and then learned this year . . . it is what students of our culture call 'an urban myth.' "

"The Dog in the Elevator"

Police Academy 3: Back in Training (1986). This movie includes a brief sequence where the training officer shouts "Sit!" to the dog, and the police recruits promptly sit on the ground.

"The Elephant That Sat on the VW"

The Corpse on the Dike by Janwillem van de Wetering (Boston: Houghton Mifflin). A police procedural novel published in 1976.

"The Hare Drier"

"An Absolutely True Bunny Story" by Judith Gorog. In *On Meeting Witches at Wells* (New York: Philomel, 1991), 99–101.
Bad Hare Day. This 12-minute film, directed by Graeme Lynch, tells the story of pets being left to fend for themselves overnight. What could possibly go wrong?

"The Mexican Pet"

Murphy Brown (1995). In the segment "Window on America" of this television series, Murphy Brown and her co-workers have to contend with rats. When told a version of "The Mexican Pet," Murphy denounces the story as an urban legend.
Pet Sematary by Stephen King (Garden City, NY: Doubleday, 1983). This novel and the resulting movie are based on a similar motif: cats, dogs, and, finally, humans buried in a magical spot revive, dig themselves up, and return as an evil resurrection.

"Spider Bites"

Bliss (1985). An Australian film based on the novel of the same name tells the story of a spider bite. Also includes the legend of the "Elephant That Sat on the VW."

The Nature of the Beast (1987) directed by Franco Rosso. Adapted from the novel of the same name, this movie uses the legend as the basis for the tale and features a 14-year-old protagonist.

REFERENCES

Ammer, Christine. 1989. *It's raining cats and dogs . . . and other beastly expressions*. New York: Paragon House.

Baker, Ronald L. 1982. *Hoosier folk legends*. Bloomington: Indiana Press.

Barden, Thomas E. 1991. *Virginia folk legends*. Charlottesville: University Press of Virginia.

Barnes, Daniel R., and Paul Smith. 1992. The contemporary legend in literature: Towards an annotated checklist, part 2. *Contemporary Legend* 2: 167–79.

Beidermann, Hans. 1992. *Dictionary of symbolism: Cultural icons and the meanings behind them*, translated by James Hulbert. New York: Facts on File.

Bishop, Amanda. 1988. *The Guicci kangaroo and other Australian urban legends*. Hornsby, N.S.W.: Australasian.

Black widow spiders in grapes. 1991. *FOAFTALE NEWS* 23 (September): 14.

Brunvand, Jan Harold. 1984. The choking Doberman: A new legend. In *Perspectives on contemporary legend, Vol. #1*, edited by Paul Smith. Sheffield, England: University of Sheffield.

———. 1989. *Curses! Broiled again! The hottest urban legends going*. New York: W. W. Norton.

Campion-Vincent, Veronique. 1989. Complots et avertissements: Legendes urbaines dans la ville. *Revue Francaise de Sociologie* 30: 91–105. Translated from the French by Suzette Weinburger.

———. 1990. Contemporary legends about animal releases in rural France. *Fabula* 31: 242–53.

———. 1992. Appearances of beasts and mystery-cats in France. *Folklore* 103, no. 2: 160–83.

Carroll, Michael P. 1984. Alligators in the sewer, dragons in the well and Freud in the toilet. *Sociological Review* 32, no. 1 (February): 57–74.

Check tub before entering. 1993. *The Edmonton Journal* (September 14): A2.

Clarke, Kenneth. 1964. The fatal hairdo and the emperor's new clothes revisited. *Western Folklore* 23: 249–52.

Coleman, Loren. 1979. Alligators in the sewers: A journalistic origin. *Journal of American Folklore* 92: 335–38.

Crossley-Holland, Kevin. 1985. *Folk tales of the British Isles*. New York: Pantheon.

Dale, Rodney. 1984. *It's true, it happened to a friend: A collection of urban legends*. London: Duckworth.

Department store snakes. 1991. *FOAFTALE NEWS* 22 (June): 12.

Dickson, Paul, and Joseph C. Goulden. 1993. *Myth-informed: Legends, credos, and wrongheaded "facts" we all believe*. New York: Perigee.

Elevator incident. 1992. *FOAFTALE NEWS* 27 (September): 11.

Fergus, George. 1980. More on alligators in the sewers. *Journal of American Folklore* 93 (April–June): 182.

Goss, Michael. 1992. Alien big cat sightings in Britain: A possible rumour legend? *Folklore* 103, no. 3: 184–202.

Kapferer, Jean-Noel. 1990. *Rumors: Uses, interpretations, and images*. New Brunswick, NJ: Transaction.

Klintberg, Bengt af. 1985. Legends and rumours about spiders and snakes. *Fabula* 26: 274–87.

Leach, Maria, ed. 1972. *Funk & Wagnalls standard dictionary of folklore, mythology and legend*. New York: Funk & Wagnalls.

Lindahl, Carl. 1986. Psychic ambiguity at the legend core. *Journal of Folklore Research* 23, no. 1: 1–21.

Marchalenis, Shirley. 1976/77. Three medieval tales and their modern American analogues. *Journal of the Folklore Institute* 13/14: 173–84.

Mayor, Adrienne. 1992. Ambiguous guardians: The "omen of the wolves" (A.D. 402) and the "choking doberman" (1980s). *Journal of Folklore Research* 29, no. 3 (September–December): 253–68.

Monger, George. 1992. Dragons and big cats. *Folklore* 103, no. 2: 203–6.

Morgan, Hal, and Kerry Tucker. 1984. *Rumor!* New York: Penguin.

Puppy jumps off high-rise balcony. 1992. *FOAFTALE NEWS* 26 (June): 11–12.

Pynchon, Thomas. 1963. *V*. Philidelphia: J. B. Lippincott.

Schechter, Harold. 1988. *The bosom serpent: Folklore and popular art*. Iowa City: University of Iowa Press.

Smith, Paul. 1983. *The book of nasty legends*. London: Routledge Kegan Paul.

———. 1986. *The book of nastier legends*. London: Routledge Kegan Paul.

Smith, Paul, and Danielle Roemer. 1988. The alligators are back. *FOAFTALE NEWS* 9 (March): 1–3.

Snakebite rumor at Knoebels Grove. 1991. *FOAFTALE NEWS* 24 (December): 12.

Snakes and bananas. 1992. *FOAFTALE NEWS* 28 (December): 10.

So there's this guy, see . . . 1991. *Maclean's* 104, no. 48 (December 2): 80–81.

South Africans in elevators. 1990. *FOAFTALE NEWS* 20 (December): 10.

Spiders in plants. 1992. *FOAFTALE NEWS* 27 (September): 10.

Thigpen, Kenneth A. 1979. Folklore in contemporary American literature: Thomas Pynchon's *V* and the alligators-in-the sewers legend. *Southern Folklore Quarterly* 43: 93–105.

Weigle, Marta. 1982. *Spiders & spinsters: Women and mythology*. Albuquerque: University of New Mexico Press.

Woman runs from snake intruder. 1990. *The Edmonton Journal* (April 16): B2.

10 THREATS TO OUR CHILDREN
STOLEN BODY PARTS, AIDS, ABDUCTIONS, AND TATTOOS

(Vienna) Children are now being sold so that their vital organs can be used in transplants, the UN special investigator stated on the sale of children. The investigator, Vitit Muntarbhorn of Thailand, told the World Conference on Human Rights on Monday that advances in technology have created new kinds of horrific crimes against children.

Muntarbhorn noted that for some time children have been sold or kidnapped to work as slaves and prostitutes, and to be the subject of pornographic films. But now, he said, youngsters are taken to supply organs for transplants and others are used to grow fetal tissues for medical treatment. (Children Sold for Transplants 1993, A1)

One of society's major fears is of threats to our young. Contemporary legends, therefore, often reflect this deep-seated anxiety, which is caused by the general public's misunderstanding of medical innovations, drugs, and "ambiguous" diseases. But our fears and anxieties are much wider than that. We are not only concerned about medical dangers to our children but also attacks from outside forces. The danger may be hidden in large impersonal institutions or brought in by "foreign" invaders. With the aid of the mass media, isolated "cases" of attempted kidnapping of children and young adults from shopping malls and large entertainment theme parks have become perceived as a widespread epidemic of organized crime.

Legends of stolen kidneys and baby body parts, AIDS, the kidnapping of children, and LSD-laced tattoo transfers all relate the same message: *Take care of your children, protect them at all costs!*

For young adults the message is also very strong: *Be careful, this could happen to you!* In many instances, young adults do not entertain thoughts of mortality and think that the legend could never involve someone of their age. For example, many young adults consider AIDS as an adult disease or a homo-sexual disease and disregard the warnings and information transmitted through official channels and the media. "AIDS-lore legends" incorporate the same warnings and have a significant impact on the young adult audience.

Also, because of the numerous instances of three threatening contem-porary legends being treated as news in the media, it is essential to under-stand the possible roots and symbolism behind these legends. Young adults need to become critical consumers of news agencies and not accept news either unconditionally as truth or dismiss it as "silly stories." The people who tell these legends believe them and pass them on, not to shock or horrify the listener, but in the hope that some action can be taken to protect the innocent victims. Their concern should be applauded and not dismissed lightly because they are gullible retellers of a migratory tale.

"THE STOLEN KIDNEY" AND OTHER MISSING BODY PARTS

The legend cycle of "The Stolen Kidney," "Baby Parts," or "Organ Transplants" alleges that children are taken from third-world countries by evil foreigners and treated as a natural resource: spare-parts for the wealthy and influential (Campion-Vincent 1993, 245). The legend not only circulates extensively and is thoroughly believed, but is often the cause of excessive anger and ostensive "retaliation."

(Guatemala City) An Alaskan woman caught up in the rumors that Americans are stealing children was transferred to a hospital in the Guatemalan capital Wednesday after suffering severe injuries at the hands of a rural mob. . . . [She] was the third foreigner known to have been attacked in Guatemala in recent days over rumors that children are being stolen. Some versions allege foreigners are taking children to sell body parts for transplant operations. U.S. officials say no evidence has been found to support the stories. . . . [She] was attacked . . . after a woman screamed that the American tried to steal her eight-year-old boy. The boy turned up later at a Holy Week celebration. (Guatemalans Beat Suspected Child-Snatcher 1994, B10)

History of "The Stolen Kidney"

The legend cycle emerged at the beginning of 1987 in Latin America and was used as a propaganda weapon against the Western world. Folklorists have devoted considerable research to the legend, focusing on its transmis-sion, functions, and historical antecedents. Others are equally fascinated with evidence of the role of the media in dissemination of the legend. It is "an example of systematic disinformation and of the dysfunctions of the international media" (Campion-Vincent 1990, 10).

The first reported news item appeared in the Honduran newspaper *La Tribuna* on January 2, 1987. The article included a quote allegedly from L. V. Bermudez, the general secretary of the official welfare agency in Honduras, stating that the trafficking of human body parts and the kidnapping of young children was a pressing problem in his country. The following day, Bermudez's denial was published and the story was picked up, minus the denial, by Latin American media. In early February, a police officer in Guatemala denied the legend in the media, but this denial was also ignored by the general public.

In April of the same year, a Mexican correspondent who spoke of thousands of Honduran children disappearing and becoming sources for organ "donations" was quoted in *Pravda*. The article was picked up by Tass news agency and reported worldwide. Several U.S. agencies (the Department of Justice, the Federal Bureau of Investigation [FBI], the Food and Drug Administration [FDA], the National Institute of Health [NIH], the Department of Health and Social Services [DHSS], and the Immigration and Naturalization Service [INS]) denied that the legend had any foundation in truth.

Circulation subsided for several months, until, in 1988, the legend began circulating again. Two new allegations (and prompt denials) were issued in Guatemala and Paraguay. In September, a French-based, non-governmental human rights organization investigated the legend and concluded that while no proof of organ trafficking had been found, trafficking in children for adoption was a widespread practice. At the end of 1989, the legend was no longer considered a legitimate story but rather an "anti-American" tale (Campion-Vincent 1990, 10–14).

However, the media did not let it rest! In an article entitled "To Market, To Market to Buy a Fine Child," a discussion on the trafficking of children for adoption in Western countries included this statement:

> Those who are not answering the insistent call for babies to adopt from rich countries are bought by those who peddle in pornography, prostitution or drugs, or by those involved in the growing international trade in human organs. (O'Shaughnessy 1993, E1)

A quote from the Salvador government Procurer for the Defence of Children substantiates the author's premise. "We know there is a big trade in children in El Salvador, for pornographic videos, for organ transplants, for adoption and for prostitution" (O'Shaughnessy 1993, E2). Further, the article describes several different practices in neighboring countries:

In Honduras . . . the practice is for baby farmers to adopt retarded children and use their organs as human "spare parts." In Guatamala City, the fire service and the undertakers are notorious for trading in the organs of the dead, young and old. . . . According to a report published last month by the European parliament in Strasbourg, only a quarter of the 4,000 Brazilian children authorized for adoption in Italy were really adopted. The rest, it is claimed, were chopped up for their organs in undercover hospitals in Mexico and Europe by the order of the Camorra, the Mafia of Naples. (E2)

Another article that appeared in the newspaper on the same day mentioned a Canadian clergyman who had problems convincing the family that he wanted to help a 28-year-old man by sponsoring a trip to Canada for medical attention:

[The family] feared Hutton meant to kill Gonzales, 28, for his organs so they could be sold for medical transplants. . . . Hutton said the family's fears were based on stories of people in the slums being lured away to the United States with promises of a brighter future. According to the rumor, they are later found dead, floating in the Rio Grande with some of their organs missing. It's a revolting crime that is known to happen in India and some Latin American countries. (Oosterom 1993, A3)

Although the rumors and legends about organ trafficking have been continually refuted, in April 1994, O'Shaughnessy wrote about the practice in another newspaper article:

A children's home in St. Petersburg, Russia, is giving away children in its care to foreigners and does not bother to register the addresses to which they go. The evidence, though circumstantial, points strongly to the orphans being robbed of their organs and tissues. . . . As advances in science make spare-part surgery common, and new pharmaceutical products allow organs and tissues to be preserved for increasingly long periods, demand is outstripping supply and waiting lists, particularly in Europe are growing fast. This is producing a booming market in organs, obtained in many cases by violence or murder, or from the corpses of executed murderers. (1994, G3)

Julio Cesar Araoz, health minister of Argentina, confirmed that organ trafficking was widespread. However, he clarified, most of the kidneys and corneas have been offered for sale by destitute Argentineans. Unscrupulous doctors are also rumored to be the source of the offered organs. "There are cases in which bodies are found to be stuffed full of paper when they are handed over to the family or of people opening the coffin to find it is empty" (Abducted Latin American Children 1992, 11).

A frequent visitor to Guatemala, John Shonder, followed the rumors and the resultant attacks on Western tourists. He states that, like most rumors, there are elements of truth in this case: children *do* disappear as there is apparently a large trade in illegal adoptions. But this legend has acquired further strength based on two additional factors: belief in the folklore of La Llorona, the "weeping woman" who is looking for her murdered children (the subject of chapter 14), and irresponsible journalism (1994, 2). While it may be easy to dismiss the news stories as contemporary legends and careless reporting, caution must be exercised. Human organs are sold on the market today and, human behavior being what it is, who can tell what may develop. After all, "remember how rumors about Kentucky Fried rats and strange bones in Chinese restaurants were followed by real-life product tampering and splintered glass in baby food in Great Britain" (Campion-Vincent 1990, 24).

Structure of the Legend

Because of the media intervention in the formulation and transmission of this legend, the basic structure of the variants is very consistent:

Orientation: A discovery of the widespread disappearance of children from poor homes or orphanages. Sometimes the story becomes "known" because of the discovery of clandestine foster homes sheltering kidnapped or bought babies.

Complicating Action: Commentary on event by middle-level officials. Prompt denials by same officials stating lack of hard evidence (speculations, suppositions, and assumptions stated were erroneously quoted by press). Reinforcement of these denials by the hierarchical superiors of these middle-level officials (Campion-Vincent 1990, 14).

Result: Denials ignored by general population (and mass media). Legend continues to circulate and to be used as an explanation for the inexplicable.

Plausible Elements of the Legend

Variants of the "Baby Parts" legend usually circulate in areas of high infant mortality and in areas that feel oppressed by the Western world (Stevens 1991, 27). The legend "rings true" for a multitude of reasons. Among other things, it reflects the "perception that a politically and economically powerful population feels entitled to strengthen itself by destroying the bodies of citizens from weaker populations" (Turner 1993, 148).

Adoptions

The recent, and common, practice of obtaining children for adoption in Western society from third-world countries facilitates the belief in, and the spread of, the legends about stolen baby parts. Hostility exists against the elite class of people who can afford to adopt ("buy") a child, and this hostility is heightened with racial and nationalistic sentiments, as many of these "fortunate" people are foreigners. Under the hostility lies a genuine anxiety about the future of the children (Campion-Vincent 1990, 15).

Marketing of Human Organs

The demand for organ transplants far exceeds the supply, and destitute (as well as unscrupulous) people have taken "advantage" of this fact. Some cultures have strong taboos against the removal of organs from cadavers, leaving the selling of organs from live donors the only avenue available. In Brazil, Turkey, and India, kidneys and corneas are advertised for sale. In North America, where the sale of human organs is illegal, authorized gifts from "relatives" can often be obtained (Campion-Vincent 1990, 17).

Popular Culture

Not only has the news media maintained a fascination with the story and the theme, but popular culture has also adopted the legend and refurbished the horror and the tragedy through film, television series, novels, and modern bogeymen such as the "mad scientist." Medical horror is a developing subgenre, and novels such as Ridley Pearson's *The Angel Maker* and the film and novel *Coma* have been written based on the oral legend. "This modern denunciation of evil medicine, enhanced by a general uneasiness towards the accelerated pace of change in technologies of life and death, has created a climate of suspicion that has spread over the whole planet" (Campion-Vincent 1990, 18).

Latin American countries import North American popular culture and incorporate into it anti-American feelings, expressing the familiar themes and anxieties about safety and future of the children that the "Baby Parts" legend reflects.

The Fear of the "White Ogre"

The "white ogre," an evil white man with supernatural powers, has a long history in many third-world countries; he is believed to be particularly needy of the blood and organs of the colored people he dominates (Campion-Vincent 1990, 19). The character resembles a traditional Spanish child-stealer, *Mantequero*, who sleeps all day and, during the night, steals the fat from sleeping natives. Foreigners, such as monks and priests, have been accused of this crime since colonial times. In Peru, the character, known as *Pistaco*, goes out at night carrying a long knife, with which he cuts up the Indians. He uses their fat to oil his machines and sells the blood to blood banks (Campion-Vincent 1990, 19).

In 1988, a new "white ogre," *Sacojos* (eye-robbers), appeared in the folk culture. *Sacojos* carves the eyes out of the children and sells them abroad for dollars "to help settle the external debt" (Campion-Vincent 1990, 20). When this story began to circulate, people panicked and took their children out of school. However, anger eventually replaced fear, and tourists and welfare workers were thought to be fair game by hostile locals (Campion-Vincent 1990, 20).

The "white ogre" character is not associated with Mexican or Guatemalan mythology, but these cultures do believe in cannibalistic child-stealing witches called *naguals*. These traditional folk characters help to form a basis for the distrust of white foreigners. But what of the urban and educated population who do not share these beliefs?

"The Blood Libel"

In other parts of the world, too, legends of ritual murders of children have a long history. The central theme of "The Blood Libel" is the kidnapping and murder of children of one group by another. Historically, such accusations have been leveled against the Christians by the ancient Romans; against the Jews by the Christians from the Middle Ages on; and against satanic cults or ethnic groups by anxious citizens today (Campion-Vincent 1990, 21). The legend always incorporates the popular scapegoats of the time, the theme of absolute evil versus complete innocence, and the destruction of a culture through the draining of its children's blood. "The Blood Libel" is discussed in greater detail in the following chapter.

Popular Fascination with Real Criminals

People have always had a fascination with criminals and criminal behavior, and popular culture serves to enhance this "glorification" of the criminal element. "Burker" stories, told by the "travelers" in Scotland to warn their children about the dangers from the larger society, are based on the real-life criminals Burke and Hare, who murdered people to obtain cadavers for a medical school during the early 19th century. Robert Louis Stevenson's *The Body Snatchers* (1884) is based on this pair of "entrepreneurs." Mass-murderers also pique the interest of the public, and they provide "invaluable" copy for the media and the entertainment industry. Because people are surrounded by these examples of the prevalence of criminal behavior, they are predisposed to believe in the legends once they appear in the media and in conversations.

Variants of "Stolen Body Parts"

There are several parallels between stolen body parts involving the kidnapping of children, and UFO abduction stories, in which aliens kidnap humans for medical examination and experimentation. The core elements of the legend remain constant regardless of the location of the tale. Interesting variations occur, however, when the theme of "innocents abroad" is incorporated into the legend. For example, the legend being told around Australia in the early 1990s incorporates the image of innocent young men coming to grief in the United States or Europe while on holiday or at business conventions:

Two Austalian men went on holiday to Los Angeles, USA. They went out one evening drinking in the bars and met up with some local people. One of the men decided to go off with one of the women whilst his companion returned to their hotel room. His friend didn't return for a few days. When he finally showed up, he complained of not feeling well and of being unable to remember what had happened. They thought that maybe he had been drugged and robbed, but he still had his wallet. As they also discovered a cut on his back, they decided to go to a doctor. After various tests, it was discovered that one of his kidneys had been removed.
(Moravec 1991, 6)

Canadian Variants

The greatest danger of cross-border shopping has just come to light. A man and a woman from the Toronto area travelled to Buffalo to shop. On arriving, they went their separate ways. When the woman finished her errands she returned to the car. The man didn't show up. An hour passed. And another. . . . Another hour passed, the parking lot was emptying. All the imagined horrors that lurk in American cities loomed in the woman's mind. With a jittery sense that something dreadful had happened, she waited another hour. By

> *now thoroughly terrified, she was about to call the police when she saw the man coming toward the garage. He was groggy and disorientated and having trouble walking. Trembling with relief she helped him into the car. He couldn't recollect where he had been since they parted. When he sat in the passenger seat, he felt severe discomfort and clutched his back. She opened his shirt and found, above his left hip, a surgical dressing. Under the dressing was what looked like an incision, still raw, closed by 23 stitches. He also had a bruised lump over his left ear. Mystified, but wanting to get away from the place as quickly as they could, they returned to Toronto and the next morning the man went to his doctor. The doctor ran tests and made the most appalling discovery of his medical career. The man's left kidney was gone. It had been stolen.*
>
> (Buffalo's a City with a Heart 1992, A2)

All of the versions of this legend that I have heard in Canada imply that, while this is a fairly common occurrence, it takes place elsewhere, not at all within the borders of Canada. Like the versions circulating in Australia, the legend reflects the Canadian concern with people going away and getting involved in dangerous situations (which could never happen at home). This version, however, is the only one I know that points out the dangers of cross-border shopping!

Mongolian Variants

"As Turks, Arabs and Germans in Polish tales or Western Europeans in Russian tales are the notorious kidnappers, so in Mongolian tales this role is reserved solely for the Chinese":

> *A young child disappeared from the street. Rumor struck among people that the child was taken for blood. Old and rich Chinese make themselves younger in that way. Many children in Mongolia have disappeared. People say that their kidneys were snatched for exchange for those Chinese. They're poor in China, but there are also some very rich people. And those rich and old need spare parts. And they get it from our children. I hear young blood helps old get younger. I've been hearing about it for three years now. It is not one single fact, I've heard about it many times.* (Czubala 1993, 4)

Polish Variants

---

*Two men (Polish priests, foreigners, or simply strangers) lure a
child or children to a black or red car where they take their blood or
different body organs for Arabian sheiks or people in the West.*
(Czubala 1991b, 1)

This variant was immensely popular in Poland during the 1970s and
early 1980s. "It was a time of panic among children, parents and teachers,
intensified by the mass media without any positive results" (Czubala 1991b, 1).
FOAFTALE NEWS editor Bill Ellis commented that the same legend was
reported in an article on Polish legends published in 1987. "The [Polish] press
reprinted this rumor as a joke, but many readers missed the irony of these
news articles, assumed the story was a genuine news item, and spread it
further" (Czubala 1991b, 2). The Polish variant demonstrates a relationship
between the child abduction/murder motif and the Anglo-American satanic
motifs of the blood, fat, or vital organs of children (especially babies) being
necessary for occult rites (Czubala 1991b, 3). Further, this legend was active
at the exact same time as the "animal mutilation" panic, the first major satanic
flap to erupt in the western United States.

Russian Variants

The story was also popular in the Soviet Union during the same period.
The first variant, collected in Minsk, July 1990, has a familiar ring, reminiscent of recent stories circulating in North America:

---

*A boy was walking along the road, a car was going by and the
passengers asked him the way. They asked him to get in and show
them the way. He got in and they went away. Later he was found in
the woods without kidneys. He had been put to sleep by chloroform
and then they cut out his kidneys. When he awoke they were gone.
He was immediately taken to a Moscow hospital by air. He survived
because he was very strong. He gave all the details of his kidnapping,
what the people looked like. There was a special gang of people who
delivered different body organs to hospitals.* (Czubala 1991b, 2)

Another Russian variant refers to Canada:

> *The Canadian Press release of 17 February 1991 reported a rumor, published in Irish and Soviet newspapers, that Russian hospital workers were secretly removing thousands of organs from the bodies of people killed in automobile accidents and sending them to Montreal to use for organ transplants and for making cosmetics. Sources at Montreal cosmetic firms dismissed the rumor as "completely absurd."* (Czubala 1991b, 3)

"CHILD ABDUCTIONS"

> *It seems that a woman went shopping with her little boy, and in that crowd of people, she lost track of him. She turned her back for a moment and he was gone. . . . The woman spoke to the guards, and they closed all the exits, locking everyone inside. . . . The guards finally found the child in a bathroom . . . his hair had been dyed blond. . . . "And the kidnappers dressed him as a girl?" [he] asked, recalling a parallel story he had heard in the Chicago area years before. "No," his friend replied, "like a clown!"* (Body Parts Panics in Guatemala 1994, 17)

Large shopping centers and theme parks are the usual setting for this legend. However, although I have known this legend for years, when I was in Rome with my family and someone tried to separate me from my very blond six-year-old daughter on public transport, I have to admit my first impulse (other than holding her hand tighter) was to think, "My blond baby! They're taking my blond baby." Needless to say, they couldn't care what color her hair was, they just wanted to distract me so they could lift my wallet. I was chagrined, not only because my pocket was picked, but because of the fact that the legend surfaced so quickly and colored my actions. My daughter was just angry: "If you would have let go of my hand nothing would have happened. I'm strong!"

Other abduction legends are of a darker nature. In Sicily, people believe that *"there's a black ambulance driving around the city trying to kidnap our children!"* (Stilo and Toselli 1991, 5). These legends about child abductions circulated throughout Italy and escalated when they became combined with the legend of stolen body parts in 1990. Circulars were said to have gone to schools (no such circular exists) warning authorities about allowing children to leave the school with men disguised as police or medical personnel.

Although the legend mirrors modern concerns about violence and the safety of children, a similar expression of the same fears and concerns circulated in Paris in May 1750:

Police using covered wagons were kidnapping children off the streets; they were never seen again. Some said they were sent to the Americas; according to others, the unfortunate children were drained of their blood, which was being used to cure a sick prince at the Royal Palace. (Stilo and Toselli 1991, 6)

"WHITE SLAVE TRADE"

Apparently, solitary sunbathing can be dangerous on the beach at Cancun, Mexico. According to a Pennsylvania woman, Sharon McCormick, she was spending her honeymoon in the Caribbean resort, and was lying on the beach, when she was chloroformed and kidnapped. She says she was dragged to a construction site by her abductors and managed to escape with minor injuries. But she told Pennsylvania state Rep. Michael Gruitza that she had seen three other American women in the kidnapper's hideout. They were heavily sedated, she said. Gruitza contacted the U.S. embassy and the FBI, which is now conducting an investigation with Mexican authorities. The FBI says it has no hard evidence of a possible white slavery operation in Cancun. Without further evidence, the State Department says, it can't issue a travel advisory to American vacationers. (Just In! White Slavers in Mexico 1989, 1)

The legend of the "White Slave Trade" circulates mainly among young adolescent girls who have very little experience with city life and social reality, and among senior citizens who have misgivings about modern trends and living conditions (Kapferer 1990, 88). While rather dormant in the early 1990s, the legend as been popular in France in the past. Basic elements in the legend are paralleled in other popular legends such as "Pin-Prick Panic" and "The Snake in the Produce," shown in the following chart that breaks down the French versions of these legends:

The Rumor's Eternal Return

The Myth's Basic Structure	Orlean's-Type Variant ("Pin-Prick Panic")	Typical Variant: Child Bitten by a Snake ("Snake in the Produce")
Strangers in the group	Jews, shopkeepers	Third-world immigrants, entertainers
Sexual violence	Biting, hypodermic needles	Snakes, scorpions, spiders
Deporting	White slave trade	Death
Victims	Girls, young women	Little girls, children
The site of inescapable temptation	Fashionable clothes stores	Supermarkets, fairs
Sites of the myth's return	Various locations in France from 1966–1985	Various locations in France from 1981–1986

(Kapferer 1990, 121)

Rumors and legends continue to resurface and circulate as long as their message is relevant to the audience. Their "eternal return" is tied to the fate of scapegoats who are always foreigners, people who are not well integrated into the collective community and who do not share the same beliefs and values of the wider community (Kapferer 1990, 122).

AIDS-LORE

The hotel barber, he used to be somebody. And now? No one goes there for a shave any more. I'm telling you, they're scared of AIDS! You used to make real money in that business. When you got a foreigner in the chair—well, he paid. It was worth it, standing there in the apron just for the tips they gave you. Today nobody goes, nobody will even let the razor touch their skin. It might all be contaminated. And, you know, it's even worse when you're a skinny barber—forget it! At Novotel [a luxurious motel chain] the barber went bankrupt. He was so skinny everybody suspected he had it. Who knows, maybe the hotel workers ruined his reputation, why not? I wouldn't go there myself. I tell you, there's no way you can pull the razor over the skin without scratching, and you got all kinds of races and types sitting on that chair. (Czubala 1991a, 1–2)

In fear of AIDS and HIV-carriers, Polish citizens actively demonstrated in protest against possible contamination. This fear is also seen in the form of the legends and rumors circulating in Poland during the early 1990s. "As the number of those infected and infecting increases, so are the situations, places and institutions in which people believe the disease can be spread" (Czubala 1991a, 1). In addition to avoiding such locations as dental clinics, hospitals, prisons, and public eating places, people have even stopped going to barber shops for a shave.

HIV carriers are thought to be a threat to society because many believe they willfully spread the disease: by biting the officers that arrest them or by assaulting unsuspecting teenage victims. "Two of them hold a girl's hands, while the third kisses her on the mouth and passes on the virus with his saliva" (Czubala 1991a, 2). Then again, it is not always folklore:

An HIV-infected man who smeared his blood onto a teenage girl's cuts and told her she was going to die was acquitted Monday of attempted murder. . . . [The Crown] ruled that there wasn't "adequate judicial knowledge" about whether such smearing of blood could infect a healthy person with HIV, the virus linked to AIDS. . . . [The defendant] told the girl that he was HIV-positive and she had just "joined his club". . . . The Crown did not lay charges against [him] for failing to tell the girl he had the HIV virus before having sex with her. (Baker 1995, A8)

Another variant tells of a drug addict who, upon hearing about his infection, threw a party and added tainted blood to the drinks to ensure that all his friends were in the same boat as himself. Others, according to the legends, deliberately spread the disease through sexual contact:

A girl slept with a guy and did not ask for money: instead she left a farewell message on the mirror. When the boy woke up, he read "Welcome to the AIDS club." (Czubala 1991a, 3)

In other instances, AIDS is said to be transmitted by people armed with infected syringes traveling on crowded public transportation or by enterprising thieves who use the syringe to discourage pursuit, allowing them to retreat safely from the scene of the crime:

> *A robber brandishing a full syringe threatened to infect a west-end*
> *bank teller with tainted blood Tuesday night if she didn't turn over*
> *the money. "To our recollection, we don't believe we've ever had a*
> *similar robbery before," said police information officer Annette*
> *Bidnaik. . . . He pulled out a full syringe and warned the teller that*
> *it was loaded with infected blood. "He didn't say what it*
> *was infected with," Bidniak said.* (Bank Robber Warns
> Teller Syringe Had Tainted Blood 1994, B3)

Although the bank robber was later apprehended, the "unknown" substance was never identified in the media; however, the local citizens did not question what it was.

My daughter first heard the legend from her teacher in her fifth-grade, sex-education class in 1989. It was presented as a true story that happened to one of the teacher's friends:

> *The friend met a man in Montreal, developed a relationship with*
> *him and then, the day before she left to return to Alberta, she spent*
> *the night with him. At the airport he handed her a gift and was told*
> *not to open it until she was in the air. The gift consisted of a*
> *container (my daughter does not remember what it was) and*
> *the message "Welcome to the wonderful world of AIDS."*

The tale was told to warn the girls to avoid casual relationships as well as unprotected sex. The legend-telling did not prompt any classroom dialogue at the time, but my daughter has not forgotten the tale itself. Perhaps, as she thinks back five years, the girls were too young to really understand the horror and the message completely. But at the same time she retains the warning; as she said, "AIDS is out there, why take chances?"

AIDS-Lore as Contemporary Legend

AIDS-lore can be classified as a contemporary legend because it demonstrates common elements of the genre. AIDS-lore is told about a specific place but anonymous people, it functions as a cautionary moral tale about revenge, and it includes traditional motifs such as writing on the mirror (Smith 1990, 113). The present cycle began circulating in the mid-1980s in both North America and Europe. Adaptations were almost immediately incorporated, including the beliefs that male prostitutes deliberately infect both their customers and their procurers and that HIV-carriers threaten to "spit" on their enemies and unsuspecting victims (Smith 1990, 119). As Paul Smith writes, "Contemporary legends about AIDS are, in part, the product of static and evolving *belief systems* and static and evolving *health systems*, both of which directly influence the content of the tales" (1990, 122).

Historical Antecedents

Sexually-transmitted diseases are not a recent phenomenon, nor are plagues that attack large segments of the population. Throughout history, people have used rumors, legends, and gossip to try to come to terms with the spreading of diseases. The body of folklore that surrounds accounts of cholera, polio, and the Black Plague provides a prototype for the folklore surrounding AIDS (Fine 1987, 192).

The view of AIDS as "the greatest killer-plague" of this century has parallels in Daniel Defoe's *Journal of the Plague Year* (1722). Defoe provides an eye-witness account of the 1665 plague and points out that there was a lack of adequate information about the cause of the plague and possible cures; that rumors circulated widely about compulsory segregation of the inflicted; that social tensions and prejudices figured largely in the rumors; and that the "explanations" for the epidemic were based on notions of Divine retribution (Smith 1990, 132). Plagues and other disasters have long been attributed to the notion of Divine retribution. Giovanni Boccaccio, in the introduction to his collection of stories *The Decameron* (1348), states that, "Some say that [the plague] is descended upon the human race through the influence of heavenly bodies, others that it was punishment signifying God's righteous anger at our iniquitous way of life" (quoted in Smith 1990, 133). The medieval belief in the healing power of storytelling and story listening prompted Boccaccio to place his 10 characters outside the walls of plague-infected Florence to tell stories to each other. The 100 stories in the collection reflect the legends, gossip, and rumors of Italy at that time.

Other tales of sexual revenge similar to much of the AIDS-lore legends have been with us throughout history, but "most have been excluded from the conventional tale type and motif indexes" (Smith 1990, 127).

Elements of AIDS-Lore

Some of the earliest lore about AIDS centered on popular misconceptions about the transmission of AIDS (by mosquitoes, sneezes, toilet seats) and jokes about homosexuals. As the disease spread outside the homosexual community, the nature of some of the folklore changed. While jokes still center on homosexuals, contemporary legends focus on heterosexual activity, "reflecting new levels of concern" (Fine 1987, 193).

Origin of AIDS

Because AIDS is a "new" disease that was (and still is) misunderstood by the general population, a popular folklore evolved to explain its development and transmission. Some of these suggestions may sound foolish today, but certain segments of the population still subscribe to them. Legends about the origin of AIDS, documented by Paul Smith (1990, 124–25), include stories that it:

1. originated in green monkeys in Africa;
2. spread from specific ethnic groups—such as Haitians;
3. is an out-of-control germ warfare virus that escaped;
4. has been put in the fluoride of our drinking water;
5. was put in K-Y Jelly by the Centers for Disease Control to eliminate homosexuals;
6. was developed by the CIA;
7. was developed by the Russians; and
8. was created in Hitler's laboratories.

Gender Roles

In a large percentage of AIDS-lore variants, the woman is the stated aggressor, knowingly transmitting AIDS to the man. Early variants circulating in the armed forces suggest that "armed forces personnel coping with their casual sexual encounters might have been the first group for which this theme was psychologically relevant" (Fine 1987, 193). The fact that this aspect of the legend does not correspond to reality in this instance is worth remarking upon. At the time of Fine's research, very few cases of transmission of AIDS from women to men had been recorded; the usual transference in a heterosexual relationship is male to female (Fine 1987, 195).

Delivery of Message

Writing the message on the bathroom mirror in red lipstick is the most cited method of delivering the message about contamination. Gary Alan Fine (1987, 195) notes that red lipstick on the bathroom mirror is significant for several reasons:

1. It makes for an aesthetically pleasing story. The setting changes, from the bedroom to the bathroom, enhancing the suspense when the woman is missing and the horror when the note is found.

2. The motif has long been popular in popular folklore and the mass media. A magazine advertisement for Bill Blass men's underwear,

issued at the same time as the legend began circulating, incorporated a handsome man in bikini briefs finding a [more positive] note from his lover written in red lipstick on the bathroom mirror.

3. A woman wearing lipstick, and particularly red lipstick, has traditionally conveyed an image of sexuality, mystery, and possibly, danger—as in the idea of a "scarlet woman."

In more recent variants, the message is conveyed in the form of a "good-bye" gift, to be open privately after the couple's parting. The surprise package is, alternately, a gift-wrapped box (the size of an engagement ring), a coffin-shaped package containing a rose, or an expensive greeting card.

The message basically welcomes the "victim" to his new cultural group: "Welcome to the world of AIDS"; "Welcome to the wacky world of AIDS"; "Welcome to the AIDS family"; and "Welcome to the AIDS club." "They suggest that having AIDS (testing positively for the virus) cements the person into a social (or folk) community, from which one can never escape and which will expand" (Fine 1987, 196).

Plausibility

The threat of AIDS is no longer confined to an isolated, marginal group of individuals; it has become the concern of the wider population. A backlash against the attitudes of the sexual revolution of the 1960s and its perceived consequences (e.g., herpes, the increased availability of pornography, and increasing numbers of divorces and rapes) have people scrambling for a "new age" of responsibility and changing sexual mores. AIDS-lore warns about casual sexual encounters and sexually transmitted diseases, but this warning is only one function of this legend. Depending upon the gender of the narrator, the legends reflect a worldview about rape (females) and paranoia towards women (males).

Many women feel that they are vulnerable to the attacks of males, particularly in the kind of anonymous "dates" described in these texts. Many women feel they have little control because accusations of forced sexual intercourse can easily be countered as having been mutually consensual. "Stories such as those cited here are, for women, a subtle revenge against men, a revenge, perhaps, in which they are not aware that they are engaged. The rape is turned on its head. . . . The woman is in total control" (Fine 1987, 196–97).

The variant that males tell "plays on their collective paranoia toward women" and indicates to men that their illusion of control may be just "an illusion" (Fine 1987, 197). The legend is easily believed because people are frightened and angry. The disease has interfered with one of the strongest human needs—security—and the aggression against, and aggression attributed to, those carrying the HIV virus are part and parcel of belief systems and defense mechanisms (Czubala 1991a, 4).

AIDS-Lore and African Americans

Research states that African American AIDS-lore reflects fears of "organized" contamination (infection) from a domineering group. The virus has been interpreted in two central ways: 1) as "the aftermath of a biological warfare experiment that was tried out on Africans or Haitians"; or 2) as "an intentional use of biological warfare *intended* to diminish the African or Haitian population" (Turner 1993, 158).

AIDS, according to one variant, was introduced into the third world through smallpox vaccinations sponsored by the World Health Organization (Legends and Life: AIDS 1992, 8). This may not be as farfetched as it sounds:

> Vaccines developed against the polio virus during the 1950s were grown in tissue cultures made from fresh-killed monkey kidneys, and outbreaks of least three fatal diseases have been linked to simian viruses that were transferred to humans through preparing or receiving polio vaccinations. The African green monkey, one of the animals used in early research, is believed to be the ultimate source of HIV (the AIDS virus). (Legends and Life: AIDS 1992, 8)

Tensions erupted on American campuses between African Americans and the Jewish community after accusations were made accusing Jewish doctors of injecting black babies with AIDS-infected blood (African-American Legends 1991, 11). This is, perhaps, a recent adaptation of historical allegations against the Jews in "The Blood Libel" legend.

"Hold the Mayo"

> *A young man, working in a metropolitan area Burger King, learns that he has AIDS. Unwilling to die alone, he ejaculates into the mayonnaise and so contaminated the unsuspecting patrons.*
> (Langlois 1991, 153)

Several features of this variant are worthy of further contemplation. People see AIDS and its victims as pollutants and therefore are willing to believe that they would contaminate food given to the "healthy" population. These legends combine two types of contemporary legend: "a sex revenge narrative in which the AIDS victim becomes the victimizer through his or her attempts to contaminate others" and the "foreign object in the food" subset of the cycle of contaminated food legends (Langlois 1991, 158).

Similarities also exist between this variant and the legend of "Church's Fried Chicken," which blends food contamination legends and conspiracy beliefs (Langlois 1991, 164). Burger King was a target of this variant because of their 1987 decision to develop regional and ethnic toppings for their burgers. "Burger King's addition of chili beans and barbecue sauce in franchises within the ethnic neighborhoods themselves, then, may be comparable to Church's offering fried chicken within African-American communities and so appropriating and stereotyping food choices" (Langlois 1991, 165).

By 1990, "Hold the Mayo" cited Domino's Pizza as the place of business in which the infected food-server worked. Mayo on pizza? In Great Britain, this legend has been transferred onto local curry houses:

After having her stomach pumped out after feeling ill, the patient is asked by the doctor if she had oral sex that night as her stomach contained a heavy amount of semen. "Explanation: the restaurateurs, annoyed at these [Caucasian] customers, decided to 'cream their curry' with something special." (Have You Heard: Creamed Curry, 1994, 16)

A Case Study: AIDS-Lore in Newfoundland, Canada

Newfoundland, the tenth Canadian province to join confederation, is situated on an island with a population of predominantly Irish and English ancestry that has been traditionally isolated from contact with both the Old World and the New. Modern technology is beginning to overcome the isolation, but the population remains island people (Goldstein 1992, 26). This study, undertaken in 1992, demonstrates how the function of legends adheres to the culture that is transmitting them.

The headline "Bizarre AIDS Story Likely a Concocted Tale" in the St. John's *Evening Telegram* (April 29, 1990) discusses a rumor about a person who knowingly transmitted the HIV virus and the subsequent investigation by the Royal Newfoundland Constabulary. The variant reflects the island culture and contains different elements from those commonly circulating elsewhere. "The message was the same, but the story itself was quite different":

A young woman . . . goes on vacation in the United States, has a one time affair, returns to Newfoundland, and some time later receives by mail a package containing a miniature coffin with a note "Welcome to the world of AIDS." (Goldstein 1992, 23)

Because of their isolation, Newfoundlanders know each other; therefore, in order for the action to take place, the victim must go off island. In variants from other parts of the globe, the participants in the legend meet in local bars and meeting places. This does not make sense within the borders of Newfoundland, where anyone infected with the virus would be made immediately known to the population at large.

The AIDS-lore of Newfoundland demonstrates that the people perceive AIDS as a mainland disease. The Newfoundland variant "appears to be as much a story about the dangers of the world outside the island, as it is about AIDS" (Goldstein 1992, 28). The story is also about Newfoundlanders as innocent victims. "Great pains are taken by the narrators to portray the protagonist as pure, respectable and proper" (28). In the Newfoundland variants, the couple are never involved in a one-night stand but rather have developed a relationship over at least a two-week period, usually longer, and the gift that she receives is, before opening, thought to be an engagement ring. Mainland protagonists are not so innocent: they participate in casual sexual encounters.

A third major difference is the gender of the victim. In Mainland variants, the male is usually the victim, while in the Newfoundland versions, it is the female who suffers. "Newfoundland women, like women in many traditional communities are expected to be the level-headed controlling factor in sexual relationships. Men, on the other hand, are accepted as sexually active or even promiscuous" (Goldstein 1992, 31). Therefore, culturally, in order for Newfoundlanders to accept the story as plausible, the narrative requires that a woman be the victim. "If you put a man into the role of victim, the protagonist loses innocence and credibility and therefore jeopardizes the image of the Newfoundlander tainted by the mainland" (Goldstein 1992, 31). The narratives in Newfoundland that did involve men as victim also included the motifs of one-night stands and "lipstick on the mirror" messages. They also include the fact that the men did not leave the island for their adventure. AIDS victims, in these legends, as documented by Diane Goldstein (1992, 33), are

1. mainlanders;

2. innocent Newfoundlanders who go to the mainland;

3. Newfoundlanders who engage in intimate relations with mainlanders at home; or

4. Newfoundlanders who engage in taboo behavior and who might therefore be said to be "behaving as mainlanders."

Recently, in my local newspaper (nearly on the other side of Canada), evidence shows that the beliefs of the Newfoundlanders have not changed since the study was conducted:

Newfoundlanders are awakening to the threat of AIDS, but a top Red Cross official warned Wednesday that many still view the syndrome as a mainland problem. . . . Since 1984, a total 144 residents of Newfoundland have tested HIV positive. Forty-two have developed AIDS. Thirty-three have died. . . . Teenagers do not identify HIV and AIDS as something that is infecting and affecting them. "We strongly feel that a lot of adolescents look at this as an adult disease and something that is not a part of their lives at this time," warns the head of the Newfoundland and Labrador AIDS committee. (Many in Newfoundland Believe Island Safe from AIDS 1994, A9)

And in the Media . . .

ET and AIDS

AIDS: The Last Great Plague (American West Distributors) is volume 6 of a 10-volume series allegedly received by short-wave radio from extraterrestrials concerning the last days on earth, and transcribed verbatim. Mixing journalistic and pseudo-scientific sources, the extraterrestrials explain that it was the World Health Organization that spread AIDS through contaminated smallpox vaccine. Further, the book alleges, the true extent of the disease is being hushed up by world governments, as is the fact that it is primarily spread by the Asiatic Tiger Mosquito, "which in fact, was intentionally introduced into America specifically to spread the disease" (41). Fortunately, since viruses are crystals, the ETs reveal that they can be destroyed by irradiating them with the correct sound frequency (Special Publications 1990, 14).

FOAFTALE NEWS remarks about this book, that it's "a fascinating example of intellectual bricolage, fabricating folk religion out of a network of contemporary legends and popular science" (Special Publications 1990, 14).

Spanish Playboy Cult

A British AIDS counsellor warned that infected playboys at Spanish resorts had formed a cult devoted to giving the disease to vacationing girls. He said that in two cases British girls, after a holiday affair in Spain, were given little farewell gifts to carry with them onto the plane home. The packages contained a small wooden coffin inscribed with "Welcome to the death club. Now you've got AIDS." The two girls are said to be undergoing three months of testing to see if they have in fact caught the disease. (Sun, March 6, 1990, 5)

"AIDS Mary" Murder

> *When Jeffrey Hengehold came up for trial in Cincinnati, Ohio, for murdering Linda Hoberg on 25 August 1990, his attorney asked that the charges be reduced. Hengehold had picked up Ms. Hoberg at a bar, had sex with her, then as they parted, the woman allegedly said to him, "Welcome to the world of AIDS." "I felt dead," the sobbing Hengehold testified, "I didn't understand how a person could do that to somebody else. I lost all self-control. I started hitting her. I was angry and I couldn't live with the fact that somebody had given me AIDS and I have to die slowly." No evidence was presented that Hengehold had the disease, though, and Ms. Hoberg's body could not be tested for the virus because Hengehold had incinerated it after the crime. Prosecutors countered that the defendant was either making up the story, or that the woman had made the remark as a joke. The presiding judge found him guilty, and he was given 17 years to life.*
> [*Cincinnati Enquirer*, January 29, 1991; *Cincinnati Post*, January 30, 1991] (Legends and Life: "AIDS Mary" Murder 1991, 9)

"AIDS Mary" on Dallas Radio Talk Show

> *After* Ebony *magazine (September 1991) printed a letter from "C. J.," a Dallas, Texas, woman "who claimed that after contracting AIDS she had become obsessed with picking up men in nightclubs, in order to pass the deadly virus on," she appeared on a broadcast of a Dallas radio talk show. She had no remorse about her actions. Local health officials noted that the controversy led to increased attendance at AIDS education seminars and a boost in HIV testing. The Dallas Police Department said that knowingly trying to transmit AIDS was a felony, but it was not investigating C. J.'s claims because no one had ever filed a complaint against her. Patrons of nightclubs became "more aware" stating that, "There could be a lot of C. J.'s out there."* [*New York Times*, October 1, 1991, A16]
>
> *By late October, police proved that both C. J.'s (two different women) perpetuated a hoax. The author of the letter, a 15-year old who had recently lost a family member to AIDS, admitted she wrote it to raise community consciousness of the disease. The other woman, 29, said she called the radio show as a joke and "didn't mean [the hoax] to take the turns it did." Neither woman was infected and no charges were filed. A Dallas health department source commented, "I look at what happened with C. J. as a fire drill, something that had made people aware of danger and risk."* [*New York Times*, October 23, 1991, A14] (Stop me if you've heard . . . 1992, 11)

"LSD-LACED TATTOO TRANSFERS"

Drug dealers were distributing tiny pieces of "tattoo paper" in the form of blue stars or cartoon characters which were intended for use by children. But the "tattoos" had been soaked in the hallucinatory drug LSD. Children were said to buy the tattoo stickers and put them in their mouths or on their skin and immediately begin to hallucinate. In some instances, persons stuck the tattoo papers on unsuspecting kids. (Dickson and Goulden 1993, 185)

The "LSD-Laced Tattoo Transfer" legend, usually transmitted by circulars, warns parents, educators, and medical workers about small sheets of white paper containing "tattoos" of blue stars or cartoons being sold to school children. These tattoos are supposedly soaked in LSD and are very dangerous.

The warning circulars have been in existence since at least 1980 in North America and are regarded as credible because they are attributed to, and are often printed on the letterhead of, a police force, hospital, or school board. Both in North America and Europe, the major agents of transmission have been educated officials that belong to one of two social groups: those in the medical and social professions, "whose members feel a responsibility toward public health," and educators, "who feel threatened" (Renard 1991, 15). "Those responsible for redirecting the memo were trained security guards and police officials who took care to 'authenticate' the facts and were willing to defend its reliability by referring to apparently reputable sources" (Ellis 1989, 3).

The lack of authenticity would not be difficult to establish once the attempt was made.

Police have now traced the path of the flyer, which has been buzzing around Europe for a year. The result? The French hospitals and police departments, which the warning named as sources, for the most part do not exist. The ones that actually do exist deny that the "clarification" came from them (Elendt and Metzner 1989, 3).

In 1987, a flyer containing the warning circulated in the northeastern United States. It was then translated into French in a memo to ALCAN (Aluminum Company of Canada) Montreal employees on November 18, 1987. By April of the following year, a memo based on the French translation appeared in France, apparently brought over by a doctor who had attended a conference in Montreal. Flyers then crossed over to Belgium (September), to Switzerland (October), and to Germany and Luxembourg (January 1989). However, the circular was paying a return visit to Germany as it had circulated through the U.S. armed forces bases in Germany in 1984 (Ellis 1989, 4).

The circular joined the computer networks in early the 1990s in a transmission from "SSGT REYNOLDS." A second computer network variant circulated to preschools and universities and added "Bart Simpson" to the list of cartoon characters to beware of; the list already included Mickey Mouse and other Disney characters (Stop me if you've heard . . . 1990b, 10).

The Canadian public received a professionally printed version of the flyer in mid-October of 1990. The flyer, dated September, claimed to quote information from New York's Beth Israel Medical Center and told readers to telephone their local R.C.M.P. officers. Beth Israel officials denied responsibility for the flyer and the R.C.M.P. recognized the warning because they had received similar reports since 1983 (Stop me if you've heard . . . 1990b, 10).

Aspects of the Legend

Once the original content of the LSD tattoo legends became suspect, a new element was added to the stories. Details about the "background" of the legend started to circulate as well. "The many rumors *about* the LSD tattoo transfer rumor include one accurate and three inaccurate pieces of information" (Renard 1991, 17):

1. LSD tattoo legends were a practical joke started by medical students. Research on the history of the legend demonstrates that this is a false assumption.

2. The legends were a political maneuver "attempting to worry parents before the election" because transmission of the flyer took place during an election year. This rumor was also disproved.

3. The LSD tattoo legends came from a legend of "antiquity." By relating the legend to an historical event, the legend can be discredited as its novelty is disputed.

4. The legend was disseminated by credulous authorities. The press disclosed, accurately in most cases, that authorities (university professors, the Lyon town hall, senators, etc.) had believed in the rumor and had been "trapped."

The speculation *about* the legend changed the image of the legend itself. "The agent diffusing the flyer was no longer a well-informed person worried about prevention, but a naïve individual disclosing an old story, or a practical joker, or worse still, a political manipulator" (Renard 1991, 18). When physicians proved the medical inaccuracy of the flyer, the focus of the rumor turned to the health professions, the major source of diffusion, who then stopped verifying and diffusing the flyer for fear of appearing incompetent (18).

Inaccuracies and Improbabilities

Before an examination of the inaccuracies and improbabilities of the legend can take place, the following facts, documented by Jean Bruno Renard (1991, 19), must be recognized:

1. LSD or "acid" is a drug causing a hallucinogenic "trip";

2. LSD is often packaged in blotters stamped with drawings;

3. LSD is ingested by placing a piece of laced blotter on the tongue;

4. LSD-laced "blotters" featuring Mickey Mouse or blue star images have been found (but not tattoo transfers for children).

The general populace may be aware of these accurate facts but base their anxieties on a misunderstanding of medical and financial inaccuracies that are inherent in the legend. LSD is not lethal to humans and, consequently, an "overdose" of LSD is impossible. While individuals under the influence of LSD have died, the drug is only indirectly the cause. The second central fear transmitted by the legend, that small children will ingest the drug by licking the LSD-soaked tattoos, has also been proved erroneous. It is impossible to absorb LSD through the pores of the skin. Even someone licking paper soaked with the substance would not absorb an active dose of LSD; users put the entire "blotter" into their mouths (Renard 1991, 18).

Because LSD does not cause physical dependency, there is no danger of users becoming "hooked." The premise, therefore, of the tattoos being made available to young children to build a future clientele is not plausible. At the same time, the prohibitive costs of soaking the transfers with LSD would make it extremely expensive to sell and far beyond the means of school children.

Beyond these inaccuracies within the legend is the fact that no one has been able to find any concrete evidence of the existence of these tattoos. In all the flyers and media coverage of the legend, not one tattoo transfer or photograph of a tattoo transfer laced with LSD has come to light. No one questioned this lack of concrete evidence as they transmitted the legend. Additionally, not a single instance of LSD poisoning of a child has ever been verified in North America or Europe.

Functions of the Legend

Fear is the major force driving this legend, and "several types of fear overlap, all related in one way or another to the fear of contamination" (Renard 1991, 20). Four major fears have been identified: fear of the "deceptive mundane," fear of drugs, fear of satanic influences, and fear of foreigners.

The "Deceptive Mundane"

Fear of the "deceptive mundane," "a menace or a danger [that] lurks behind banal, trivial, everyday occurrences," can be identified in many of the contemporary legends (Renard 1991, 20). It is the juxtaposition of two polar elements that produces the shock element of the legend: the innocent world of the child versus the perverted world of drugs.

Fear of Drugs

Drugs have become a scapegoat for the ills of modern society, and this "active" fear melds with a second fear to produce the "credible" legend of "LSD-laced tattoo transfers." A poll conducted in France in May 1988 showed that those surveyed felt that the two gravest and most condemnable activities imaginable are the "sale of drugs" (98 percent) and "the exploitation of children" (97 percent) (Renard 1991, 21). Fears about drugs incorporate other collective fears as well. Drugs impair health as does industrial and urban pollution; drugs hamper educational and professional achievement, also affected by industrial pollution and economic crisis; drug users are usually young adults, and fear of drugs incorporates the fear youth revolt; and the use and sale of drugs leads to crime and violent behavior, leading in turn to an increase in insecurity (Renard 1991, 21).

It is significant that LSD, not marijuana or heroin, is the drug mentioned in the rumor and in the flyers. For to the public at large, LSD is the drug that makes people crazy. An attack against an individual's mind is often thought to be worse than an attack against the body. LSD is also the anti-establishment drug, associated with numerous American movements of the 1960s (Renard 1991, 21).

Fear of Satanic Influences

Contemporary ills have also found a scapegoat in Satan and satanic cults. Fundamentalists, coping with rebellious youth and declining church attendance, are quick to cite satanic influences at work. "The fears that a child could become a drug addict, a juvenile delinquent, a mentally disturbed youth, all embody the same fear of the loss of parental authority" (Renard 1991, 22). Other aspects of the fear of Satan are discussed in the following chapter.

Fear of Foreigners

Another popular scapegoat for society's malfunctions are foreigners. The threat always comes from "away," brought to our society by foreigners who have either "infected" our citizens while on holiday or have deliberately moved to our shores. One popular explanation of the LSD-laced tattoo transfers was a modern application of the "Trojan horse." "Using this trick, the foreigner gains entrance into a city and annihilates its future: its children" (Renard 1991, 23). The fear of foreigners is an active ingredient in a wide array of today's legends (e.g., "Kentucky Fried Rat," "Doggie Dinner," "Department Store Snakes").

Historical Antecedents

Several historical antecedents have been mentioned in connection with this legend. The first, involving contaminated glue, is closely related in content. The second, cartoon characters and drugs, shows just how easily the general population assumes that a "connection" provides the concrete evidence for the authenticity of the legend as it circulates.

Infectious Stamps

Gummed postage stamps labeled "penny blacks" or "Queen's heads" were introduced in Britain in 1840. The glue was reputed to be poisonous and "those so rash as to lick the Queen's head were in danger of contacting cholera" (Dickson and Goulden 1993, 186). The fear of a new "innovation" again lends itself to rumors and gives voice to anxieties.

Drugs and Cartoon Characters

A common illustration on the warning flyers about the LSD-laced tattoo transfers shows Mickey Mouse as "The Sorcerer's Apprentice" from Disney's animated feature *Fantasia* (1940). The re-release of the film in the 1970s attracted college-age audiences, who found the impact of the surreal film enhanced by the use of marijuana, LSD, and other drugs (Ellis 1989, 4).

A sequence in *Dumbo* (1941) includes a "trip" taken by a baby elephant who accidently drinks water spiked with champagne. The *Dumbo* character is also frequently identified with the LSD tattoos (Ellis 1989, 4). Because of these established connections, it is much easier for the general public to accept the correlation between cartoon characters and the drug trade!

A Case Study of the "LSD-Laced Tattoo Transfers" Legend

The migration of the LSD tattoo transfer legend was traced from the United States, into Canada and, through the province of Quebec, into France in the late 1980s. Renard's examination of the early transmissions of the legend in North America (1980–1987) shows that the legend may have been the result of an honest misunderstanding. Individuals "mistakenly transformed the accurate fact that one means of preparing LSD *resembled* children's cartoon stamps into the misconception that children's cartoon stamps *did* contain LSD" (Renard 1991, 4). Warning flyers were immediately disseminated and newspapers reported the information as a public service without verifying the flyers' origins or authenticity (4).

The dissemination of the flyer into Canada and Quebec led to its translation into French in 1987; this translation was the source for the majority of flyers that circulated in France and Europe (Renard 1991, 6). This assumption is based on several "Canadianisms" in the French flyers. The most obvious Canadianism is the name "Mickey Mouse"; the same character is known only as "Mickey" in France.

The flyers were circulated throughout the French educational system, but when the schools closed for the summer, transmission of the legend did not slow. "Extensive travelling during vacation allowed for an extended oral diffusion of the rumor" (Renard 1991, 10). A popular woman's magazine, *Enfants Magazine*, published the flyer in August 1988 under the heading "Good Things to Know from Kindergarten to High School." A retraction was published the following month stating that "the rather worrisome information about the circulation of children's tattoo transfers laced with LSD . . . is in fact erroneous" (Renard 1991, 10). However, this did not stop the circulation of the legends and, by November 1988, the Ministry of Education requested that its officials inform parents and children that the rumor was unfounded (12). Legal action was threatened for anyone circulating the legend, and the flyer quickly stopped circulating in France.

Further research, conducted by Kapferer, demonstrates the persuasiveness of this legend in France. The three basic channels for dissemination were the media, the education system, and the workplace, where circulars and faxes can be easily received and read. Kapferer discovered that it was, in fact, the printed format of the circular that lead to its widespread belief. Kapferer (1993, 98–99) isolates several possibilities for the persuasiveness of the written flyers:

1. The anonymous leaflets soon became official circulars complete with stamps of official health and law officials.

2. The leaflet "visualizes the seal of authentication" supporting the contents of the rumor.

3. Written documents convey a greater quantity of information and have clarity of transmission.

4. The written text allows readers time to absorb the information at their own speed.

Written transmissions still allow for variants, however. Recently, just after conducting workshops on contemporary legends in a local high school,

I sat in the staff room where teachers were discussing the written warning they had received that morning:

The RCMP have advised us that LSD is circulating in [this area] on sugar cubes. They advise staff not to leave their coffee cups unattended in classrooms, etc.

When I mentioned that it seemed to be an extension of the LSD transfer legend, the teachers regarded me as something less than intelligent. . . . Afterall, the circular would not be transmitted if it was not true! Those teachers were not about to leave their coffee cups anywhere out of sight!

And in the Media . . .

"Kids Sold Drug Laced Biscuits"

Police along Sydney's northern beaches have stepped up their hunt for someone they call "the Baker" who sells biscuits laced with deadly drugs to school children for $5 each. The cookies are home-made and contain everything from heroin and LSD to heavy am-phetamines and pot, police said yesterday. Several young people who have eaten the cookies have had to have emergency treatment at Manly Hospital. Constable Trevor Otten said "the Baker" had been a police target for almost a fortnight. "We know that he's been selling the things from a lime-green Holden (car) or sometimes a Ford," Constable Otten said. He warned that anyone eating one of the spiked snacks risked death from asphyxiation or shock, halluci-nations or other reactions. [Brisbane Courier-Mail, August 17, 1987] (Re Mickey Mouse LSD Rumor 1989, 5)

Many school administrators decided against sending copies [of the flyer] home with students because they remembered distributing the same letter in 1982. But the principal of the Normandie Christian School in Los Angeles felt "that if it was something that concerned the safety and well-being of our students, then the parents ought to know about it." One parent of a seven-year-old child said she was frightened: "He's always going to the store to get candy and a sticker." [Los Angeles Times, December 9, 1987, 1, 4] (Mickey Mouse LSD Rumor Update 1989, 6)

> *The principal of a private school in Tinton Falls, NJ, hesitated before distributing copies to parents, but went ahead when she learned that the principal and nurse of the local public elementary school had circulated it under their names. She commented, "you don't want even one child to fall victim to this." Parents agreed, one saying, "Drugs are everywhere today. You can't assume that your child is safe." [New York Times, December 9, 1988, B1, 5] (Mickey Mouse LSD Rumor Update 1989, 6)*

> *An Edmonton school principal thought he was giving parents the low-down on children getting high. [The] school principal . . . warned parents in letters sent home with 364 students Wednesday that LSD-laced tattoos were circulating in the community. . . . But visions of youngsters taking the hallucinogenic drug are just that, said police. "To the best of my knowledge this is the third or fourth year in a row a letter has been sent out (in the community) and there's nothing to it," Sgt. Mike Tabler said Thursday. The warning was sent with the best of intentions after a parent alerted the principal to a similar note circulating in [a nearby county] schools. [The principal] sent the note home with pupils before talking with police who have labelled the phony warning "a scare tactic.". . . "It's a matter of erring on the side of caution," [the principal] said. Another note setting the record straight went out Thursday.* ("Principal's Warning About LSD-Laced Tattoos False Alarm," *Edmonton Journal*, September 21, 1991)

LITERARY AND VISUAL ADAPTATIONS

"AIDS-Lore"

Via Appia (1992). A German film directed by Jochen Hick, in German, Portuguese, and English, with subtitles. "This film concerns a young homosexual airlines steward who has a one-night stand with a young man. The morning after, he wakes to find his partner gone and 'Welcome to the AIDS Club' scrawled in soap on the bathroom mirror" (Media Versions 1992, 11).

"The Stolen Kidney"

The Angel Maker by Ridley Pearson (New York: Delacorte 1993)."They stitched her back up. But they took X-rays. She's missing a kidney. . . . No hospital record of any such operation. . . . She has no memory of any surgery. None. No explanation at all" (p. 10). The novel explores the greed for recognition that drives a doctor to perform surgical operations to remove kidneys and other organs for sale on the black market.

Coma. (Film and book by Robin Cook). Patients are sent to a mysterious hospital and placed in an irreversible coma to enable the harvesting of their organs as "spare parts" for others.

"Dick Tracy." During 1991, this comic strip featured a plot focusing on stolen body parts.

The Harvest (1992). This film, written and directed by David Marconi, involves a visiting American in Mexico who becomes the intended victim for an organ-smuggling ring.

Law and Order. Television series, first shown on April 2, 1991. The basic plot was suggested by co-producer Robert Palm to scriptwriter Joe Morgenstern and based on a newspaper clipping (unseen by Palm). Morgenstern "concocted a story of a wealthy philanthropist whose daughter is dying of a kidney disease, but her tissue type is so rare that she can't have a transplant unless someone finds a perfect match" (More Stolen Body Organs 1991, 7).

Les Miserables by Victor Hugo (Middlesex, England: Penguin, 1976). While not an adaptation of the contemporary legend, the story is based on a common theme, the exploitation of the poor. The destitute have nothing left to sell but bits and pieces of themselves. "Fantine sells her beautiful hair, her perfect four front teeth and finally herself as a prostitute to raise enough money to take care of her child" (Campion-Vincent 1990, 18).

REFERENCES

Abducted Latin American children. 1992. *FOAFTALE NEWS* 26 (June): 11.

African-American legends. 1991. *FOAFTALE NEWS* 22 (June): 10–11.

Aids Mary on Dallas radio talk show. 1992. *FOAFTALE NEWS* 25 (March): 11.

Baker, Geoff. 1995. HIV-blood smearing man wins acquittal. *Edmonton Journal* (February 21): A8.

Bank robber warns teller syringe had tainted blood. 1994. *Edmonton Journal* (August 11): B3.

Body parts panics in Guatemala. 1994. *FOAFTALE NEWS* 33/34 (June): 17.

Buffalo's a city with a heart—and it may be yours. 1992. *Toronto Star* (January 23): A2.

Campion-Vincent, Veronique. 1990. The baby-parts story: A new Latin American legend. *Western Folklore* 49 (January 1990): 9–25.

———. 1993. Demonologies in contemporary legends and panics: Satanism and baby parts stories. *Fabula* 34, no. 3/4: 238–51.

Children sold for transplants. 1993. *Edmonton Journal* (June 22): A1.

Czubala, Dionizjusz. 1991a. AIDS and aggression: Polish legends about HIV-infected people. *FOAFTALE NEWS* 23 (September): 1–5.

———. 1991b. The "black volga": Child abduction urban legends in Poland and Russia. *FOAFTALE NEWS* 21 (March): 1–3.

———. 1993. Mongolian contemporary legends: Field research report, part 2: Political rumors and sensations. *FOAFTALE NEWS* 29 (March): 1–7.

Dickson, Paul, and Joseph C. Goulden. 1993. *Myth-informed: Legends, credos, and wrongheaded "facts" we all believe.* New York: Perigee.

Elendt, Gerd, and Wolfgang Metzner. 1989. Warnings about supposed LSD stickers for children terrify parents. Police call it a horror story. *FOAFTALE NEWS* 16 (December): 3–4.

Ellis, Bill. 1989. Editor's note. *FOAFTALE NEWS.* 16 (December): 4.

———. 1989. Mickey Mouse LSD tattoos: A study in emergence. *FOAFTALE NEWS* 14 (June): 3–4.

Fine, Gary Alan. 1987. Welcome to the world of AIDS: Fantasies of female revenge. *Western Folklore* 46 (July): 192–97.

Goldstein, Diane E. 1992. Welcome to the mainland, welcome to the world of AIDS: Cultural viability, localization and contemporary legend. *Contemporary Legend* 2: 23–40.

Guatemalans beat suspected child-snatcher. 1994. *Edmonton Journal* (March 31): B10.

Have you heard: Creamed curry. 1994. *FOAFTALE NEWS* 35 (October): 15–16.

Just in! White slavers in Mexico. 1989. *FOAFTALE NEWS* 12 (February): 1.

Kapferer, Jean-Noel. 1990. *Rumors: Uses, interpretations and images.* New Brunswick, NJ: Transaction.

———. 1993. The persuasiveness of an urban legend: The case of Mickey Mouse acid. *Contemporary Legend* 3: 85–101.

Langlois, Janet. 1991. "Hold the mayo": Purity and danger in an AIDS legend. *Contemporary Legend* 1: 153–72.

Legends and life: AIDS. 1992. *FOAFTALE NEWS* 27 (September): 8–10.

Legends and life: "AIDS Mary" murder. 1991. *FOAFTALE NEWS* 22 (June): 9.

Many in Newfoundland believe island safe from AIDS. 1994. *Edmonton Journal* (August 18): A9.

Moravec, Mark. Organ kidnap stories. 1991. *FOAFTALE NEWS* 23 (September): 6.

Media versions. 1992. *FOAFTALE NEWS* 27 (September): 11–12.

Mickey Mouse LSD flyers. 1990. *FOAFTALE NEWS* 20 (December): 10.

Mickey Mouse LSD rumor update. 1989. *FOAFTALE NEWS* 15 (September): 6.

More stolen body organs. 1991. *FOAFTALE NEWS* 23 (September): 6–7.

Oosterom, Nelle. 1993. Samaritan had to overcome suspicion. *Edmonton Journal* (October 3): A3.

O'Shaughnessy, Hugh. 1993. To market, to market to buy a fine child. *Edmonton Journal* (October 3): E1–2.

———. 1994. Murder and mutilation supply human organ trade. *Edmonton Journal* (April 2): G3.

Re Mickey Mouse LSD rumor. 1989. *FOAFTALE NEWS* 13 (March): 5.

Renard, Jean-Bruno. 1991. LSD tattoo transfers: Rumor from North America to France. *Folklore Forum* 24, no. 2: 3–26.

Schmidt, Sigrid. 1989. *Bild* and the Mickey-Mouse LSD rumor. *FOAFTALE NEWS* 16 (December): 1–3.

Shonder, John A. 1994. Organ theft rumors in Guatemala: Some personal observations. *FOAFTALE NEWS* 35 (October): 1–2.

Smith, Paul. 1990. "AIDS—Don't die of ignorance"—Exploring the cultural complex. In *A nest of vipers: Perspectives on contemporary legend, vol. V,* edited by Gillian Bennett and Paul Smith. Sheffield, England: Sheffield Academic Press. 113–41.

Special publications. 1990. *FOAFTALE NEWS* 17 (March): 13–14.

Stevens, Phillip, Jr. 1991. The demonology of satanism: An anthropological view. In *The Satanism Scare,* edited by James T. Richardson, Joel Best, and David G. Bromley. New York: Aldine de Gruyer, 21–39.

Stilo, Giuseppe, and Paola Toselli. 1991. The kidnappers and the black ambulance: Child abduction legends from Sicily. *FOAFTALE NEWS* 23 (September): 5–6.

Stop me if you've heard . . . 1990a. *FOAFTALE NEWS* 18 (June): 10–11.

———. 1990b. *FOAFTALE NEWS* 20 (December): 10–11.

———. 1992a. *FOAFTALE NEWS* 25 (March): 11–12.

———. 1992b. *FOAFTALE NEWS* 26 (June): 10–12.

———. 1994. *FOAFTALE NEWS* 33/34 (June): 17–18.

Turner, Patricia A. 1993. *I heard it through the grapevine: Rumor in African-American culture.* Berkeley: University of California Press.

11

MODERN CONCERNS
SATANIC LEGENDS

To be sure, legend types such as the mutilation lore and similar complexes attached to Halloween sadists, Satanic cults, and UFO abductions do seem to function differently from "classic" contemporary legends like "The Stolen Grandmother" and "The Surpriser Surprised," which circulate primarily as complex narratives in a variety of conversational contexts and do not imply any kind of social crisis. But many kinds of legend incorporate both narrative and social action (especially dormitory mass-murder legends, adolescent trips, and mercantile legends). And even legends involving minimal narrative content but elaborate social activity, like Halloween sadism reports, have been analyzed fruitfully as contemporary legend. (Ellis 1991a, 42)

Contemporary legends involving satanic cults and devil-worship are important social commentaries that need to be addressed. This chapter briefly discusses the different aspects of satanic folklore and the "universals" reflected in all variants: "the evil others kidnap our children, obscenely torment them in horrible rituals, sacrifice them to some higher power by slashing them with knives; dismember them; drink their blood and eat their flesh and vital organs" (Stevens 1990, 129). A look at the historical antecedents of satanic legends demonstrates that demonologies appear whenever society is undergoing rapid changes in economic, social, and environmental spheres. Belief in satanic scapegoats has wide-ranging consequences, from challenging Halloween celebrations, to challenging reading materials in school libraries, to the increasing fear of those who are "different" from others in the community.

Satanic cult activity draws the attention of both those who condemn it and those who wish to embrace the lifestyle and act out the legends. Because the majority of satanic folklore relies on personal-experience experience narratives rather than hard evidence, people will believe what they wish to hear—formulating their own justification for their behavior and the behavior of others. There are many parallels between contemporary satanic and ritual abuse investigations and the witchhunts of earlier times. In both cases, social scientists agree, the fear represented by these concerns is indicative of intolerable social stress (Stevens 1991, 22).

There is also a strong connection between satanic cults and other traditional scapegoats such as vampires and werewolves, who like the witch, have an uncontrollable hunger for human flesh and blood, particularly those of young, innocent victims (Stevens 1991, 26). It is interesting to note that these traditional "horrors" have become increasingly popular with young adults today. The themes are being expanded in popular fiction and on the screens, building on and spreading the allusions to satanic activity that makes the legends familiar and therefore, more believable (Campion-Vincent 1993, 244).

DEFINITION OF TERMS

Before we delve into an investigation of rumors and legends incorporating satanic and demonic behavior, certain terminology should be clarified. While several of these terms are used broadly in popular culture, they remain ambiguous to say the least.

Cults

The popular and current meaning of "cult" is a derogatory label imposed on the new religions, particularly non-Christian religions, that have been emerging since the 1960s. Labeled as "cults," these "new age" religious groups lack legitimacy in the eyes of traditional faiths. Indeed, they signal heresy to many traditional groups. But, in addition to the implication of heresy, the term represents "dangerous, secretive, manipulative and conspiratorial" action to mainstream North Americans (Victor 1989, 40).

These negative connotations have been reinforced by the mass media coverage of Jim Jones' Peoples' Temple mass suicide and, more recently, of David Koresh and his followers. A cult "came to mean a group, led by a manipulative fanatic and having mindless followers, who were brainwashed into submission to his authority" (Victor 1990, 62).

Reactions to the cult movements of the 1970s and concerns about drug abuse and violence in middle-class young adults triggered a widespread overreaction to concerns about missing children and sexual child abuse and created stereotypes of "satanists" and "satanic cults." Within the decade, the ambiguous "satanic cult" became "a socially constructed "fact"—their existence had become a taken-for-granted, consensually validated, social reality for millions of Americans" (Victor 1990, 73). Our current identification with cults and adolescent behavior is, in part, the result of ostension—small local gangs of predominantly middle-class young adults who, along with their involvement with drug abuse, evoked symbols of black magic and ritual sacrifices of animals.

Youth turning to criminal behavior and cruelty to animals are not new phenomena, but what is new, is the "use of satanic ideology as a justification for aggression" (Victor 1990, 63). In the mid-1980s, the generic label "satanic cult" became a familiar stereotype that merged together "notions about satanic religion and bizarre criminal activity to invent a new category of criminality: ritual or occult crime" (Victor 1990, 63). "The symbolic meaning of the term 'satanic cult' is now clear. It refers to a secretive, conspiratorial group having occult powers, which manipulated otherwise innocent children into a demonic heresy" (Victor 1989, 40).

However, while most people associate the word "cult" with an anti-Christian message, others profess that cults exist within organized religious groups as well. The following passage was printed in *The Chronicle of Higher Education* (November 15, 1989):

> Some colleges have begun programs warning students against fundamentalist Christian groups like the Maranatha Christian Fellowship that attract young people and then use them in aggressive recruiting and fund-raising activities. The Cult Awareness Network had received many complaints from families and friends of Maranatha members, who have witnessed radical personality changes, falling grades, and frequent arguments that family members are not "being Christian enough." A survey of student-affairs administers showed that students who earlier might have been drawn to groups like the Hare Krishnas are now being attracted to fundamentalist churches that often use "cult-like" practices to retain them. Experts claimed that "cults deceive people when they try to recruit them and then trap them psychologically, making it extremely difficult to leave. . . . Any group that relies on such practices should be classified as a cult—regardless of its ideology or religious beliefs." (Gazdik 1989, A42)

Demonology

> [Demonology is] an elaborate body of belief about an evil force that is inexorably undermining the society's most cherished values and institutions. The evil it describes may be embodied in and perpetuated by a specific group, a minority which becomes the scapegoat for the people's pent-up frustration. Or the evil force may be a set of ideas, often exaggerated or totally imaginary: an ideology which spreads as if driven by a will of its own, or by a supernatural will. The perceived threat may be given credence as certain deviant individuals or groups are attracted to it as a source of power or enhanced identity, and attempt to act it out. Examples of such persecuted minorities in Western history are the Jews—over and over again; or Bolsheviks; or Japanese-Americans. Examples of the

other, the pervasive ideology of evil, include various late medieval heresies, including witchcraft; Communism in the 1950s and— Satanism today. (Stevens 1990, 128)

Modern demonology, as defined by Stevens, is a legend that contains both ancient and contemporary elements and is firmly embedded in Western popular culture through popular literature, films, and heavy metal lyrics and album covers. Demonologies serve to distract us from immediate yet alarming social problems (Stevens 1991, 30). Instead of addressing serious problems that are affecting young adults, the search for "demonic ritual abusers" becomes a primary concern for some parents and authorities.

ASPECTS OF THE SATANIC RUMOR/LEGEND

Impartial investigators of satanic cults have had difficulty obtaining hard evidence of the existence of wide-ranging cults. In fact, all that can be found are the rumors and legends about the cults. In light of this information, Jeffrey Victor researched newspaper articles in an attempt to discover how the rumors and stories became so prevalent. As his analysis of the data is useful to anyone involved with young adults, I am including a full discussion of his findings and interpretations. Hopefully, this information will initiate class (and family) discussions, enabling a fuller understanding, on both sides, of a very contemporary issue.

Victor expresses his conclusions in several articles published in the late 1980s and early 1990s. His investigation of news items isolate a core of 31 newspaper articles across the United States that report real investigations into satanic activity and contain confirmable evidence. His research establishes the following pattern: The reported satanic cult panics were a rural, rather than an urban, phenomena that revolved around the kidnapping and ritual sacrifices of children; all of the reported incidents were triggered by specific events, usually Friday the Thirteenth or Halloween; and the allegations helped to explain local incidents that bewildered the inhabitants (Victor 1990, 73–75). Also, all the newspaper reports quote local authority figures who lend credibility to the legend. Two basic themes kept appearing: animal mutilations (approximately 75 percent) and the kidnapping and ritual sacrifice of children (65 percent). More than 40 percent of the kidnapping stories refer to the kidnapping of blond, blue-eyed children or virgins, cultural symbols of innocence and purity (Victor 1991, 226).

Victor isolates four common aspects of the satanic cult legend: teenage suicide, the ritual killing of cats, kidnapping, and ritual murders.

Teenage Suicide

One of the darkest fears of parents of young adults is the specter of teenage suicide caused by a satanic cult or listening to heavy metal rock music. These rumors both reflect and foster parental concerns about outside influence and lack of parental control. "Beyond the obvious meaning that rumors about teenage suicide have as a reflection of parental fears, such rumors can be interpreted as cultural metaphors for the loss of the family function to protect children" (Victor 1989, 37). In response to these rumors and legends, parents and other authority figures have declared war on the music and lifestyles of rebellious youth. In an effort to protect the children, "offensive" and "dangerous" music, reading materials, and films have been identified and censoring attempts have been the result. Some parents have misplaced the blame squarely on the outside influences without due consideration to other circumstances.

A judge in Reno, Nevada, ruled on 24 August 1990 that the recordings of Judas Priest, a British heavy metal rock group, did not contain subliminal instructions for listeners to commit suicide. The parents of two Nevada teens who shot themselves in 1985 had asked $6.2 million in damages from the musicians and their distributors, CBS records, claiming that recordings on the 1978 album *Stained Glass* deliberately contained "backmasked messages." Similar cases against Ozzy Osbourne, focusing on his recording "Suicide Solution" had failed because courts ruled that the lyrics of his songs were protected under U.S. Constitution freedom of speech. But attorneys in the Nevada case successfully argued that messages recorded backwards were not protected by law.

Defense attorneys pointed out that both teens had been the victims of domestic assaults, one having been beaten repeatedly by his parents. Both were known to use cocaine and other drugs regularly. Under cross examination, the other boy's mother admitted that she had never heard her son mention Judas Priest and did not know whether he had actually listened to their albums.

The judge's ruling conceded that subliminal messages were possible, but he threw out the case because the plaintiffs did not show that the messages on this album were deliberate. His ruling was seen as a precedent for future lawsuits based on subliminal messages. ("Backmasked" Album Exonerated 1990, 7–8)

The Ritual Killing of Cats

Newspaper articles annually announce that, around Halloween, people are not allowed to adopt cats, especially black cats, from local animal shelters. These announcements fuel the legend that members of satanic cults kill cats at secret ritual gatherings, bringing another level of symbolic meaning to the legend: the persistent European folk belief linking cats and witchcraft (Victor 1989, 37). Often cats are mutilated and killed as result of ostension: mock-sacrifices carried out by youths acting out the legends and stories they have heard about the satanic rites (Campion-Vincent 1993, 241).

Cats play a sizable role in other contemporary legends as well. They are eaten, run over, and, in the case of larger species, run wild and attack animals and children.

Kidnapping

A third recurring element of the satanic cult legends is the kidnapping of innocents. Victor recognizes this as a persistent traditional folk motif in legends that have been preserved from generation to generation, adapting to reflect current societal anxieties. As with the other elements, rumors of kidnappings reflect parental fears and communicate, in metaphor, the age old lesson: "beware of strangers" (1989, 38). Common to the kidnapping aspect of the legend is the physical appearance of the victim: blond, blue-eyed, and virgin. The symbolic interpretation of the victim is offered below. What is glossed over, by the media and the content of the legends, is that most children who disappear are either runaways or have been kidnapped by non-custodian parents. The satanic cult legends focus on a more universal anxiety, the children of "everyman," which is much more frightening because any child can be threatened by the random choice of a diabolical stranger (Campion-Vincent 1993, 240).

Fears about the kidnapped children and young women are reflected in many other legends and are discussed in other chapters.

Ritual Murders

Another constant motif in the satanic cult legends is ritual murders. The killing of cats and mutilation of farm animals are only stepping stones to the actual sacrifice of blond virgins. Blond, blue-eyed children remain a symbol of attractiveness and beauty in North American culture (Victor 1989, 39). This symbol represents innocence, purity, and the opposite of evil. "Placed in the story of a kidnapping and ritual murder by a satanic cult, the overall metaphor seems to carry the message: Our cherished values are being threatened and may be destroyed by mysterious forces of evil" (Victor 1989, 39).

Chart of Rumor Story Interpretations

To summarize his findings, Victor devised a chart comparing the elements of the satanic cult legend (rumor) with both the symbolic cultural meaning and metaphoric interpretation.

Rumor Story Symbolism	Symbolic Cultural Meaning	Interpretation as Metaphor
Teenage Suicide	Failure of the family as a shield against a dangerous world for children.	Loss of the family to protect children.
Ritual Killing of Cats	The practice of witchcraft for evil purposes.	An omen of imminent danger from sources of evil.
Satanic graffiti; black roses; list of people to be sacrificed.	Threats are being made against certain people.	People are being warned that they are in danger.
"A blond, blue-eyed virgin . . .	Innocence, purity, rare beauty and high esteem . . .	"Our most cherished values . . .
. . . will be kidnapped and ritually murdered by . . .	. . . are threatened and may be destroyed, by . . .	. . . are threatened and may be destroyed, by . . .
. . . a satanic . . .	. . . a very powerful, evil force in rebellion against the moral authority of God and capable of the most demonic immorality; . . .	. . . very powerful, evil forces that threaten the legitimate moral order of society."
. . . cult."	. . . a dangerous heresy, that is secretive, manipulative and conspiratorial.	
[The rumor stories taken together as a whole.]		The moral order of society, especially the family, is being threatened by mysterious evil forces (and we have lost faith in society's authorities to deal with the threat).

(Victor 1989, 42)

HISTORICAL ANTECEDENTS

Although history will not give us "exact parallels" to contemporary satanic legends, a look at historical antecedents brings to light disturbing similarities between actual and perceived trends in the modern world and trends that contributed to the Inquisition in the later Middle Ages (Stevens 1990, 131). Looking even further into history, the motifs of kidnapping and ritual sacrifices of children are drawn from the ancient blood ritual myth ("The Blood Libel") and the myth of Satan's conflict with God. This combination of symbolism arises in times when "societies are undergoing a deep cultural crisis of values" (Victor 1990, 72). The power of this combination is that it offers symbols that are both secular and sacred, thereby appealing to both secular professionals and religious traditionalists, as presumed satanists can be regarded as either social deviants or agents of supernatural evil or both (Victor 1991, 232). The danger in this powerful subversive mythology lies in the demand to identify scapegoats (232).

"The Blood Libel"

The central element of "The Blood Libel" is that a child is "mutilated and usually killed by members of a minority group whom the majority, for reasons of racial or religious—or one might suspect financial—prejudice, has cause to hate" (Ridley 1967, 153). The blood libel has been traditionally identified against Jewish transgressors who "need" the blood of a Christian child to make their Passover matzos (unleavened bread). Several examples have been cited throughout history and the world of literature.

Thomas of Monmouth, before 1200, lay the 1144 murder and mutilation of young William of Norwich at the feet of the Jewish community, claiming they had sacrificed the child in accordance with their Passover preparations even though there was no evidence to support the libel. All of London was up in arms over the alleged murder, but wholesale slaughter of the Jewish community was prevented by John the Sheriff. William's murder was never positively solved (Ridley 1967, 153).

In another historical example of the blood libel, Matthew Paris recorded the story of the death of Hugh of Lincoln in 1255. The pattern was similar to that of William of Norwich's murder, but the murder of eight-year-old Hugh did not go undetected, and the murderers were caught and punished (Ridley 1967, 154). The ballad "Sir Hugh, or the Jew's Daughter" tells the garnished story. The most celebrated version of the tale was composed by Chaucer in "The Prioress's Tale." The little Christian boy, in the tale, has to cross through the Jewish ghetto and does so while sweetly singing praises to Mary:

> The constant dinning of a Christian hymn in the ears of those who dwell there so arouses Satan in their hearts that they hire an assassin to waylay the boy, to slit his throat and cast his body into a privy, thinking by this means to stop his song forever. (Ridley 1967, 155)

The crime is not left unpunished; Mary, herself, helps to bring the murderers to the dock.

There were more than 27 analogues of this tale in medieval England and almost as many that dealt with the deaths of Hugh and William. Ridley enumerates the continued popularity of this tale. By her count, the story resurfaced "five times in the twelfth century, fifteen in the thirteenth, ten in the fourteenth, sixteen in the fifteenth, thirteen in the sixteenth, eight in the seventeenth, fifteen in the eighteenth, and thirty-nine times in the nineteenth century" (Ridley 1967, 155). Indeed, the stories of William of Norwich and Hugh of Lincoln, the two "martyrs," were not allowed to fade and, as recently as 1947, Benedictine monks of Ramsgate listed them in a calendar of saints, and placed a plaque commemorating St. Hugh's martyrdom at the cathedral in Lincoln (Ridley 1967, 154).

According to *Brewer's Dictionary of Phrase and Fable,* edited by Ivor H. Evans, Saint Hugh (13th century), a boy of about ten years of age, was allegedly tortured and crucified in mockery of Christ. The story goes that the affair arose from his having driven a ball through a Jew's window while at play with his friends. The boy was finally thrown into a well from which he spoke miraculously. Eighteen Jews were purported to have been hanged. The story is paralleled at a number of other places in England and on the continent and forms the subject of Chaucer's *The Prioress's Tale* (1981, 575).

Ridley goes on to illustrate the parallels between the above blood libels and the Nazi propaganda of the 20th century. They "issued periodical warnings to the general population to take special care of their children at Passover time in view of Jewish ritual requirements" (Ridley 1967, 155). Of particular concern to Ridley was the revival of this legend in the United States in the 1960s. Her concern arose because, as she stated, the tale has too often fueled the persecution of innocent people. She quotes Paul Coates, reporting on April 20, 1965:

> There was a rumor spreading all across Southern California that a little white boy had been assaulted and mutilated in a public restroom by a band of adult Negroes. The location of this "atrocity" depended upon the person who was passing along the story. . . . The age of the child varied with the teller [and] . . . the color of the suspects varied according to the district. If there was a Negro neighborhood nearby . . . the suspects were Negroes. If there were Mexican-Americans living in the section, the suspects were Mexicans. (Ridley 1967, 156)

A more recent variant on the theme is the tale of "The Castrated Boy," in which a young boy goes into the washroom at a local shopping center alone. He fails to emerge and, when finally found, it is discovered that he has been castrated by some minority group member. Upon researching the legend, Dorson found that it was part of an initiation legend, in which members had to emasculate a young white boy (Ellis 1983, 200). Because this legend functions as a justification for racial hatred, folklorists quickly connect it to the older blood libel tale that Ridley discussed over a decade earlier.

Folklorists Joseph Jacobs, in 1902, and Hippensteel, in his 1969 examination of the Hoosier version of the "Ballad of Sir Hugh," claimed that the legend had its roots in ancient Greece and that it was not specifically attached to Jews until late Medieval times, although according to the earlier Greek analogues, a few Jews, along with Christians and pagans, were guilty of ritually castrating children. This legend may be the oldest continuously circulating recorded legend, with variants being found as early as 63 B.C. (Ellis 1983, 200). Ellis (1983, 201) documents four basic traits of the early Greek variants, found in an analysis of the legend by two lawyers, Terullian (ca. A.D. 150–220) and Minucius Felix (second or third century A.D.).

1. They spread rapidly as accounts of actual, recent happenings.

2. Official investigations found no firsthand witnesses and no factual substantiation for any of the stories.

3. The culprits were ethnic, religious, or political groups rising in prominence.

4. The stories expressed the existing anxieties and taboos of the established majority rather than knowledge of the scapegoated group.

Only the identity of the villain has changed over time. Today, the fear of castration does not mean a literal emasculation but rather a symbolic one that threatens to "take away the power of the majority" (Ellis 1983, 206).

Satan

"Satan and Hell, we should be reminded, are uniquely Christian developments; they are *not* ordained in . . . the Old Testament" (Stevens 1989, 4). In the first thousand years of Christianity, Satan was relatively unimportant, gaining prominence only in the years approaching the millennium. Historical records show an acute similarity between the social and economic conditions of that time and those of today: urban over-crowding; high unemployment and inflation; weakening of kinships and other social networks; rapid increase in ethnic and cultural heterogeneity; alienation of ordinary people from government, Church, and upper classes; and the Inquisition (Stevens 1989, 4).

The belief that Satan sent demonic agents to work evil through human agents was reinforced by publication of Dante's *Inferno* in 1312, and by the Black Death of 1348 (Stevens 1989, 5). A scapegoat had to be found to rationalize the devastation that the plague had inflicted on people:

> As in all persecutory movements, the Great Witch Hunt focused blame first on people so culturally different from the mainstream that allegations of conspiratorial intentions about them were credible. (Stevens 1989, 5)

Ready at hand were the Jews who kidnapped children for Satan and defiled Christian sacraments at secret rituals (Stevens 1989, 5). Subsequent purges built on this groundwork found many kinds of people to fear and suspect. Those scapegoats were

> Gypsies, homosexuals, eccentric widows or spinsters, bad-tempered or immoral women, the mentally or physically disabled, ordinary peasants of both sexes and all ages, and any targets of envy or spite; and moving inexorably up the social ladder until by the end of the 16th century no woman or man of any station or social class was immune from suspicion. (Stevens 1989, 5)

The Age of Reason in the 18th century helped to lessen the credibility of the satanic demonology, but it was quickly replaced by new forms of satanism, including occultism and the Black Mass (Stevens 1989, 7). Occult leaders of the 19th century included Aleister Crowley and authors William Butler Yeats, Algernon Blackwood, Sir Edward Bulwer-Lytton, Arthur Machen (whose tales of evil and horror would become popular later), and Bram Stoker (of *Dracula* fame) (Stevens 1989, 7).

The demonology of satanism is a European-Christian phenomenon (Stevens 1991, 35). Evidence for this theory can be found by studying the North American black community and their image of Satan. Satan, in the black culture, has maintained strong African influences that contradict the image of the European Christian Satan kept alive for centuries through Inquisitions and witch hunts. The first missionaries to Africa identified the trickster deities with Satan, and the New World blacks retain the trickster elements in their idea of Satan (see chapter 9 for further discussion of Anansi the Spider, an African trickster deity): "he is clever, even dangerous, but he had human foibles and he can be outwitted—more a principle of unpredictability than of evil" (Stevens 1991, 35). In fact, most of the world's religions, with the exception of Christianity, have no counterpart to Satan or to Hell (Stevens 1991, 35).

THE POPULARITY OF
SATANIC LEGENDS TODAY

Although satanic legends are not at all new, they are popular as both something to be feared (and blamed for today's ills) and something to be sought out (ostensive action by young adults and other thrill-seekers). The pervasive mass media and "global village" atmosphere of the modern world has intensified both the power and the awareness of the legend today.

The legends endure because they offer "universal appeal to the latent fears of parents everywhere" (Victor 1990, 60). Incorporated into the age-old legend, embellished by the teller, are the following symbols of evil: graveyard robberies and the mutilation of corpses; secret meetings of people engaged in secret rituals; strange incantations; strange symbols on walls; and people clothed in black with black cats, making ritual animal sacrifices, and, occasionally, eating human body parts in cannibalistic rites (Victor 1990, 60).

Satanic and "baby parts" legends are disturbing because their horrible contents trigger deep and powerful emotional responses in people, seriously disrupting the flow of life in whole communities, and because they can motivate and justify persecutory movements against individuals or groups (Stevens 1990, 128).

One of the major reasons for the renewed popularity of these legends is the social and economic flux that Western society is experiencing. With both social and economic values undergoing swift and, in some cases, incomprehensible, changes, people struggle to find something to hold onto. Because satanic legends take symbolism from both secular and sacred realms, the battle against satanic movements can join often antagonistic groups, eliciting condemnation by religious fundamentalists as well as social workers, law enforcement, and journalists (Victor 1989, 40).

Both secular and religious groups react to a loss of faith in society's authorities and values. Satan has always been a symbol in Western culture for loss of faith. Rural areas react more strongly to this lack of faith, because values are more central to the moral order of society in rural areas, where community and common goals unite the population. Urban areas are conglomerates rather than united social units.

Economic stress is related to family problems and is a symptom of the decreasing cohesiveness of family bonds in rural communities. Social uncertainty has, throughout history, inspired development of demonologies about evil forces undermining the most cherished values and institutions of society (Stevens 1989, 1). The world is given constant reminders that we face severe social, economic, and environmental problems and that the future is dire. As Phillips Stevens points out, there are reasons to believe that the future looks bleak:

Signs that the *true* Millennium is coming soon: terrorism, drugs, sexual promiscuity, homosexuality, AIDS, poverty and homeless-ness, economic deterioration, political corruption and ineptitude, social unrest, earthquakes, environmental disasters, radically changed weather patterns and constant warnings from scientists and "experts." (1989, 9)

And as in eras past, people concoct their own plausible explanations for things that are beyond their understanding and acceptance. Thus, in the view of many, the evil in the world is the result of Satan, the result of the thwarting of institutions and youth by members of satanic cults! And there is plenty of evidence for these beliefs, especially in the form of anecdotes. The fact that there is no hard evidence does not deter the promoters of satanic cult rationalization. However, for the legends to circulate and be believed, certain conditions must be in place, noted by Jeffrey Victor (1990, 72):

1. Isolated, local claims about satanic cults have to find a channel to reach a broad, mass audience.

2. Some kind of "carrier" group must take up the rumor stories as a cause and persist in disseminating them over many years, in the face of strong skepticism.

3. Some kind of authority figure has to legitimize the rumor stories, by endorsing them as true.

The mass media demand for unique and dramatic issues satisfy the first condition. The legends are constantly reworked in the media and popular culture to entertain the masses. The horror stories and movies that young adults thrive on keep the ancient legends (and the fears of the parents and authorities) alive. The "carrier" groups of the second condition are both sacred and secular individuals who attempt to explain the world's ills as caused by supernatural or, at the very least, unnatural organized phenomenon. The third condition is met in the form of authority figures and "experts" who travel the world giving lectures and advice (and in many cases, causing panic themselves) about satanic phenomena. At any time that these three condi-tions come together in a time of social and economic uncertainty, the legend will flourish.

"The satanic cult legend says, in symbolic form, that our moral values are threatened by evil forces beyond our control, and that we have lost faith in our authorities to deal with the threat" (Victor 1991, 221). Unexplained local events, such as teenage suicide, desecration of churches and grave-yards, and mysterious graffiti, fuse with the instability created by economic and social stresses to form rumors, gossip, and speculation about satanic cults. Thus, satanic cult legends function as "improvised news" to provide an explanation for ambiguous sources of shared social stress and provide scapegoats for frustration, anger, and the feeling of powerlessness (Victor 1991, 223).

The media plays a large part in igniting and promoting satanic cult panics. The following report adequately demonstrates how large a role they can play:

> A nurse arriving at a geriatric center . . . found a young German shepherd wandering around wounded and muddy, with a short piece of rope dangling from its neck. The rope was knotted to a stake that witnesses suspected had been used to pin the dog to the ground. The animal was identified and taken to the local veterinarian, who at first was quoted as saying that it had been stabbed twice in the throat with a small knife. It was treated and returned to its family.
>
> [Two days later] . . . two local television stations had announced that "the mutilated body of a German shepherd was found . . . and police were investigating whether satanic activity was involved." Local emergency personnel were told to be alert for other incidents that suggested cults, but to "keep quiet about the wounded shepherd for fear that publicity would cause copycat crimes." This factor, however, was news to authorities, who disclaimed any information linking the incident to cults. A state police trooper issued a statement saying "Contrary to reports from local TV the dog was *not mutilated* and is very much alive and doing well." Also *no* evidence of any cult activity was discovered. The vet also requested a retraction: he had found only one small cut or puncture, the cause of which could not be determined. (Dog Mutilation 1993, 8)

CONSEQUENCES OF THE LEGENDS

Understanding the symbolism of satanic cult legends is made more important when one considers the harm caused by concerned citizens who overreact and form informal vigilante groups (satanic cult hunters).

Censorship Issues

Through my involvement with censorship issues in Alberta schools, I have become aware of the rise of parental concern about which reading materials children have access to and about Halloween celebrations. Parental and religious overreaction to satanic legends has resulted in "witch-hunts" against anything that they deem "satanic," from traditional folktales to "new age" symbols such as the "rainbow." Groups have demanded the removal of books that they claim promote the occult and satanism. A survey conducted by People for the American Way found that this claim has now become the most common threat to American students' freedom to use libraries. Indeed it has become the most common claim in Canadian libraries as well.

From the top-ten list of the most frequently challenged books in schools for the last few years, three involve retellings of contemporary legends aimed at upper elementary school students: *Scary Stories to Tell in the Dark* by Alvin Schwartz (#1), *More Scary Stories to Tell in the Dark*, also by Schwartz (#2), and *Scary Stories 3: More Tales to Chill Your Bones*, also by Schwartz. The same three titles are high on my list of recommended books for reluctant young adult readers!

Increase in Gun Sales and Fear of Others

Rumor-panics result in the widespread buying of guns in communities that perceive danger from satanic influence. A secondary reaction is for people to prevent their children going to public places (Victor 1991, 222). Though protecting children should not be seen as a negative, the aggressive nature of the responses to rumor-panics can be construed no other way. Incidents of group attacks on people perceived to be threats (or simply different from the majority) and destruction of property also increase in such communities.

Ostension

Three types of ostension are associated with satanic cult legends: ostension, pseudo-ostension, and quasi-ostension. Ostension proper involves legend-tripping in which young adults commit ritual acts suggesting satanism as an invocation of the supernatural. These ritual acts include vandalism and animal mutilations. Pseudo-ostension occurs when students fabricate incidents of satanic activity to frighten peers or parents. In these cases, young adults impersonate satanists or act out satanic cult rituals but do not believe that they, themselves, are part of a cult. The third type, quasi-ostension, occurs when authorities misinterpret normal adolescent acts such as graffiti (the number 666, pentagrams, and peace emblems) and "altars" (meeting places) as being part of satanic rites (Ellis 1991b, 282).

Much of what is labeled as satanic cult activity, therefore, is the result either of young adults "playing a role" to shock the adult community and entertain themselves or of worried authorities overreacting and misinterpreting the behavior of young people.

Propaganda

The propagation of satanic legends by influential people can be an authentic expression of beliefs and convictions, but well-intentioned people may also use the legends as good propaganda, or scare tactics, believing that the belief in such horrors will bring the public back to God (Campion-Vincent

1993, 242). Many of these forces of dissemination are retired policemen who have lucrative careers as lecturers on the cult crime circuit and television talk shows. Others are "escaped" cult members and victims who have publicized their experiences, often with lucrative results. There is evidence that not all disseminators of satanic legends do so out of true belief or a desire for the public's best interest:

> Harvest House Publishers, a Christian Press, has stopped publishing Lauren Stratford's *Satan Underground: The Extraordinary Story of One Woman's Escape* and has called in all copies of it from the book stores. The book described the author's involvement in a satanic cult and her eventual break for freedom. Reporters from *Cornerstone*, an evangelical Christian magazine, were disturbed by inconsistencies in her account and made efforts to verify her story. Failing to do so, they confronted Stratford, who admitted that she had fabricated the account. (Cult "Survivor" Book Withdrawn 1990, 9)

Later reports confirmed that the book had been withdrawn but that neither the publishing house nor the author admitted to fabrication. The book was withdrawn to end the controversy that detracted from the real issue of "compassion for the abused" (More on Lauren Stratford 1990, 6–7).

And in the Media . . .

The following news releases demonstrate the commonality of the reaction to satanic legends in various communities in Western society.

In the School Environment

> School officials in at least six local schools prohibited clothing that included the "peace symbol" made famous in the 1960s. After attending a seminar on cults held at the University of Houston during the spring, officials became concerned that the symbol had been adopted by satanists as "Nero's Cross," an inverted cross with broken arms. One spokesperson said that the cult slayings in Metamoros reinforced their doubts about the symbol, "but the awareness was already there. . . . We'd pick up little signs, like students doodling things on desk tops . . . or rumors of some students involved in cult practices." Classes affected by the bans included mainly 11- and 12-year-old students. [*Time*, July 23, 1989, 23]

> According to "Attacks on the Freedom to Learn," an annual survey of parent-school confrontations published by People for the American Way, accusations about witchcraft and satanism provoked the

largest number of complaints against readings or audiovisuals used in American classrooms. In nearly half the instances, parental complaints were successful in banning or restricting use of such materials. Items found objectionable were *Halloween ABC* (exposes elementary school pupils to "satanic influences"), *The Witch Grows Up* (makes "witchcraft look like a viable lifestyle"), *Devils and Demons* ("might lead children to a life of devil worship"), and *Stars, Spells, Secrets and Sorcery* (features "step-by-step instructions to set up an occult group"). (Satanism in the Library 1989, 7)

In the Legislature

Among bills filed by Louisiana state legislators was one to increase maximum jail terms for grave desecration from six months to five years. The sponsor, Rep. Cain for Dry Creek, introduced the bill after reports of devil-worship and grave disturbing increased in the New Orleans area and southwest LA. Later he added a bill to outlaw blood-drinking, cannibalism, and animal mutilation. "You stick one of those devil-worshippers pretty good with the bill, and word will get out we're not just slapping 'em on the wrist," Cain commented. (*New Orleans Times-Picayune*, April, 28, 1989)

The British Driving, Vehicle and Licensing Center agreed on 2 February to stop distributing car license plates containing the number 666 after numerous motorists complained that the plates had brought them bad luck. Jeff Mumford, senior executive officer of the Center's policy branch, cited a number of cases in which motorists blamed the plates for misfortune. In one case "a lady . . . claimed the car actually took hold of her and she couldn't control it. It reversed, mounted the doorstep, and squashed her son's scooter. She said she stopped it only in time to prevent it from crashing into the kitchen." In other cases, a North Wales man had his house robbed, his car wrecked by a garbage truck, and his water supply contaminated, within a week of receiving the plate. A mother complained that her "quiet, home-loving boy" changed into a murderer after his job made him drive a van with a 666 plate. British TV also reported that after another man bought a car with such a plate, he lost his family, home and business. Mumford said that the Center would not recall the thousands of 666 plates now in circulation, but he said the center would consider "sympathetically" complaints that the plate had caused motorists distress. A similar dispute arose in Davidson County, Tennessee, in 1988, when the officials tried to distribute license plates with the number on it. During the same year, after retiring from the White House, Ronald

Reagan changed the number of his private residence in California from 666 to 668 St. Cloud Drive. [AP release, February 3, 1990]

In Deer Park, a neighbor of Houston, Texas, residents complained when the number of their voting precinct was changed to "666." On 3 April, the city council unanimously passed a resolution asking that the precinct be renumbered, "so that all voters may enter the precinct and vote freely." The county clerk knew of no case in which a precinct was renumbered simply because "people didn't like it," but officials agreed to ask the US Justice Department to change it to Precinct 673. During the primary election on 10 April only 15% of normal voters turned out, some reluctantly, noting that the voting booths were located on 13th Street. [*Houston Chronicle*, April 11, 1990]

In the Technical Environment

Computer terminals are now being blamed by fundamentalists for more than health hazards. According to a scenario heard in a church seminar at Corpus Christi, Texas, Satan uses such terminals to emit invisible X-rays that burn "the mark of the beast" on users' foreheads (under the skin so that they can't be easily seen). After this rumor circulated on the alt.folklore.urban computer list, a fellow user recalled hearing this "proof" of the satanic origin of computers from a Mormon classmate at West Hills College, Coalinga, California in 1982:

If A = 1 x 6; B = 2 x 6; C = 3 x 6 . . . Z = 26 x 6, then

$$
\begin{array}{rcrcrcr}
C & = & 3 & \times & 6 & = & 18 \\
O & = & 15 & \times & 6 & = & 90 \\
M & = & 13 & \times & 6 & = & 78 \\
P & = & 16 & \times & 6 & = & 96 \\
U & = & 21 & \times & 6 & = & 126 \\
T & = & 20 & \times & 6 & = & 120 \\
E & = & 5 & \times & 6 & = & 30 \\
R & = & 18 & \times & 6 & = & \underline{108} \\
& & & & & & 666
\end{array}
$$

(More Signs of the Beast 1990, 8–9)

The Manitoba [Canada] Telephone System has abandoned plans to assign numbers beginning 666—because customers refused to accept them. (Signs of the Beast 1991, 13)

ANIMAL MUTILATIONS

During the 1970s rumor-panics about large-animal mutilations filled the media. Cattle were found dead and mutilated with all the soft parts (lips, ears, tongues, udders, and genitals) removed, apparently by a very sharp instrument like a razor or a scalpel. In many reports, the animals were completely drained of blood, and there were no blood stains on the ground. There was very little else on the ground either—no evidence of footprints or animal tracks. Numerous theories abound about the cause of the mysterious animal deaths, documented by Bill Ellis (1991a, 39):

1. Satanic cults are killing cattle as part of their rites.

2. The U.S. government is killing cattle as part of a secret project to monitor experiments.

3. Aliens from outer space are killing cattle as part of biological experiments.

By far, the most accepted explanation was the first: satanic cults and devil-worshippers became the popular answer. "And soon thereafter, prominent promoters of Satanic hysteria arrive on the scene to lend a new credibility to people's fears" (Carlson and Larue 1988, 51).

Again, as with other instances of alleged satanic worship, the rumor-panics are not new. In the 1500s, in France, a series of unexplained attacks on sheep led to extended hunts for *loup-garoux*, werewolves. "Authorities obtained confessions from several werewolves who freely confessed changing into animal form, then mangling as many sheep as they could under the instigation of the devil" (Ellis 1991a, 46).

The rumor-panics surrounding cattle mutilations gained prominence in the United States during the summer of 1973 in north-central Kansas. An investigation by Kansas State University and the brands commissioner cited the cause of the deaths as a combination of natural causes and predators. The cattle died from diseases, eating poisonous plants, and ordinary hazards such as rattlesnakes. The soft parts were eaten by small predators with, as microscopic examination revealed, razor-sharp teeth. Blood that appeared to be drained completely away had actually coagulated in the animal after its death. Statistical studies concluded that there was no actual increase of animal deaths in the area under investigation (Victor 1990, 64).

However, in spite of these findings, the general rural population were not too sure about this "pat" answer. An article in the *Kansas City Times* on December 22, 1973, "aired many of the fears of rural farmers, especially focusing on the 'eerie pattern' that had been observed: nearly all the deaths had involved cows with black hides, sex organs had been cut from both bulls and heifers, and in many cases ears had been cut off" (Ellis 1991a, 47).

The next spring, when cattle mutilations occurred in Nebraska, *Newsweek* gave the satanic rumors nationwide coverage and by 1980, special investigations had been conducted in Iowa, Oklahoma, Texas, Colorado, and New Mexico, as well as in the provinces of Alberta and Saskatchewan (Ellis 1991a, 47). At the height of the rumor-panics, mass media and propagandists such as local police and satanic "experts" fed the flames of the legends in spite of scientific evidence to the contrary. The panics offered much more drama than the scientific facts and sold more papers and garnished more interest in both the broadcasts and the workshops and lectures that were conducted by the "experts" during that time (Victor 1990, 65). These experts linked animal mutilations to kidnapping of children and ritual sacrifices, adding to the anxiety of the general population. However, in 1979, when former FBI agent Kenneth Rommel conducted a year-long federal investigation on the cattle mutilations, he debunked the rumor-panic, citing mass hysteria as the major culprit. This study virtually ended mass-media attention and the rumor-panics abated (Ellis 1991a, 48).

Evidence had been found, in a few cases, of actual attempts of animal mutilations after the animal had died. This was discovered to be the result of copy-cats and legend-tripping young adults who, through ostension, helped to keep these rumors and legends alive (Ellis 1989, 205). "No informant provided any firsthand accounts of the rites, but nearly everyone knew a cautionary story telling how 'someone' spied on the cult and came to a bad end" (206). Today, in specialized interest groups, the topic is still very much alive; for the average North American citizen the rumor-panic is an historical event.

SATANISM IN CHILD CARE CENTERS

Warnings about the menace posed by Satanists focus on some unusual elements. In particular, threats to children receive considerable attention; Satanists supposedly kidnap children to use them as human sacrifices or objects in ritual abuse orgies. It seems striking that, in a world where apocalyptic warnings of nuclear holocaust, ecological catastrophe and economic collapse are commonplace, the forces of the Prince of Darkness are thought to concentrate on child molesting. In this view, Satanists may belong to a vast conspiracy, but their evil deeds take the familiar form of random, irrational attacks. (Best 1991, 116)

The animal mutilation rumor-panics were followed by another panic: ritual abuse in child care centers in the United States and Great Britain. Ritual abuse is defined as "abuse which involves a series of repeated physical, emotional and/or sexual assaults combined with the systematic use of symbols, ceremonies or machinations" (Carlson and Larue 1988, 61).

Media attention was first caught by the McMartin Preschool case in 1984, which ignited numerous investigations and allegations of day care centers. Investigations that resulted in convictions did not reveal any involvement with devil worship but, rather, "involved a single paedophile or pornographer who, working alone, used ritualistic trappings to frighten children into participating and not revealing the abuse" (Carlson and Larue 1988, 62). The accusations were based only on the fears of parents and the testimonies of very young children and "some reporters have noted the curious resemblance to the Salem witch trials, which also were brought on by the accusations of children" (Victor 1990, 67). A study of 36 cases of accused ritual sexual abuse in children, conducted by Memphis Tennessee *Commercial Appeal* reporters Tom Charlier and Shirley Downing, concluded:

> Allegations of satanism—of rites involving mutilation, infant sacrifice and devil worship have since emerged in more than 100 child sex abuse cases across the country. . . . In four years, though, investigators have found no evidence to support fears that cults are preying on the nation's children. The *Commercial Appeal* studied ritual sexual abuse allegations in 36 cases and found instead that many of the stories labeled "satanic" or "ritual" have the hallmarks of urban legends. (Victor 1990, 68)

By 1986, the media realized that the cases alleging ritual abuse had been blown out of proportion and an attempt was made to provide more balanced coverage. However, when Geraldo Rivera, in a program aired on October 25, 1988, titled "Satanism—Exposing the Devil's Underground," focused on the McMartin Preschool case, Rivera presented a very one-sided view. While he admitted that charges had been dropped against most of the defendants, he did not explain that the charges were dropped because there was no evidence of ritual abuse or how this affected the case. Instead, he publicized the parental concerns of satanic involvement. "This is the type of coverage that allows rumors and lies to become accepted as facts in the public mind" (Carlson and Larue 1988, 68).

In their discussion of "anti-satanic hysteria," Carlson and Larue list the damage it has done so far: wasted tax dollars; wasted hours of police and law enforcement personnel; rumor-panics (Halloween and Friday the 13th); harassment and discrimination against minority religions (many of the current "experts" on satanic crime are fundamentalist Christians); and increased teen "satanism" (Carlson and Larue 1988, 81–89). The authors point out that the media attention of satanism has *itself* fostered an interest in the occult that wasn't there a few years ago.

Then, American "experts" offered their assistance in Great Britain. Sandy Hobbs and Bill Ellis examine the public controversy in Britain over the role of social workers in claims of ritual satanic child abuse. They attribute the beginning of the panic to the seminar held in Reading during September of 1989. Satan-hunters gave lectures to child care workers to aid them in recognizing signs of ritual child abuse. The lectures were followed by a series of locally organized workshops that culminated in a statement by the National Society for the Prevention of Cruelty to Children (NSPCC) on March 13, 1990 that said that satanic child abuse was common in Great Britain.

Social workers, armed with rumors, raided homes and removed the children, taking them into custody. "Since initial news coverage of the incident had given (authorities felt) too many clues to the families' identity, they obtained an injunction preventing parents from seeing their children or making official inquiries about the charges against them" (Rochdale: Row over Ritual Child Abuse 1990, 6). News media were also blocked from publishing information or making inquiries, but on September 9, 1989, *The Mail* denounced the investigation as "totalitarianism . . . creating an atmosphere which is beginning to be reminiscent of the days of the Nazis" (Rochdale 1990, 6).

The ensuing public uproar led police to confirm that the children showed no medical signs of abuse and that no hard evidence had been uncovered. *The Mail* speculated that several key investigators had gone to a three-day conference held in Reading in September 1989, a conference that had been presented in an atmosphere of "hysteria." It was later confirmed that three members of NSPCC's child sexual abuse team had presented papers at the conference. The funding for the NSPCC was withdrawn by Manchester, and the same action was pending in Rochdale at the time of this report. Both communities had been involved with the removal of children from parental care (Rochdale: Row over Ritual Child Abuse 1990, 6–7).

Though the social workers defended their actions, the courts finally threw out the cases in March 1991 because no evidence had come to light to justify any action. Manchester Justice Douglas Brown stated that "no evidence had ever been produced of missing, dead or mutilated babies and that the worst parents had done was to allow young children to watch horror videos" (Hobbs and Ellis 1991, 1).

Sandy Hobbs, Bill Ellis, and Gillian Bennett created three checklists of newspaper articles from quality presses dealing with stories of ritual abuse. Bennett explains the purpose of these checklists in the second report:

> This checklist cites articles appearing in the quality press rather than the tabloids because this allows readers to see what opinion-leaders were making of the reports. It also shows how claims of ritual abuse were politicized by involving the National Society for the Prevention of Cruelty to Children (NSPCC), a high-profile, quasi-official charity, and how, after an initial period of universal credulity, "informed opinion" gradually began to reject the claims. (Bennett 1991, 8)

The first checklist in the series, compiled by Hobbs and Ellis, deals with the Orkney Islands ritual abuse controversy, which started as the Rochdale case was dissolving. The second report, by Gillian Bennett, presents a checklist that covers the Rochdale and (the less publicized) Nottingham Affairs during the period of February 1989 to April 1991.

In the third checklist of the series, Bennett, Hobbs, and Ellis continue the examination of the Orkney Islands case. The checklist is divided into three categories: "The Arrest and Dismissal: 1 March to 5 April 1991"; "The Reversal: 6 April to 16 June" (social workers overturn sheriff's decision); and "The Inquiry: 20 June to 7 November" (investigation on the handling of the case by social workers). In their prologue, the three authors explain the initial removal from their homes of the children on the island of South Ronaldsay:

> Children were not allowed to take personal belongings because toys might carry a "possible symbolic meaning" that would limit their ability to describe their experiences. For the same reason, messages from parents to children were intercepted and letters from children were never delivered. Even Easter eggs sent by parents were broken to see if they concealed anything. (Bennett, Hobbs, and Ellis 1991, 1)

The final report on the Orkney Islands Affair was issued on October 28, 1992, concluding that adults, not children, should be investigated and that the terms "satanic" and "demonic" abuse, as used in the inquiry, did not have "any relevance to the present case" accept to add "further colour or detail to the concept of ritual abuse" (Orkney Report Issued 1992, 7). The report concluded that the use of such inflammatory labels clouded the thinking and actions of the social workers involved and the presumption of innocent until proven guilty should have been maintained. A booklet collating and extending the checklists of British newspaper reports is available from The International Society for Contemporary Legend Research. ISLR's Occasional Publication #1: The Orkney Islands SRA Case. Queries directed to Philip Hiscock, Folklore and Language Archive, Memorial University of Newfoundland, St. John's NFLD. Canada A1B 3X8.

SATANISM AND THE CONSUMER

The average consumer has also had contact with rumors and legends about satanic corporations. Large corporations have always been popular targets of rumors, both positive and negative. The corporations targeted by satanic rumors are usually those that deal directly with consumers. They are usually manufacturers of food or household products and are leaders in their product area, either in sales or prestige (Fine 1990, 135). This dominance creates a reaction, on the part of the general public, against the large "unfriendly" big businesses. "By associating corporations with extreme religious and political groups, believers are saying, in effect, that these corporations are outside of the moral boundaries of society" (Fine 1990, 135).

The cult rumors and legends fall into two broad categories: first, that the corporations are involved with what the teller considers a religious fringe group or second, that the corporation is involved with or supports an extremist political group. There is virtually no crossover of the two groups in any corporation and, in fact, the two categories are essentially different folk traditions (Fine 1990, 136). The following chart demonstrates these findings.

Mercantile Rumors Linking Corporations and Extremist Groups

I. RELIGIOUS RUMORS

Arm & Hammer	Satanists
Celestial Seasonings	Unification Church (Moonies)
Century 21	Unification Church
Coca-Cola	Mormons
Exxon	Satanists
Gorton Seafood	Unification Church
Johnson & Johnson	Satanists
McDonalds	Satanists
Marriott Hotels	Mormons
Ralph's Super Market	Mormons
Safeway	Mormons
Wendy's	Unification Church

II. POLITICAL RUMORS

Adolph Coors Company	American Nazi Party
	Contras
	Iran Arms Sales
	Ku Klux Klan
	Moral Majority
	Gun Control
Church's Fried Chicken	Ku Klux Klan
Kentucky Fried Chicken	American Nazi Party
	Ku Klux Klan
Pepsi-Cola	Palestine Liberation Organization (PLO)
R.J. Reynolds Co.	Contras
Stroh's Beer	Gun Control
Uncle Ben's Rice	Ku Klux Klan
	PLO
Welch's Food	John Birch Society

(Fine 1990, 136)

Several studies have examined how corporations handle rumors about their satanic involvement.

Proctor & Gamble

A couple from Topeka, Kansas, had been sued by Proctor & Gamble for reproducing and distributing a flyer stating that the company's trademark contains satanic imagery. The flyer states that the president of P & G "gave Satan all the credit for his riches" and adopted their well-known logo as a satanic symbol. The crescent moon was actually a "ram's horn" and that the thirteen stars, if connected by lines, form the number 666. [The flyer] continues, "Christians should always remember that if they buy any product with this symbol, they will be taking part in the support of the Church of Satan."

The two are distributors of Amway Home Products, a line of privately sold alternatives to commercial household products. Proctor & Gamble has asked for more than $50,000 in damages and had requested an injunction to stop the flyer's circulation. "These lies have persisted now for 10 years," the firm's CEO stated, "and we will file further suits if necessary." In 1985, the company filed suits against Amway distributers in Virginia, Pennsylvania and Kansas for distributing similar flyers. Soon after, it began to phase out its use of the trademark. (Proctor & Gamble & Satan 1990, 7)

Proctor & Gamble, the largest American manufacturer of cleaning and food products, is a frequent target of religious cult rumors. The rumors can be divided in two parts: the first part describes the satanic symbolism of their product logo, and the second alleges that the man in charge of the company (that "president" or "owner" is never named, since this individual has always had a low public profile) appeared on a leading television talk show (usually "Donahue," occasionally "60 Minutes," "20/20," or "Merv Griffin") and announced that the company was in league with the devil, or associated with the Church of Satan, adding that there weren't enough Christians in America to affect their sales (Fine 1990, 137).

The rumors were first noticed in 1978 when the logo of the moon and stars first came to be identified with the Unification Church, the "Moonies." The rumor alleged that the company had been purchased by the Unification Church, a plausible connection to the "moon" and to the fact that the Unification Church was known to be wealthy and committed to American-style capitalism (Fine 1990, 138). Research into the rumor found that its early transmission was mainly through informal communication networks such as small-town bulletins and conversations. Later, flyers and newspaper articles picked up the warnings and rumors and expanded upon them.

The persistence of the Proctor & Gamble satanist rumor stories demonstrates the power and pervasiveness of the religious traditionalist communication network. By researching the newspaper and media reports of the last decade, students can plot this complex communication network, and follow Proctor & Gamble's reactions to the campaign against them.

Liz Claiborne, Inc.

On 9 June a reader wrote in to an information column in the Austin American-Statesman *asking if it was true that the fast-growing clothing firm Liz Claiborne was in league with the devil. She wrote: "My boyfriend saw Liz Claiborne interviewed recently on the Oprah Winfrey show. She said 40 percent of the profits on her sales go to Satanism. The screen went black then switched to a commercial. After the commercial, Liz Claiborne was gone." The columnist debunked the rumor, citing a spokesperson for the Oprah show, who confirmed that Claiborne had never been on the nationally syndicated show. "Sounds like the Proctor & Gamble moon and stars rumor." (Liz Claiborne Rumor Continues 1990, 7)*

Similar rumors began circulating in early 1990s about the noted American sportswear manufacturer. The structure of the rumors closely resembled those that were being spread against Proctor & Gamble. Sarah Patterson, the company's public relations manager, stated, "There's absolutely no truth to these rumors" (Another "Satanic" Corporation 1990, 9). As with the former rumor campaign, the guest lists of the talk show were examined and revealed that Liz Claiborne had never been a guest. But within a very short time, the nature of the rumor shifted from satanism to racism with the onset of a different rumor about a Liz Claiborne appearance on the "Oprah Winfrey Show."

Film director Spike Lee . . . insisted that he had seen [Liz Claiborne] on the show stating that "she didn't make clothes for black people." The show was stopped and Winfrey threw Claiborne off the set. He concluded his statement that "it definitely happened. Get the tape." This is an adaptation to an earlier rumor stating that Liz Claiborne said that her dresses do not fit black women because their "hips are too big." (Liz Claiborne Rumors 1992, 11)

This rumor remains quite active.

A few readers have called Flair [the fashion section] recently to ask if it was true that fashion designer Liz Claiborne openly supported the Ku Klux Klan . . . revealed on Oprah. [It] sounded bizarre to us, first of all because Claiborne is no longer in the public eye, having retired five years ago from designing and the business that still bears her name. . . . We called Harpo Productions, the company that produces Oprah. From the tone in the research manager's voice, it was evident the question had been asked before. The answer left no doubt: "Ms. Claiborne has never been a guest on this show." (Say it ain't so, Liz 1994, B3)

"DEVIL AT THE DANCE"

Neide's Bar is a huge dance hall in the populous bairro of Jardim Eldorado in the city of Porto Velho, Brazil. . . . By 1990, when the lambada had spread all over Brazil, a hot competition for the best lambada dancer took place every weekend at Neide's.

On a Friday night in 1990, Neide's Bar opened normally at 10 P.M. to run to its usual closing time of 4 A.M. Everything would have run normal indeed, if a superb lambada dancer had not made an appearance that night: a slim man elegantly attired in black, who danced so well he would cause envy in any dancing instructor. All the ladies wanted to dance with the stranger. At a given moment, all present were shaken by a terrible scream, and the girl dancing with the stranger fainted. People ran to her aid, but what had happened to her partner? He had disappeared, leaving only the smell of sulphur.

The girl was taken to the hospital. After recovering, she said that she had danced without looking at her partner. When she finally did look, she saw that he had flaming eyes and the features of a demon.

The news came out the following days in the Estadao and Alto Madiera, the major newspapers of Porto Velho, and over the radio. A few weeks later, a similar occurrence took place in another dance hall. This time, the police managed to get their hands on the stranger. It turned out that after he was arrested he succeeded in escaping, disappearing mysteriously from the jail house. He was a strange character, so it was concluded that the dancer was really the devil—and the lambada his favorite dance! Ladies who were at the dances where the strange events took place affirmed that they had heard from the dancer that the lambada was his favorite dance and that he was going to take the best dancing partners down to the depths of hell. (Nineve 1992, 4)

In Brazil, "there is widespread moralistic opposition to the lambada, a sexually explicit dance that had been condemned by Pope John Paul II as immoral" (Nineve 1992, 4). Therefore, the "Devil at the Dance" legend functions as a cautionary tale in communities that have sanctions about dancing. Variants of this legend are not found only in rural communities but were popular in North American urban settings as well. The kernel of the story remains constant in all variants, as documented by Herrera-Sobek (1988, 152):

1. Young person

2. Disobeys parents

3. Goes to dance

4. Devil appears

5. Punishment

In Mexican American variants of this legend, the devil is recognized by his feet (the only part of his body he cannot transform when he takes a human shape) (Glazer 1984, 121). In many of the recent variants, the devil wears his customary black attire but it is most elegant and fashionable. Mark Glazer (1984, 123) notes the three major areas of Chicano culture reflected in this legend:

1. Relationship between parents and children characterized by strict discipline. Children who do not obey their parents are severely punished.

2. Religion and sacred days of observance include the prohibition of cooking, washing, and dancing. Many of the variants take place on one of the most important days, Good Friday.

3. Cultural perception of evil makes the devil a force to battle and to be kept at bay.

"It is . . . symbolically important to behave in a pure manner which fits the cultural patterns and not to pollute one's behaviour with evil activities such as disobeying a parent or dancing on Good Friday" (Glazer 1984, 123).

The figure of the devil disguised as a handsome young man has traditional symbolism. "The devil is *par excellence* the symbol of evil in Western civilization: in Christian myth it is Satan, in the form of the serpent, who appears to tempt Eve into tasting forbidden fruit from the tree of knowledge" (Herrera-Sobek 1988, 153).

Peter Theroux, commenting on his first experiences in Saudi Arabia in the early 1980s, recalled visiting a friend of his and finding the house in an uproar, the father praying, the sisters weeping, the mother talking excitedly on the phone. "*IT* had happened to their two girlfriends":

> *They had been strolling down the block and were attracted by the sound of music from the Festival Place in this flat Arabian suburb of Slueimanya. The girls peeked in to see almost a hundred elegant unveiled women dancing to tribal wedding music. "Come in— join us!" called one of the tallest and lightest-skinned women—a princess surely. The girls pulled off their veils and were about to start dancing when one of them grabbed her friend's elbow. "Look at their legs!" All the women had the legs and hoofs of donkeys.*
>
> *The girls snatched their veils and ran out of the ranch-style place, through the marble courtyard and gardens, to the sidewalk where a little yellow taxi was parked under the fizzing amber streetlights. "Get the police! And get a sheik—there's a party of demons in the Festival Palace!" screamed the girls.*
>
> *"How do you know they were demons?" asked the driver placidly.*
>
> *"They were dancing and had donkey legs!"*
>
> *"Like this?" The driver lifted the hem of his thobe, the ankle-length white shirt Saudi men wear, to reveal his hirsute donkey hoofs. The girls ran screaming home and phoned all their friends.*
> (Meanwhile, back in Riyadh 1991, 10)

Theroux comments, in his book *Sandstorms: Days and Nights in Arabia*, that this was the first, and last, urban legend he heard in Saudi Arabia that did not involve foreigners (Meanwhile, back in Riyadh 1991, 10). Unless, of course, you call the demons at the dance foreigners!

An earlier variant of this legend circulated in Danzig in 1875:

*It is said that one of the last Sundays [before Lent] a servant
woman went to confession and communion. Despite the reprimands
of her mother, an honest laundress, who warned her not to desecrate
the day by mundane festivities, she couldn't resist the temptation
and was going that same night to dance at The Vineyard [a ball-
room situated in an inner suburb of Danzig].*

*The punishment for her impiety came quickly. Around midnight,
she saw a handsomely dressed stranger with black hair and eyes
that glistened like onyx, coming towards her to ask her to dance.
She took his arm with pleasure as they began to dance with perfect
grace, but faster and faster. . . .*

*One of the musicians watched the dancing people carefully, and one
can imagine how he felt when he noticed that the stranger had the
cloven hoof of Satan! He drew his comrades' attention to it, and in
the very middle of the waltz they were playing, they changed the
tune and broke into a religious hymn. The clock struck twelve, the
devil pulled his partner close to him and in a frantic whirl crossed
with her to the other side of the room and crashed through the window.
The girl was found lying on the green grass in the garden covered
with broken glass. The devil had disappeared.* (Renard 1994, 2)

REFERENCES

Another "satanic" corporation. 1990. *FOAFTALE NEWS* 18 (June): 9.

"Backmasked" album exonerated. 1990. *FOAFTALE NEWS* 19 (October): 7–8.

Bennett, Gillian. 1991. Satanic ritual abuse in the United Kingdom: A checklist of newspaper reports, part two: The Rochdale and Nottingham affairs. *FOAFTALE NEWS* 23 (September): 7-11.

Bennett, Gillian, Sandy Hobbs, and Bill Ellis. 1991. Satanic ritual abuse in the United Kingdom: A checklist of newspaper reports in England and Scotland, part three: The Orkney Islands ritual abuse case continued. *FOAFTALE NEWS* 24 (December): 1–4.

Best, Joel. 1991. Bad guys and random violence: Folklore and media constructions of contemporary deviance. *Contemporary Legend* 1: 107–21.

Brewer's dictionary of phrase & fable. 1981. Edited by Ivor H. Evans. New York: Harper & Row.

Campion-Vincent, Veronique. 1993. Demonolgies in contemporary legends and panics: Satanism and baby parts stories. *Fabula* 34, no. 3/4: 238–51.

Carlson, Shawn, and Gerald Larue. 1988. *Satanism in America: How the devil got much more than his due.* El Cerrito, CA: Gai Press.

Cult "survivor" book withdrawn. 1990. *FOAFTALE NEWS* 18 (June): 9.

Dog mutilation. 1993. *FOAFTALE NEWS* 31 (November): 8.

Ellis, Bill. 1983. De legendis urbis: Modern legends in ancient Rome. *Journal of American Folklore* 96, no. 380: 200–208.

———. 1989. Death by folklore: Ostension, contemporary legend and murder. *Western Folklore* 48 (July): 201–20.

———. 1991a. Cattle mutilation: Contemporary legends and contemporary mythologies. *Contemporary Legend* 1: 39–80.

———. 1991b. Legend-trips and satanism: adolescents' ostensive traditions as "cult activities." In *The Satanism Scare*, edited by James T. Richardson, Joel Best, and David G. Bromley. New York: Aldine de Gruyer.

Fine, Gary Alan. 1990. Among those dark satanic mills: Rumors of kooks, cults and corporations. *Southern Folklore* 47: 133–46.

Gazdik, Tanya. 1989 Some colleges warn students that cult-like methods are being used by Christian Fundamentalist groups. *The Chronicle of Higher Education* (November 15): 1, A42. Quoted in Not all cults are satanic. 1990. *FOAFTALE NEWS* 171 (March): 11.

Glazer, Mark. 1984. Continuity and change in legendry: Two Mexican-American examples. In *Perspectives on contemporary legend, vol.I,* edited by Paul Smith. Sheffield, England: Sheffield Academic Press, 108–27

Herrera-Sobek, Maria. 1988. The devil in the discotheque: A semiotic analysis of a contemporary legend. In *Monsters with iron teeth: Perspectives on contemporary legend, vol. 3.,* edited by Gillian Bennett and Paul Smith. Sheffield, England: Sheffield Academic Press, 147–57.

Hobbs, Sandy, and Bill Ellis. 1991. Satanic ritual abuse in the United Kingdom: A checklist of newspaper reports in England and Scotland. Part one: The Orkney Islands case. *FOAFTALE NEWS* 22 (June): 1–3.

Liz Claiborne rumor continues. 1990. *FOAFTALE NEWS* 19 (October): 7.

Liz Claiborne rumors. 1992. *FOAFTALE NEWS* 28 (December): 11.

Meanwhile, back in Riyadh. 1991. *FOAFTALE NEWS* 21 (March): 10.

More on Lauren Stratford. 1990. *FOAFTALE NEWS* 20 (December): 6–7.

More signs of the beast. 1990. *FOAFTALE NEWS* 19 (October): 8–9.

Nineve, Miguel. 1992. The devil does the lambada: Another visit to Brazil. *FOAFTALE NEWS* 27 (September): 4.

Orkney Report issued. 1992. *FOAFTALE NEWS* (December): 7.

Proctor & Gamble & Satan. 1990. *FOAFTALE NEWS* 19 (October): 7.

Renard, Jean-Bruno. 1994. Old contemporary legends: 19th-century French folklore studies revisited. *FOAFTALE NEWS* 32 (February): 1–4.

Ridley, Florence H. 1967. A tale told too often. *Western Folklore* 26: 153–56.

Rochdale: Row over ritual child abuse. 1990. *FOAFTALE NEWS* 20 (December): 6–7

Satanism in the library. 1989. *FOAFTALE NEWS* 16 (December): 7.

Say it ain't so, Liz. 1994. *Edmonton Journal* (September 6): B3.

Signs of the beast. 1991. *FOAFTALE NEWS* 23 (September): 13.

Stevens, Phillip, Jr. 1989. Satanism: Where are the folklorists? *New York Folklore* 15, no. 1-2: 1–22.

———. 1990. "New" legends: Some perspectives from anthropology. *Western Folklore* 49 (January): 121–33.

———. 1991. The demonology of satanism: An anthropological view. In *The satanism scare*, edited by James T. Richardson, Joel Best, and David G. Bromley. New York: Aldine de Gruyer, 21–39.

Victor, Jeffrey S. 1989. A rumor-panic about a dangerous satanic cult in western New York. *New York Folklore* 15, no. 1-2: 23–49.

———. 1990. Satanic cult rumors as contemporary legend. *Western Folklore* 49 (January): 51–81.

———. 1991. The dynamics of rumor-panics about satanic cults. In *The satanism scare*, edited by James T. Richardson, Joel Best, and David G. Bromley. New York: Aldine de Gruyer, 221–36.

12

SCARY STORIES

A young woman must return home from college in the middle of the night because of a sudden illness in her family. Her nervousness increases after she pulls into a filling station because the attendant keeps looking at her in an odd manner. After he pumps the gas, he insists that she get out of the car. She resists, but he finally convinces her to get out and see because it could be "a major problem with the car." As she gets out, he grabs her, pushes her into the gas station office, and locks the door behind them. As she opens her mouth to scream, he says calmly, "I'm sorry I had to do that, but there's a man lying on the backseat of the car with a knife." (Dickson and Goulden 1993, 165)

While most adults find no harm in tales about Santa Claus and the Tooth Fairy, many of these same people censor a child who breathlessly relates her experiences with UFOs and faeries. In the opinions of those adults, these children are "letting their imaginations run away with them" (Grider 1979, 137). These children will continue to relate imaginative stories as young adults, but instead of "harmless" supernatural helpers, they tell each other stories of gross, horrific events that are intended to shock and thrill and above all, entertain.

Horror tales, like the horror and ghost genres that comprise their favorite reading material, are often ridiculed and frequently censored by "responsible" adults who wish only the best for their students and children. But young adults, like the characters in their stories, are nebulous by nature, as they are caught between worlds, searching for their identity and place in the social order. "The legends [and the horror genre] reflect the tensions in the adolescent tug-of-war between childhood and adulthood" (Peters 1988, 231).

SCARY STORIES DEFINED

The contemporary legends in this chapter are known by a variety of labels: slumber party stories (designated by setting of narration); ghost stories (designated by content); gross stories (by tone); and scary stories (by the effect upon the audience) (Roemer 1971, 1). Danielle Roemer asked females between the ages of 10 and 20 to list the characteristics that define scary stories. Roemer (1971, 1) created the following list based on those interviews:

1. The teller claims that the story is true.

2. The main character is a female (she may be accompanied by a male character) who is threatened by some extraordinary person or thing.

3. The ending causes surprise, fear, or at least respect for the confrontation.

The villains in scary tales include both supernatural and extranatural foes. Supernatural refers to those beings that are "above or beyond what is natural; abnormal or extraordinary and an action [which] intervenes in the natural order" (Roemer 1971, 2). They are the ghosts and spirits that populate some of the tales. The extranatural, however, refers to "humans or semi-humans such as murderers, dog men and wild men." These beings are not part of a natural, ordinary life and "their presence disrupts the other characters' expectations for an ordinary way of life; their full nature and the extent of their posers are unknown and they can be described as extraordinary" (Roemer 1971, 2).

THEMES OF SCARY STORIES

Scary stories reflect universal concerns nearly as old as storytelling itself. The legends not only illuminate these anxieties but also serve to instill and ingrain them in the members of each new generation.

Concealed Danger

Concealed danger is a common motif in most contemporary legends. The threats range from snakes or spiders in clothing or rugs to rats in chicken batter to killers in the backseat of cars. Because of the potential for suspense and fear, concealed danger is probably the most common feature of scary legends.

Helpless Females

The scary stories revolve around an isolated "victim" or main character who is basically helpless. Females are traditionally portrayed as helpless by the media and in the world of contemporary legends. Several scary legends feature a lone woman in danger of being attacked ("The Boyfriend's Death," "The Baby-Sitter," "The Killer in the Backseat," and "The Roommate's Death").

Men may distrust women who look (and act?) strong and independent (like men?), and these stories are told by men to keep women "in their place" as the women experiment with nontraditional sexual roles and occupational roles. Some stories, however, may distrust the "new man" who has been socialized to be more emotionally expressive and compassionate. This distrust is reflected in legends that contain violence that lies "just below the surface" and will attack the unsuspecting female (Seelhorst 1987, 36). "The emotional core [of the story] . . . depends upon the victim's helplessness—in our society, on being an undefended woman, as she is still commonly perceived" (Rosenberg 1991, 227).

Fear of the Unknown

Contemporary legends are concerned with the theme of people's fear of the unknown, especially that unknown that exists within oneself. Not only does the content of the scary story provide us with evidence of this fear, but the occasion of the storytelling event also demonstrates that people are afraid of being separated from the secure and the ordinary.

FUNCTIONS OF SCARY LEGENDS

Scary stories, particularly those that make reference to the supernatural, have been the target of the recent censorship movement that has attacked North America. This is unfortunate because scary stories serve a variety of beneficial functions for the emotional and psychological maturity of young adults.

Warning Against Danger

Contemporary legends transmit cautionary and traditional wisdom that has been handed down through the generations. The social messages are simple: choose friends carefully, don't stay out too late, be brave, be strong, be truthful, be loyal, and heed your elders' warnings (Young and Young 1993, 167). Scary legends also warn the listener to always be cautious of being separated from the group, and be aware of any unconventionality in a situation (Roemer 1971, 9).

Confronting Fear

The need to come to terms with fear, but to make it bearable inside a stylized framework, gives rise to a complex set of storytelling conventions that grow and change as children move toward adolescence. Scary stories related by younger children are usually "jump" tales and funny-scary stories. As the child matures and is able to confront frightening phenomena, the legends told become horrifying, without any cushioning. "The transition from one kind of storytelling to the other is an important one, handled with care by the children themselves" (Tucker 1981, 141).

Because the cellar and the attic are not part of our general living space in the home, they are mysterious and threatening and are therefore frequently featured in the stories told by "pre-driving" storytellers. Both the attic and cellar represent early fears: fear of the dark, fear of being left alone, and the fear of the unknown hidden in shadows (Tucker 1981, 143). Once the young adult is mobile, the scary settings change, portraying fear of relationships (lover's lanes), fear of disobeying parental wishes ("Devil at the Dance"), and fear of being isolated on dark deserted roads ("The Killer in the Backseat").

> Closer to the fearful associations of storytelling is the feeling of transition between one spot of firm ground and another. The outdoor equivalent of the staircase is the bridge, so often said to be haunted by ghosts or other frightening figures. Both the bridge and the staircase serve as a connector between one place and another, but also as a connecting link with the supernatural. (Tucker 1981, 143)

The delight that children find in scary stories can be attributed in part to their indirect mastery of fear, as well as their gradual acquisition of the idea that spooky and scary manifestations can be fun. Horror movies on television, children's books, and such yearly phenomena as Halloween spookhouses are important examples of this concept (Tucker 1977, 101).

Releasing Tension

Scary story sessions help young adults release tension in a socially acceptable manner. "Tension is channelled into a narrative which produces fear and excitement, but which is socially acceptable because it also serves as a warning and reinforces the rigid moral standards of the home" (Greenburg 1972/73, 135). Young adults are free to react safely to whatever fears they are experiencing without having to acknowledge the fears to their peers. Without this tension, however, the legend would not survive (145).

Stepping Towards Maturation

The guidance, education, and limits of behavior that the tales impart to the young adult audience are a necessary component of maturation. Young adults need more than to be simply told stories that are "good for them"; they need to tell and listen to the stories that reflect their growth and understanding as well as their fears and misconceptions. While many of my contacts have been concerned with their students' fascination in the horrifying and the gross, they should realize that this is another aspect of maturation. As students move from junior high school through high school and post-secondary education, their tastes in contemporary legends also mature to reflect their "new" fears, interests, and concerns. These legends focus less on the gross and more on the plausible aspects of horrifying elements in our modern society.

Affirming Beliefs

Contemporary legends, on the whole, reflect a number of stereotypes held by the general population. In a time when solidarity with the group is of utmost importance, young adults are reassured to have stated beliefs that they can recognize and acknowledge. These stereotypes are particularly potent in the scary legends: the dangerous madman, the helpless female, and the violent male.

STRUCTURE OF SCARY LEGENDS AND THE LEGEND-TELLING EVENT

Contemporary legends that are classified as "scary stories" not only have common functions, they share a common structure and a common pattern for the telling of the stories.

General Structure of the Legend

The general structure of the scary story can be divided into three parts:

Isolation. The main character (narrator) is separated from a group and may become increasingly isolated throughout the story. The isolation may be psychological (apprehension about safety; butt of prank or joke) or geographical (separated from parents, friends, home; or departing from a cultural norm). "The 'group' or the character's 'security base' can be viewed as a place, person or group of persons or as a social norm which provides a character with a sense of security" (Roemer 1971, 5).

Encounter. While isolated, the main character becomes involved with either a supernatural or extranatural character or situation. A warning may be given to the character. The encounters are all psychologically unnerving to both the characters and the audience that is caught up in the telling.

Consequence. The warnings and the approaching danger are not heeded, and any plans, expectations, or rationalizations that the character may have had are fulfilled in a surprising manner (Roemer 1971, 5). The audience's expectation of being shocked and surprised is also fulfilled.

General Structure of the Legend-Telling Event

The settings of the legends and the legend-telling event are often the same: haunted houses, haunted bridges, and ghostly graveyards. Audiences remember and value the legends that threatened or frightened them the most. The structure and content of the legends and the skill of the storyteller help provide the optimum scare, but the "best" stories are experienced under ideal conditions.

I have found that telling scary stories at night in a dark, preferably rural and outdoor location, gives to optimum results. The same stories do not have the same effect within the safe environment of the school library or music room! The legends are also most effective when the audience is separated from their elders and their everyday routine. This is why camp counselors can spin such scary tales around the campfire. Our imaginations are much freer in the dark.

The typical legend-telling session (if such a thing exists) among college girls includes the following features: the use of dramatic emphasis (story-telling skills), audience reaction and participation as both the teller and the audience create the story, informal stories that are interspersed with conversation, a flowing transition from story to story, and a definite closure of the session (Grider 1973, 15).

The stories are told simply, usually in past tense with the active voice approximating everyday speech. Because the success of the legend depends on the credibility and believability of the content and teller, the story must be delivered in a straightforward manner without distracting artistic embellishments. The legend cannot sound as if it is a polished performance piece. However, it should be localized with people and places that the audience can identify and relate to easily.

THE LEGENDS

The following legends include the contemporary legends that young adult audiences have appreciated the most. The amount of discussion on the individual legends is dependent upon the amount of research literature available. The legends are organized alphabetically but do not include "The Vanishing Hitchhiker" or "La Llorona" ("The Weeping Woman"), which are discussed individually in chapters 13 and 14, respectively.

"THE BABY IN THE OVEN"

> *Parents leave their baby son with a new baby-sitter, a teenage girl who seems distracted. The woman phones from the party and asks whether everything is all right. The girl says yes and adds that the turkey is in the oven. The parents rush home in time to save their son only because the girl had not turned the oven on. She was high on LSD.* (So There's This Guy, See . . . 1991, 81)

This is a legend that I heard told frequently when I was growing up during the "drug-days" of the 1960s. Brunvand states that the legend represents the parents' ambivalent feelings towards their children; guilt for leaving them with strangers; a deep-seated distrust of strangers; and a fear of technology (1980, 62).

A recent adaptation to this legend tells about parents who can no longer wait for the arrival of the baby-sitter, who is late; so they tie the child into the high chair and catch the airplane as planned. They, of course, assume that the sitter will arrive momentarily. Unfortunately, this is not the case and when they return from their holiday, the parents find their child dead, still strapped to the chair. Either the baby-sitter was in an accident and hadn't regained consciousness or there was a confusion of dates, accounting for the baby-sitter's absence. Both of these tales, although usually featuring teenage baby-sitters, are told among parents to frighten themselves!

My husband first heard a version of "The Baby in the Oven" when he was 10 years old. He still recalls his horror at the grotesque nature of the tale, which he believed implicitly. As an adult, he now surmises that what he was experiencing was "separation anxiety." When he heard the legend again, he was a decade older, but he recognized it and easily recalled his initial emotional response. This time he realized it was a legend and just laughed. But then again, he knew it couldn't happen in Canada!

"THE BABY-SITTER"

While baby-sitting two youngsters one night, a young teenage girl received a few phone calls. The calls came after she had put the two children to bed upstairs. After having listened to two or three calls from a man breathing heavily and using obscene language, the girl called the operator to see if she could trace the number. A few minutes later, the operator called her back. She said for the girl to get out of the house as fast as she could because the calls were coming from an upstairs extension. The girl got out safely, but by the time she had gotten help the two children had been murdered. (Samuelson 1984, 2)

When I first told this legend, I told one of three different endings depending on which audience I was addressing. If I was speaking to an audience of mixed ages (adults and young adults), both the baby-sitter and the children survived. However, if I was speaking to a high school audience, the baby-sitter was the lone survivor. The junior high audience, for some reason, preferred the ending where no one survived. But as time went by, though, my own daughters started baby-sitting and I, unconsciously, stopped including the tale in my repertoire.

Although it has had enormous exposure through the various movies and retellings, the story is still very effective. Upon telling "The Baby-Sitter" in a special school for junior-high-aged offenders, one member of the audience had something to add to the tale. This audience made up of incarcerated youths acted so tough, but this story demonstrated a different side of them. The girl said, "You know that baby-sitter story? I know it's just a story, but you know what happened to me? My friend's parents were out of town and we were going to spend the weekend at her house. Well, we got everything ready and then sat around telling each other scary stories. I just finished that one ["The Baby-Sitter"] when the phone started ringing and ringing and ringing. We just looked at each other, grabbed our stuff, and ran over to my mom's. We stayed there all weekend, too. Don't know who tried to phone us!"

Elements of "The Baby-Sitter"

The elements of the core legend, as noted by Sue Samuelson (1984, 2), are

1. the babysitting situation;
2. the telephone calls;
3. the tracing of the call; and
4. the discovery of the caller's presence in the house.

The action usually takes place in a suburban home that is isolated from the neighbors because there are no other people in the legend until the telephone operator. The children are already upstairs and asleep. Although the children provide the reason for the sitter's presence, they do not feature as characters at any time.

As a mother of two teenage daughters, I know how important the telephone is to a young adult audience. The baby-sitter assumes the calls are pranks, which would not be at all unusual, either. The most frightening aspect of this legend is that the baby-sitter is not in control at any time; the caller multiplies the anxiety that the baby-sitter is already feeling as the responsible person in the household. The possibility that this could *actually* happen is never far from the mind of any baby-sitter.

Technology

The actual limits of the technology for tracing telephone calls is disregarded in this legend. It takes almost three minutes to make a trace, and it is doubtful that an obscene caller would remain on the line that long. "These technical aspects are downplayed in order to preserve the continuity of the legend. Most people know very little about the workings of the telephone, so the trace motif is acceptable" (Samuelson 1984, 4). Today's technology will eventually change the face of this legend—with "call-trace" and "call-display" features on most telephones, the baby-sitter would know immediately where the call was coming from and would have no need to call the operator.

Functions of "The Baby-Sitter"

The most obvious function of this legend is to frighten the audience. People have an intense desire to face challenges and be frightened, but we seek our thrills vicariously through horror movies, roller coaster rides, and ghost stories (Samuelson 1984, 6). An outgrowth of this is the desire to be frightened in a communal situation, which increases the feeling of community and togetherness, helping to reduce anxiety: "I am not alone."

A secondary function of "The Baby-Sitter" is the exploration of such hazardous elements in modern Western society as random violence and prank calls (Samuelson 1984, 7). It also contains a warning to baby-sitters that they must be capable and in control of any situation that they may encounter while they are in charge and responsible for the children. For this reason, the legend is usually told by females to female audiences. The legend reflects insecurity and fear of failure, not only as a baby-sitter, but as a young adult on the road to adulthood. However, most young people who relate this tale are unaware of the underlying messages, telling it just for the thrill of frightening and being frightened. "Baby-sitting is such a common practice among teenage girls that it is not unusual that it should be incorporated into adolescent folklore" (Samuelson 1984, 8).

"THE BOYFRIEND'S DEATH"

There was this boy and this girl. They were driving along this back country road. They were lovers trying to find a place where no one would see them kissing. Pretty soon the boy's red Corvette broke down. They waited for awhile but no one came along, so the boy said he would go and get some help. He told the girl to crawl into the back seat, get down on the floor so no one could see her, and lock all the doors. The boy was gone a long time and the girl was beginning to wonder what had happened when she heard a scratching noise on top of the car. She thought it was only a branch from the tree at the side of the road. Pretty soon she heard a "drip—drip—drip." She looked out the window and saw a car coming which had its headlights on. A policeman got out of the other car and told the girl to come in with him and not look back. But she did and saw her boyfriend hanging from a tree by the car with his head cut off.
(Bronner 1988, 148)

"The Boyfriend's Death" is told to shock and frighten the listener and plays on fears about the dark, abandonment, the unknown, and physical assault.

Most commentators have described this story as a cautionary tale about the dangers of parking, especially during the period of increased sexual freedom in the 1960s and 1970s. After all, the boy "gets it in the neck" for his wish to neck with his girlfriend. But another element is the girl's disregard of the strange noises outside the car. So the story suggests that the boy should have been less foolishly macho and that the girl should have been more aware of what was happening outside the car (Bronner 1990, 170).

Elements of "The Boyfriend's Death"

North American variants of "The Boyfriend's Death" consistently incorporate the following stable elements: parked couple, abandoned female, mysterious scratching or dripping sound, the daybreak rescue, and the horrible climax. The variables involve the precise location, the reason for the girl's abandonment, and the nature of the rescuers (Brunvand 1980, 51).

Types of the Legend

Through an examination of the legend in various communities and cultures around the world, it was found that there are two basic types of this legend, North American and European.

Type A: North American

Type A is typically told by female young adults in North America and follows the pattern established in the example at the beginning of this discussion. The chief function of this type of legend, like "The Hook," is to warn teenagers of the dangers of parking in lover's lane. The basic structure, as noted by Mark Glazer (1987, 93), includes the following elements:

1. A couple in lover's lane cannot start car when they wish to depart.

2. The boyfriend decides to go for help.

3. Before leaving, he instructs the girl not to open the door or leave the car.

4. He does not return as the hours go by.

5. She becomes increasingly terrified as she hears strange noises on the roof of the car.

6. The police arrive in the morning and a policeman tells her to get out of the car and not to look back.

7. She disregards advice and looks back to see her boyfriend hanging, dead, over the car.

Type B: European

A young couple were motoring through Italy when the car ran out of petrol. It was late at night but the boy remembered that there was an all-night garage not far back, so he decided to walk back, leaving the girl safely curled up under a blanket on the back seat of the car. She slept without difficulty but, all of a sudden, was rudely awoken by someone rocking the car and banging on the roof. Even though the doors were locked she became very frightened and hid under her blanket. Suddenly, the interference stopped and the girl dropped into an uneasy sleep. Dawn broke, and she looked out to discover that she was surrounded by policemen, of whom one had a loudhailer. When she looked out he said, "We want you to get out of the car as quickly as you can, run over here and on no account look behind you." Petrified, she did as she was told, but when she reached safety she turned back and there on the top of the car was a wild, dog-like madman. The police later told her that the man had escaped from an asylum and the noises that she had heard were the sounds of him decapitating her boyfriend and bouncing his head on the roof. (Dale 1984, 86)

Type B stories are most often told by males. Other differences from type A, as noted by Glazer (1987, 94), include:

1. The relationship between the characters: in Type B, the couple is either married or engaged.

2. The reason for the driver to leave the safety of the car: they are not parked but ran out of gas on a deserted road while traveling.

3. The nature of the horror: the husband is usually beheaded and the head is left in a bag or box on the hood of the car.

4. The bag or head is sometimes pounded on the car.

5. The gruesome discovery of the head when the bag is opened by the spouse or policeman.

A common link between the two tales is the running out of gas. Our modern culture rejects the poor planning that allows anyone to "run out of anything" or "be without" anything. Therefore, because the males neglected their machinery (cars), they were appropriately punished. "This relationship is reminiscent of that between humans and animals in folktales where the hero who treats animals well is rewarded, while the individuals who mistreat them are punished" (Glazer 1987, 106). The car has replaced the animals of folktales and the lesson to learn from this tale, according to this interpretation, is that being left without gas in a remote place may be dangerous.

> Although the story at first seems to be dealing with proper sexual behaviour, the real danger to the young man results from his having to leave the car to obtain gas. The real reason for his death is his not giving proper attention to his car. Had he fulfilled the necessary preliminaries for success, nothing would have happened to him. (Glazer 1987, 107)

In type A versions of this story, told in the United States and Canada, the noise that the girl hears can be the scraping of the boy's heels as he sways above the car, the scratching of his fingernails if he is hanging from his heels, or his blood dripping on the roof of the car. But in all scenarios, the boyfriend is found hanging from a tree that conveniently hangs over the car. In European versions (type B), the sound is a monotonous thumping of the madman pounding the severed head into the roof of the car. "The change mirrors real cultural differences: lynching is common in American folk law but utterly rare in Scandinavia, where knifing is the most common form of murder" (Barnes 1966, 312).

"Don't Look Back!" and Other Ancient Warnings

In his introduction to *The Scary Story Reader*, Jan Harold Brunvand explains that contemporary legends follow the tradition of tales told in the past. The warning "don't look back" is prevalent in mythology. The biblical story of "Lot's Wife," the Greek myth of Orpheus and Eurydice, and "The Boyfriend's Death" all share that message. The taboo against looking is also part of an older tradition and includes "Pandora's box," "Bluebeard," and "Peeping Tom" from the legend of Lady Godiva. Disobeying the warning constitutes breaking a taboo, creating the tension of the plot, and as a result, such stories, beyond being just scary, also describe the consequences of not following orders (Young and Young 1993, 7–8).

An analogy between this legend and tarot cards has also been drawn: the boyfriend who dies hanging upside down over the girlfriend and the car can be compared with the image in the tarot of the "hanged man," who is inverted, hanging by his feet. The card is often interpreted as a symbol of total defeat and impotence and is also viewed as a punishment for lack of interest and promises not kept. The swinging of a hanged object is a symbol of unfulfilled longing or tense expectation. His preoccupation with the girlfriend, spouse, or other situation has caused the driver to forget to fill the car's gas tank and he is punished, rather severely, by hanging (Glazer 1987, 106).

A Mexican American Adaptation of "The Boyfriend's Death"

The story has been adapted in the Mexican American community to fit its unique cultural values and expectations. "The society being acculturated brings its own traditions into play and changes the items being incorporated to fit its own needs" (Glazer 1985, 297). Young women in these communities do not have the same freedom as Anglo women. Therefore, the couple must be married and because they are, the couple does not need to seek lover's lane. To advance the story, the car must malfunction or run out of gas so the young man can leave the safety of the car and lose his life (Glazer 1985, 294). Thus, the type B variant is the most common among the Mexican American community.

My cousin told us about a young couple that was driving home one night when they ran out of gas. The young man told his wife to lock herself inside the car and also gave her a gun for self-protection. Some time after the young man had left, three evil-looking men tried to break into the woman's car. When she pointed the gun at them, they set a bag on the hood of the car and fled. Shortly after dawn a police officer arrived and asked the woman what was the matter. After the woman explained the situation, the police officer curiously picked up the bag on the hood of the car and reached inside. As he pulled the decapitated head of the young man out of the bag, the woman went into hysteria. According to my cousin, this is a true story and he swears the woman is in a mental hospital in Dallas. (Glazer 1985, 294)

Similarities Between "The Boyfriend's Death" and "The Hook"

"The Boyfriend's Death" is one of a group of contemporary legends that are similar in content and function. The setting in both "The Hook" and "The Boyfriend's Death" is the same: a deserted country road or lover's lane and the same type of activity is taking place. Both tales involve an interruption: "The Boyfriend's Death," a malfunction of the car or a lack of gasoline; "The Hook," a radio announcement. In both tales, there is a change of scene: the boyfriend, in the first legend, leaves the girl in the car to get more gas or help, while the second boyfriend leaves the scene complete with car and (angry, frightened) girlfriend. In both legends there is a horrifying climax to the adventure (Samuelson 1981, 137).

Both tales also follow the general structure discussed previously, as noted by Sue Samuelson (1981, 137):

Isolation. The couples are isolated (on purpose) from the rest of society and become increasingly isolated throughout the action of the tales.

Encounter. The extraordinary threat of being stranded in an isolated area without means of returning home because of car problems is only heightened by the strange sounds above the car when the girl is hiding in the backseat in "The Boyfriend's Death." The extraordinary encounter in "The Hook" involves the possible threat of an escaped madman.

Consequence. The surprising ending of "The Boyfriend's Death" leaves the girlfriend in shock after seeing her boyfriend's dead body swaying above the car that was her sanctuary. In "The Hook," both characters survive, but barely, as the bleeding hook is left hanging on the passenger's door handle.

"THE DARE"

> *There was a girl who hung around with a group of kids. They were all talking about this graveyard outside of town that was real spooky. She said she wasn't afraid and to prove it she would go out and stick a knife in one of the tombstones. She got out there and stuck the knife in and when she turned to get up, she thought a ghost or something was holding her and she died of fright. The next morning, when they found her, they found the knife stuck in the edge of her skirt.* (Bronner 1988, 146)

This is not a story about a ghost per se, but rather a tale that "shifts attention to the believers" (Bronner 1988, 260). This tale is extremely popular with young adult audiences because of their ability to identify with the situation. Their hyperactive imaginations are constantly misinterpreting pranks or practical jokes that are being played on them (Grider 1979, 569).

Not all the tellers are young adults, though. One version, told by a 65-year-old woman, tells of a girl who took a kitchen fork to the cemetery and put it through her apron. The informant stated: "This is a story that has been told to me for at least fifty-five, sixty years. As to whether there's any truth to it, I don't know, but I've heard it many a time" (Burrison 1989, 215). A coda to this tale, and others that involve the supernatural, may be stated: do not mess around with such powers. Even attempting to find out who one will marry constitutes a violation of this rule (Barden 1991, 15).

Elements of "The Dare"

"The Dare" is listed as Tale Type 1676B: "clothing caught in graveyard (man thinks that something terrifying is holding him and dies of fright)." Baughman, in *Type and Motif Index of the Folktales of England and America*, lists 15 references circulating between 1900 and 1959. The variations include stakes, sticks, knives, forks, swords, and nails into a grave or coffin (1966, 43). The legend follows the general structure of the scary tale:

Isolation. The young person purposely removes him/herself from the rest of the group to show his/her bravery.

Encounter. The supernatural being encountered in this tale is one of imagination. The protagonist is so frightened that very little encouragement is needed to visualize the potential danger.

Consequence. The protagonist pays a heavy price for the privilege of trying to prove a point and accepting a dare. The surprising ending is the result from the natural death from fright rather than anything "horrifying" happening.

Antecedents and Innovations

This legend is second only to "The Vanishing Hitchhiker" in number of appearances in collections of supernatural stories. In these collections, several recent modifications to the legend can be seen. The first involves the gender of the protagonist. The older tales involve a male who tries to prove his bravery; the more recent variants cite a female character who dies of fright in her attempt to prove herself. Perhaps this is indicative of the social order: more females may find it necessary to go out into the world to prove to themselves and others that they are equal.

The second modification involves the tone of the telling and cannot be conveyed by the "bald" printed versions. From her research in the Jewish community of Toronto, Kirshenblatt-Gimblett provides a transcript of "The Dare" told to demonstrate the superstitions of the Old World. She theorizes that when the story was first told, the emphasis was on the dangers of challenging tradition and of being skeptical of the old beliefs. In this case, the stake is pinned the young man's *kapote* [long coat traditionally worn by orthodox Jews] (1972, 119). The more contemporary version was told in an off-hand manner: "isn't it silly what these old people believe."

An early variant however, shows the strength of belief in justice:

Charlie Carter said that his father lived in the days of the Civil War. He said that there was a thief that caused much trouble and could not be caught up on. There was a very wealthy man that died and he had some very expensive jewelry and the man requested that this jewelry be buried with him, so his request was granted. There was no thought of anything or anybody, depredation of the grave, but just a short time later someone went to the grave, and when they got there, they found the grave opened. The corpse [coffin] had been opened and all of the jewelry [was] out. A man was laying across the box which had contained the corpse. His coat was fastened to the box with the screw that fastened the top of the box. He was dead. Apparently he was scared to death. So this was thought to be the thief that was causing the trouble in the community.
(Barden 1991, 308)

"EMBALMED ALIVE"

This lady died, and she wasn't very old. A couple of her sisters went out to buy a dress to bury her in, and they couldn't decide between this yellow one or the purple one, so they took both of them to get approval from the rest of the family. They left both dresses at the funeral home and later decided on the purple one, so they called the undertaker. I don't know if the undertaker didn't understand, but he had the yellow dress on her the next morning when the family came in. They told him about the mistake, and he exchanged the dresses, and they returned the yellow one to the store. A few days later a girl bought the yellow dress and wore it to a dance. During the dance she began sweating because the place was really full. After a few minutes she dropped dead. The stuff the undertaker had used had been so thick on the dress that it killed her. (Baker 1982, 215)

This legend has been circulating since at least 1933 and reflects a fear of the negligence of modern institutions such as large department stores. The name of the store varies with the actual location of the teller, but the story usually names one of the largest and most prestigious department stores in the community. Most frequently, the story relates the death of a young girl who buys a dress for a special occasion. Only after a great deal of dancing (and perspiring) does the girl succumb to either formaldehyde or embalming fluid left on the dress from a previous occasion. Now that young adults are purchasing secondhand clothes in great quantities, perhaps the department store will fade from the picture and the consignment shop will enter. Some variants provide the young girl with a brand new garment:

A woman bought a new dress at a large department store downtown. The first night she wore it, she noticed a strange smell. As the evening wore on, she began to feel sick. Then she fell over and died. It turned out that the store had bought some surplus shrouds from an undertaker and made them into dresses. Formaldehyde fumes lingering in the cloth had killed the woman. (Morgan and Tucker 1987, 192)

There is a close parallel between this legend and the Greek myth of Hercules, who died when his wife Dejanira secretly soaked his shirt with the blood of the centaur Nessus. Hercules had killed Nessus, but the dying centaur had tricked Dejanira, convincing her to save a vial of his blood as a love potion. Some time later, Dejanira felt jealous and soaked Hercules's shirt in the blood, taking care to wash out any visible stain. When he wore the shirt, Hercules's body heat warmed the poison and it worked its way into his body, causing great agony. He burned himself on a funeral pyre (Brunvand 1984, 113–14).

"THE HATCHET IN THE HANDBAG"

A girl was going to get some groceries. She parked far away because she wanted to protect her new car. She locked the doors and went inside. She got her groceries, came outside and looked towards her car. She thought she saw a shadow in her car. Walking closer, she noticed a little old lady sitting in her backseat. As she approached the car, she asked the lady, "What are you doing in my car?" "I've been walking so long, and my feet are very tired. Would you be so kind as to drive me home? I just live up the street." The girl thought, "Well, sure I could do this for this poor old lady," when suddenly she remembered that she had locked her car doors, and there was no way [the old lady] could have gotten in there. Remembering this, she replied, "Sure, just a minute. I forgot my keys. Let me go get them. I'll be right back, and then I'll give you a ride home." She went into the store and got the store's security men. They came out, but the little old lady was gone! After searching her car, they found a hatchet in the back seat. Later on, she found out about a man who was supposed to have been wanted in California for murder believed to be dressed up like a little old lady. (Bronner 1988, 149–59)

This legend was adapted for BBC radio broadcast early in 1978 from a literary short story written by Christine Herring:

The author of the broadcast story swears in a letter to me that the original legend is true, because she was told it (in its standard form) by a doctor friend who knows the nurse who was the driver; but the author goes on to say that she is unable to divulge the doctor's name because of the ethics of the medical profession. (Sanderson 1981b, 16)

This claim isn't true; in fact, the legend has been told in England for a much longer time. The *Stamford Mercury* of April 11, 1834, reports the same tale: "The driver is a gentleman in his gig, who on opening the supposed female's reticule finds to his horror a brace of loaded pistols inside" (Sanderson 1981b, 10).

The legend also reverberates louder in a country that has had a long history of mass murderers of women: Jack the Ripper and, more recently, the Yorkshire Ripper (1981). During the period when the Yorkshire Ripper was murdering women, reports of this legend were received in at least 17 police stations. The public urged the police to contact the driver and get a full description from her of the hatchet carrier (Sanderson 1981a, 164). The legend was first disseminated orally, then through local and national newspapers. The printed versions helped to both confirm people's belief in the tale and to spread it further. Journalists commented that, upon inquiries at various police stations, they could not verify that the incident took place as reported (Sanderson 1981a, 164).

Students tell this story about West Edmonton Mall, the mighty shopping complex in my home town that has acres and acres of parking:

> *Apparently a young girl was late to work at her part time job at the mall and had to park far away from the entrance. She worked late and by the time she went out to the car, the parking lot was deserted. She had, in her haste to get to work, left the car doors unlocked but was still surprised and dismayed to find an old woman sitting in the passenger seat. Being a quick thinker, the girl replied to the woman's request for a ride, with a smile and a promise for a quick return after she telephones her parents that she will be a little late. The security guard telephones the police and they go to the car with the driver. The old woman is still in the car. They explain that the girl has to go straight home and that they will give her a ride home. As they help her out of the car, the old woman's wig gets caught in the door molding, and they realize that it is not an old woman at all. It's not even a woman. They arrest the man and search the girl's car. Under the seat, in a large carpet bag, they find a bloody hatchet, or axe, or knife . . . or all three.*

The usual coda ascribed to this tale is that it is important to lock your car doors and therefore it serves a similar function as "The Killer in the Back Seat."

"THE HOOK"

This young couple is out parked on a country road. The girl is real nervous and uneasy. It seems that there had been a report about an escaped criminal in the area. He was supposed to be dangerous, a mad killer. They called him "The Hook" because one of his hands was missing and he wore a hook in place of it. He was supposed to have used it on all of his victims. Anyway, the girl was real uneasy for some reason. Supposedly, they were not aware of the escaped killer. She kept saying she had an uneasy feeling but she did not know why. The guy finally got mad at her. He thought she was just making up excuses because she didn't want to park. Finally he lost his temper and stepped on the gas. He really tore out of there fast. He didn't say a word on the way home. When they get to the girl's house, he just got out and went around to open her door. When he got to the door, there was a hook hanging on the handle.
(Baker 1982, 201)

The legend of "The Hook" has been the subject of much deliberation by scholars of contemporary legends for many years. The focus of this discussion revolves around the interpretation of the legend as well as the inclusion of "The Hook" in the corpus of contemporary legends.

Interpreting the Legend: A Dialogue

In the late 1960s, Linda Degh explored 44 variants of "The Hook" and the reasons the tellers gave for telling the tale. She hypothesizes that males tell the story while parking in lover's lane to add "spice" to the experience. Some of the tellers dwelled on the horrible looks of the "hookman" while others emphasized the argument between the couple in the car. She identifies the most persistent motif as that of the boy "gunning" the car and taking off in a hurry, providing a the credible and plausible explanation for the wrenching of the hook off the arm of the "madman" (1968, 98).

Alan Dundes refutes Linda Degh's analysis of "The Hook," stating that she makes "no real attempt to *interpret* the content of the legend but rather limits herself to *surveying* the content" (1971, 29). One clue to the meaning of the legend, he argues, is the fact that the principal tellers and audience of this legend are female. Thus the tale functions as a warning of the double-standard still facing young women today. "It is not the fear of an escapee from a mental institution but the fear of sexual attack of the girl's date which provided the emotional raison d'etre of the story" (31).

Gary Alan Fine discusses both interpretations in an article entitled "Evaluating Psychoanalytic Folklore: Are Freudians Ever Right?" Fine reminds us that, according to Dundes, the legend's primary focus is the girl's anxiety about the sexuality of the boys that she dates and *her* control of the situation (1984, 14). The hook is seen in Dundes's interpretation as a phallic symbol and also represents both the escaped maniac and the boyfriend, who are each temporarily removed from institutionalized constraints of society and are thus out of control. However, Fine reminds us, Dundes did not analyze a real text in a real legend-telling session but his own reconstruction of one that was grounded on the 44 texts in Degh's study (15).

Bill Ellis has concluded that "The Hook" is not a contemporary legend at all, although it does have many features of legends. His interpretation of "The Hook" is as a legend *parody,* and, therefore, he believes that it functions only as entertainment for young adults, who usually tell the story at "slumber parties" (1991, 65). Because of his understanding of the setting of the storytelling session, Ellis concludes that the tale is told as "untrue" and therefore does not belong to the canon of contemporary legends.

"Traditional belief legends and most contemporary legends aim to modify the actions of the listener directly: don't gamble on Sundays; watch your children at malls" (1991, 65). Contemporary legends are constantly in flux, growing out of social contexts that they tend to alter. "By contrast, legends like 'The Hook' are static in that they describe and indeed incite the very action they describe as taboo: parking and sexual experimentation" (65). Ellis explains that "The Vanishing Hitchhiker" is told in response in "emergency" situations, but that "The Hook" has not provoked any real-life panics or hunts for one-armed maniacs. Because the essential truth of the legend is not believed, Ellis continues, "The Hook" is a legend-trip core narrative "which promise[s] dire consequences of visiting spooky sites and performing certain rituals—only to encourage the listeners to carry them out" (66).

In a firm rebuttal of Ellis's article, Linda Degh questions his theory, stating that if a legend is indeed static, then it is "irrelevant, temporarily or permanently defunct, that is, nonexistent, dead" (1991, 72). "The Hook," she argues, is still one of the favorite tales for retelling, not only by teenagers but by cartoonists (Gary Larson's *Far Side*) and contemporary authors of adult fiction.

> Memories of summer camp as an 8-year-old: "The first night around the campfire, after we sang 'Kumbayah' about six times, they told me about this poor girl camper who had drowned two years before, and one who'd had an allergic reaction to a bee sting and nearly died, and another who broke her arm falling out of a tree. Also one of the counsellors had been parked with her boyfriend necking when the radio announcer told about this escaped raving maniac and after they rolled the car window up and drove away quick, there was his hook right in the window." (Sue Grafton, *"H" Is for Homicide* 1991, 213)

The legend was also alluded to in a skit on *Saturday Night Live*. The skit, situated around a campfire, actually begins with the end of the telling of the legend. Obviously, the writers of the skit assume that their audience knows "The Hook."

Ellis maintains that the legend has been told, for the last 20 years, mainly by children as a Halloween scare-tale in formal structured events:

> It shows up among girls in the ten to thirteen age group, an age just before they engage in the rituals of courtship. Boys, interestingly, circulate the legend a bit later, during the fourteen to seventeen age group, suggesting that among male groups it may serve as a way of daring others to park or to brag about their experience. (1994, 68)

I remember my mother telling me this legend as a cautionary tale when I first started dating boys with cars. In a small town, after cruising mainstreet eight or nine times, what else was there to do but go to "lover's lane"? My mother wanted to make sure that I thought twice about going.

General Structure of "The Hook"

Like the other scary stories, "The Hook" can easily be divided into three parts:

Isolation. The couple is isolated from the rest of society and they are engaged in a common activity of young adult culture: kissing, necking, making out, or intercourse. "The possibilities realistically reflect the ranges of choice open to teenagers and the one that an informant uses usually reflects the degree to which that person engages in romantic activity" (Samuelson 1981, 135).

Encounter. The tone for the encounter is set by the interruption on the radio and the warning of the dangerous maniac. The girl tries to heed the warning, but the boy is reluctant to leave and tries to pressure the girl into staying.

Consequence. The surprise ending is the discovery of the hook. A major difference between this legend and others that we are discussing is the fact that the major characters are not physically harmed in any way. Perhaps this is because, regardless of how angry the young man may be, he finally heeded the warning given him.

But some variants do not contain any sign of dissension between the couple at all:

One evening, a young couple was parked on the secluded Finchville Road, just at the time that a prisoner escaped from a state prison in nearby LaGrange. His description was broadly circulated in a matter of minutes, but, of course, the young lovers were not listening to the radio. It was thought that the prisoner would be captured quickly, because he was so easily identified— he had a hook in place of his left hand.

Around midnight, the youngsters, preparing to leave, turned on the radio, and, of course, heard the exciting news of the escape of a convict earlier in the evening. At the very minute that the announcer concluded the day by signing off the air, the girl turned, hearing something like a low groan. She was frozen in terror at the sight of a hook shaking in the moonlight, and framed in the window directly behind her. By the time she had forced a scream, scaring the boy into a hasty departure, the hook had disappeared. He managed to convince the girl that their scare had been a natural reaction to hearing the grotesque description of the escaped prisoner.

The next morning, the prisoner had still not been captured and had apparently made a successful getaway—the only trace he left was his hook, bent and bloody, which the boy had found attached to his rear bumper the next morning. (Stephens 1963, 7)

Functions of "The Hook"

The apparent functions of this legend are as varied as the interpretations accorded it in the literature:

1. It serves to provide the thrill of a good scare.
2. It reflects the fears of young adult females about parking with their boyfriends.
3. It is used as a warning by parents to their daughters of the possible dangers of parking with their boyfriends.

"THE KILLER IN THE BACKSEAT"

Research shows that one true case of "The Killer in the Backseat" did occur in 1964 in New York City, when an escaped murderer hid in the backseat of a car. The car, ironically, belonged to a police detective who shot the man. Though the differences between the legend and the true occurrence are vast (the real occurrence did not feature a lone female; it didn't necessarily happen at night; and no third person was involved), the legend may have sprung out of this actual happening (Drake 1968, 109). This legend maintains its popularity because it is so plausible and reflects the fears of women driving alone at night.

The legend has been identified as a "female's story" because it always involves a woman driving at night in relatively unsafe surroundings (Cord 1969, 50). The story is told by females to females because it involves both a character and a situation with which women can easily identify. The "killer" and the rescuer are always male. The legend has sexual overtones for both the teller and listener because of the situation (late at night, lone "helpless" woman) and because of an unstated fear of sexual assault that lies at the back of the mind (Cord 1969, 51). Although unstated, the woman is not concerned that the man who is following her will kill her but that he will violate her, which heightens the climax of the tale. Her fear is totally misdirected! What she fears the most is fear itself (Rosenberg 1991, 227).

Types of "The Killer in the Backseat" Legends

In addition to the primary version (type A) about the gas station attendant (earlier in this chapter), there are four other types:

Type B

A trucker follows the woman's car because he can see the man in the backseat from the higher vantage point of his truck cab.

Type C

One of the most common variants told today: an ordinary citizen in a parking lot follows the woman's car because he sees a man get into the backseat while she is in the store.

Type D

Here we have more than one rescuer. The woman, aware that she is being followed, summons a police man or security guard, who confronts the man following her. The man tells the woman and the officer about the killer in the backseat (Cord 1969, 48–49).

Type E

A new type has surfaced recently. A new gang initiation tale has been circulating about Phoenix, Arizona on the computer network (alt.folklore.urban, Sept. 25, 93). According to the network, this adaptation of "The Killer in the Backseat" has been circulating around in California and North Carolina.

Two interwoven themes are conveyed by all five types of this legend: a safe and supposedly private place may not be either safe or private, and nothing is as it seems. There is a suggestion "that in reality there is no safe warm haven of the kind all human beings long for" (Barden 1992, 163).

A woman fills her tank at a self-serve station. When she goes to the cashier's booth to pay, the cashier warns her that somebody had gotten into the backseat of her car. He advises her to fumble with her purse to stall while he calls the police. The police arrive and arrest a teenager who confesses that, as part of his gang initiation, he must sneak into the cars of two women at gas stations in order to rape and kill them. (Just In: The Killer in the Back Seat 1993, 6)

Structure of the Legend

Isolation. The (always) female driver is alone in a dark and isolated area, either a country road, deserted highway, or empty suburban street.

Encounter. The threat is of a suspected assailant either following her in another vehicle or in the gas station itself. The climax is heightened by the stranger's repeated "aggression" against the woman.

Consequence. The warnings that the woman misunderstood as aggression lead to a surprising turn of events: her fear was misdirected and the danger came from somewhere much closer than she realized, the backseat of her own car!

"THE PICKLED HAND"

This story took place in a hospital which was quite near Boswell, and concerned a nurse, called Jane in the story. For some reason Jane was unable to get along with the other nurses in the hospital, and was constantly quarrelling with people. They purposely did things to annoy her because they felt she deserved it. One night after Jane had been particularly trying, they decided to do something particularly unpleasant. One of the nurses on surgery duty agreed to bring an arm which had been amputated that day to Jane's room and slip it in her bed after she was asleep. They knew this would frighten her, but they thought perhaps it might force her to be more agreeable in the future.

The arm was carefully and quietly put in the bed and Jane did not wake up. The next morning she did not appear, and no sound came from her room. The nurses, thinking she might be sick, went to investigate. They opened the door slowly and saw Jane sitting on the bed. Her hair, which had been black, was now completely white, and she was gnawing on the arm, making low gurgling noises all the while. (Baughman 1945, 31)

Originally referred to as "The Cadaver Arm," this story told of an arm "lifted" from a body that was going to be dissected. The arm was placed in the victim's bed and, upon discovery, drove the victim to madness (Baughman 1945, 30).

The story was well known on the Indiana University campus in 1933, and it is the first one that I can actually remember being told. I was 11 years old and at camp for the first (and last) time. I knew no one at the camp but one of the counselors (all medical students) was from my home town. So when we were told the story, around the fire, and my acquaintance was looked at as an authority (he was one of the people "involved!"), what could I do but completely accept the story, true as told. It took me a few years to understand (in their version) the problem with the nursing student, but I remember vividly the image of her eating the hand. I remember also wondering why, with such an evil trick, the medical students were not punished!

According to this early research, there are two basic types of this legend: 1) the victim is a nurse, the setting is a hospital residence; and 2) the victim is a female medical student, the setting is the victim's campus room (Baughman 1945, 30). The placing of the arm varies slightly as well; in the majority of collected variants, the arm is placed in the victim's bed, several had the arm attached to the light cord, and in one it is placed in a dresser drawer. In the majority of these early variants, the entire arm is used. The results of the prank are consistent as well. The victim goes mad, her hair turns completely white, and she is found gnawing on the cadaver limb (Baughman 1945, 30).

Cadaver Stories

Frederic Hafferty discusses this legend and others even more gross, graphic, and sexist when he analyzes how medical students are given information about anatomy labs ("Cadaver Stories"). These narratives serve as an important source of information about anatomy lab classes and remain virtually unchanged through time. "Whether the storyteller is a medical-student friend, a fellow applicant or one's favorite biology professor, cadaver stories are a major source of information about the anatomy-lab experience" (Hafferty 1991, 56). Like other contemporary legends, these tales are anchored in reality with a specific setting, specific people, and a specific time.

Types of Cadaver Stories

1. Medical students carrying cadavers or cadaver parts outside the lab to shock nonmedical people.

> *A group of medical students cut off a cadaver's hand, carry it to the bus stop, board a bus, and extend the hand, clutching the fare, to the unsuspecting bus driver. When the driver realizes that he is holding not only the anticipated fare but also a severed human hand, he screams and either faints or drops dead from fright. The medical students, now engulfed in laughter, make their getaway unencumbered by either the hand or any feelings of guilt or remorse.*
> (Hafferty 1991, 57)

In variants of this type of cadaver story, medical students drop various body parts into a woman's shopping bag or place a limb in a public washroom. "The punch line always involves a lay victim who reacts with shock, partly because of the animate qualities of the body part" (Hafferty 1991, 57). The medical students are immune to shock and revulsion because of their "scientific detachment." This is a popular variant of "The Pickled Hand."

2. In-lab manipulation and/or mutilation of sexual organs, almost always by male students against unsophisticated (therefore weak) female medical students.

3. "Resurrection" stories, in which cadavers appear to be, or become, alive or more lifelike. Often the cadavers are dressed up and taken to a campus-based activity.

4. Student is about to dissect the body, then discovers that the cadaver is a relative or friend. In some cases, the face is revealed after the dissection takes place. This type of story is unique, as there are no perpetrators, the event is accidental rather than staged, and it is the only type that routinely features male medical students as victims.

5. Cadaver-as-food story told in-lab to female victims.

> *One such story tells of the shocked reactions of one or two labmates as a male dissector unexpectedly cuts off a piece of cadaver flesh and pops it into his mouth, chewing vigorously and swallowing with a smile.* (Hafferty 1991, 58)

An out-of-lab version relates the story of a male medical student cooking a cadaver's kidney for dinner and serving it to his unsuspecting guests. The guests do not have to know what they are eating for the audience to get the joke.

Functions of Cadaver Stories

Cadaver stories, told as true accounts, have several functions. The stories play a large part in the emotional socialization of medical students. "The activities described in cadaver stories reflect a triumphant victory over an adversary (the cadaver) who has caused them no small amount of emotional anxiety" (Hafferty 1991, 59). It is the height of scientific detachment. The stories define boundaries between insiders (medical students) and outsiders (unsophisticated medical students and the world at large). The stories aid in the development of an emotional toughness that protects the students from projected stress, becoming too involved with their patients. "By telling and listening to cadaver stories, medical students and students-to-be can visualize, articulate, and thus vicariously experience a variety of medical norms governing emotional competence well in advance of lab itself" (Hafferty 1991, 61). The stories also foster a sense of common group identity and offer warning that "weak" students are the victims of pranks.

Hafferty asserts that medical students believe the stories because they can identify with the anxieties that underlie the accounts. The listeners are expected to find the stories funny and laugh as proof that they are not afraid of anything. At the same time, stories told to laypeople are not expected to get a laugh, as laypeople are expected to react with shock and revulsion and fail to see any humor at all. The stories "continually reinforce the message that medical students are different from laypeople and that the stresses and strains of medicine require this distinction" (Hafferty 1991, 75).

"ROOM FOR ONE MORE"

A young woman on her way up to town broke her journey by staying with friends at an old manor house. Her bedroom looked out to the carriage sweep at the front door. It was a moonlight night, and she found it difficult to sleep. As the clock outside her bedroom door struck twelve, she heard the noise of horses' hooves on the gravel outside, and the sound of wheels. She got up and went over to the window to see who could be arriving at that time of night. The moonshine was very bright, and she saw a hearse drive up to the door. It hadn't a coffin in it; instead it was crowded with people. The coachman sat high up on the box: as he came opposite the window he drew up and turned his head. His face terrified her, and he said in a distinct voice, "There's room for one more." She drew the curtain, and ran back to bed, and covered her head with the bedclothes. In the morning she was not quite sure whether it had been a dream, or whether she had really got out of bed and seen the hearse, but she was glad to go up to town and leave the old house behind her.

It was a shopping expedition that she was going on, and she was shopping in a big store which had a lift [elevator] in it—an up-to-date thing at that time. She was on the top floor, and she went to the lift to go down. It was rather crowded, but as she came up, the liftman turned his head and said, "There's room for one more." It was the face of the coachman of the hearse. "No, thank you," said the girl, "I'll walk down." She turned away, the lift doors clanged, there was a terrible rush and screaming and shouting, and then a great clatter and thud. The lift had fallen from the top to the bottom of the building and every soul in it was killed.
(Briggs and Tongue 1965, 67–68)

This version was first told to Katherine Briggs in 1912 by a visitor from London, England. An updated version was included in Bennett Cerf's *Famous Ghost Stories*. His tale is set in South Carolina and the New York visitor scurries back to her doctor on the 18th floor of an office building. He laughs at her "nerves" and sends her to the elevator, which of course, she does not get on—even if there was "Room for One More."

The fear of technological advancement seems to be the catalyst for this tale. The fear of the elevator and the safety of the people in the confined space held up by cables contributed to the story's popularity. Contemporary retellings focus on the "spooky" figure and the warning that the protagonist receives.

"THE ROOMMATE'S DEATH"

---

*This story takes place in a sorority house on this campus, during
Christmas vacation when most of the girls had gone home. There
were two or three girls left in the sorority house. It was late at
night and the girls decided that they were hungry, so two of the
girls went downstairs to the kitchen. One of the girls went back to
the room to rejoin the other girl, leaving one girl downstairs in the
kitchen. A little bit later on, say about half hour later, the two girls
in the room started wondering about the other girl 'cause she
hadn't come back yet. So they went out on the landing and they
heard something moving around downstairs. So they called down
and nobody answered, the person or whatever it was moving
around was still heard. They were afraid to go downstairs, so they
locked themselves in their room and waited for morning. They
actually waited about an hour when they decided to try it again.
They were going to open the door, when they heard a noise outside—
like scratching, so they got scared and didn't open the door. The
scratching was like somebody dragging somebody down the steps.
They were afraid to leave the room 'cause someone was out in the
hall. They stayed in their room till early the next morning until the
mailman came around, and they hailed the mailman out the window. The mailman came in the front door and went up the stairs,
and told the girls to stay in their room that everything was all right
but they had to stay in their room. But the girls didn't listen to him
'cause he had said it was all right, so they came out into the hall.
When they opened the door, they saw their girlfriend on the floor
with a hatchet in her head. (Emrich 1972, 335)*

The legend is told by girls who are in transition between adolescence
and a "safe" existence in the family home and that of independence and
responsibility as a college student (Degh 1969, 55). The elements of this
legend remain very stable through different versions with the major differences relating to the skill of the storyteller.

Structure of "The Roommate's Death"

The legend focuses almost completely on the "torturous fantasy of one
girl left alone for the night in an empty dormitory" rather than on the victim,
and the audience never really hears details about what happened to the
victim (Degh 1969, 66).

Isolation. The girls are left alone in a deserted college dormitory, usually at a major holiday such as Christmas. One girl leaves the room to go "elsewhere" to ultimately be the victim. The girl who is "safe" in her room is the focus of the legend as her protective confinement ultimately contributes to the tragedy.

Encounter. The "victim" hears strange noises and scratching outside her door and refuses to find out what is causing them.

Consequence. Upon finally gathering enough courage to open the door (or with the aid of a male helper), the girl discovers the dead victim. The surprising turn of events is revealed when the girl realizes that if she had opened the door earlier, her friend might still be alive.

The contrast of silence and the frightening noises play an important role in the story—"scratching" on the door and other noises are usually attributed to a faceless killer ("The Hook") but in actuality are caused by the frantic, wounded girl's fingernails (Degh 1969, 67).

Analysis of the Legend

The primary fear is not of the unknown killer but an over-identification of the audience with either protagonist (Grider 1973, 31). The tragedy occurs not only because the women are in a threatening environment without protection, but because the survivor reacted "emotionally" rather than "logically" to the situation. "The survivor became scared and refused to open the door; that is, she refused to 'use her head' and take responsibility in the situation which might have saved the other girl's life" (Crane 1976, 146). Members of the audience realize that they, too, would have probably reacted the same as the guilt-ridden survivor of the legend. Two implicit points of value are made by the legend: 1) if women wish to depend on traditional attitudes and responses they had best stay in a place where those attitudes and responses are best able to protect them; and 2) if women do choose to venture into the realm of equality with men, they must become less dependent, more self-sufficient, more confident in their abilities and, above all, more willing to assume responsibility for themselves and others (Crane 1976, 147).

"The Decapitated Roommate"

This legend is a variant of "The Roommate's Death":

I guess some girl had gone out on a date, but her roommate stayed in that night. When the girl returned, her roommate was in bed all covered up so she didn't turn on any lights but just got ready for bed. Then her roommate started humming. For a while she just ignored it. Then she really became angry and asked the girl if she would please be quiet, that she was tired and had to get to sleep. The roommate kept humming. Finally the girl became furious—she went over and pulled the covers off the roommate, only to find that she was decapitated. But there was still humming. She looked over and right by the door stood a man holding a big butcher knife and the roommate's head. (Degh 1969, 67)

In this reversal of the traditional legend, the girl who leaves the room is safe, while the one who stayed behind the locked door is not (Degh 1969, 68).

"THE STOLEN LIVER"

[There's] this little kid, his mom gives him some money to go get some liver and he always buys candy because she gives him extra money and he always goes and buys candy with it. So he went to the store and he bought, he goes up there and buys a bunch of candy. And he don't have enough money left to buy the liver with. And he goes to this graveyard and digs up this man. He goes, he takes the liver home and his mom fries it and everything else and his mom goes, "Johnny aren't you gonna eat any?" And he goes, "No, I'm not hungry." And so that night that little kid, their whole family was asleep and in bed and he heard something, "Johnny, I'm on the first step. Johnny, I'm on the second step. Johnny, I'm on the fourth step." Finally he gets to the top of the stairs. "Johnny, I'm walking down the hall. Johnny, I'm at your doorway. Johnny, I'm by your bed. Johnny, I'm getting closer. Johnny, I GOTCHA!" (Grider 1980, 12)

Identified as Tale Type 366, "The man from the gallows," the story in which a corpse returns to punish the theft of part of his body or an article of clothing, has been collected throughout North America and western Europe. The underlying folk belief in the legend is ancient: a dead man or animal can not find rest until the physical remains are intact. The search for that which is lost is often the *raison d'etre* for ghost stories and the "just" punishment for such a crime is severe, especially if a grave was disturbed in the process (Burrison 1968, 3).

"The Stolen Liver" has, through the passage of time, become almost exclusively a children's tale, although the traditional motifs reflect ancient taboos and anxieties, combining "fearsome features of grave-robbing, cannibalism, and supernatural retribution" (Grider 1979, 197). The older tales revolve around the story of the man who feeds the stolen liver of a criminal to his wife. The tale develops an almost unbelievable tension as the revenant moans for the loss of his liver and carries off the man responsible for the deed. Contemporary versions include a "jump" ending ("I GOTCHA!"), releasing the tension within the telling of the tale.

Functions of "The Stolen Liver"

Did [this legend] originate as a "jump" tale or scare story, in which suspense is built up through the repetition of the ghost's formulaic cry or through dramatic dialogue containing incremental repetition, to be broken suddenly by the ghost's shouted accusal and the tale teller springing at the audience, or did this form evolve from a more mundane moralistic legend or belief tale? (Burrison 1968, 8)

Contemporary variants of "The Stolen Liver" can be classified as "funny-scary" stories rather than as truly frightening tales. This subgenre of scary stories provide comic relief within the framework of mock-frightening occurrences. Like jokes, funny-scary stories have a "jump" ending, "usually a humorous remark that effectively neutralizes the fearfulness of the initial situation" (Tucker 1977, 121).

This type of story is popular with children from the first grade on up. They provide a training ground for young children, preparing them to handle the concept of "a good scare" before they move on to the more serious supernatural narratives that they will meet in upper elementary school. Both Grider and Tucker found, in fact, that the popularity of the funny-scary stories began to wane around the fifth grade, when children began to prefer contemporary scary legends instead. By the following year, the children were demanding "real scary stories!" (Tucker 1977, 122). However, the funny-scary stories were still retold, once in awhile, as a safety valve when the tension became unbearable.

It is my hypothesis that children have been an important vehicle for carrying "The Golden Arm" [a variant of "The Stolen Liver"] into modern American society. This becomes more likely when we see that the tale, in the earliest records and on the folk level, was told by adults (nurses or grandparents rather than parents, who would have greater inhibitions about frightening their children), but on the urban level it is told almost exclusively by children and adolescents to those of their own age group. (Burrison 1968, 16)

Though modern children and young adults no longer believe in the disastrous consequences of disturbing the dead, the legend still serves as a warning. It warns against greed that is strong enough to motivate a person to desecrate a grave and it warns against not listening to those who care for you and your well-being (parent or spouse). If one sees children's lore as a preparation or practice for the responsibilities and realities of adult life, then one might view this tale as conditioning the child to some of the realities of death and to the code "crime does not pay" (Burrison 1968, 18).

Types of "The Stolen Liver" Variants

The basic theme of "The Stolen Liver" remains intact in the modern variants of the legend, told either in this form or as "The Golden Arm," which was made famous by Mark Twain (Burrison 1968, 3). There are two subtypes that are based on two different motivations for the removal of the limb or organ.

Type A. Intentional Theft for Cannibalism

The body has been vandalized to use as food. Variants that fall into this category include: "The Man from the Gallows" (Germany); "The Bone" (England); and "Johnny and the Dead Man's Liver" (America). A subsection of this type includes the accidental discovery of the limb in the ground and the (unintentional) cannibalism when it is used for soup or some such food. The most common variant of this subtype is "The Big Toe" (America).

Type B. Avarice for Precious Body Part or Item from Grave

Greed is the downfall of the characters in this type of the legend. The body is dug up for access to a limb made of precious metal. The most common variants are "The Golden Leg" (Europe) and "The Golden Arm" (America) (Burrison 1968, 4).

Mark Twain and "Brer Rabbit"

Mark Twain, who enjoyed performing this tale, a variant based on the tale retold by Joseph Jacobs in *English Fairy Tales*, for the delight (and suspense) of his audiences, remembered it from his childhood. Twain gave advice for the presentation of these tales to Joel Chandler Harris, who retold it in *The Tales of Uncle Remus*:

It adds, however, certain stylistic devices of the expert tale-teller for heightening the drama, such as the use of sound effects, repetition, words expressing the sensations of sight, sound, and feeling so that the listener empathizes with the thief, and the dragging out of the suspense to make the ending more breath-taking. (Burrison 1968, 10)

The instructions for the telling of the legend "The Golden Arm" first came to print in *How to Tell a Story and Other Essays* (1892) by Mark Twain. He published the essay to demonstrate an important storytelling technique: the pause. Harris's "coins" version was printed as the 29th tale in *Nights with Uncle Remus: Myths and Legends of the Old Plantation* (1881) and is presented within the natural context of a legend-telling session. Burrison states that Twain came to the story in a traditional way, reaching into a childhood memory, but Harris made a conscious effort to seek out the legend once Twain brought it to his attention (Burrison 1968, 13). Either way, the legend has become one of the most popular tales in North America.

RELATIONSHIPS BETWEEN SCARY STORIES

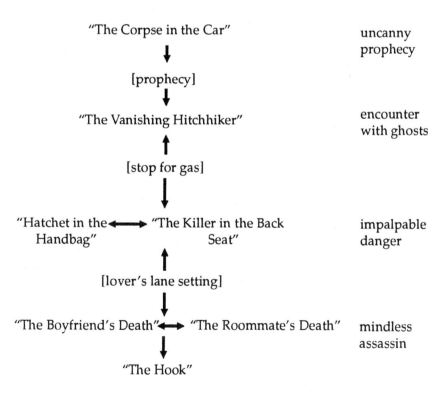

(Rosenberg 1991, 229)

This chart demonstrates the various similarities among the different "scary" contemporary legends: their emotional cores, the setting, and the ease with which they exchange episodes (Rosenberg 1991, 228). "The Boyfriend's Death" has no hero, only a terrorized woman. "The killer" functions "merely as an agent to kill the boyfriend, whose corpse functions only to terrorize the girl, which terror is the emotional core of this story" (Rosenberg 1991, 226). The real terror in "The Hook" is very similar; it is not realized until the danger has passed and the girl returns home to find the hook on the car door. "Both stories end on notes of terror, though soon alleviated, because in both cases the terrorized victim has escaped" (Rosenberg 1991, 227). The boyfriend is killed in the first tale but the real victim of the legend is the girl: frightened but not harmed.

"The Killer in the Back Seat," regardless of type, has a victim, hero, and villain (Rosenberg 1991, 227). The hero is not revealed until the end of the tale (he is usually suspected to be a villain throughout the narrative), and the actual villain never appears as a particularized individual, a man who wishes to do her harm. The victim is a woman alone, isolated from protective society, and in a frightening and "dark" situation. "Nighttime isolates, removing one from contact—however much dependent on sight—with others, and with safety" (Rosenberg 1991, 228). This fear of the dark is a very old anxiety in our culture.

The *revelation* of the specific danger is an affective element common to all the legends under discussion. To the woman driver, it is when the presence of the man in the backseat is revealed. To the accommodating driver, it is the discovery that his hitchhiker is a revenant. To the lovers who rush away from their secluded spot, it is the discovery of the proximity of the hookman. To the girl left in the stalled car, it is the delayed knowledge that the scraping she has heard throughout the night is from the feet (or the fingernails) of her boyfriend's corpse. Revelation forces the victim to consider the danger that was narrowly escaped and gives the legend's audience "that chill which is one of these legend's most consistently maintained messages" (Rosenberg 1991, 232).

Another common element is the fact that the pivotal character in all these legends is not the hero but the victim (Rosenberg 1991, 232). This is revealing of life in contemporary urban America; only the victim has been accorded any personality. The villain (real or implied) is mute and one-dimensional, and the rescuer is almost marginal, providing relief for the victim but never brought to life by the narrator (Rosenberg 1991, 232).

LITERARY AND VISUAL ADAPTATIONS

"The Baby-Sitter"

Adventures in Babysitting (1987). The story is told in this movie by the baby-sitter to amuse her charges.

The Dumb Waiter (1979). The babysitter is terrorized in this movie by an assailant who travels between floors in the dumb waiter.

Lisa (1990). The scenario of this movie is analogous to the legend as the killer stalks his potential victims to see where they live. Just before he strikes, he leaves a message on their answering phone: "Hi! I'm Richard. I'm in your apartment, and I'm going to kill you." While the victim is listening to the message, he does just that.

The Sitter (1977). A film short dramatization of the legend by Fred Walton.

When a Stranger Calls (1979). This film is an expanded version, by Fred Walton, of his short film *The Sitter*. The opening sequence is a dramatization of the legend, and the final sequence is a replay of the opening segment, when the escaped psychopath returns to threaten the same woman and her children (Danielson 1979, 219).

"The Boyfriend's Death"

Dead Poet's Society (1989). In this movie, at the first meeting of the society, one of the boys attempts to tell the legend but is shouted down by the rest of the group as they all know it. One boy comments, "I got that in camp at sixth grade."

"The Hook"

Dinky Hocker Shoots Smack! by M. E. Keer. New York: Dell, 1972. This novel also includes "The Pickled Hand." Both legends are told as "true but weird happenings."

Meatballs (1980). In this movie, Tripper, a character played by Bill Murray, tells the story around the campfire. He concludes that the hookman had never been apprehended, and people believe he is still around "waiting for a chance to kill again." He pauses and then says, "And they're right!" and lifts his arm to reveal a metal hook. After the screaming dissolves into laughter, the group briefly talk about other variants.

"The Killer in the Backseat"

Mr. Wrong (1984). Based on the short story of the same name by Elizabeth Jane Howard, the film primarily uses "The Vanishing Hitchhiker" motif but incorporates elements of this legend along with others. For a discussion on the short story and its relationship with contemporary legends, see Rosenberg's chapter 14, "Urban Legends," *Folklore and Literature: Rival Siblings*.

Nightmares (1983). The first segment of this collection of four short films focuses on this legend.

"The Stolen Liver" and "The Golden Arm"

Tales of the Supernatural (1970). A film by Sharon R. Sherman, featuring a storytelling session of 11 tales told by children. "It uses film footage to test hypotheses about the functions of telling ghost and horror tales generally classified as contemporary legends" (Bennett, Smith, and Widdowson 1987, 203). Three of the tales included are "The Vanishing Hitchhiker," "The Hook," and "The Boyfriend's Death." The film focuses on the function of telling scary stories, the legend-telling session dynamics, and the process of localizing the legends.

RECOMMENDED RESOURCES

The following retellings of scary stories are frequently found in collections in school libraries and in those owned by the students themselves. Once students have read varied retellings of the same tale, they should feel free to create their own adaptations and reworkings of the tales. They should be reminded, however, that the tales in the collections are protected by copyright and are to be used as examples only. The students should begin with only the basic story structure of the tales and let then their imaginations flow. These stories can be retold by students from various points of view in a variety of formats: short story adaptations, poetry, and dramatic plays.

"The Baby in the Oven"

Cohen, Daniel. "Oven Ready." *Southern Fried Rat & Other Gruesome Tales*. New York: M. Evans, 1983, 33–37.

"The Baby-Sitter"

Schwartz, Alvin. "The Babysitter." *Scary Stories to Tell in the Dark*. New York: Harper & Row, 1981, 69–71.

Young, Richard, and Judy Dockrey Young. "The Call from the Downstairs Phone." *The Scary Story Reader*. Little Rock: August House, 1993, 27–30.

"The Boyfriend's Death"

Young, Richard, and Judy Dockrey Young. "Don't Look Back!" *The Scary Story Reader*. Little Rock: August House, 1993, 16–19.

"The Dare"

Cohen, Daniel. "The Hand of Charity Hawthorne." *Southern Fried Rat & Other Gruesome Tales*. New York: M. Evans, 1983, 97–102.

de Vos, Gail. "The Graveyard Dare." *Storytelling for Young Adults: Techniques and Treasury*. Englewood, CO: Libraries Unlimited, 1991, 106.

Downer, Deborah L., ed. "The Girl Who Was Scared to Death." *Classic American Ghost Stories*. Little Rock: August House, 1990, 84.

Leach, Maria. "The Dare." *The Thing at the Foot of the Bed and Other Scary Tales*. New York: Dell, 1977, 37–39. (Reprint of 1953 edition.)

San Souci, Robert D. "Scared to Death." *Short and Shivery: Thirty Chilling Tales*. New York: Doubleday, 1987, 78–83.

Schwartz, Alvin. "The Girl Who Stood on a Grave." *Scary Stories to Tell in the Dark*. New York: Harper & Row, 1981, 41–42.

Watson, Julie V. "The Fork in the Grave." *Ghost Stories & Legends of Prince Edward Island*. Willowdale, ON: Hounslow Press, 1988, 85–87.

Young, Richard, and Judy Dockrey Young. "She's Got Me!" *Favorite Scary Stories of American Children*. Little Rock: August House, 1990, 37–39.

"Embalmed Alive"

Cohen, Daniel. "The Secondhand Evening Gown." *Southern Fried Rat & Other Gruesome Tales*. New York: M. Evans, 1983, 23–27.

Schwartz, Alvin. "The White Satin Evening Gown." *Scary Stories to Tell in the Dark*. New York: Harper & Row, 1981, 65.

Young, Richard, and Judy Dockrey Young. "The White Dress." *The Scary Story Reader*. Little Rock: August House, 1993, 160–62.

"The Hook"

Schwartz, Alvin. "The Hook." *Scary Stories to Tell in the Dark*. New York: Harper & Row, 1981, 62–63.

Young, Richard, and Judy Dockrey Young. "Hook-Arm." *The Scary Story Reader*. Little Rock: August House, 1993, 21–22.

"The Killer in the Back Seat"

Schwartz, Alvin. "High Beams." *Scary Stories to Tell in the Dark*. New York: Harper & Row, 1981, 66–68.

Young, Richard, and Judy Dockrey Young. "The Killer in the Back Seat." *The Scary Story Reader*. Little Rock: August House, 1993, 42–44.

"The Pickled Hand"

Schwartz, Alvin. "The Dead Man's Hand." *More Scary Stories to Tell in the Dark*. New York: Harper & Row, 1984, 56–57.

"Room for One More"

Roberts, Nancy. "Room for One More." *This Haunted Southland: Where Ghosts Still Roam*. Columbia: University of South Carolina Press, 1988, 44–51. [Reprint of 1970 edition. An airplane is the setting of this variant.]

Schwartz, Alvin. "Room for One More." *Scary Stories to Tell in the Dark*. New York: Harper & Row, 1981, 47–48.

"The Roommate's Death"

Schwartz, Alvin. "Oh Susanna!" *More Scary Stories to Tell in the Dark*. New York: Harper & Row, 1984, 49.

Young, Richard, and Judy Dockrey Young. "Outside the Door." *The Scary Story Reader*. Little Rock: August House, 1993, 39–41.

"The Stolen Liver" and "The Golden Arm"

Cohen, Daniel. "The Stolen Liver." *The Restless Dead: Ghostly Tales from Around the World*. New York: Archway, 1984, 95–100.

Leach, Maria. "The Golden Arm." *The Thing at the Foot of the Bed and Other Scary Tales*. New York: Dell, 1977, 33–36. (Reprint of 1953 edition.)

Schwartz, Alvin. "The Big Toe." *Scary Stories to Tell in the Dark*. New York: Harper & Row, 1981, 7–9.

———. "Cemetery Soup." *More Scary Stories to Tell in the Dark.* New York: Harper & Row, 1984, 71–73.

———. "Clinkity-Clink." *More Scary Stories to Tell in the Dark.* New York: Harper & Row, 1984, 20–24.

———. "Just Delicious." *Scary Stories 3: More Tales to Chill Your Bones.* New York: Harper & Row, 1991, 12–14.

Wilkerson, Tyrone. "Johnny and the Liver." In *African-American Folktales for Young Readers,* collected and edited by Richard Young and Judy Dockrey Young. Little Rock: August House, 1993, 148–55.

Young, Richard, and Judy Dockrey Young. "Dame, pues, mi asadura." *Ghost Stories from the American Southwest.* Little Rock: August House, 1991, 92–78.

———. "Dottie Got Her Liver." *The Scary Story Reader.* Little Rock: August House, 1993, 129–32.

———. "Give Me Back My Guts!" *The Scary Story Reader.* Little Rock: August House, 1993, 149–53.

REFERENCES

Baker, Ronald L. 1982. *Hoosier folk legends.* Bloomington: Indiana University Press.

Barden, Thomas E., ed. 1991. *Virginia folk legends.* Charlottesville: University Press of Virginia.

Barden, Thomas E. 1992. Early Virginia analogues of some modern legends. *Contemporary Legend: The Journal of the International Society for Contemporary Legend Research* 2: 155–64.

Barnes, Daniel R. 1966. Some functional horror stories on the Kansas University campus. *Southern Folklore Quarterly* 30: 305–12.

Baughman, Ernest Warren. 1945. The cadaver arm. *Hoosier Folklore Bulletin* 4: 30–32.

———. 1966. *Type and motif index of the folktale of England and North America.* The Hague: Mouton.

Bennett, Gillian, Paul Smith, and J. D. A. Widdowson, eds. 1987. *Perspectives on contemporary legends, vol. II.* Sheffield, England: Sheffield Academic Press, 203–4.

Briggs, K. M., and Ruth L. Tongue. 1965. *Folktales of England.* Chicago: University of Chicago Press.

Bronner, Simon. 1988. *American children's folklore.* Little Rock, AR: August House.

———. 1990. *Piled higher and deeper: Folklore of campus life.* Little Rock, AR: August House.

Brunvand, Jan Harold. 1980. Heard about the solid cement Cadillac or the nude in the camper or the alligator in the sewer or the snake in the K-Mart? *Psychology Today* (June): 50–62.

————. 1984. *The choking doberman and other "new" urban legends*. New York: W. W. Norton.

Burrison, John A. 1968. *"The golden arm": The folk tale and its literary use by Mark Twain and Joel C. Harris* (Research paper, no. 19, School of Arts and Sciences Research Papers). Atlanta: Georgia State College.

————. ed. 1989. *Storytellers: Folktales and legends from the South*. Athens: University of Georgia Press.

Cerf, Bennett, ed. 1974. (Reprint of 1944 edition), pp. 13-46. *Famous ghost stories*. New York: Vintage Books.

Cord, Xenia. 1969. Further note on "The assailant in the back seat." *Indiana Folklore* 2: 47–54.

Crane, Beverly. 1976. The structure of value in "The roommate's death": A methodology for interpretive analysis of folk legends. *Journal of the Folklore Institute* 13: 133–49.

Dale, Rodney. 1984. *It's true, it happened to a friend: A collection of urban legends*. London: Ducksworth.

Danielson, Larry. 1979. Folklore and film: Some thoughts on Baughman Z500–599. *Western Folklore* 38: 209–19.

Degh, Linda. 1968. The hook. *Indiana Folklore* 1, no. 1: 92–100.

————. 1969. The roommate's death and related dormitory stories in formation. *Indiana Folklore* 2: 55–74.

————. 1991. Speculations about "The hook"—Bill Ellis doesn't need any more theoretical concepts. *Folklore Forum* 24, no. 2: 68–75.

Dickson, Paul, and Joseph C. Goulden. 1993. *Myth-informed: Legends, credos, and wrongheaded "facts" we all believe*. New York: Perigee.

Drake, Carlos. 1968. The killer in the back seat. *Indiana Folklore* 1, no. 1: 107–9.

Dundes, Alan. 1971. On the psychology of legend. In *American folk legend: A symposium*, edited by Wayland Hand. Berkeley: University of California Press.

Ellis, Bill. 1991. Why "The hook" is *not* a contemporary legend. *Folklore Forum* 24, no. 2: 62–67.

————. 1994. "The hook" reconsidered: Problems in classifying and interpreting adolescent horror legends. *Folklore* 105: 61–75.

Emrich, Duncan. 1972. *Folklore on the American land*. Boston: Little, Brown.

Fine, Gary Alan. 1984. Evaluating psychoanalytic folklore: Are Freudians ever right? *New York Folklore* 10, no. 1–2 (winter–spring): 5–20.

Glazer, Mark. 1985. The traditionalization of the contemporary legend: The Mexican-American example. *Fabula* 26: 288–97.

————. 1987. The cultural adaptation of a rumor legend: "The boyfriend's death" in South Texas. In *Perspectives on contemporary legends, vol. II*, edited by Gillian Bennett, Paul Smith, and J. D. A. Widdowson. Sheffield, England: Sheffield Academic Press, 93–108

Greenburg, Andrea. 1972/73. Drugged and seduced: A contemporary legend. *New York Folklore Quarterly* 28/29: 131–58.

Grider, Linda. 1973. Dormitory legend-telling in progress: Fall, 1971–winter, 1973. *Indiana Folklore* 6: 1–32.

Grider, Sylvia. 1979. *The supernatural narratives of children.* Ph.D. diss., Indiana University.

———. 1980. Gotcha! *Center for Southern Folklore* (winter): 12.

Hafferty, Frederic W. 1991. *Into the valley: Death and the socialization of medical students.* New Haven, CT: Yale University Press.

Just in: The killer in the back seat. 1993. *FOAFTALE NEWS* 31 (November): 5–6.

Kirshenblatt-Gimblett, B. 1972. *Traditional storytelling in the Toronto Jewish community.* Ph.D. diss., Indiana University.

Morgan, Hal, and Kerry Tucker. 1987. *More rumors!* New York: Penguin.

Peters, Nancy Krammer. 1988. Suburban/rural variations in the content of adolescent ghost legends. In *Monsters with iron teeth: Perspectives on contemporary legend, vol. III,* edited by Gillian Bennett and Paul Smith. Sheffield, England: Sheffield Academic Press, 221–35

Roemer, Danielle. 1971. Scary story legends. *Folklore Annual* 3: 1–16.

Rosenberg, Bruce. A. 1991. *Folklore and literature: Rival siblings.* Knoxville: University of Tennessee Press.

Samuelson, Sue. 1981. European and American adolescent legends. *ARV* 37: 134–39.

———. 1984. "The man upstairs": An analysis of a babysitting legend. *Mid-America Folklore* 12, no. 3: 2–10.

Sanderson, Stewart. 1981a. From social regulator to art form: Case study of a modern urban legend. *ARV* 37: 161–66.

———. 1981b. *The modern urban legend* (Katherine Briggs Lecture #1). London: Folklore Society.

Seelhorst, Mary. 1987. "The assailant in disguise": Old and new functions of urban legends about women alone in danger. *North Carolina Folklore Journal* 34, no. 1 (winter–spring): 29–37.

So there's this guy, see . . . 1991. *Maclean's* 104, no. 48 (December 2): 80–81.

Stephens, James. 1963. Belief tales. *Kentucky Folklore Record* 9: 7–10.

Tucker, Elizabeth G. 1977. *Tradition and creativity in the storytelling of pre-adolescent girls.* Ph.D. diss., Indiana University.

———. 1981. Danger and control in children's storytelling. *ARV* 37: 141–46.

Young, Richard, and Judy Dockrey Young. 1993. *The scary story reader: Forty-one of the scariest stories for sleepovers, campfires, car & bus trips—even for first dates!* Little Rock, AR: August House.

13

"THE VANISHING HITCHHIKER"

One rainy and wintery night, a man was driving down this road and slowed up to come into this curve. As the headlights flashed around the curve, they showed that a young girl was standing in the road waving. The man stopped immediately and offered the girl a ride home, and she accepted by simply nodding her head.

The man was overwhelmed by the girl's beauty and fell in love with her before she ever spoke a word. The young girl directed the man by pointing her finger and never saying a word. The man thought she was just shy and didn't press for conversation. They finally reached her house, which was about five miles off the main highway, and the man got out to go around and open the door.

When he reached the other side of the car, he discovered that the young girl was no longer in the car. Thinking that she has already gone in the house, he went up and knocked on the door. An old, tired-looking lady came to the door and asked him in. When he asked to see her daughter, she looked surprised and began to explain that her daughter was killed on that very night just five years ago. She was on her way home from a party when it happened. She explained that this same thing had happened on the four previous years before now: she had been picked up, brought home, and disappeared for another year. (McNeil 1985, 106)

This version of "The Vanishing Hitchhiker" was collected in 1959 as an example of one of the many ghost stories the informant was told by his junior high school football coach while traveling to games (McNeil 1985, 188). "The Vanishing Hitchhiker," says McNeil,

> is an example of a narrative constantly readapted to changing times (to take newer technology into consideration, among other things) but ultimately derived from earlier European legends about eternally wandering ghosts such as "The Flying Dutchman." (190)

The adaptable "Vanishing Hitchhiker" is the focus of this chapter, which looks at the legend, possible antecedents and relatives, and international variants and their roles in the communities in which they are told.

This disappearing-ghost story is very flexible, allowing for technological advances the individual needs and socio-cultural heritage of the storyteller and the audience (Goss 1984, 14). It is also one of the most popular and widespread ghost stories still being told today. "The Vanishing Hitchhiker" appears in almost every collection of "true" ghost stories that I can find as well as in literary retellings aimed for the young adult market.

Guiley, in her *Encyclopedia of Ghosts and Spirits*, notes that "The Vanishing Hitchhiker" probably originated in Europe with legends about phantom travelers but that it also appears in Asian folklore, in which a young woman, following a man to the home of her parents, vanishes upon reaching their destination (1992, 248). The restless phantoms travel according to the mode of transportation of their time: they walk; ride horses, bicycles, or motorcycles; or drive carriages, cars, buses, or trucks (252).

MAJOR TYPES OF "THE VANISHING HITCHHIKER"

Four major versions of "The Vanishing Hitchhiker" were established in 1942 by Beardsley and Hankey in their study of this legend. Research since that time consistently refers to the work by the two scholars.

Type A

One day a Mr. Barron was driving home from work. He lived quite a distance from town. After leaving the city limits and travelling for about five miles, he saw a girl coming toward the car. The girl was very beautiful, and she wore a white formal under a black cape. Mr. Barron slowed the car down and the girl motioned for him to stop the car. Mr. Barron stopped the car and asked her what she wanted. The girl asked him if he would take her to 215 Woodlawn Park estate [Informant heard various addresses and various names for the driver.] and he said he would.

All the time they were riding the girl never said a word, and just before reaching the estate, Mr. Barron turned toward the girl to say something; but she was gone. Being very mystified, Mr. Barron decided he would go on to the estate. He found the estate very easily, and went up to the door and knocked. An elderly gentleman came to the door and asked what was wrong, but for awhile Mr. Barron could say nothing. Then he explained to the elderly gentleman what had happened to him when he was driving toward home. The elderly gentleman looked rather sad, and began to tell Mr. Barron a story. "It was exactly a year ago today that my daughter went to a dance with some friends and on the way home on that same road her car was hit, and she was killed, and you are the fourth young man today to come and tell me about seeing her." (Jansen 1943, 2)

The informant had heard this story several times, the first no later than 1936. "It has been a favorite Hallowe'en story, and in the various times she has heard it she has noticed only one variation: That the girl sometimes comes up to a car already stopped at an intersection" (Jansen 1943, 2).

Type A, the most common variant of this story, involves a driver who picks up a strange girl on a street or highway, and then, during the course of the ride, realizes that the hitchhiker has disappeared. Upon going to the address the hitchhiker gave him as her destination, the driver discovers that the passenger had been dead for years. The climax of this version hinges on this unexpected revelation and is heightened by the contrast between the ordinary and explicit details given at the beginning of the tale and the final realization of the passenger's identity (Beardsley and Hankey 1942, 318).

Like many of the previous contemporary legends that we have explored, type A of "The Vanishing Hitchhiker" has been assigned its own identification number:

> Motif E 332.3.3.1. *The Vanishing Hitchhiker*. Ghost of young woman asks for ride in automobile, disappears from closed car without the driver's knowledge, after giving him address to which she wishes to be taken. The driver asks person at the address about the rider, finds she has been dead for some time. (Often the driver finds that the ghost has made similar attempts to return, usually on anniversary of death in automobile accident. Often too, the ghost leaves some item such as a scarf or travelling bag in the car.) (Baughman 1966, 148)

Type B

> *In February 1602 an unnamed vicar and two farmers were travelling back from the Candlemas fair in Vastergotland (at this time of year the vehicle they used must have been a sleigh). On the road to Vadstena they were accosted by a "nice" and "lovely" female dressed like a serving-girl who asked for (and was given) a ride. At a wayside halting-station they all alighted to get some food; the girl, however, only wanted something to drink. A jug of beer was procured for her. The vicar observed she did not take it up and found it was filled with malt. A second jug mysteriously changed from beer to acorns and a third—apparently under the vicar's nose—to blood. At this point the serving-girl announced (as if interpreting these omens): "There will be good crops this year. There will be enough fruits on the trees. There will also be many wars and plague." With which she vanished. (Goss 1984, 46)*

Type B includes stories in which the hitchhiker, often an elderly woman, prophesies disaster or the end of a battle or war (Goss 1984, 360). The initial difference between type A and type B versions of the legends is in the character of the hitchhiker: not usually a young female but, instead, an older woman. Two other significant deviations are that the event occurs during the hours of daylight (rather than at night, and often a stormy one at that) and instead of a single man, there are usually several people in the vehicle.

The prophesy is an addition that completely shifts the climax of the tale. The climax of type A, the discovery of the supernatural aspect of the hitchhiker, is of only minor importance in type B, as it becomes an element of proof that the prophet, because she was supernatural, knew of what she was speaking (Beardsley and Hankey 1942, 321).

The early variant, above, is an example of type B, although the fact that the woman does not disappear from the vehicle but from the close proximity of witnesses is characteristic of type C. The credible hitchhiker (serving girl) hitches a ride in the standard mode of transportation for the time and geographic area and prophesies something of immediate interest to her fellow travelers (Goss 1984, 47).

Type B variants are considered a subset of the type A legend in the motif index:

> Motif E332.3.3.1(d). Woman or old woman given ride in automobile, makes a prediction or prophesy; she disappears suddenly or gives other evidence of ghostly nature. (Baughman 1966, 148)

Commenting on the research by Beardsley and Hankey, Louis Jones explains that type B variants of the legend are complicated by another group of stories that parallel them in both historical and geographic distribution. He calls them "type BX" stories, tales that center on a dual prophesy, though there is no revenant. The first prophesy concerns the end of the war; the second, the prediction that the driver's vehicle will contain a corpse before the end of the day, is offered as proof of the first prophesy's validity (1944, 285). The emphasis in this variant is not on the first prophesy (as in type B) but upon the event that confirms the prophetic power of the hitchhiker: the corpse in the car (286).

Type C

There was a taxi driver, who, one day, after work was done, went on a spree. He drove all around the town, up one street and down another, and finally he came upon a dance. He stood for a long time in the doorway, seeing what he could see, and finally noticed a very pretty and charming girl. He went up to her and asked her to dance with him. She accepted, and they danced until very late. Then she decided to leave, and the taxi driver offered to take her home in his car. She accepted, and on the way home, she felt very cold. He took off the coat and gave it to her to put around her shoulders.

When they reached her home, she asked him to let her out at the garden gate. The girl got out, opened the gate, and went inside. The taxi driver went on home and went to sleep. Next morning when he awakened, he recalled that he did not have his coat and decided to go to the girl's house to ask for it. He rapped on the door, and a woman answered. He said to her, "I'd like to speak to the young lady who lives here. We were dancing together last night."

> *The woman was a bit surprised and told him that her only daughter had been dead for many years. The driver protested that such was not possible, because they were dancing just last night and she had brought his coat home with her. The woman replied that she was sorry but that her daughter had died a long time ago. "Come with me," she said, "and I will show you her tombstone." So the mother and the taxi driver went to the cemetery. How surprised they were to find that upon the tombstone was hanging his coat!*
>
> *The man fell ill, and a few days later he was dead.*
> (McNeil 1985, 108–9)

Similar to type A but with significant differences, type C is composed of stories in which a girl is met at some place of entertainment (dance) instead of on the road and when she leaves the vehicle she either leaves something behind or takes with her some token (often an article of clothing borrowed from the driver), later found on her grave as proof of the experience and her existence (Goss 1984, 36). Beardsley and Hankey state that this version becomes "a romantic tale of distinctly macabre quality" (1942, 323).

Type D

> *There is a legend in Kona [Hawaii] that one should be very careful about picking up old ladies that one may see walking alone at night. The reason for this is that one moonlight night three people saw an old lady walking down the road leading to Kona on the same evening but at different times. The first man drove right by and passed her. The second man passed her too, without giving her a lift. The third man gave her a lift, and went along for about half an hour and turned back to ask her where she wanted to get off. To his surprise there was no one in the back seat of the car and he began to think that he was imagining it all. He returned home safely and told people about the strange woman who wasn't there, to whom he had given a lift. A few days later the lava flow hit Kona and burned the homes of the two men who had not given the old lady a ride, but the home of the third man who had given the old lady a lift was spared by a miracle. The lava flowed right up to the house and split, to flow around the house, and left the house untouched. All the people said that the old lady was Pele in disguise who showed her wrath to the people who were rude and selfish by burning their homes to cinders.* (Luomala 1972, 44)

Stories in which the hitchhiker is later identified as a local deity are classified as type D variants:

Motif E332.3.3.2(a). Ghostly rider is Hawaiian deity Pele, whose appearance foreshadows the eruption of Mauna Loa. (Baughman 1966, 149)

The most frequent identification is Pele, the Hawaiian goddess of volcanoes, discussed in the section on international variants below.

FUNCTIONS OF THE LEGEND

As one of the world's most common ghost stories, "The Vanishing Hitchhiker" serves, first and foremost, as a tale told for sheer entertainment. Michael Goss believes it is mainly told as a means of flattering the ego: to make the teller seem important, to give the teller center stage, or to hoax the listener:

There are many social situations when ghost stories are invented (or re-invented) purely to conform with the topic of conversation; the fabricator contributes partly from the desire to impress, partly to be sociable. (1984, 77)

The legend is often told, however, as either a modern cautionary tale about the dangers of picking up hitchhikers or a validating tale that supports the existence of the supernatural. One of the reasons why this tale is still so popular is the fact that the form is readily adaptable to the "needs of the hour." Those needs may be personal, national, or spiritual.

In terms of both function and behavior, the vanishing hitchhiker is a very conventional ghost: "one who matches popular expectations of what a ghost is, what it does and why." Because of her tragic and untimely demise, the ghost has as her primary purpose the completion of her interrupted journey. This teaches us that death, perhaps, is not the final chapter in the human story (Goss 1984, 118).

Although there is a vast body of work available on "The Vanishing Hitchhiker," most early discussions focus on either textual variation or annotated collections of variants (Limon 1983, 192). Only recently have researchers concentrated on socio-cultural meanings and functions of the tale. These will be explored in the discussion of international variants later in the chapter.

STRUCTURE OF THE LEGEND

Although there are four distinct types of "The Vanishing Hitchhiker" legend, the structure of all variants remains fairly stable.

The Basic Structure: A Comparison of Schemata

This schema, developed in 1942 by Beardsley and Hankey (noted by Gillian Bennett [1984, 51]), provided a blueprint for legend scholars to work from:

1. Introductory remarks
2. Description of driver and vehicle
3. Character of hitchhiker
4. Circumstances of the pickup
5. Disappearance
6. Explanation of disappearance
7. Narrator's concluding remarks

An alternative structure developed by Jan Harold Brunvand (1981, 25) enumerates eight stable story units in "The Vanishing Hitchhiker":

1. Driver
2. Hitchhiker
3. Address
4. Choice of seat
5. Authentification
6. Disappearance
7. Curiosity or concern
8. Identification

A final way of considering the structure of the legend is to apply Labov's structural elements. This model has been applied to the majority of contemporary legends under examination in this book and is discussed in chapter 5.

1. *Abstract*: a brief summary of the whole story in one or two clauses at the beginning of the telling. *What is this about?*

2. *Orientation*: the introduction of the setting, characters, and problem addressed in the story. *Who, when, what, where?*

3. *Complicating Action*: the narrative proper, the main body of the story. *Then what happened?*

4. *Evaluation*: reveals the attitude of the narrator towards the narrative by emphasizing some narrative units over others. *So what?*

5. *Result or Resolution*: follow the evaluation to wrap up the problem or conflict. *What finally happened?*

6. *Coda*: returns the audience to the "real" world and out of the world of the story. The coda is found less frequently than other elements of the narrative.

The following table demonstrates how the structural schemata of Beardsley and Hankey and of Brunvand fit into Labov's paradigm:

Labov	Beardsley and Hankey	Brunvand
1. abstract ⟶	narrator's introductory remarks	
2. orientation ⟶	description of driver and vehicle ⟶	driver
3. complication ⟶	character of hitchhiker ⟶	hitchhiker
	⟶ circumstances of pick-up	⟶ address
		⟶ choice of seat
4. evaluation ⟶		⟶ authentication
5. resolution ⟶	disappearance ⟶	disappearance
6. coda ⟶	explanation of disappearance ⟶	curiosity
		⟶ identity

(Bennett 1984, 52)

The only elements from Labov's model that are essential to "The Vanishing Hitchhiker" are the complication, evaluation, and resolution. The remaining elements are included at the narrator's discretion (Bennett 1984, 53). For the legend to be most effective, the teller includes the proof of the supernatural state of the passenger at the conclusion of the telling.

Elements of the Legend

The majority of "The Vanishing Hitchhiker" variants include the following stable elements.

Setting

The action of "The Vanishing Hitchhiker" (types A, C, and D) almost always occurs at night and often in inclement weather. It is possible that, when the teller relates the tale, the incident is so unusual that it seems to require an eerie setting. The bad weather often provides a logical reason for the hitchhiker to be either hiking or offered a lift (Beardsley and Hankey 1942, 308). Nocturnal motorists frequently mistake natural objects for supernatural ones, perhaps because they have been "preconditioned" or influenced by subconscious memories of horror films or stories (Goss 1984, 82).

Gender of Driver and Hitchhiker

The gender of the driver is dependent on which of the four types of legend variants are being related. Types A and C usually involve a single male while type B frequently involves a married couple or a family (Beardsley and Hankey 1942, 309). The hitchhiker is most usually a female character and is often described in elaborate detail. The description of the hitchhiker frequently shows that she has a legitimate reason for needing a ride: an armful of books, heavy basket, and so on. This burden often serves as the concrete proof left in the car after the hitchhiker vanishes (Beardsley and Hankey 1942, 310).

Nature of the Revenant

The classic vanishing hitchhiker is a passive and purposeless revenant whose only terror lies in the thrill of discovery after her appearance (Bennett 1984, 50). The revenant can be classified as a "helpful ghost," but traditionally, helpful ghosts haunted *people* rather than *places* (Bennett 1987, 198). However, the nature of revenants has been modified over the centuries. The ghosts of the 16th century came back to fulfill a duty or mission, but later they confined themselves to aimlessly terrifying people in graveyards and "haunted houses" (Kapferer 1990, 126). In the mid-19th century, this ghost became a "stranger-ghost" attached to locations, and for the first time, a person might not recognize that the ghost *was* a ghost, and might mistake it for a living person (Bennett 1987, 198). In fact, the most important aspect of the ghost is that she cannot be readily identified as a supernatural being but is thought to be a normal person (Goss 1984, 43). This is a fairly new phenomenon in ghost lore. Before this century, ghosts were always easily identifiable as such. Therefore, according to Beardsley and Hankey, this aspect of the legend as we know it today points to its recent development (1943, 14). From 1900 onwards, there was a proliferation, in both "tradition" and collections of ghost lore, of ghosts of the phantom hitchhiker and ghostly guardians types (Bennett 1987, 198).

The ghost could also be considered a "warning ghost." In medieval times, the principal role of revenants was to reinforce the teachings of the Church about purgatory. After the Reformation, when the doctrine of purgatory was rejected by Reformist theologians, the British warning ghost took on a more secular role, a role that became increasingly emasculated in succeeding centuries until it became geared to purely domesticated concerns (Bennett 1987, 62).

The story of the deity or heavenly messenger who travels in the guise of a human being is as old as mythology. The Olympians of Greece were fond of traveling incognito; angels appeared to Lot, who took them to be men (Genesis 19: 1–16); and Jesus appeared to two of his disciples on the road to Emmaus and was not recognized by them (Luke 24: 13–35). The vanishing hitchhiker legend in the New Testament (Acts 8: 26–39) is strikingly similar to the contemporary version: Philip is picked up by an Ethiopian who is driving a chariot. They discuss religious matters and the Ethiopian asks to be baptized. Philip does as he requests and then the Ethiopian vanishes (Fish 1976, 5). Stories of the "helpful saint" have several motifs in common with earlier versions of "The Vanishing Hitchhiker": the prophesy of the end of the war (often found in texts collected during World War II) and the recognition of the apparition by a photograph (Fish 1976, 6).

The Vehicle

The vehicle in the legend reflects the current mode of transportation during the period and in the country of origin of the telling. Thus, early tales tell of horses, wagons, and carts, while recent renditions mention automobiles, vans, buses, motorcycles, and airplanes.

The Disappearance

The listener is drawn into the tale by the sudden and inexplicable disappearance of the hitchhiker. If the hitchhiker does not disappear directly from the vehicle, a wide variety of motives are given for the driver to return to the destination to discover that indeed he had given transportation to a ghost (Beardsley and Hankey 1942, 314). This information is often delivered as a "punch ending."

The Evidence

It is not the actual disappearance of the ghost that distinguishes this legend from other ghostlore. Rather, it is the explanation for the disappearance and the physical evidence that is left behind. The most frequently cited evidence found, either in the car or on the tombstone, is a jacket or sweater that had been borrowed from the driver (Glazer 1987, 33).

The search for and discovery of the hitchhiker's identity are not the keystone of the story but are structural devices made necessary by the passive and silent behavior of the ghost. For modern society to credit that a supernatural visit indeed took place, concrete evidence must be put forth: address and identification at the address and the article left behind (Bennett 1984, 55).

Further collaboration of the experience is often attributed to a visit to the local police station to report the alarming experience. The police respond favorably to the report, reassuring the driver and traveling to the scene, but unfortunately, finding no evidence. Because they believe that the police took the event seriously, listeners believe that the adventure actually took place.

AN ANALYSIS OF THE RESEARCH

The vast volume of research and discussion on "The Vanishing Hitchhiker" legend complex demonstrates a wide diversity of opinion. Beardsley and Hankey's study stresses their belief that "The Vanishing Hitchhiker" is a modern legend, not historically linked to disappearing ghosts of the past. However, subsequent discussion demonstrates that, although the tale is "dressed in modern conveniences," it is indeed an old tale.

Louis C. Jones's work on "Hitchhiking Ghosts in New York" demonstrates that one of the important features of this contemporary legend, the automobile, is a matter of surface detail only. This also means that the hitchhiking aspect, also a recent innovation, is not an essential ingredient, but a modern adaptation to provide a credible reason for the ghostly event. In cultures where hitchhiking is not possible, for example, the vanishing hitchhiker gathers rides in other ways (1944, 288).

Additional studies of "The Vanishing Hitchhiker" legend illustrate culturally variable aspects. Luomala's research in Hawaii "shows the nature of the supernatural character changing from ghost to goddess under the influence of dominant supernatural traditions." William Wilson's research discusses the legend in relation to the traditions of the Three Nephites. And finally, Lydia M. Fish explores the identification of the hitchhiker as Jesus or an Angel of God, which may be a response to the influence of "born again" Christianity in the United States (Bennett 1984, 47).

In variants studied by Fish, instead of a female hitchhiker, a male, "young bearded and with long hair looking like a hippie in blue jeans or all in white," is picked up and warns the driver of the vehicle that the second coming is imminent. In several cases, he identifies himself as Jesus. This variant was particularly popular during the spring of 1971 and winter of 1972, coinciding with a period of religious revival on American campuses (1976, 8).

Since 1984, other explorations of the legend as it is told in Mexican American communities, Native American traditions, and in Israel and South Africa demonstrate that the legend is not only flexible but important in the lore of those cultures.

VARIANTS

A driver named Powell picks up a hitchhiker and they discover a mutual interest in chess. The hitchhiker offers to show the driver an interesting chess problem and gives his name and address. If he isn't at home, [he says], the chess problem will be found in his tobacco jar. Later that day the driver calls at the house.

The woman who answered the door invited him in, then hearing his story, looked somewhat taken aback. "Can you describe him?" she queried. The description was of her husband. Puzzled, she said "That's strange, he died three days ago." Mr. Powell noticed the alabaster tobacco jar on the mantlepiece and asked permission to open it, to which the widow agreed. Inside was the chess problem written on a sheet of paper, just as his passenger had described. (Hobbs 1978, 75)

This variant of the legend does not fit comfortably in any of the type categories that were devised in the 1940s. Instead of a female, young or old, we have a male hitchhiker who, while not making a prediction or prophesy, manages to leave a message for his helper.

Other revenants that have been identified as part of "The Vanishing Hitchhiker" legend complex include "Resurrection Mary" from Chicago's Resurrection Cemetery, in which she is said to be buried (Guiley 1992, 280). Resurrection Mary walked out on her boyfriend after an argument in the 1930s. She was accidently killed while hitching a ride and, because she has never had a chance to make peace with her boyfriend, she cannot rest.

Cultural contouring, "the process by which a phenomenon is interpreted in the light of a specific consensus pattern," allows the vanishing hitchhiker to support whatever message or teaching fits the group circumstances. Thus, the vanishing hitchhiker is interpreted as an angelic prophet by Mormons and Catholics in the United States, a vampire in Malaysia, a deity of volcanoes in Hawaii, and an agent of apocalypse in Europe (Goss 1984, 14).

In her analysis of 82 vanishing hitchhiker narratives, Gillian Bennett (1984, 48–49) discovers a myriad of variations that reflect the culture of the teller and listener. Cultural variations surfaced in the following elements:

- The setting (all narratives collected in urban centers set the hitchhiker on city streets, the Mormon variants take place en route to the Temple, and rural versions take place on unlit, deserted roads).

- The sex and number of travelers.

- The gender and appearance of the hitchhiker (in societies where prophets are male, the hitchhikers are male, but where the prophets are female, the hitchhiker is also female). The hitchhiker, in the most common variants of the legend, is a passive revenant; once she indicates the address of her destination, she rarely speaks again. Variations on this behavior include: predictions or prophetical warnings, provisions, threats, helpful ghosts, and ghosts who seduce the living, endangering their immortal souls.
- The mode of transport used by the traveler.
- The method by which the hitchhiker obtained the lift.
- The behavior of the fellow-traveler while on the journey.
- The outcome (if any) of the encounter.
- The length of, and number of, motifs in the story.

"The Vanishing Hitchhiker" in the United States

Several studies have attempted to determine the method and amount of cultural adaptation one of the world's most popular tales has undergone in the United States.

Hawaiian Variants

Pele, the Hawaiian goddess of the volcano, is portrayed as a restless and violent-tempered wanderer. In her wanderings, she rewards those who are kind to her and punishes severely those who are not. The legends of Pele teach that not only should Pele be instantly obeyed, but that all strangers should be treated with kindness and respect (Luomala 1972, 29). The contemporary legend also contains a warning about kindness. The homes of those who treat Pele well are saved from the lava flow during a subsequent eruption.

> Fiery, impulsive and unpredictable, this holdover from the ancient Hawaiian religion is said to appear as a hitchhiker, sometimes young, sometimes old, often smoking a cigarette or sipping coffee or gin. Not to pick her up is bad luck, but when you do, she vanishes from the vehicle before the destination is reached. (Vanishing Hitchhiker Update, 1989, 2)

In the body of legends examined by Luomala, two major divisions are distinguished: 1) the goddess actually vanishes from the conveyance while it is in motion; and 2) the hitchhiker leaves the vehicle at the destination and her supernatural nature is discovered later (Luomala 1972, 35).

Mexican American Variants

In the year 1940 a Santa Monica, California, cab driver was
stopped by a woman dressed in black who asked him to take her to
the cemetery. She paid her fare with a check for $100 and gave him
the name of a store where he could cash the check. When he arrived
at the store, he noticed that the check was for $1000 rather than
$100. The store owner recognized the signature on the check as that
of his mother, who had been dead for twenty years, and agreed to
give the cab driver the money, since it was his mother's wish. The
cab driver, however, bothered by the idea of spending the money
of a dead woman, became quite ill and died the following year.
(Miller 1973, 94)

Folklore is colored by traditional beliefs and customs. Several of the
most common elements of this legend are missing in Mexican American
variants. The ghost did not disappear from the vehicle and the identity is not
established until the driver tried to find it a second time. Because the hitchhiker did not disappear, other reasons are given to account for the driver
searching the ghost out again. Versions from South Texas, as documented by
Mark Glazer (1987, 33), provided 13 distinct reasons for the driver to seek out
the hitchhiker again:

1. The hitchhiker does not come to the rendezvous.

2. The person who rode in the ghost's station wagon wants to thank
   the revenant.

3. A terrible noise comes from the ghost's house.

4. The driver tries to pick up an item forgotten at the hitchhiker's
   home.

5. The driver likes the hitchhiker and wants to see him or her again.

6. The hitchhiker forgets an item in the car and the driver tries to
   return it.

7. The driver attempts to retrieve a garment loaned to the hitchhiker.

8. The driver wants both to take back an item and visit the hitchhiker.

9. The driver wants to find out why the hitchhiker disappeared into
   the darkness.

10. The taxi driver is tired of waiting for a nun to come back to the car
    and decides to investigate.

11. The driver is not curious at all and finds out, by coincidence, that the hitchhiker was a ghost.

12. The taxi driver is given a note with an address where he can pick up his money.

13. The taxi driver is given a crucifix to help him collect the money.

A major difference between the outlook of Anglo-Americans and Mexican Americans is that the former have a great deal of anxiety about ghosts, while there are a large number of friendly ghosts in Chicano folklore (Glazer 1987, 33). Additionally, the belief in miracles is strong in Mexican American culture beliefs. The cause of these miracles is a religious vow made to a saint or one of the personifications of the Virgin Mary. In return for a request for aid, the individual promises personal sacrifices, prayers, and presents to the saint. The nonfulfillment of the promise after the request has been granted can have dire consequences. "An individual who dies before fulfilling the vow becomes a ghost who will search for a way, and sometimes for a human, to help him or her, to pay the debt to the saint" (Glazer 1987, 34). This belief is frequently attached to the legend of "The Vanishing Hitchhiker" in Mexican American culture.

> *A woman engaged a hack on the night of Holy Thursday for the purposes of attending various churches. When she has finished these activities, she asks to be taken back to the spot where the carriage picked her up. She alights at the entrance to a cemetery but finds that she has no money to pay the driver. She then writes an address on a slip of paper and assures the driver that someone at that address will pay what she owes. She then disappears into the cemetery. The next day the driver goes in search of the fare owed him and learns that his passenger of the night before has been dead for a year.* (Robe 1980, 130)

Other cultural adaptations involve the nature of the hitchhiker. Because it would be unlikely for a Mexican American woman to hitchhike, the ghost becomes a customer in a taxi. Often she goes to seven churches to pray as a retribution for a vow broken by her untimely death. Hopefully, with the fulfillment of the vow, the revenant can rest for eternity (Glazer 1987, 35).

Navajo Variants

Keith Cunningham and Kathryn Cunningham studied the legends of the Ramah Navajo society. In their article "The Appearing Hitchhiker," they find that "The Vanishing Hitchhiker" was one of the stories that was recognized and retold most frequently in that community (1989, 223). They found that the Navajo had adopted and adapted the legend—it has a striking similarity to a traditional Navajo form, *ch'iidii* stories. *Ch'iidii* are "the evil part of the spirit of a dead person." The Navajo believe that the evil in each person (except for children who died before they spoke and old people who have lived blameless lives and died natural deaths) is released at the time of death and is the primary cause of illness, disharmony, and most of what is wrong with the world (223).

Unfortunately, the article doesn't contain an example of the Navajo narrative, but the authors report that in those tales, the *ch'iidii* would linger near the body's resting place, but they were not easily recognized by those who knew them when they were alive. The *ch'iidii* do not communicate with people and appear and disappear without explanation. Although they were not known as hitchhikers, they were believed to have jumped onto horses behind the riders and to have ridden with them (226). Today, like the hitch-hiker revenants in other parts of the globe, *ch'iidii* have adapted to modern transportation and ride in vehicles.

"The Vanishing Hitchhiker" in Europe

European antecedents abound in stories of vanishing ghosts and phantom travelers. Contemporary versions of "The Vanishing Hitchhiker" are also common and appear in the media and are told to warn people about the dangers of picking up hitchhikers.

French Variants

In May 1982 there were numerous reports of a monk hitchhiking along France's Atlantic coast in the Vendee region. The monk is always sighted in the evening or at night and when picked up, sits in the backseat of the car. He says very little for a long while and then makes several statements that sound like predictions: "We'll have a hot summer and a bloody fall." The driver or the passenger in the front seat turns around but finds that the backseat is empty, although the vehicle has never stopped. The driver goes to the closest police station and reports the event. He is informed that others have had the same experience. In reality, however, an investigation showed that no one had made any reports at the police stations. Two things are certain, though: monks do travel in the region, and they are often seen there beside the roads (Kapferer 1990, 31).

German Variants

The following article appeared in one of the largest regional newspapers in southern Germany in December 1981:

> *An enigmatic "black lady" has, of late, been worrying the citizens of the Salzburg districts Pinzgau and Pongau, as well as the archdiocese of Salzburg. According to reports by automobile drivers, this uncanny woman appears at night on the Pinzgauer national highway and signals cars to stop. One distressed driver reported that, after driving a few hundred meters after he had picked the hitchhiker up, she told him: "If you hadn't stopped and taken me along, you would have had an accident." At that moment she disappeared, without a trace. Going by the descriptions, many living in the area believe that the mysterious woman is the resurrection of a young waitress from St. Viet, who was killed in the previous year in an accident on the Pinzgauer highway. The car of the 23-year-old driver had crashed off the road directly onto the train tracks running parallel to the highway and was hit by a train that came through in the next instant. According to police reports, the young woman was not immediately killed and her piercing screams filled the air. The archdiocese also reacted to the rumours: this type of appearance is often the result of a deception of the senses, an overexcited imagination or hallucinations. Only a fraction of such apparitions, the archdiocese concluded, fall into the category of "true hauntings." (Petzoldt 1990, 51)*

Dutch Variants

> *A man driving along a busy motorway sees a hitchhiker and stops. The hitchhiker gets in and straightaway announces the End of the World. The way he speaks makes a deep impression, but when he says he is an angel, the driver looks round at him incredulously, and at that very moment there is no one there; he has dissolved into thin air. The driver's surprise is immense. He stops the car, looks around him, and sees a police car approach. "You are by no means the first to tell me this story," says the officer when the driver tells him his tale. (Jans 1991, 5)*

One of the early versions of this tale that circulated through the Netherlands for several months was first told in Evangelical circles, moving on to secondary schools affiliated with the Reform circles. The Dutch press tried to confirm the story but was constantly referred to a "friend of a friend." *Koers*, a weekly magazine, received reports from various parts of the country, some dating it to the Wednesday when the Iraqi ground war began, others to Christmas 1990 (Jans 1991, 5).

"The Vanishing Hitchhiker" in Israel

A driver proceeds with his eye on the Geha highway which connects Jerusalem with Haifa, on a rainy winter night. At the gathering station for soldiers who want a "lift," with great difficulty he perceives a person and stops his vehicle. A wet female soldier gets in. The driver begins a conversation with her. She tells him that, as usual, she wants to go from the military base to her home in Ramat Gan and thus the ride passes in a friendly manner. However, the driver has difficulty in steering, owing to the bad weather conditions. The driver says to the young woman that in such weather he will bring her to her home and she tells him her address. When they arrive at the house, the driver stops and wants to tell the young woman that they have arrived, but he perceives that she is not in the car and only her military coat is left. Bewildered, he knocks at the door of the house and tells a woman who opens it what has happened. The woman is not surprised and tells him that three years ago her daughter, then a soldier, was killed, in a road accident on the Geha highway and from then on, on rainy nights, like the present-one, a driver appears who tells he took her in his car and brings part of her clothing which she left in it. (Shenhar 1984, 203–4)

To understand the cultural adaptations in the example, we should consider that it comes from a country that requires all youth, male and female, to serve national aims and values by serving in the army. Death in the line of duty, especially for a son, is accorded public mourning with troop reviews, ceremonies, and memorial monuments. "The Vanishing Hitchhiker" involves a female soldier, rather than male, who meets death in a road accident and whose death, therefore, is not marked by public ceremonies. It is an antithesis to stories of war and heroism (Shenhar 1984, 205). The story functions as catharsis while focusing on the increasing number of deaths in road accidents as well as the guilt about hapless female victims whose death goes unremarked (Shenhar 1984, 207).

Thirty-seven versions of "The Vanishing Hitchhiker" were collected in Israel with the help of students at Haifa University from 1980 to 1983. Twenty-six of the legends collected were similar to the above example, while the remaining eleven were varied. In one familiar version, a motorcyclist takes a woman hitchhiker from one of the *kibbutzim* (communal settlements) and lends her his sweater so she will not be cold. She disappears before arriving at the *kibbutzim* and so he goes in to look for her. When he is informed that she was killed the previous year at the exact spot that he picked her up, he does not believe it. He finally goes to the cemetery and finds his sweater on the grave (Shenhar 1984, 204).

"The Vanishing Hitchhiker" in Asia

Japanese Variants

> *Late one night in Kyoto, a young and inexperienced taxi-driver picked up a beautiful young woman dressed in exquisite kimono and obi at a lonely spot beside the Kamogawa River. The lady gave him the address she wanted to go to, which she said was a house right next to a famous temple. Like all Kyoto taxi-drivers, the young man knew quite well where the temple was, so he was confident he could find the house without difficulty.*
>
> *During the drive, the woman kept silent. The driver tried to start a conversation, but she would not reply. She kept brushing the folds of her kimono with her hands, as if trying to brush something away. The driver fell silent, deciding she must be a little crazy.*
>
> *As he approached the temple, he saw that the house next to it was burning. It was completely devoured by flames. The firemen were helpless against such a great conflagration. The driver turned to the woman to warn her that her house was on fire, but found that she had vanished. But as Japanese taxi doors are automatic, and controlled by the driver, who alone can open them to let a passenger out, the driver was baffled. That very moment, a dead body was being carried out of the house by the firemen, and to the taxi-driver's horror, he saw that it was the woman he had driven in his taxi from Kamogawa. Her body was burned and dripping with water from the firemen's hoses, but her face was still plainly recognizable.*
>
> *Terrified, the driver sped away, back to his taxi company headquarters. When he got back there, shaking with fright as he told his story, one of his fellow drivers called: "Hey! Look here! The back seat of your taxi is all soaking wet!" As the taxi-driver gazed in stupefaction at the pools of water on the backseat and the floor, he saw that they were swimming with charred cloth exactly like that like that of the woman's kimono. Then he fainted clean away.*
> (Kirkup 1989, 3–4)

Mongolian Variants

"The Vanishing Hitchhiker" is a common motif in Mongolian folklore, demonstrating "a unique stigma of the vast Mongolian steppes" and the process of *contemporizing*, or adapting traditional folklore to contemporary life conditions. "This evolution proceeds slowly towards replacing the magic thinking by causal thinking, though apparently this process is slower in Mongolia than in Europe" (Czubala 1992, 2–3). Roads in Mongolia are typically "trails winding through the steppes, deserts and mountains, whose pavement consists mainly of potholes, bumps, loose boulders and a rich assortment of similar entrapments" (2). Vehicles are often in the same state of disrepair and drivers must be proficient mechanics. Drivers must also be knowledgeable of the sections of roads that have magic power. "Both drivers and passengers alleviate their fear of those places by depositing offerings on special roadside mounds, rocks and trees" (2).

The types of Mongolian vanishing hitchhikers include the man with half his head shaved who appears by the cars parked in the steppes while their drivers are either making repairs or resting; the "fast-runner," who runs so fast that he catches up to the moving car and frightens the driver; a naked girl who stands by the road in the steppes or runs alongside the car and jumps on the sideboard and later disappears; and the "girl in the red dress."

Mongolian vanishing hitchhikers establish eye contact with the driver, who doesn't stop the car on the road, and they never actually get into the car. They are dangerous. "Demons, semi-demons and other non-personified and dangerous forces that are poised to strike the Mongolian driver are a clear reflection of magic thinking, which seems to be still a strong cultural trait in Mongolia" (Czubala 1992, 3).

Bill Ellis comments that the Mongolian "fast-runner" variant provides an interesting parallel to the "skin-walker" beliefs. "This motif has been adopted by Anglo-American adolescents, who say that 'skin-walkers' will run alongside speeding vehicles, pacing their speed and often knocking on the car windows, laughing demonically, or trying to drive the auto off the road." A possible allusion to this motif is a scene from the movie *Superman*, where the adolescent hero tests his powers by running alongside a speeding train and waving to the passengers (Czubala 1992, 5).

"The Vanishing Hitchhiker" in South Africa

The story of Maries Roux of Uniondale is possibly the best docu-mented ghost story in the world. Marie, a passenger in a car driven by her fiance G. M. Pretorius, was killed on Easter morning, April 12, 1968. Her ghost has been sighted since Easter of 1973 and investigated by Uniondale's magistrate Andries Vermeulen. "He chronicled sightings and showed those involved pictures of Marie. He came to the conclusion that the ghost exists." (Vanishing Hitchhiker Update 1989, 3)

Five story elements can be distinguished in the legend complex of South Africa, as noted by Sigrid Schmidt (1990, 2):

1. A girl dies in a car accident.

2. A couple, stopping by chance by the accident site around midnight, sees the transparent, white-dressed ghost of a girl.

3. A car driver gives a girl a ride but she vanishes from the car.

4. A motorcyclist gives a girl a ride but she suddenly vanishes, leaving his spare helmet, which she was wearing, clipped to the luggage rack.

5. A university scientist sets the spirit at rest.

The tale, popular in the late 1970s, incorporated variations in the type of vehicle and the sound that the hitchhiker made just before she disappeared (repetition of her death cry or laughter). What did not vary was the setting of the event.

The stories are a striking example of the importance of the press in connection with contemporary legends. The South African press transformed the legend into an official report. The actual person who experienced the occurrence was interviewed, not a friend-of-a-friend. The validity of these "interviews" were reinforced by police statements again and again, making the story even more official. The press did not adapt the core legend to local places and persons but constantly connected it to Uniondale (Schmidt 1990, 3).

Another South African hitchhiker is known to have a more dangerous aspect:

> A girl hitchhiker is also supposed to haunt the verges of Du Toit's Kloof, but she is not as well authenticated as Uniondale's lady—for no one who meets her lives to tell the tale: It is said that whoever takes her in their car is always involved in a fatal accident.
> (Schmidt 1990, 2)

COUSINS OF "THE VANISHING HITCHHIKER"

While not exactly variants of "The Vanishing Hitchhiker," the following legends are peopled with close relatives to the legendary revenant.

Malaysian Legends

The *langsuyar* is a type of female vampire who lurks by the side of the road, usually by the dense jungle or a graveyard, and seduces young men into offering her a lift. The *langsuyar* persuades the driver to stop and promptly soars off into the night uttering blood-curdling screams (Goss 1984, 128).

Russian Legends

A miracle that occurred in St. Petersburg during December 1890 was reported in at least five newspapers at the time. The reports have a close similarity to "The Vanishing Hitchhiker" but are a different legend. In this tale, a young priest came to a certain apartment after mass carrying the holy sacraments. A young man opens the door. The priest tells him, "I was asked to give the sacraments to a sick man." The young man replies that the priest must have the wrong house as no one is there but himself. The priest notices a photograph of a woman on the wall. "Look," he points, "that is the woman who asked me to come." "But," the young man gasps, "that is my mother, but she has been dead for several years." Awe, fear, and terror seized the young man, and he took communion. That evening he lay dead (Edgerton 1968, 39).

English Legends

An English ballad and folktale tells of a girl who is given a lift to her door on horseback by her recently-deceased lover. The ghost lover leaves a token to show that he was really with her. He borrows the girl's handkerchief to bind his head. When his parents exhume the coffin, there is the handkerchief just as she saw it (Goss 1984, 45). The ballad "The Suffolk Wonder" concludes:

Affrighted, then they did behold
His body turning unto mold;
And though he had a month been dead
This handkerchief was 'bout his head. (Goss 1984, 46)

LITERARY, RECORDED, AND VISUAL ADAPTATIONS

"The Vanishing Hitchhiker," long a part of Western society's popular culture, has been transformed by the mass media to reach new generations. The legend has provided inspiration for *Twilight Zone* episodes, television sit-coms, and movie shorts, as well as numerous popular songs.

Literary Adaptations

Traditional literary adaptations of this legend can be found in such older works as:

"The Lady with the Velvet Collar" (1824) by Washington Irving, also known as "The Adventure of the German Student," found in *Tales of a Traveller* (1849). In the preface to this edition, Irving remarks that the latter part of this story is based on an anecdote related to him as being current somewhere in France (Short Story Index Reprint Series 1977).

"The Lavender Evening Dress" by Carla Carmer. In *Folklore in American Literature*, edited by John T. Flanagan and Arthur Palmer Hudson. Evanston, IL: Row, Peterson, 1958, 99–101. Also in *The Life Treasury of American Folklore*. New York: Time-Life, 1961, 252–56. "Every year the girl in the long lavender dress is sighted somewhere in the United States, a quick flicker of color on a nocturnal country road. She is one of the most enduring and romantic figures in modern American folklore" (*The Life Treasury of American Folklore*, 252).

Contemporary adaptations can be found in the following resources:

Brien, Jean. "The Girl in the Rose-Colored Shawl." *The Unseen: Scary Stories*, selected by Janet Lunn. Toronto: Lester, 1994, 26–28.

Cohen, Daniel. "The Most Famous Phantom." *Railroad Ghosts and Highway Horrors*. New York: Cobblehill Books, 1991, chapter 1.

Gregory, Nan. "No-Post." *Next Teller: A Book of Canadian Storytelling*, collected by Dan Yashinski. Charlottetown, P.E.I.: Ragweed Press, 1994, 197–200.

Justice, Jennifer. "The Vanishing Hitchhiker." *The Ghost & I: Scary Stories for Participatory Telling*. Cambridge, MA: Yellow Moon Press, 1992, 105–11.

Young, Richard, and Judy Dockrey Young. *Ghost Stories from the American Southwest*. Little Rock, AR: August House, 1991, 33–34, 138–39.

———. "The Lady from the Lake." *The Scary Story Reader*. Little Rock, AR: August House, 1993, 53–55.

———. "The Lady in White on Mount Hood." *The Scary Story Reader*. Little Rock, AR: August House, 1993, 93–94.

———. "Last Kiss." *The Scary Story Reader*. Little Rock, AR: August House, 1993, 34–36.

Recorded Adaptations

"Blommetjie Gedenk aan My" [Oh, My Flower, Remember Me]. A South African popular song about the "real" Uniondale vanishing hitchhiker incidents.

A wicked wind blows over the n'goenie bushes
On the road near Uniondale.
There a ghostly girl waits, every Good Friday night
As the eternal autumn winds howl. . . .
And she stands there, begging for a ride.

Chorus:
As the Kammanassie ghost
Rolls rocks down the mountain,
The phantom girl of Uniondale
Thumbs a ride and sadly sings:
"Oh, my flower, remember me!"
As she holds her thumb in the air:
"Oh, my flower, remember me!"
Sings the ghost of the Little Karoo.

Easter is an autumn holiday in South Africa because the seasons are reversed south of the equator. "Easter week, particularly the night of Good Friday, takes on the atmosphere of Halloween in Europe and North America" (de Bruyn 1990, 4–5). The Kammanassie mountains are just west of Uniondale. "Karoo" is a Hottentot word meaning "dry country." The Big and Little Karoo are arid plains located on the southern tip of the continent, the Little Karoo lying between the coast and a range of mountains near Oudtshoorn (de Bruyn 1990, 5).

"Bringing Mary Home" by Billy Edd Wheller (1966), from his album *Goin' Town and Country.*

"Hitchhiker of Karoo." Jazz bassist Brian Torff explained this title cut song title on the liner notes to his 1987 instrumental album:
A few years ago, in South Africa, I came across this strange story in a local newspaper. It seems a woman with long blonde hair died in a motorcycle accident while traveling across the Karoo desert. Since then, so the story goes, there have been numerous incidents of a biker picking up a blond-haired woman along the road and when she gets on, the motorcycle suddenly speeds up to over 100 mph [170 km/h] and the biker hears a hysterical laughing coming from behind him. When he turns around, the woman is gone. She is "The Hitchhiker of Karoo." (Uniondale on Disk, 1992, 8)

"Laurie (Strange Things Happen)" by Milton C. Addington; recorded by Dickie Lee (Twentieth-Century Fox, TCF 102-ZTSP 91656). "Laurie" reached number 14 in 1965's *Billboard's* Top 100 and remained on the charts for 13 weeks (McNeil 1985, 191). "Laurie" is a fine example of an old theme having been given new currency; even the replacement of an overcoat with a sweater as proof-item is no accident. At the time the record was released, stylish seaters were a vital article in the average teenage trendsetter's wardrobe (Goss 1984, 41).

"Laurie (Strange Things Happen)"

Last night at the dance I met Laurie,
So lovely and warm, an angel of a girl.
Last night I fell in love with Laurie,
Strange things happen in this world.

A strange force drew me to the graveyard.
I stood in the dark. I saw the shadows wave,
And then I looked and saw my sweater
Lying there upon her grave.

"Phantom 309" by Red Sovine. In this song, the legend is being "told from the hitchhiker's point of view; this time, the trucker who picks up the hitcher is the ghost" (Uniondale on Disk, 1992, 8).

"Taking Mary Home" by the Country Gentlemen. (Only the girl's name has changed!)

Visual Adaptations

Our habit of trivializing the supernatural through popular culture for the sake of commercial gratitude has resulted in our popular notion of ghosts. They are tameable and friendly (Casper); frauds and fakes; tourist attractions; and threatening only to those who deliberately seek a thrill (entertainment) (Bennett 1987, 210). Several film versions of "The Vanishing Hitchhiker" use the legend elements solely to entertain the viewers.

Pee-Wee's Big Adventure (1985). Incorporates the "other perspective" variant of this tale.

Return to Glennascaul (1951). Features Orson Welles as a man who tells the story of this "true" experience.

Mr. Wrong (1984). Based on the short story of the same name and also includes other contemporary legends in the story line. The story has been dramatized for radio and was broadcast in Great Britain in 1983 (Smith and Hobbs 1990, 147).

REFERENCES

Baughman, Ernest Warren. 1966. *Type and motif index of the folktales of England and North America.* The Hague: Mouton.

Beardsley, Richard K., and Rosalie Hankey. 1942. The vanishing hitchhiker. *California Folklore Quarterly* 1: 303–35.

———. 1943. A history of the vanishing hitchhiker. *California Folklore Quarterly* 2: 13–25.

Bennett, Gillian. 1984. The phantom hitchhiker: Neither modern, urban nor legend? In *Perspectives on contemporary legend, vol. 1,* edited by Paul Smith. Sheffield, England: Sheffield Academic Press.

———. 1987. *Traditions of belief: Women, folklore and the supernatural today.* New York: Penguin.

Brunvand, Jan Harold. 1981. *The vanishing hitchhiker.* New York: W. W. Norton.

Cunningham, Keith, and Kathryn Cunningham. 1989. The appearing hitchhiker: Narrative acculturation among the Ramah Navajo. In *The questing beast: Perspectives on contemporary legend, vol. IV,* edited by Gillian Bennett and Paul Smith. Sheffield, England: Sheffield Academic Press, 213–30.

Czubala, Dionizjusz. 1992. Mongolian contemporary legends: Field research report, part one. *FOAFTALE NEWS* 28 (December): 1–5.

de Bruyn, Pieter. 1990. Blommetjie gedenk ann my: A South African vanishing hitchhiking song. *FOAFTALE NEWS* 20 (December): 4–5.

Edgerton, William B. 1968. The ghost in search of help for a dying man. *Journal of the Folklore Institute* 5, no. 1: 31–41.

Fish, Lydia M. 1976. Jesus on the thruway: The vanishing hitchhiker strikes again. *Indiana Folklore* 9: 5–13.

Glazer, Mark. 1985. The traditionalization of the contemporary legend: The Mexican American example. *Fabula* 26: 288–97.

———. 1987. Mexican-American culture and urban legend: The case of the vanishing hitchhiker. *Urban Resources* 4, no. 3 (spring): 31–36.

Goss, Michael. 1984. *The evidence for phantom hitch-hikers.* Wellingborough, Northhamptonshire: Aquarian Press.

Guiley, Rosemary Ellen. 1992. *The encyclopedia of ghosts and spirits.* New York: Facts on File.

Hobbs, Sandy. 1978. The folktale as news. *Oral History* 6, no. 11: 74–86.

Jans, B. O. 1991. Hitchhiking angels in Holland. *FOAFTALE NEWS* 22 (June): 5–6.

Jansen, William Hugh. 1943. Folklore items from a teacher's notebook. *Hoosier Folklore Bulletin* 2: 1–8.

Jones, Louis C. 1944. Hitchhiking ghosts in New York. *Western Folklore* 3, no. 4: 284–92.

———. 1983. (Reprint of 1959). *Things that go bump in the night.* Syracuse University Press.

Kapferer, Jean-Noel. 1990. *Rumors: Uses, interpretations and images*. New Brunswick: NJ: Transaction.

Kirkup, James. 1989. Truth stranger than legend: Contemporary legends in Europe and the Orient. *FOAFTALE NEWS* 15 (September): 2–4.

Limon, Jose E. 1983. Legendry, metafolklore, and performance: A Mexican-American example. *Western Folklore* 42: 191–208.

Luomala, Katharine. 1972. Disintegration and regeneration, the Hawaiian phantom hitchhiker legend. *Fabula* 13: 20–59.

McNeil, W. K., ed. 1985. *Ghost stories from the American South*. New York: Dell.

Miller, Elaine. 1973. *Mexican folk narrative for the Los Angeles area* (American Folklore series, vol. 56). Austin: University of Texas Press.

Petzoldt, Leander. 1990. Phantom lore. In *Storytelling in contemporary societies* (Script Oralis, 22), edited by Lutz Rohrich and Sabine Wienker-Piepo. Tubingen: Narr, 51–58.

Robe, Stanley L. 1980. *Hispanic legends from New Mexico: Narratives from the R.D. Jameson collection* (Folklore and Mythology series, 31). Berkeley: University of California Press.

Schmidt, Sigrid. 1990. The vanishing hitchhiker in South Africa: Additional notes. *FOAFTALE NEWS* 17 (March): 1–3.

Shenhar, Aliza. 1985. The Israeli versions of the vanishing hitchhiker. In *The 8th Congress for the International Society for Folk Narrative Research*, vol. II, edited by Reimund Kvideland and Torunn Selberg, Bergen, Norway, June 12-17, 203–9.

Smith, Paul, and Sandy Hobbs. 1990. Films using contemporary legend themes/motifs. In *Contemporary legend. The first five years*, compiled by Gillian Bennett and Paul Smith. Sheffield, England: Sheffield Academic Press.

Uniondale on disk: More on South African vanishing hitchhiker music. 1992. *FOAFTALE NEWS* 26 (June): 8.

Vanishing hitchhiker update. 1989. *FOAFTALE NEWS* 13 (March): 2–3.

LA LLORONA— THE WEEPING WOMAN

La Llorona was a beautiful Indian woman who had several illegitimate children. When her lover rejected her, she went out of her mind and drowned his children in a river. After her death, she was compelled to search for them every night. Nowadays, she appears like a ghost near watery places or on the streets, screaming and crying, "Ay, mis hijos! [Oh, my children!]" She is very attractive, is dressed in a long, white, flowing robe and has long hair hanging freely down to her waist. (Arora 1981, 25)

For centuries ghosts have been the subject of legends and folklore worldwide. In many times and in many cultures, people believed very strongly in such supernatural figures. Today, most people, especially in the Western world, scoff at supernatural presences, at least consciously. However, subconsciously, many people are just not sure about the (in)validity of these specters. In North America, the most frequent type of ghost is revenants, "the dead who return from the grave." Revenants manifest themselves in various ways, from the popular concept of ghosts as wispy, filmy beings to solid forms that appear to be living figures (Guiley 1992, 282).

Elaine Miller categorizes four types of revenants in folk narratives according to the nature of their mission (if any). The first two categories, the *anima*, or soul, and the *espiritus*, rather generalized ghosts, do not concern us here. The other two categories consist of revenants common to contemporary legends. The living corpse, Miller's third category, is defined as

> a deceptively natural-looking apparition who interacts with the living in a perfectly normal way, disappears, generally in a mysterious manner, and is later discovered to have been a dead person; and whose mission is best explained as a vague compulsion to make periodic appearances at specific times or places, such as on an anniversary or at the site of an accident in which he was killed. (1973, 55)

This type of revenant is easily identified as "The Vanishing Hitchhiker" and the subject of the previous chapter. The fourth classification is the *llorona*, the wailing woman, and the focus of this chapter.

La Llorona is the second most common supernatural presence in the narratives of the Mexican American population. The first is the devil and the third is "The Vanishing Hitchhiker" (Glazer 1985a, 205). The legend of La Llorona and its different aspects, functions, possible historical antecedents, and variants provide a fascinating look at a constantly evolving legend.

ASPECTS OF LA LLORONA

La Llorona is not an easy revenant to define because stories about her are most likely a complex of legends and involve at least three aspects of the main character. The identity that she assumes in a given situation or rendition of the legend depends on the age, gender, and purpose of both the storyteller and the listener of the tale.

The Grieving Mother

The most popular aspect of the weeping woman is that of a grieving mother who is forever wandering, usually around a body of water, looking for her murdered children. In most versions, La Llorona herself was guilty of her children's murder as a reaction to her unfaithful lover. When she realizes what she has done, she is full of remorse and dies of grief, but she cannot rest until she is reunited with her children, who cannot be found. She is often seen and heard around bodies of water providing a "reason" for parents to warn their children away from potential danger at the water's edge.

The Dangerous Lady

In these tales, La Llorona's purpose is not limited to her search for her children; she has a more malevolent function as well. Besides punishing disobedient children, she can be also dangerous to animals and causes car accidents (Russel 1977, 208). In this aspect she can be compared to the bogeyman of other cultures, warning children against disobeying their parents: "If you are not home before dark, La Llorona will catch you!"

The Siren

La Llorona sometimes manifests as a desirable woman who lures men to their deaths in the jungle or by drowning. In these variants, she is portrayed as a beautiful woman who, at the last moment, reveals her true face to her prey. The last glimpse those luckless souls catch is that of a skull or the head of a horse. While not technically a woman who weeps, this siren does use her voice as lure to attract the attention of the men (Robe 1971, 113).

STRUCTURE OF THE LEGEND

The structure of the "La Llorona" legend complex has been the focus of various studies. These studies reveal that there are six distinct ways that the legend is told, as noted by Donald Ward (1991, 301):

1. a specific belief (*"The river bed is haunted . . ."*);

2. an etiological legend (*"A woman once drowned her children there . . ."*);

3. a background legend (*"That is why we don't go to the river at night."*);

4. a cautionary narrative (*"Be careful, you may meet La Llorona."*);

5. an experience legend (*"My grandfather was riding his horse there many years ago when . . ."*); and

6. a personal narrative (*"While I was driving by that spot last week . . ."*).

In addition to the ways in which the legend is transmitted, the elements of the legend have been classified. Not all elements appear in each narrative. The inclusion (and exclusion) of the elements depends on the way the legend is told, by whom, and for what purpose.

Ralph S. Boggs devised a classification system for the "La Llorona" texts in 1944. Stanley Robe later added four subcategories to accommodate additional variants that he had uncovered (Robe 1971, 110). The two major aspects of "La Llorona," the weeping woman and the siren, have individual classification systems.

Classification of "La Llorona," The Weeping Woman

    I. Where she appears.
       a. On streets
       b. Woods
       c. Beside rivers (or streams)

   II. When she appears.
       a. At midnight
       b. Any time of night
       c. By day

  III. Form in which she appears.
       a. In ordinary clothing
       b. In a shroud

    c. Is not seen; only her laments are heard
    d. As a ball of fire
    e. As a figure clothed in white
    f. As a woman with the face of an animal

IV. Why she wanders.
    a. She is looking for her lost child
    b. She is looking for her child that she has drowned
    c. She is condemned to wander after death for having killed her child(ren)

V. What she does to those she meets.
    a. Attracts men and kills them in some desolate place
    b. Asks them if they have seen her child
    c. Does nothing to them
    d. Frightens those who follow her (Robe 1980, 94)

Recently, additional adaptations to this classification system have been suggested. Mark Glazer's research concentrates on how La Llorona came to be. The most common reason given for her state is the death of her children, usually by infanticide, but what interests Glazer are the reasons that are used to explain why she murdered her children (Glazer 1985a, 207). The adapted entries are as follows:

I. How she came to be (reason for death of children).
    a. Poverty
    b. Unfaithful husband or lover
    c. Neglectful mother
    d. Immoral woman, most commonly a prostitute, who does not want children and kills them to lead the life she desires

II. Where she appears.
    a. Bodies of water
    b. Railroad tracks

III. When she appears.
    a. Any time of night

IV. Form in which she appears.
    a. A woman in white
    b. A woman with a face of an animal

Certain elements of the legend are more important than others, depending on the locality of the community. It is significant to note that the reason for the wailing of the La Llorona is not always an important factor in the tale. The most contemporary adaptations demonstrate changing economic considerations and lack of the extended family, as "La Llorona" illustrates what can happen to poverty-ridden nuclear families who do not have the support of the larger family unit.

Classification of "La Llorona," The Siren

I. A young man at night.
    a. Is on his way to a dance
    b. Is in violation of a taboo
        1. Going to a dance during Lent
        2. Being drunk on Holy Thursday
    c. Is riding home from a dance
    d. Is a taxi driver on duty
    e. Is one of a group of soldiers

II. He encounters a woman.
    a. She has particular characteristics
        1. Well dressed
        2. Dressed in white
        3. Dressed in black
        4. Wearing a black veil
        5. She is old
        6. She is cold
        7. Has long fingers and nails
    b. She is alone
        1. Walking on a country road
        2. Walking on a street at night
        3. At an abandoned house
        4. At a church
        5. At a bridge
        6. Leaving the young man's house
        7. At a river
        8. Asking for a match
        9. Picked up as fare

III. Unusual features of the encounter.
    a. Woman is a skeleton
    b. Skeleton leaves automobile while it is moving
    c. Woman turns into a skeleton
    d. Woman is the devil
    e. Woman has the face of a horse
    f. Woman disappears

IV. Reason for woman's presence.
    a. She has drowned her children in a river and God has sent her to look for them
    b. She is looking for a priest to baptize her illegitimate children
    c. She is a witch

V. Consequences of encounter.
   a. Rider rushes home as fast as he can
   b. He faints
   c. Men resolve never to follow strange women (Robe 1980, 459)

The siren aspect of the "La Llorona" legend has not adapted to modern concerns in the same way as the weeping woman aspect; therefore the elements have remained fairly stable.

FUNCTIONS OF THE LEGEND

Whatever its age or origin, the legend of La Llorona is unquestionably "a living part of Hispanic tradition, and as such needs to be examined in light of its functions and adaptations in its contemporary environment rather than its relationship to a conjectured past" (Arora 1981, 36).

When stories of La Llorona are related by children to their peers, they are told as horror stories to produce a scare. When told to children by adults, they are told as cautionary tales to encourage proper behavior or to warn against possible danger. The legends also function as morality tales to promote correct behavior in adults, particularly young married couples, young mothers, and young men with wanderlust. Thus, as with the varied aspects of La Llorona, the functions (and the content) change depending on the age, gender, locality, and purpose of the teller.

"La Llorona" as Bogey-Woman

The most interesting stories that came from my childhood were the stories that the parents and grandparents would tell you to keep you in line and were passed on to my father from his grandfather. They had to do with when they wanted to emphasize certain points, when they didn't want you out at certain days of the month, specifically on the dangerous nights of the month, like Friday night and Saturday night. They had these stories about the wailing woman, who was condemned to walk the streets late on Friday and Saturday nights, wailing because she had killed her two children. The grandparents would tell these stories with all the children around them. And I mean, you just don't question your grandmother. So they really sunk in. (Valdez 1982, 41)

Numerous sources of this tale, recalling a childhood in which the Llorona functioned as an effectively terrifying bogeyman, have mentioned specifically that she was used to keep children away from river banks, lakes, dams, or similarly dangerous spots (Arora 1981, 35). The stories, presented as true, are told to the children to warn them about what could really happen if they are outside in the dark. These versions do not dwell on the history of the woman: it is enough to know that she is outside, wailing and weeping, and looking for foolish children.

The first acknowledged appearance of La Llorona as a "scare figure" was in the first part of this century. Village priests told the stories to warn boys against attending parties or dances late at night. "And with this they motivated fear and prompted the children and boys to return home early" (Barakat 1965, 294). The warnings were not directed towards girls, as they would not have been allowed to attend dances and parties in the first place.

"La Llorona" as a Socializing Agent for Married Couples

Holly Mathews explores "La Llorona" as a morality tale in the Mexican community of Ocacan. Morality tales "attempt to inhibit immoral behaviour by depicting the terrible consequences that stem from the failure to achieve culturally prescribed goals" (1992, 139). They not only contain a great deal of information about cultural expectations for behavior but provide the basis of individual motivation. The study of this particular legend is appropriate because daily conversations are peppered with the tale, as community members use its message to both interpret local events and socialize their young. There is "an interesting divergence between the genders with respect to the way the tale is told" (127). The tales told by women detail the main character as achieving their own valued life and marital goals: being devoted wives and mothers. Children are the most important mark of achievement of adult status for the woman (141). Success for the men in the community is measured by their public status and the tales told by men reflect their important goals: providing well for their children, being well-liked in the community and having a faithful and devoted wife (144). "Although each of these stories begins with the conventionalized scenario of how marriage should proceed, the body of the plot . . . is devoted to explaining how and why the marriage goes wrong" (144). The blame always rests on the opposite sex of the teller, while the character of the same sex is always a virtuous achiever of life goals of the teller.

"La Llorona" is told to instruct unmarried youngsters about their future roles in marriage as well as to illustrate potential problems for newly married individuals. "La Llorona" is also told as a warning to spouses to respect their marriage vows and can be used to interpret ongoing marital disputes and to justify actions taken to settle the disputes (Mathews 1992, 127).

"La Llorona" as a Socializing Agent
for Young Mothers

The weeping woman in these tales would not harm a contented child but, rather, is drawn to harm children who are crying and suffering from neglect. The child is in danger from La Llorona because of the mother who does not adequately care for her child. Young mothers, faced with this graphic illustration of dire consequences, cannot afford to ignore the physical and mental well-being of their children.

There is tremendous pressure on Mexican American women to have large families. While the fathering of large families is considered to be an extremely masculine achievement, many women face unresolved fears of childbirth, poverty, and isolation. The story of "La Llorona" has two distinct functions for young mothers, depending on who is telling the tale. It functions as a catharsis for the women telling the story but also as a reinforcing message on the maternal role of mothers (Jordan 1985, 39).

"La Llorona" as a Socializing Agent
for Romantic Young Females

Young adult females who may have romantic ideas above their "station in life" are also targeted audiences of these tales (West 1988, 76). When this is the case, the telling emphasizes the wailing woman's history so the listener can benefit from the implied lesson. She learns not to harbor romantic notions about wealthy young men but instead to respect her parents' wishes and marry a suitable spouse.

"La Llorona" as a Socializing Agent
for Males

The siren aspect of La Llorona, in which she lures men to their deaths, focuses on directing the behavior of immoral married men. Virtuous men would not follow such a creature, even if she is enticing and almost irresistible. The message is loud and clear: Stay faithful to your wives and girlfriends and you will be safe from danger.

HISTORICAL ANTECEDENTS

Numerous scholars attempt to trace "La Llorona" back to its mythological roots and have described connections to the myths of the Aztecs and the tales of Europe. Several studies demonstrate a grafting of the "New World" myths on the "Old World" tales. The long history of this legend and its antecedents shows how pertinent the themes have been in the past, and suggests that the tale will have a long future, as well, as long as the theme is still pertinent to the culture in which it is being told.

New World Connections

"La Llorona" has been identified with both Aztec goddesses and Mexican "historical" figures.

Chalchiuhtliycue (Lady Precious Green)

The storm goddess and personification of whirlpools and youthful beauty in Aztec mythology is known as Chalchiuhtliycue (Mercatante 1988, 169). "She is particularly involved as a guardian goddess of young women and is responsible for unpredictable events" (Jordan 1993, 54).

Coatlicue or Cihuacoatl (The Serpent Lady)

Another Aztec goddess often identified as the ancestor of La Llorona is the mother goddess, responsible for giving the people "poverty, mental depression and sorrows," who often appears in the marketplace carrying a cradle that she leaves behind as she disappears into the lake. Inside the cradle will be found a lance point or sacrificial knife (Mercatante 1988, 183). Her voice was believed to summon war and "roar out at night as an omen" (Kirtley 1960, 164).

Dona Marina (Malinche)

Malinche is a "historical" figure instrumental in the conquest by the Spanish, led by Cortez, of her people and her land. She apparently had a son with Cortez, but after the conquest was complete, she was abandoned and never saw her lover or son again. This identification of "La Llorona" as Malinche, weeping in everlasting remorse over her betrayal of her people to the Spanish conquerors, owes more to literary sources and political symbolism than to oral tradition (Arora 1981, 27). The "Cortes variant is especially savored by militant Chicanos who have adapted it to focus resentment against the non-Mexican elements in their culture" (West 1988, 75).

Old World Connections

"La Llorona" has a possible relationship to a European legend, the story of "The White Lady," and to several ballads.

The White Lady

A very convincing argument is made for the identification of "The White Lady," of a German tale, with "La Llorona" as the grieving mother. In the story of the White Lady, a young girl becomes pregnant, gives birth, and is then abandoned by her high-born lover. In a fit of grief she murders the child and then goes insane with remorse. She dies a violent death and returns as a malign ghost and, at other times, as a siren, and is an omen of death to anyone who sees her (Kirtley 1960, 159). "La Llorona" employs European social and moral values rather than those of the New World. The Aztec social system incorporated polygyny and concubinage as acceptable forms of alliance. If not based on European values, the tragedy could not have taken place: the mistress would not have been disgarded for a more acceptable wife, she would have simply been added to the household. "The fierce sexual alliance, the intricate scruples and conventions resulting from an involved double moral standard and the intense attachment to a concept of honor felt by the legend's characters are European, and the sentiments alone give the tragedy a rationale" (162). The legend of the White Lady traveled to the New World with the explorers and local adjustments were made, incorporating a "weeping woman" from the Aztec pantheon into the legend (168).

Ballads

The motif of infanticide by either drowning or stabbing is a principal element in the "La Llorona" legends. Several European ballads also feature these "traditional" means of murdering ones' own children (Arora 1981, 29).

Frances James Child, a professor at Harvard, collected 305 distinct ballads in British tradition. "His thick five-volume collection is the basic repository of the folk ballad in English, and it is customary in ballad books to refer to a child-type ballad by the number it bears in Child's Collection, even though the title may vary from his and the version may be one he did not know" (Friedman 1956, xi).

"The Cruel Mother" (Child Ballad #20)

A young mother gives birth to two (or three) children and puts them to death by stabbing them, drowning them, or burying them alive. The ghosts return on the mother's wedding day and accuse her of murdering them. The mother responds that the devil may come for her if this is true, and he does. In other variants, the children spell out her penance:

> *"Seven years a fish in the sea,*
> *And seven years a bird in the tree.*
> *Seven years to ring a bell,*
> *And seven years porter in hell."*

"Mary Hamilton" (Child Ballad #173)

The identity of the historical Mary Hamilton is not actually known (much like La Llorona). The story tells of a young maid who is executed for drowning her newborn child, who was fathered by an aristocrat.

Literary Antecedents

Several early dramatic scripts have been credited with shaping of the contemporary image of "La Llorona" as an innocent young woman who pays dearly for her transgressions.

La Llorona: Drama en Tres Actos y un Epilogo
by Francisco Neve

Neve's drama was first presented in 1893 and has been performed as a theatrical production, a puppet play, and a motion picture. Six elements of the traditional legend have been influenced by this work, as noted by Shirley Arora (1981, 26):

1. The heroine is named "Luisa."

2. She is described as an extraordinarily beautiful but humble and virtuous young woman (not of Indian blood as in the prototype).

3. The play is set in Mexico City during the early years of the Viceregal period.

4. Luisa's lover is identified as a Spaniard of noble blood who eventually leaves her to marry a woman of his own class.

5. Luisa stabs the child or children of their union.

6. Luisa is executed or dies just before her execution, and the faithless lover also dies or commits suicide.

La Llorona *by Toscano*

Carmen Toscano modified Neve's plot in 1958 by introducing themes of racial conflict that were never part of the early versions. He did this by making Luisa of mixed blood (Arora 1981, 26).

La Llorona *by Don Vicente Riva Palacio*

This is a composite blending of the legend and a historical tragedy of Viceregal times (Janvier 1910, 164).

CASE STUDIES

Comparing two case studies of the "La Llorona" legend vividly demonstrates how the role of the storyteller and the demographics of the audience shape the legend variant and its function. Not surprisingly, in a study of adolescent girls, Bess Lomax Hawes discovers that her informants focus on the aspects of the legend that most closely relate to their own circumstances and fears and anxieties. A second study, involving young parents, illustrates the relationship, equally well, between the form of the legend, its function, and the circumstances of the community.

> After listening to only a few variants of the story told by my informants I realized that the *llorona* is an endlessly changing legend, modified by storytellers to address themes central to their own psycho-social development and lifestyles. (Jones 1988, 197)

"La Llorona in Juvenile Hall"

Bess Hawes conducted her study at the Las Palmas School for Girls, a residential facility of the Department of Correction of the County of Los Angeles, in 1965. She mentions a surprisingly large number of stories featuring malevolent female revenants, most frequently "La Llorona." Most North American revenants, Hawes points out, are indifferent male figures (1968, 154). For these girls, "La Llorona" takes on the form of either a siren or a pitiful creature who has murdered her children.

> The themes that occur most frequently are infanticide and other aggressive crimes committed *by* women, punishment or aggressive crimes committed *against* women, inconsolable grief or loss, and mutilation (another kind of loss). (164)

Rather than a clear distinction between the traditional aspects of "La Llorona," the girls embody their tales with a "multifaceted, loving-hating ghost-mother" that reflects the emotional conflicts of the delinquent female young adult (165).

"La Llorona in Oregon"

Pamela Jones interviews young immigrants from Mexico living in Southern Oregon and compares their versions of the legend complex to those of Hawes. Jones (1988, 195) finds that the legend serves a different function in this community made up of young mothers coping with poverty, children, and being far from home. In this community, the legend functions

1. as a release for parental frustrations and tensions when coping with several children;
2. as an expression for unconscious anxieties about childcare; and
3. as articulation of the difficulties of caring for children while living in poverty.

The mothers in Jones's study clearly identify with "La Llorona" as a mother figure, while the students in Hawes's study relate to her as siren and lover. The following chart shows how the different groups accounted for the disappearance of La Llorona's children.

Motivation Behind the Disappearance of La Llorona's Children

Possible Causes	Mothers	Students
Related to lover	1	10
No explanation	11	7
Due to her negligence	2	1
Due to her poverty	3	1
Disliked/tired of children	2	1
To continue her "wild life"	1	1
	20	21

(Jones 1988, 210)

Jones concludes that each group, while retaining the framework of the traditional legend, places emphasis on those details relevant to their own social roles. For example, the majority of the student group, composed of young, unmarried women, placed the greatest emphasis on the lover. The group of married mothers placed little emphasis on the role of the lover in the tragedy. Thus the legend "changes subtly in its message and its function within each group" (Jones 1988, 210).

VARIANTS OF "LA LLORONA"

The shift in population from rural to urban centers has effected a change to the legend complex. La Llorona no longer haunts only waterways. A new non-traditional site has been adopted into the legend complex: the city dump. For women in urban areas, abandoning unwanted babies in garbage dumpsters is a more modern and "efficient" method for disposing of them than drowning (Walraven 1991, 209). Dumpsters are convenient and are emptied regularly, disposing painlessly (and anonymously) of unwanted items. This method of disposal seems more "believable and appropriate to the surroundings than drowning" (211).

The term "trashcan babies," referring to this phenomenon, appeared in a letter to Ann Landers in July 1989 and was readily understood by her readers. "It would appear to fall into that category along with 'Vanishing Hitchhiker' and 'Kentucky Fried Rat' which, in a word or two, conjure an unmistakable image" (Walraven 1991, 211). The function of this variant remains the same. It is used as a scare tactic to protect children and to keep them away from dangerous places, and it serves as a moral lesson for neglectful mothers (Walraven 1991, 214).

Clarissa Pinkola Estes devotes a chapter in her book *Women Who Run with the Wolves* to "La Llorona." Estes states that the legend complex builds on the fears, anxieties, and economic conditions of each generation. Estes (1992, 301) makes references to several recent variants but does not include substantiating texts. The variants mentioned are

1. the female protagonist in a union-busting war in the north woods;

2. those involved in the forced repatriation of Mexicans for the United States in the 1950s;

3. a spook story in which she wanders and wails through a trailer park at night; and

4. a "prostitute with AIDS" tale.

Estes includes an interesting variant of "La Llorona" told by a ten-year-old boy in Colorado:

> *While pregnant with twins fathered by the rich factory owner, the young woman drank from the river which is polluted by the factories of her lover. . . . The twins were born deformed. . . . The mother was thrown over by lover [and] in her grief, she threw her children into river "because they would have such a hard life." . . . [She] fell down dead from grief, condemned to wander. . . . "Now "La Llorona" looks and looks through the polluted river for her children, but she can hardly see, for the water is so dirty and dark. Now her ghost drags the river bottom with her long fingers. Now she wanders the riverbanks calling for her children all the time."*
> (Estes 1992, 302)

Other variants have been influenced by the modern issue of border crossings between the United States and Mexico. In these variants, La Llorona's children died while crossing the border illegally (Glazer 1985b, 296). Comparing the variants with the prototype legend at the beginning of this chapter exemplifies the divergent nature of the "La Llorona" legend complex.

The weeping woman was a young Mexican woman who had an illegitimate baby. The father of the child took it away from her and drowned it in a small lake. This caused the young woman to go crazy, and she drowned herself in the same lake. She now appears during the summer months in the lake not far from shore, weeping and wailing. When a man goes out to save her, she drifts towards the middle of the lake just out of his reach. When they get to the middle of the lake, the man is exhausted. He at last reaches her and grabs her so he can bring her back to shore. But she hugs him and starts to laugh, and they both go down together. (Barakat 1965, 271)

She is a widow whose only son was lost playing near a flooded river. Insane from grief, she seeks to kidnap any small child that she sees. Often her fingerprints are found on windows, or screens are torn where she tried to enter homes. (Leddy 1948, 274)

An Indian girl, of peasant heritage and dissatisfied with her status, dresses in elaborate white garments on fiesta occasions and dances gaily with one and all. She is criticized by her peer group for leaving her two or more small children unattended on these occasions. Being resentful of these circumstances, she, in anger, drowns her children in a well, stream, or lake. . . . After the murder of her two children, the "white lady" kills herself in remorse or dies a natural death. Unable to rest in her grave, however, the ghost of the "white lady" roams as La Llorona, "the woman who weeps." (Agogino, Stevens, and Carlotta 1973, 27)

> *The llorona in this version was bathing one of her three children when she heard the phone. She answered the phone, ran out to her car, drove away and returned. The child in the bathtub drowned while unattended and the mother accidently ran over the other two with the car, one on the way out and the other on her way in. The poor woman was the victim of a series of household accidents, for which she held the blame; however she was depicted as willfully negligent.* (Jones 1988, 208)

> *In El Paso children speak of a real woman in their neighborhood who is known as La Llorona ("The Crier"). According to the story, her son was killed by a boy playing with a slingshot. Every night at eight she weeps, and if you speak while passing her house, she will put a curse on you.* (Knapp 1976, 249)

"COUSINS" OF LA LLORONA

Other cultures have their own legends of potentially dangerous women and water spirits. Close "relatives" to "La Llorona" include:

1. Banshees are bean sidheare Irish lore's "white ladies." Their wail presages a death in families to which they attach themselves. "The Caoline, the funeral cry of the Irish peasants, is said to be an imitation of the cry of the banshee" (Mercatante 1988, 108).

2. Chatalem is a supernatural temptress from the Sanpoil, a Salishan tribe of northeastern Washington. She moves through the forests and lures hunters with her beautiful and sad wailing. She keeps just beyond their sight and hunters follow her until they perish.

3. Dzelarkhons is the Haida "weeping woman" because of the dirges or traditional laments attributed to her after the destruction of the village by a volcano. Totem poles show her clutching her dead child.

4. Lamia (gluttonous, lecherous), is the malign Greek temptress of males and patroness of mysteries featuring infanticide. She became a child-killer in response to the murder of her children (with Zeus) by Hera.

5. Lilith (storm goddess), of Jewish, Christian, and Islamic mythology, is the childless demon hostile to the children of others. "Lilith is a female demon, seductress, and man-hater, sometimes called the Howling One" (Ausubel 1948, 592–94).

> In medieval Europe (especially in Germany), Lilith became a popular man-devouring creature . . . who covets other women's children, and threatens to steal them. . . . [Also] she becomes in the Middle Ages a scraggy-toothless hag. . . . Though ugly and malformed she still prevails, however, as the seductress of sleeping men. (West 1988, 36)

6. Lorelei is a water nymph of the Rhine River, whose song misleads sailors into the rocks below her perch. Her story is not a myth but based on a fabrication of Klemens Brentano who wrote *Lore Lay* in 1800. Heinrich Heine's poetic retelling made the story popular in the English-speaking world. This, in turn, brought people to the Rhine River and made Lorelei a tourist attraction.

7. Nakineiu, in Finno-Ugric mythology, is "a beautiful girl who sat on the surface of the water, on a stone on the shore, or in the shadow of a tree growing near the river, combing her long golden-yellow hair" (Mercatante 1988, 470). She bewitches men and animals with her songs until they fall into the sea and drown.

8. Ran, a Norse siren, is often seen reclining on the shores combing her hair (Mercatante 1988, 549).

9. Rusulka, a northern Slavic spirit of a maiden who was drowned by accident or by force, became a demonic being haunting the spot where she died. She often entices men with her song (Guiley 1992, 288).

10. The Sirens (Greek) are three water nymphs (Ligeia, Parthenope, and Leucosia) who lure sailors to a watery grave with their singing. They are featured in the myth of Odysseus, who sailed safely past the sirens, but also managed to hear their song by tying himself to the mast so he couldn't follow their song, and plugged the ears of his sailors with wax. Orpheus defeated their songs when the Argonauts sailed through their waters. Originally they were portrayed as great birds with the heads of women but, in later Greek art, were depicted as beautiful women.

11. The "weeping woman" myth explains the origin of the salmon-eater clan of the Tsimshians, Haidas, and the Tlinkits (Kirtley 1960, 165). The Gitrhawn (salmon-eater) tribe originally, according to the legend, had a disagreement with the Grizzly Bear tribe over a wedding taboo. The bride, the niece of the chief of the salmon-eaters, was turned into a statue in the resulting battle. Her spirit became part of the lake and would issue warnings and threats to people on the lake and at the lake shore (Barbeau 1964, 16–21).

ADDITIONAL READINGS

Anya, Rudolfo A. 1984. *The Legend of La Llorona: A Short Novel*. Berkeley: Tonatiuh-Quinto Sol International.

Cypess, Sandra Messinger. 1992. *La Malinche in Mexican Literature: From History to Myth*. Austin: University of Texas Press.

De Aragon, Ray John. 1980. *The Legend of La Llorona*. Las Vegas: Pan American.

Kraul, Edward Garcia, and Judith Beatty, ed. 1988. *The Weeping Woman: Encounters with La Llorona*. Santa Fe, NM: Word Process.

McNeil, W. K., ed. 1985. *Ghost Stories from the American South*. New York: Dell, 103–4.

Murray, Earl. 1988. *Ghosts of the Old West: Desert Spirits, Haunted Cabins, Lost Trails and Other Strange Encounters*. Chicago: Contemporary Books, 101–8.

Weigle, Marta. 1982. *Spiders and Spinsters: Women and Mythology*. Albuquerque: University of New Mexico Press, 255–59.

West, John O. 1981. "The Weeping Woman: La Llorona." *Legendary Ladies of Texas* (Texas Folklore Society #53), edited by Francis E. Abernethy. Dallas: E-Heart Press, 31–36.

Young, Richard, and Judy Dockrey Young, eds. 1991. *Ghost Stories from the American Southwest*. Little Rock, AR: August House.

———. 1993. *The Scary Story Reader*. Little Rock, AR: August House.

REFERENCES

Agogino, George A., Dominique E. Stevens, and Lynda Carlotta. 1973. Dona Marina and the legend of La Llorona. *Anthropological Journal of Canada* 11, no. 1: 27–29.

Arora, Shirley. 1981. La Llorona: The naturalization of a legend. *Southwest Folklore* 5, no. 1 (winter): 23–40.

Ausubel, Nathan. 1948. *A treasury of Jewish folklore*. New York: Crown.

Barakat, Robert A. 1965. Aztec motifs in "La Llorona." *Southern Folklore Quarterly* 29: 288–96.

Barbeau, Marius. 1964. Totem Poles. Bulletin No. 119—Volume 1 (Anthropological series #30). Ottawa: National Museum of Canada.

Estes, Clarissa Pinkola. 1992. *Women who run with the wolves: Myths and stories of the wild woman archetype*. New York: Ballantine.

Friedman, Albert B., ed. 1956. *The Viking book of folk ballads of the English-speaking world*. New York: Viking.

Glazer, Mark. 1985a. "La Llorona" in south Texas: Tradition and modernity in a Mexican American legend. In *The 8th Congress for the International Society for Folk Narrative Research, vol. 1*, edited by Reimund Kvideland and Torunn Selberg. Bergen, Norway, June 12–17, 205–16.

———. 1985b. The traditionalization of the contemporary legend: The Mexican-American example. *Fabula* 26: 288–97.

Guiley, Rosemary Ellen. 1992. *The encyclopedia of ghosts and spirits*. New York: Facts on File.

Hawes, Bess Lomax. 1968. La Llorona in juvenile hall. *Western Folklore* 27: 153–70.

Janvier, Thomas A. 1910. *Legends of the City of Mexico*. New York: Harper and Bros.

Jones, Pamela. 1988. "There was a woman": La Llorona in Oregon. *Western Folklore* 57, no. 3 (July): 195–211.

Jordan, Michael. 1993. *Encyclopedia of the gods*. New York: Facts on File.

Jordan, Rosan A. 1985. The vaginal serpent and other themes from Mexican-American women's lore. In *Women's Folklore, Women's Culture*, edited by Rosan A. Jordan and Susan J. Kalcik. Philadelphia: University of Pennsylvania Press, 26–44.

Kirtley, Bacil F. 1960. "La Llorona" and related themes. *Western Folklore* 19: 155–68.

Knapp, Mary, and Herbert Knapp. 1976. *One potato, two potato. . . . The secret education of American children*. New York: W. W. Norton.

Leddy, Betty. 1948. La Llorona in southern Arizona. *Western Folklore* 7: 272–77.

Mathews, Holly F. 1992. The directive force of morality tales in a Mexican community. In *Human motives and cultural models*, edited by Roy G. D'Andrade and Claudia Strauss. Cambridge, England: Cambridge University Press, 127–62.

Mercatante, Anthony S. 1988. *The Facts on File encyclopedia of world mythology and legend*. New York: Facts on File.

Miller, Elaine K. 1973. *Mexican folk narrative for the Los Angeles area* (American Folklore series, 56). Austin: University of Texas Press.

Robe, Stanley L. 1971. *Mexican tales and legends from Veracruz: Introduction, classification and notes* (Folklore and Mythology Studies, 23). Berkeley: University of California Press.

———. 1980. *Hispanic legends from New Mexico: Narratives from the R.D. Jameson collection* (Folklore and Mythology Studies, 31). Berkeley: University of California Press.

Russel, Louise. 1977. *Legendary narratives inherited by children of Mexican-American ancestry: Cultural plurism and the persistence of tradition*. Ph.D. diss., Indiana University.

Valdez, George, Jr. 1982. The wailing woman. In *A celebration of American family folklore: Tales and traditions from the Smithsonian collection*, edited by Steven J. Zeitlin, Amy J. Kotkin, and Holly Cutting Baker. New York: Pantheon.

Walraven, Ed. 1991. Evidence for a developing variant of "La Llorona." *Western Folklore* 50, no. 2 (April): 208–17.

Ward, Donald. 1991. On the genre morphology of legendry: Belief story versus belief legend. *Western Folklore* 50, no. 3 (July): 296–303.

West, John O. 1988. *Mexican-American folklore*. Little Rock, AR: August House.

APPENDIX:
CLASSROOM EXTENSIONS

Contemporary legends offer a glimpse into the values and worldview of specialized groups in Western society. My focus, in writing this book, has been to provide background information to foster a more complete understanding of the functions of the contemporary legends for young adults. By putting contemporary legends in perspective, teachers, librarians, parents, and storytellers gain additional insight into Western society as a whole and into the perceived role of the young adults in particular.

One of the most fascinating aspects of contemporary legends is their versatility. The focus, shape, and ultimate message of contemporary legends revolves around a myriad of variables. The teller, the audience, the setting of the legend-telling event, and the context of the telling all play a large part in the transmission of the core legend. This versatility means contemporary legends can be referred to, studied, and told in every aspect of the curriculum. The following are suggested as possible classroom discussion topics and research topics. They can be modified for any subject area and grade level.

GENERAL TOPICS

The following exercises focus on contemporary legends in general. Students can gather contemporary legends in your school and community and compare the variants, or study the role of the legend-teller in shaping the tone and message of the legends for a specific audience or purpose.

Studying the Functions of Contemporary Legends

Six different legend functions were identified in a study by Sandy Hobbs (1987, 142). The functions are:

A. Poetic justice, in which a wrongdoer is punished in some bizarre way;

B. Anxiety justified, providing "evidence" to justify an anxiety that people may be ashamed of, or find difficult to admit to;

C. "I am in the know," allowing the tellers to know something "confidential," some special knowledge, that has been hidden from others;

D. Normal behavior in inappropriate settings, allows for the breaking of social "taboos" (farting, going nude, sex play) by showing other people performing these actions at the "wrong" time;

E. Expressing inappropriate feelings, offering vicarious expression to the inappropriate feelings when they must be "hidden" in public (finding misfortune funny, having no sympathy for the deceased); and

F. Permanent representation of feelings, supporting and "objectifying" our instinct that the world is somehow "different" because of an action that has taken place.

Hobbs charted frequency of functions in the legends discussed in Brunvand's *The Vanishing Hitchhiker* (1981). He discovered that the most common functions of contemporary legends are "anxiety justified," "poetic justice," and the "expression of inappropriate feelings" (Hobbs 1987, 146). Students can conduct a similar investigation of the legends they collect, to decipher for themselves the most frequent functions of contemporary legends in their own community.

Hobbs's Chart of Contemporary Legends and Their Functions

Legend Name	Function Categories					
	A	B	C	D	E	F
Boyfriend's Death		x				
Death Car					x	
Vanishing Hitchhiker		x				x
The Hook	x	x				
Babysitter		x			x	
Alligator in Sewer		x	x		x	
Surprise Party	x			x		
Department Store Snake		x	x			
Exploding Toilet	x			x	x	

(Hobbs 1987, 144–45)

Comparing Variants

Choose a legend that has a large number of variants, such as "The Vanishing Hitchhiker," "La Llorona," "Kentucky Fried Rat," or "The Dead Cat in the Package." After reading and discussing the variants, have students write their reactions to the legends, determining common threads that link the versions, and pointing out credible, and incredible, sections of the legend. Invite speculations on why each variant was told the way it was, and on the personalities of the characters and the tellers. Can the student discern a pattern in the history of the legend that reflects the changes taking place in Western society? Is this legend unique to North America and

Europe? Why or why not? Have students compile tables to present the elements of the legends discussed in this book, in other source material, and in the community. For example Susan Domowitz (1979, 94) suggests possible headings for a schematic comparison table for "Kentucky Fried Rat":

Variant and year

Canned or packaged food/restaurant food

Human or animal part (or body)

Discovered before or after eating

Credible

Legend believed

Source cited

Contemporary Legends in Your School

Assemble an anthology of legends gathered in the community or at school. Study the ways these versions have been localized to suit local concerns and issues. It would be interesting to see how the legends of the school have grown and changed over a period of time.

Collection guidelines should be established, and students should record each legend as precisely as possible, including the following information:

1. Personal information about the collector (own name and address, the name of the informant, and relationship to the informant).

2. Source of the story: family, friends, mass media.

3. The approximate age at which the informant heard the story (and date) and where (both town location and place where the storytelling activity took place: slumber party, kitchen-table conversation, legend trip). Collect as many details about the event as possible.

4. Who else was there when the legend was first heard?

5. The effect of the story on the listeners, noting all the emotional responses that can be remembered.

6. The tone of the legend: Was it told as true? Did the teller believe it? Did the listeners? Why?

Look for a place to publish the students' papers. Local newspapers and magazines may be interested in publishing local research. The possibility of publishing articles will encourage students in their research and writing and offer them an incentive for producing accurate work. Folklore is an inexpensive source of material for financially strapped schools.

The Role of the Storyteller

One of the most interesting aspects of the contemporary legend is the way tellers alter the elements or the tone of the legend to promote their own messages. For example, in the telling of "La Llorona," the storyteller's purpose can shift the ultimate responsibility of the infanticide to the father and increase the sympathetic reaction to the mother. This is done by including and emphasizing the reasons why the mother and children are abandoned: the father wants to marry another woman; he is of a "superior" class; or he is of a different racial background than the mother (Arora 1981, 30). Sympathy builds as the storyteller relates the reasoning behind the tragic act. The mother drowns the children because she cannot bear to be reminded of their father, whom she loved so much; she is crazed with grief; or she takes to drink to forget her loss and is not responsible for her actions (Arora 1981, 31). Kraul and Beatty state their agreement to the role of the storyteller in drawing a response from the listener: "Whether these children have been lost, accidently drowned or murdered outright by their infamous mother depends upon the storyteller" (1988, xii). Students can examine other tales to discover how the storyteller has manipulated story elements to shape the audience's response.

STEREOTYPES, CLICHÉS, AND THE WORDS WE USE

Both "stereotype" and "cliché" were originally printing terms referring to the metal sheets, developed in the late 18th century, on which whole pages of type could be cast. However, "the too obvious, too familiar formulations or observations that these terms are now used to describe, observations as invariant as the words molded on those metal stereotypes or clichés, predate the printing press" (Stephens 1988, 138). Preset, formulaic phrasings are crucial memory aids in oral cultures, but today, resorting to stereotypes and clichés exacts a cost on the news, as it does on any form of communication. "The idiosyncrasies of individual events are lost when they are illustrated by familiar pictures, described in familiar words and shaped into familiar themes" (Stephens 1988, 138).

Many of our most familiar clichés have resulted from our observations of the natural world. Because certain creatures repeatedly show up in our contemporary legends and our speech patterns, closer examination of these terms seems appropriate.

"Frog in the Throat"

This expression, which means a temporary loss of voice or extreme hoarseness, may have a literal history dating back to the time of Doctor Mor, who instructed Doctor Ban in matters connected with second sight. Dr. R. F. MacLagan, in his paper on the Macbeths of Islay, made the following reference. Notice the parallels between this tale and the legends of "contaminated water" and "diet pills" introduced in chapter 7.

Two young girls were singing at a ceilidh one harvest evening in a croft by the side of Loch Feuchian, when one of them, who had a beautiful voice, seemed suddenly to choke and complained of severe pain. A member of the Clan MacConnachair, who happened to be present, sent for Doctor Ban. . . . The doctor said "that I see that there is a frog in the girl's stomach." The girl, overhearing what the doctor had remarked, got into a dreadful state. The doctor thereupon said to her: "You must eat no meat and drink no drink till I come to you again, and make sure of that." A few hours later, the doctor returned, applied the hot lid of a pot to her stomach, took a piece of flesh and roasted it before her mouth. The girl became very sick, and the

> *animal came out of her mouth towards the flesh whenever it felt the smell*
> *of it. After putting up the frog, the girl became quite well. It was going to*
> *start back when the man put his hand on the girl's mouth and caught the*
> *beast, and told her she had drank it from the stream when she was thirsty,*
> *and when it was but small. And they took the beast away with them alive.*
> (Robertson 1964, 111–12)

Other less exotic explanations for this expression hark back to medicinal practices of the Middle Ages. Throat infections were treated by first putting a live frog head into the patient's mouth. It was thought that the frog, by inhaling, would draw out the infection into its own body (Ammer 1989, 184).

Spiders and Spinning

The English word "spider" is derived from an Old English verb *spinnan* "to spin." Words and phrases related to spiders and spinning include:

"Spinster," defined by the *Oxford English Dictionary* as a woman (or, rarely, a man) who spins, especially one who practices spinning as a regular occupation. The second definition, and the more common, was appended to names of women, originally to denote their occupation, but subsequently (from the 17th century) as the proper legal designation of one still unmarried. It now carries the connotation of an old maid.

"To spin a yarn" means to tell a story. The term is a nautical expression from the days when sailors kept themselves entertained and made the time pass a little more quickly by telling stories while sitting on the deck and making spun yarn, repairing fishing nets, and doing other rope work (Evans 1981, 1059).

"A web or the web of life" refers to the destiny of an individual from the cradle to the grave. An allusion to the three Fates who, according to classical mythology, spin the thread of life; weave the thread of life, the pattern being the events that occur; and cut the thread, ending the life (Evans 1981, 1181).

Other clichés and sayings involving spiders, spinning, and webs include: "web of deceit" and "Oh, what a tangled web we weave." Have students research the origins of these sayings, and other related words such as "cobwebs," to enrich their vocabulary and creative writing projects.

Cats, Dogs, Mice, Rats, and Snakes

Have students research the meaning (and origin, wherever possible) for the following words and phrases: "It's raining cats and dogs"; "catgut"; "catty"; "let the cat out of the bag"; "Who will bell the cat?"; "like a cat on a hot tin roof"; "kitty-corner"; "to be made a cat's paw"; "to fight like Kilkenny cats"; "to grin like a Cheshire cat"; "the hair of the dog that bit you"; "Doggone it!"; dog-tired"; "to put on the dog"; "let sleeping dogs lie"; "to lead a dog's life"; "going to the dogs"; "dog days"; "love me, love my dog"; "dogfight"; "underdog"; "dog eat dog"; "dog in the manger"; "pup-tent"; "Are you a mouse or a man?"; "build a better mousetrap"; "You dirty rat!"; "to smell a rat"; and "snake in the grass."

How do these terms reflect our preoccupations and our perceptions of these various species? As can be seen from the above examples, dogs do not fare well in the English language, and in fact, a term involving dogs is often negative and demeaning (Ammer 1989, 13). Earlier we saw that dogs are often respected in our mythology. Why is this respect not reflected in our speech?

Selective Reference Titles

Other helpful titles include:

Beidermann, Hans. 1992. *Dictionary of Symbolism: Cultural Icons and the Meanings Behind Them.* Translated by James Hulbert. New York: Facts on File.

Ciardi, John. 1987. *Good Words to You: The All-New Browser's Dictionary and Native's Guide to the Unknown American Language.* New York: Harper & Row.

Dolan, Edward F. 1992. *Animal Folklore: From Black Cats to White Horses.* New York: Ivy Books.

Freeman, Morton S. 1992. *Even-Steven and Fair and Square: More Stories Behind the Words.* New York: Plume.

———. 1985. *The Story Behind the Word.* Philadelphia: isi Press.

Leach, Maria, ed. 1972. *Funk & Wagnalls Standard Dictionary of Folklore, Mythology and Legend.* New York: Funk & Wagnalls.

Mercante, Anthony S. 1988. *The Facts on File Encyclopedia of World Mythology and Legend.* New York: Facts on File.

Weigle, Marta. 1982. *Spiders & Spinsters: Women and Mythology.* Albuquerque: University of New Mexico Press.

TRADITIONAL CONNECTIONS

The term contemporary, in reference to these legends, is very relative. Numerous connections have been made throughout the discussions in the text to possible ancestors of these legends in the world of metaphor, folklore, and history. Contemporary legends can function as *pourquoi tales;* they frequently involve traditional scapegoats and other strangers as antagonists; and they maintain our fascination with thieves and other outlaws.

Pourquoi Tales

Each culture has tales that helped early citizens understand the mysterious in the natural world around them. The explanations in these stories ranged from the stars in the heavens to the shape and size of the tails of the animals they saw each day. The stories make use of observation skills that may not be in much evidence today. Define and explore the "how and why" stories of previous cultures. How did early cultures explain scientific phenomena such as the changing of seasons, unexplained objects in the sky, and animal and plant characteristics?

Spiders in History

Several historical events and the safety of the men involved are woven into the webs of spiders. While the great Frederick II of Prussia was at Sans-Souci, he went into his anteroom to drink a cup of chocolate, but set his cup down to fetch a handkerchief. On his return, he found a great spider had fallen from the ceiling into his cup. He called for fresh chocolate and the next moment heard the report of a pistol. The cook had been suborned to poison the chocolate and, supposing he had been found out, shot himself. According to tradition, Frederick II had a spider painted on the ceiling of his room in Sans-Souci in remembrance of this event (Evans 1981, 1059).

When Mohammed fled from Mecca, he hid in a certain cave, with the Koreishites close upon him. Suddenly an acacia in full leaf sprang up at the mouth of the cave, a wood-pigeon had its nest in the branches, and a spider had woven its net between the tree and the cave. When the Koreishites saw this, they felt persuaded that no one could have entered recently and they went on (Evans 1981, 1059).

In 1306, Robert Bruce began a resistance to Edward I's domination of Scotland and was crowned King at Scone. The story is that, when in hiding on the island of Rathlin, he noticed a spider try six times to fix its web on a beam in a ceiling. "Now shall this spider [said Bruce] teach me what I am to do, for I have also failed six times." The spider made a seventh effort and succeeded. Bruce thereupon left the island (1307) with 300 followers, landed at Carrick, and at midnight surprised the English garrison in Turnberry Castle. His successes steadily grew until, in 1314, he routed the English at the great victory of Bannockburn (Evans 1981, 1059).

Discuss the different attributes of the spiders in these legends. Do we have comparable culture heroes who display these attributes? What would happen today if someone saw a spider "and it sat down beside her?"

String Games

In his classic 1907 study *Games of the North American Indians*, anthropologist Stewart Culin notes: "My informant in Zuni stated that the cat's cradle was called *pichowaini* or *pishkappoa*, the netted shield . . . which was supposed to have been carried by the War God. The idea is borrowed from the spider web, and cat's cradle was taught to the little boys, the twin War Gods, by their mother, the Spider Woman, for their amusement" (Weigle 1982, 3). The Navajos believe that the string games were taught by Spider Woman—on one condition—to be played only in the winter (Weigle 1982, 4).

Examine the traditional string games that evolved in various cultures around the world and note similarities and differences. String games are important to the Inuit (Eskimo) culture, several Native American cultures, the Aborigines of Australia, and many African tribes. Are string games still important in these cultures? Why did Spider Woman demand that the game only be played in winter?

Most North American children are familiar with the string game "cat's cradle" without realizing its long and varied history. My university students spend hours attempting to master simple figures only to realize that their hands and fingers are not as flexible as they should be!

Traditional Scapegoats

Define "scapegoats" and have students research those who have been made scapegoats throughout history. Were these scapegoats persecuted for religious, political, or economical reasons? What roles have supernatural groups such as werewolves, vampires, and witches traditionally played in societal reaction to change?

Several articles have marked the resemblance of society's reaction to modern satanic cult legends to the witch hunts of the Inquisition and beyond. One of the most famous witch hunts was in Salem, Massachusetts. How did it start and why did it finally run its course? Discuss the implications of such witch hunts to today's social and political climate.

Famous Thieves

> As noble champions of social equality, stealing the ill-gotten gains of the rich and distributing them among the poor, robbers are romantic symbols of protest against unequal distribution of property; for the psychologist, they may symbolize the rebellion of the young against authority and parental (especially paternal) power. (Biedermann 1992, 286)

Is the romantic image of the "highwayman" still valid today? Although the thieves discussed in chapter 8 are more famous for their foolishness and greed than for their cleverness, there are numerous famous thieves and thefts in folklore. Compare the exploits of the following reknowned characters. Are there any parallels? Major differences? What did they steal and why?

Hermes (Mercury)—Greek god of commerce and industry, associated especially with prosperity and the merchant class. He is both associated with profit and referred to as the god of thieves (Biedermann 1992, 220).

Till Eulenspiegel—Hero and title of a 16th-century German chapbook, a collection of satirical tales pointed at certain class distinctions of the period and region. The tales recount a long series of jests and pranks demonstrating the superior wit of the clever peasant (often under the guise of thick-headedness) over the typical townsman (Leach 1972, 1114).

Robin Hood—English ballad hero; noble robber who steals from the rich to give to the poor. He was believed to be Robert Fitzooth, the outlawed Earl of Huntington. Numerous novels, operas, and films are based on this legendary thief.

Theft of Thor's Hammer—Thor used his hammer to bless weddings on Thursday (Thor's day). The hammer, Mjolnir, was stolen by the giant Thrym who demanded the goddess Freyja as ransom payment. Thor disguising himself as the "willing" bride to retrieve his hammer makes for one of the funniest episodes in Norse mythology.

Yankee Tricksters—Originally, the sharp Yankee was a development of the green Yankee or comic countryman, who, like his prototype, the English Yorkshire clown, was often more rogue than fool. In his general capacity of "practical wag" and good-natured rogue, the sharp Yankee fitted naturally into the traditional pattern of trickster and trickster-tricked stories (Leach 1972, 1187). The most famous of all Yankee peddlers was Sam Slick, created by a Nova Scotia judge, Thomas Chandler Haliburton, in 1836.

Fox—In many folklore traditions, the fox represents cunning and trickery. In Norse myth, the fox was the symbolic animal of the trickster Loki. Many languages contain proverbial references to a fox preaching to geese—a crafty sermon in the fox's own interest. The most famous fox is Reynard, the main character of a French epic that appeared in Europe around the 11th century.

Dymas—The traditional name for the penitent thief who suffered with Christ at the Crucifixion. In Longfellow's play *The Golden Legend* (*The Miracle Play, V*), he belonged to a band of robbers who molested the Holy Family on their flight into Egypt (Evans 1981, 372).

Native American Folklore—Thefts of major and minor order form the bases for several tale plots or appear as incidents in various North American tales. One of the most popular is a tale that concerns the theft of fire, light, or the sun.

Other Strangers

How different are contemporary legends from classical and biblical myths in which disguised strangers welcomed into the home are really gods, and kindness is rewarded with riches? The modern inclination to turn away pleas for help becomes more understandable when we realize that modern communication heaps upon us more tragedies and requests for assistance than any one person can manage, either practically or psychologically. These legends are an appropriate and effective way to release the guilt and frustration arising from our inadequacy. What myths reward kindness of strangers? Do any of our contemporary legends even approach the topic?

Inadvertent Cannibalism in Mythology

Several contemporary legends make reference to inadvertent cannibalism: "The Stolen Liver," "The Pickled Hand" and other cadaver stories, and "Grandma's Ashes." This theme is not new. Research classic mythology for evidence of inadvertent cannibalism. Two myths, that of Thyestes and Tantalus, both include this element. What is the function of the cannibalism in these tales? What is the function in other tales? Does cannibalism figure in myths of other cultures as well?

The Deadly Sins

The cardinal (deadly) sins are personified in the visual arts as characters of distaste, often doing battle with the virtues. Covetousness (Avarice or Greed) is represented by a man sitting on a money-chest, and Deceit is shown as a snake with a human head and the tail of a scorpion (Biedermann 1992, 367).

What are the deadly sins? How are they portrayed? Explore the use of these symbols in the history of art. Would people today readily recognize these symbols? Or the sins?

EXPLORING MODERN ATTITUDES
AND VALUES

Our modern value systems are shaped by both traditional systems and modern speculation. However, while the beliefs surrounding AIDS-lore bear a close resemblance to the beliefs of earlier plagues, our attitude towards food and waste have undergone an almost complete reversal. The following discussion topics explore some of these dichotomies.

The Plague: Boccaccio and Defoe

Both authors were referred to when discussing the historical antecedents of the AIDS-as-plague folklore. Defoe offered an eyewitness account of the Black Plague. However, he was only a child of five or six in 1665! Thus he relied on local gossip and legend to fill in the blanks of his "memory." *A Journal of the Plague Year* brims with accounts of "old wives tales," local scandal, and gossip. Defoe stated that "I could give a great many such stories as these, diverting enough, which in the long curse of that dismal year I met with—that is, to say, true in the general for no man could at such a time learn all the particulars" (Smith 1990, 131).

Smith states that "beside providing us with an array of legends, Defoe (like Pepys and other writers) left us much more, in that they describe the health systems and belief systems which fostered the spread of the disease and the spread of rumours" (Smith 1990, 131–32).

Examine the works of these authors to ascertain the state of the health systems, the transmission of disease, and the legends and gossip included in their works.

Boccaccio, Giovanni. *The Decameron*. Translated and introduced by G. H. McWilliam. Harmondsworth: Penguin, 1972. [Mature content]

Defoe, Daniel. *A Journal of the Plague Year: Being Observations or Memorials of the Most Remarkable Occurances as Well as Private, Which Happened in London During the Last Great Visitation in 1665: Written by a Citizen who Continued All the While in London*. London: Nutt, 1772. Quotations taken from the Penguin edition (1986), edited by Anthony Burgess.

Origin of AIDS

The present head of the WHO's [World Health Organization] AIDS program refused to discuss the [green monkey] theory, saying, "The origin of the AIDS virus is of no importance to science. . . . Any speculation on how it arose is of no importance." (Ellis 1992, 8)

If the origin of the virus is of no importance, then why would the general population attempt to explain, through rumor and legend, its beginnings? Do the sciences not have a responsibility to the general population to discover not only cures but also preventive actions?

For a case of an American infected with a fatal monkey virus through Salk vaccine, see Harold L. Klawans's *Toscanini's Fumble* (New York: Bantam, 1989), 113–28.

Drugs, Magic, and the Supernatural

Contemporary legends often point to areas of concern in our society. However, they frequently refer to concerns that are not, in actuality, real threats.

The Popularity of LSD

"It seems paradoxical that this LSD alert takes place at a time when the use of the drug has reached its lowest recorded level" (Renard 1991, 19). Discuss the possible reasons for the paradox in the statement issued in response to an LSD-laced tattoo transfer alert.

Deviance

While both colonial and modern legends often center around fear, the nature of the threat has changed over the years. Supernatural elements such as witches, vampires, vengeful spirits, and ghost ships inhabit earlier frightening legends. The fear in modern legends is generated by adversaries found in the rational world of everyday life: kidnappers, demented murders, and impersonal institutions are today's enemies (Bell 1991, 114).

Crime—One of the first questions that we can ask ourselves when the topic turns to crime is: Why is there such a fascination with crime-related stories, both in the news media and in entertainment? Is this a recent trend? Is crime on the rise or is our awareness of it heightened by the mass media?

Corporate Deviance—The American public sees the potential political diversity in America, thanks to the media that tends to emphasize such divergences. Therefore, the public is willing to believe that some corporations have hidden, deviant agendas, and that they trick consumers into supporting their goals. All of these deviant groups have common elements, noted by Gary Alan Fine (1990, 143):

1. They are believed to be secret, with rites and rituals of which the public is largely unaware. They have kept their activities out of the public eye and so, the public can believe nearly anything of them: high levels of *secrecy*.

2. Members of these groups are believed to share common goals and values and to hold these strongly. Members are highly committed to the group and are willing to do whatever the authorities in the group ask: high levels of *internal coherence*.

3. These groups are believed to be working against the interests of most Americans. This provides a need for secrecy and internal coherence: perceived as *hostile*.

Fine states that these three factors, taken together, provide the rationale for certain groups to be the focal points of rumors and legends (1990, 143). In contrast, the companies themselves are well-known corporations that deal directly with the consumer. "These rumors symbolically mirror the ambivalence between knowledge of the product and ignorance of the individuals who direct the creation and marketing of these products" (Fine 1990, 144).

Degrees of Satanic Interest—Social analyses indicate that there are three levels, or degrees, of satanic interest, noted by Stevens (1989, 16):

1. The healthy curious: intelligent young people in high schools and colleges who are curious about this widespread phenomenon.

2. "Dabblers," who embrace deviant lifestyles for whatever reason: the mystery and exclusiveness of joining or establishing a "satanic cult" and the appealing fact that it is anathema to authorities. These groups meet irregularly and make haphazard use of satanic signs and "engage in concocted macabre 'rituals' often involving animal mutilation and drugs and alcohol." These dabblers are usually ephemeral but are deeply disturbing to their communities. These constitute the vast majority of satanists today, and provide nearly all the "evidence" for journalists, police, and "experts."

3. "Hard core" satanists who are of two streams: those "respectable" satanists who conduct their own versions of the Black Mass involving mainly kinky sex and no blood; and a very few deeply disturbed sociopathic individuals who may become obsessed with their versions of something like satanism or who, because of the extreme brutality of their crimes, may be so identified by the public.

Do you agree with this analysis? Why or why not?

Censorship Attempts—Classrooms and school libraries are specific targets of groups who wish to monitor not only the material their own children are hearing, reading and studying, but also the material of their neighbor's children. In a large majority of the cases, this censorship is accomplished silently and a minority of the population regulate the subject matter of books in the library collection, the type of author visits, and the subject matter researched in school projects. The major fear reflected in these censorship challenges in recent years has been that of satanic influence and worship. To understand the rationale behind these fears as well as to provide informed choices for student and parents, satanic contemporary legends can be studied in the schools. "Folklore in Education" programs should explore the *social* dimensions of this type of folklore: its power to motivate people and the development and direction of demonologies and fear that are disruptive and divisive in the school and the community (Stevens 1989, 21). Fears of satanism can be diffused by an understanding of historical antecedents as well as the role of satanic legends today.

Has the community and school had censorship challenges lately? How were the challenges handled? Who was involved in the final decision? What do these challenges tell you about the community as a whole?

Modern Ghost Beliefs

Gillian Bennett, in her exploration of the supernatural "The Vanishing Hitchhiker," maintains that one of the central aspects of the legend, the ghost's behavior, is as highly influenced by cultural and historical factors as by less significant details such as the mode of transportation. "The pattern seems to be that it is the unresponsive ghost which appears in modern city streets, prophetic ghosts which appear in rural areas, and dangerous ghosts who appear in older versions" (1984, 49). This pattern reflects the supernatural beliefs of each community: "the prevalence of the neutral, silent, unresponsive ghost in the modern story is a reflection of the prevalence of neutral, silent, unresponsive ghosts in modern urban ghost beliefs" (Bennett 1984, 49). Do you agree? Why or why not?

A further discussion on the role of ghost beliefs can be found in Gillian Bennett's *Traditions of Belief: Women, Folklore and the Supernatural Today* (New York: Penguin, 1987).

In early exploration of a "true" ghost story, "The Ghost of Cline Avenue," Philip Brandt George determines that this tale actually consists of three distinct or separate stories. The first is the *encounter* that "tells of what happens when a human meets or sees the ghost" (1972, 59). In his investigation, George found that the encounter tales were very similar to the tales of "The Vanishing Hitchhiker" but did not include the traditional denouement in which the ghost is identified. The second part of the tale is the *search*, or the description of the attempt to find the young woman who disappeared. George declares that this part of the tale is told for one of two reasons: to give proof that the ghost really exists (search parties do not gather for no reason) and to add some humor by showing that many people can be taken in by a tale (1972, 61). The final aspect of the tale is the origin, which is "the explanation of who the ghost is and why she is haunting the area" (1972, 610). The three parts of the tale are not told in any particular order and are not told as a set. They are usually part of the normal conversational flow and are stimulated by the topic under discussion. Slumber parties are the only place they are told as a whole, and they are told specifically to frighten participants. Naturally enough, in this situation, the emphasis is on the encounter.

In conversational retellings, the origin has often been neglected and, with the passing of the tale, forgotten, so the listeners have had to develop their own explanations for the ghost (1972, 67).

> Thus each group, ethnic, economic, and generational, has relied on some past known event, such as an accident or fire, or on some already known figure, such as La Llorona, or murder victim, to supply an identity and an explanation. As a result of the ethnic mixture and the transience of the population, these traditions have passed among many groups to form the complex situation as it appears now. (1972, 67)

George concludes that

> to validate this tentative explanation of events, in the future, greater attention must be paid to the understanding of the entire region in terms of its history, development, movement of ethnic groups, immigration, the role of mass media in dissemination and verification of their reports, and the nature of intergroup contacts and relations. (1972, 68)

Magic?

> One function of legend is to "name" previously undefined threats and by doing so gain psychological control over them. By extension, when people change their behavior based on such legends, they are engaging in magical practices, whether they perceive them as overtly superstitious or as "good common sense," since their actions do not act directly on the threat but simply reassure individuals that they are somehow controlling their fates. (Ellis 1990, 31)

Identify and discuss what Ellis means by magical practices.

The "Mad Scientist"

Fear of technology is evident not only in our contemporary legends but in the popular culture industries of film and horror tales. One of the characters that has had prominence since the time of Shelley's *Frankenstein* is that of the mad scientist. Another famous mad scientist is Dr. Jekyll, whose evil alter ego, Mr. Hyde, was the result of chemical experiments. Various comic book superheroes were created through misadventure with science and technology. There is now a developing subgenre in horror fiction: medical horror and the evil scientist/doctor.

Explore the historical foundation of this subgenre and examples of the motif.

Changing Attitudes Toward Food and Waste

Bengt af Klintberg comments that today's attitude toward food is opposite to that of the attitude of the old peasant self-subsistent economy. "In a time when it was possible to scrutinize all the stages of food preparation and when a shortage of food was a familiar threat, it became important to maintain the norm that nothing should be wasted" (Klintberg 1981, 157). The folklore of peasant society, therefore, teaches that food, regardless of possible contamination, should not be wasted. Compare the attitudes of the peasant society with those of today in respect to all aspects of food preparation (acquiring, preparing, and preserving) and handling of wastes related to food preparation.

"Trashcan Babies"

In the contemporary versions of the "La Llorona" legend discussed in chapter 12, briefly described is the transference of the setting from the waterways to the sanitation dumps of large urban centers. In his article on the subject, Ed Walraven asks the question, "What other factors have contributed to the concept that our children may become or have become throw-away items?" His answers (and further questions) include the dissolution of the nuclear family and traditional family values. How does the erosion of the extended family affect modern family members? Do modern urban residents have a sense of place and community?

Walraven's final question is: "Now that we may fancy ourselves too sophisticated to be scared by traditional stories of supernatural evil, do we latch on in a macabre fashion to the unnatural evil practiced by people who might live just next door, people who might scurry in the night to leave a bundle at the corner dumpster?" (Walraven 1991, 211).

UFOs

The literature on unidentified flying objects (UFOs) "provides an excellent opportunity to examine the position that rumor material interacts with, and changes into, other folklore forms" (Bird 1979, 104). Reports appear as rumors, legends, and personal anecdotes about seeing UFOs, about being "abducted," and as news items, including magazine articles, about the "cover-ups" involved. Research and discuss the various aspects of UFO-lore and its relationship to gossip, rumors, and contemporary legend. As research and publication in this area has recently accelerated, there should be no shortage of primary and secondary material for students.

COMMUNICATION

Contemporary folklore figures prominently in all aspects of modern communication, from face-to-face interaction and telephone conversations to the mass media. The following topics delve into additional facets of our modern communication channels.

Contemporary Legends on the Pulpit

Parallels have been seen between contemporary legends and stories told as examples or models in medieval sermons, and, as can be seen in the section on the "Kit Kat" legend (chapter 8), many of these tales are still being used today in sermons. FOAFTALE NEWS editor Bill Ellis argues that "preachers and ministers play a bigger role than we suspect in circulating stories such as this." He then asks the following question: "Have church-going readers encountered other legends told as sermon illustrations?" (1992, 11).

Informal Communication Networks

As mentioned earlier, reports of animal mutilations continue on specialized networks that resemble a *legend conduit*. Degh and Vazsonyi observed about legend conduits: "in a natural setting tradition-bearers did not communicate information to everyone they knew; rather, they formed specific alliances based on shared beliefs and interests, and selectively passed on messages through this conduit" (Ellis 1991, 48). The networks generate a sense of belonging, a sense of self-identity, and share specialized information in the same way as did traditional folk conduits. They supplement face-to-face communication, however, with modern communication media "such as telephones, newsletters, and personal computer listings" (Ellis 1991, 49). Compare the function of traditional folk conduits with those of modern media.

Because the primary means of transmission of "LSD-laced Tattoo Transfer" legends was through flyers and computer networks, a definite dissemination pattern can be established. Follow the legend from its apparent beginnings in North America through Europe. Some of the European transmissions originated on American military bases.

Telephone Pranks

Research telephone pranks. Ask students if they ever attempted to trick someone on the telephone. Why? What is going to happen now that technology seems intent on making sure everyone is "secure" with telephone features such as "call display" and "call screen"? For further resources on telephone pranks, see:

Dresser, Norine. 1973. "Telephone Prank." *New York Folklore Quarterly* 29: 121–30.

Dundes, Alan. 1966. "Some Minor Genres of American Folklore." *Southern Folklore Quarterly* 30: 21–22.

Jorgensen, Marilyn. 1984. "A Social-Interactional Analysis of Phone Pranks." *Western Folklore* 43: 83–103.

Gossip as Art

To balance the concept of gossip as a gender-based activity (see below), Patricia Spacks refers to a study by Roger Abrahams in Richland Park, Saint Vincent, British West Indies. There "peasants believe that gossip involves an 'art' comparable to that demonstrated in composing stories or speeches.... The behaviour involved in gossip, they feel, is potentially disruptive but vital to individual and community life." Gossip is categorized as " 'nonsense' performance, unlike the 'sensible' behaviour which demonstrates order and decorum, the products of knowledge" (Spacks 1985, 47). Is gossip a necessity? Is it a performance art in Western society? For further reading, see:

Abrahams, Roger D. 1970. "A Performance-Centred Approach to Gossip." *Man: The Journal of the Royal Anthropological Institute* 5: 291, 293–94.

FOLKLORE OF WOMEN

"La Llorona": Expressing the Worldview of a Culture

"Folklore is an important means of expressing attitudes, ideology, and world-view, whether consciously or unconsciously" (Jordan 1985, 27). Jordan suggests that people should use folklore as a source for information about values and concerns. Using the versions and discussions of "La Llorona," examine how Mexican American women view their culturally assigned roles. What are their attitudes towards maternal activities and the stresses that are related to that role? Is the historical background of "La Llorona" important in these stories? Why or why not?
Discuss the following quotation:

> Women's folklore can be an important means of indicating differences in male and female ethos and worldview and exposing ideologies that have been accepted as representing the total culture as reflecting only a male ideal. (Jordan 1985, 42)

Is this true of the "La Llorona" legend? What of other cultural interpretations of the role of women in society?

The Gender of Gossip

Patricia Spacks quotes a social anthropologist who studied a village in the French Alps:

> For men to sit around in public and gossip is quite acceptable since, it is generally assumed, that this exchange is a friendly, sociable, light-hearted, altruistic exchange of news, information and opinion. But if women are seen talking together, then something quite different is happening: very likely they are indulging in gossip, malice, "character assassination." (1985, 38)

The actual topics of discussion are never described by the anthropologist; he concerns himself only with its interpretations. "What, after all, *could* women be talking about? Lacking public occupation, with no responsibilities for the world's important affairs, they must be discussing other people" (Spacks 1985, 38). The anthropologist infers that what the women are saying must be dangerous as he makes use of an ancient metaphor, "character assassination" (Spacks 1985, 38).

Spacks comments that all attempts to relate the habit of gossip to women rests on the assumption that the act of gossiping involves weakness of character or actual sin. Contemporary women are sensitive to the stereotype of the woman gossip that men still casually evoke, even when the men know better (Spacks 1985, 41).

Are females still stereotyped as gossips? Do males gossip? What is your interpretation of a gossip? Is gossip necessarily negative?

"Passive Princesses"

The theme of the "passive princess" continues to be imbedded in our contemporary tales. Do our tales show level-headed, quick-thinking women, or do the female characters passively await rescue? Whether the passive woman is locked in a car while her boyfriend goes for help, is locked in her dorm room awaiting her roommate's return, or baby-sitting sleeping children, she is terrified but helpless to remove herself from the dangerous situation. That deed is left to someone else: a heroic rescuer who is always male.

Contemporary legends such as "The Roommate's Death" present a dichotomy for the tellers and audience. At the same time as it presents a method for coping with possible disturbing elements in the world of female students away from home for the first time, it also contributes to the anxiety and tension in the lives of these concerned individuals. Beverly Crane, in 1976, theorized that the story is popular in environments "where there is a sharp contrast between what is expected of a woman by her family and society and what is expected of her in a college or high school situation" (page 147).

Has this dichotomy shifted in the last 20 years? Are young women still receiving the same contradictory messages in the contemporary legends being transmitted today? What does this tell us about our society and the female's role? Do males face similar contradictory messages in contemporary legends?

REFERENCES

Ammer, Christine. 1989. *It's raining cats and dogs . . . and other beastly expressions.* New York: Paragon House.

Arora, Shirley. 1981. La Llorona: The naturalization of a legend. *Southwest Folklore* 5, no. 1 (winter): 23–40.

Beidermann, Hans. 1992. *Dictionary of symbolism: Cultural icons and the meanings behind them,* translated by James Hulbert. New York: Facts on File.

Bell, Michael E. 1991. I know it's true because it happened to my best friend's cousin: The modern legend in America. In *Courtly love in the shopping mall: Humanities programming for young adults,* edited by Evelyn Shaevel. Chicago: American Library Association, 109-28.

Bennett, Gillian. 1984. The phantom hitchhiker: Neither modern, urban nor legend? In *Perspectives on contemporary legend*, edited by Paul Smith, Sheffield England: Sheffield Academic Press, 45-63.

Bird, Donald Allport. 1979. *Rumor as folklore: An interpretation and inventory*. Ph.D. diss., Indiana University.

Brunvand, Jan Harold. 1981. *The vanishing hitchhiker*. New York: W. W. Norton.

Crane, Beverly. 1976. The structure of value in "The roommate's death": A methodology for interpretive analysis of folk legends. *Journal of the Folklore Institute*, 13: 133–49.

Domowitz, Susan. 1979. Foreign matter in food: A legend type. *Indiana Folklore* 12: 86–95.

Ellis, Bill. 1990. The devil-worshippers at the prom: Rumor-panic as therapeutic magic. *Western Folklore* 49 (January): 27–49.

———. 1991. Cattle mutilation: Contemporary legends and contemporary mythologies. *Contemporary legend* 1: 39–80.

———. 1992. *Legends and Life* 27 (September): 8–10.

Evans, Ivor H., ed. 1981. *Brewer's dictionary of phrase & fable*. New York: Harper & Row.

Fine, Gary Alan. 1990. Among those dark satanic mills: Rumors of kooks, cults and corporations. *Southern Folklore* 47: 133–46.

George, Philip Brandt. 1972. The Ghost of Cline Avenue: "La Llorona" in the Calumet region. *Indiana Folklore* 5: 56–91.

Hobbs, Sandy. 1987. The social psychology of a "good" story. In *Perspectives on contemporary legend, vol. II*, edited by Gillian Bennett, Paul Smith, and J. D. A. Widdowson [CECTAL Conference Papers #5]. Sheffield, England: University of Sheffield Press, 133-48.

Jordan, Rosan A. 1985. The vaginal serpent and other themes from Mexican-American women's lore. In *Women's Folklore, Women's Culture*, edited by Rosan A. Jordan and Susan J. Kalcik. Philadelphia: University of Pennsylvania Press, 26-44.

Klintberg, Bengt af. 1981. Modern migratory legends in oral tradition and daily papers. *Arv* 37: 153-60.

Kraul, Edward Garcia, and Judith Beatty, eds. 1988. *The weeping woman: encounters with La Llorona*. Santa Fe, NM: Word Process.

Leach, Maria, ed. 1972. *Funk & Wagnalls standard dictionary of folklore, mythology and legend*. New York: Funk & Wagnalls.

Renard, Jean-Bruno. 1991. LSD tattoo transfers: Rumor from North America to France. *Folklore Forum* 24, no. 2: 3–26.

Robertson, Ronald MacDonald. 1964. *More highland folktales*. Edinburgh: Oliver & Boyd.

Smith, Paul. 1990. "AIDS—Don't die of ignorance"—Exploring the cultural complex. In *A nest of vipers: perspectives on contemporary legend, vol. V*, edited by Gillian Bennett and Paul Smith. Sheffield, England: Sheffield Academic Press, 113-41.

Spacks, Patricia Meyer. 1985. *Gossip*. New York: Alfred A. Knopf.

Stephens, Mitchell. 1988. *A history of news: From the drum to the satellite*. New York: Viking.

Stevens, Phillip Jr. 1989. Satanism: Where are the folklorists? *New York Folklore* 15, no. 1-2: 1–22.

Stop me if you've heard . . . 1992. *FOAFTALE NEWS* 27 (September): 10–12.

Walraven, Ed. 1991. Evidence for a developing variant of "La Llorona." *Western Folklore* 50, no. 2 (April): 208–17.

Weigle, Marta. 1982. *Spiders & spinsters: Women and mythology*. Albuquerque: University of New Mexico Press.

LEGEND INDEX

Note: Page numbers in bold indicate legend itself, roman indicates discussion of legend, italic indicates mention of legend.

399

LITERARY INDEX

Boccaccio, Giovanni. *The Decameron,* 238, 388
The Book of Sinbad, 211
Brain, Sir Walter Russell. *Tea with Walter de la Mare,* 162
Brentano, Klemens. *Lore Lay,* 376
Brien, Jean. *The Girl in the Rose-Colored Shawl,* 355
Bull, Emma. *Bone Dance,* 94
Burgess, Anthony. *The Piano Players,* 182

Campbell, Robert. *Hip-Deep in Alligators,* 218
Carmer, Carl. *The Lavender Evening Dress,* 355
Carroll, Lewis. *Through the Looking Glass,* 67
Cerf, Bennett. *Famous Ghost Stories,* 317
Chaucer, Geoffrey. *The Prioress's Tale,* 264, 265
Claudian. *The Gothic War,* 211
Cohen, Daniel. *Railroad Ghosts and Highway Horrors,* 355
Cohen, Daniel. *The Restless Dead, Ghostly Tales from Around the World,* 328
Cohen, Daniel. *Southern Fried Rat & Other Gruesome Tales,* 181, 326, 327
Cook, Robin. *Coma,* 228, 254
Cooper, Natasha. *Poison Flowers,* 155

Daley, Robert R. *The World Beneath the City,* 218–19
Dante, Alighieri. *Inferno,* 267
de Caro. *The Folktale Cat,* 181
Defoe, Daniel. *Journal of the Plague Year,* 238, 388
de Lint, Charles. *Dreams Underfoot,* 94
de Vos, Gail. *Storytelling for Young Adults,* 327
Dickens, Charles. *The Pickwick Papers,* 155
Downer, Deborah L., ed. *Classic American Ghost Stories,* 327
Dunning, John. *Booked to Die,* 94

Estes, Clarissa Pinkola. *Women Who Run with the Wolves,* 373

The Fables of Bidpai, 211
Fitzgerald, F. Scott. *The Great Gatsby,* 4
Flagg, Fannie. *Fried Green Tomatoes,* 128

Gorog, Judith. *On Meeting Witches at Wells,* 219
Gotthelf, Jeremias. *Die schwarze Spinne,* 191
Grafton, Sue. *"H" Is for Homicide,* 309
Gregory, Nan. *No-Post,* 355

Harris, Joel Chandler. *Nights with Uncle Remus, Myths and Legends of the Old Plantation,* 323
Harris, Joel Chandler. *The Tales of Uncle Remus,* 322
Heine, Henrich. *Lorelei,* 376
Hemingway, Ernest. *The Torrent of Spring,* 181
Howard, Elizabeth Jane. *Mr. Wrong, A Collection of Short Stories,* 128, 326, 357
Howeill, Mary. *The Spider and the Fly,* 186, 187
Hugo, Victor. *Les Miserables,* 254

Irving, Washington. *Tales of a Traveller,* 355

Jacobs, Joseph. *English Fairy Tales,* 322
Justice, Jennifer. *The Ghost & I,* 355

Keer, M. E. *Dinky Hocker Shoots Smack!,* 325, 328
King, Stephen. *Christine,* 128
King, Stephen. *Pet Sematary,* 128, 219
Klawans, Harold L. *Toscanini's Fumble,* 388

Leach, Maria. *The Thing at the Foot of the Bed and Other Scary Tales,* 327, 328
Linkletter, Art. *Oops! or Life's Awful Moments,* 181
Longfellow, Henry W. *The Golden Legend (The Miracle Play V),* 387
Lunn, Janet. *The Unseen: Scary Stories,* 355

SUBJECT INDEX

403